CAVE CARSON HAS A CYBERNETIC EYE

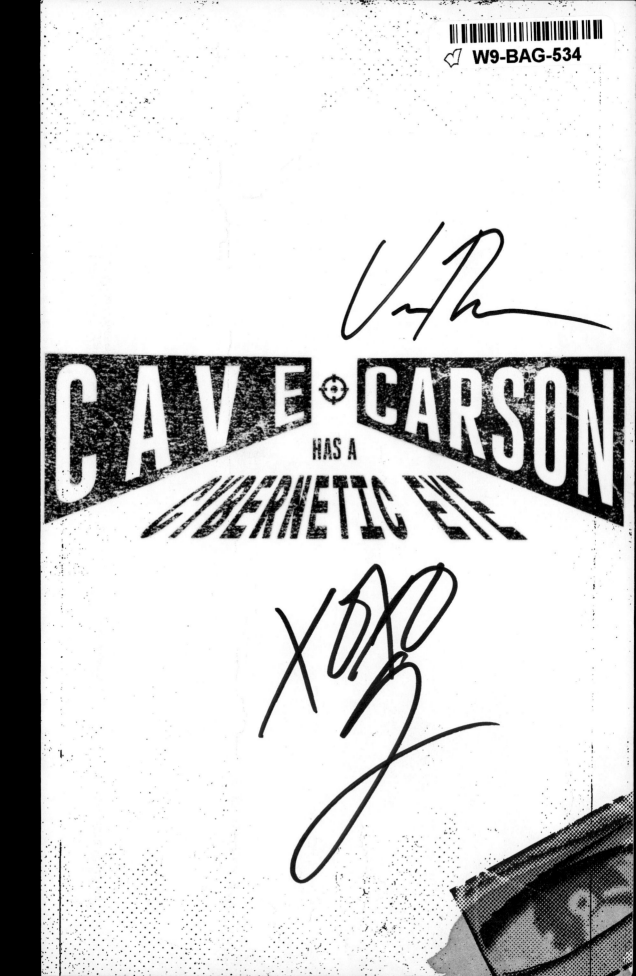

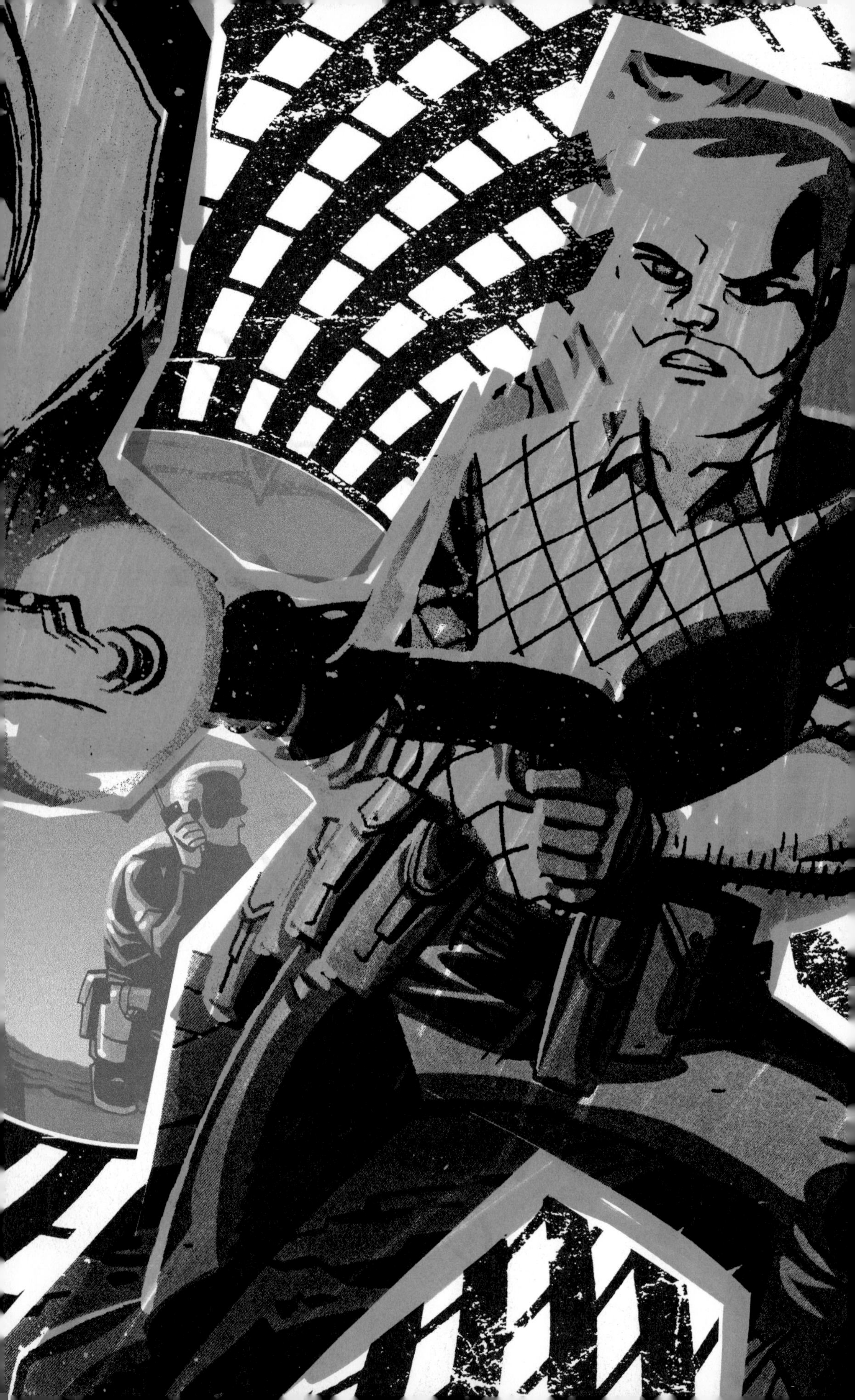

CAVE CARSON HAS A CYBERNETIC EYE

VOL. 1: GOING UNDERGROUND

JON RIVERA GERARD WAY Writers

MICHAEL AVON OEMING Artist

NICK FILARDI Colorist

CLEM ROBINS Letterer

MICHAEL AVON OEMING and NICK FILARDI Cover Art and Original Series Covers

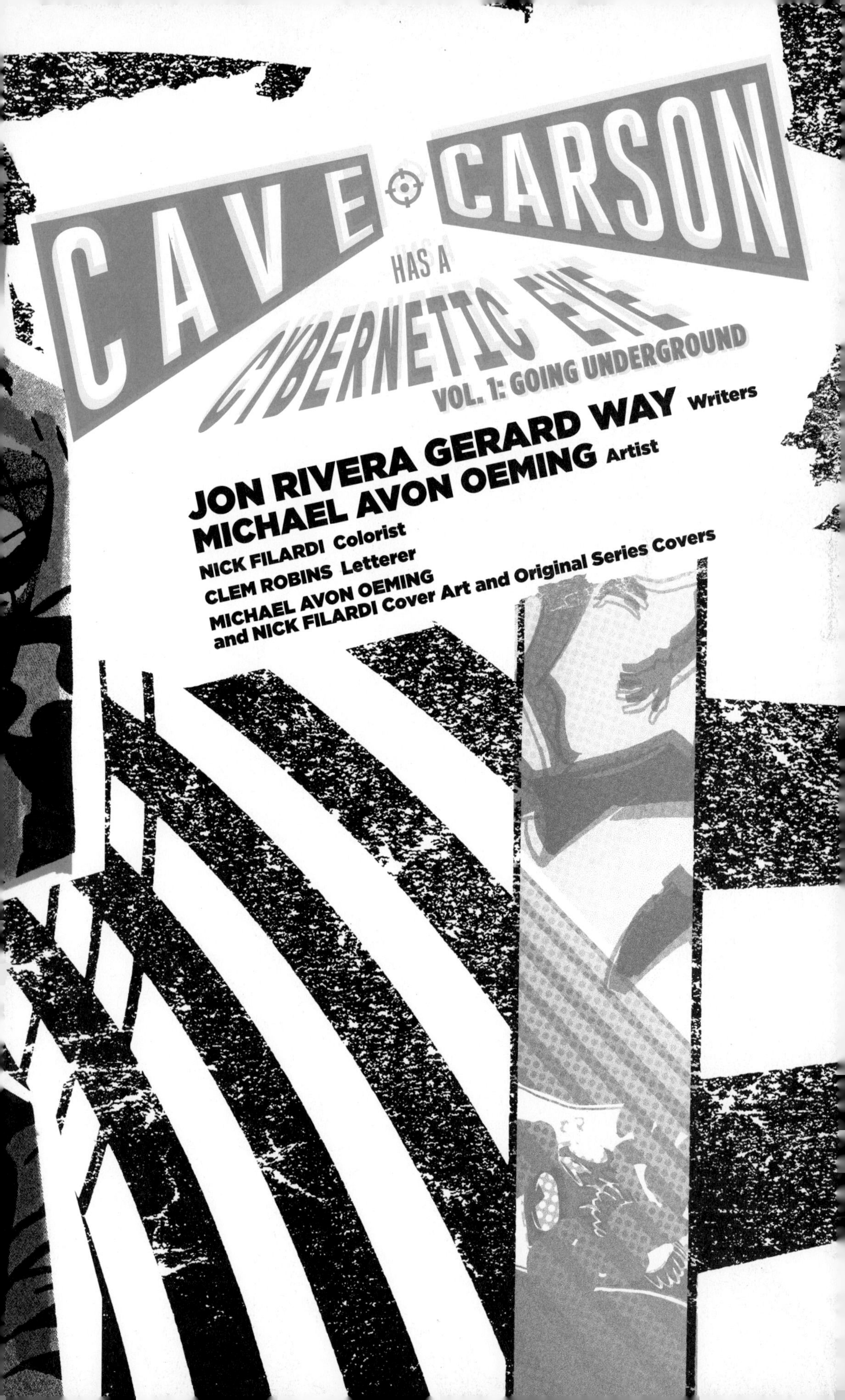

Molly Mahan Editor – Original Series
Jeb Woodard Group Editor – Collected Editions
Scott Nybakken Editor – Collected Edition
Steve Cook Design Director – Books
Louis Prandi Publication Design

Bob Harras Senior VP – Editor-in-Chief, DC Comics

Diane Nelson President
Dan DiDio Publisher
Jim Lee Publisher
Geoff Johns President & Chief Creative Officer
Amit Desai Executive VP – Business & Marketing Strategy,
Direct to Consumer & Global Franchise Management
Sam Ades Senior VP – Direct to Consumer
Bobbie Chase VP – Talent Development
Mark Chiarello Senior VP – Art, Design & Collected Editions
John Cunningham Senior VP – Sales & Trade Marketing
Anne DePies Senior VP – Business Strategy, Finance & Administration
Don Falletti VP – Manufacturing Operations
Lawrence Ganem VP – Editorial Administration & Talent Relations
Alison Gill Senior VP – Manufacturing & Operations
Hank Kanalz Senior VP – Editorial Strategy & Administration
Jay Kogan VP – Legal Affairs
Thomas Loftus VP – Business Affairs
Jack Mahan VP – Business Affairs
Nick J. Napolitano VP – Manufacturing Administration
Eddie Scannell VP – Consumer Marketing
Courtney Simmons Senior VP – Publicity & Communications
Jim (Ski) Sokolowski VP – Comic Book Specialty Sales & Trade Marketing
Nancy Spears VP – Mass, Book, Digital Sales & Trade Marketing

**CAVE CARSON HAS A CYBERNETIC EYE
VOL. 1: GOING UNDERGROUND**

DC Comics
2900 West Alameda Avenue
Burbank, CA 91505
Printed by LSC Communications, Salem, VA, USA. 5/26/17. First Printing.
ISBN: 978-1-4012-7082-7

Library of Congress Cataloging-in-Publication Data is available.

MIX
Paper from
responsible sources
FSC® C132124

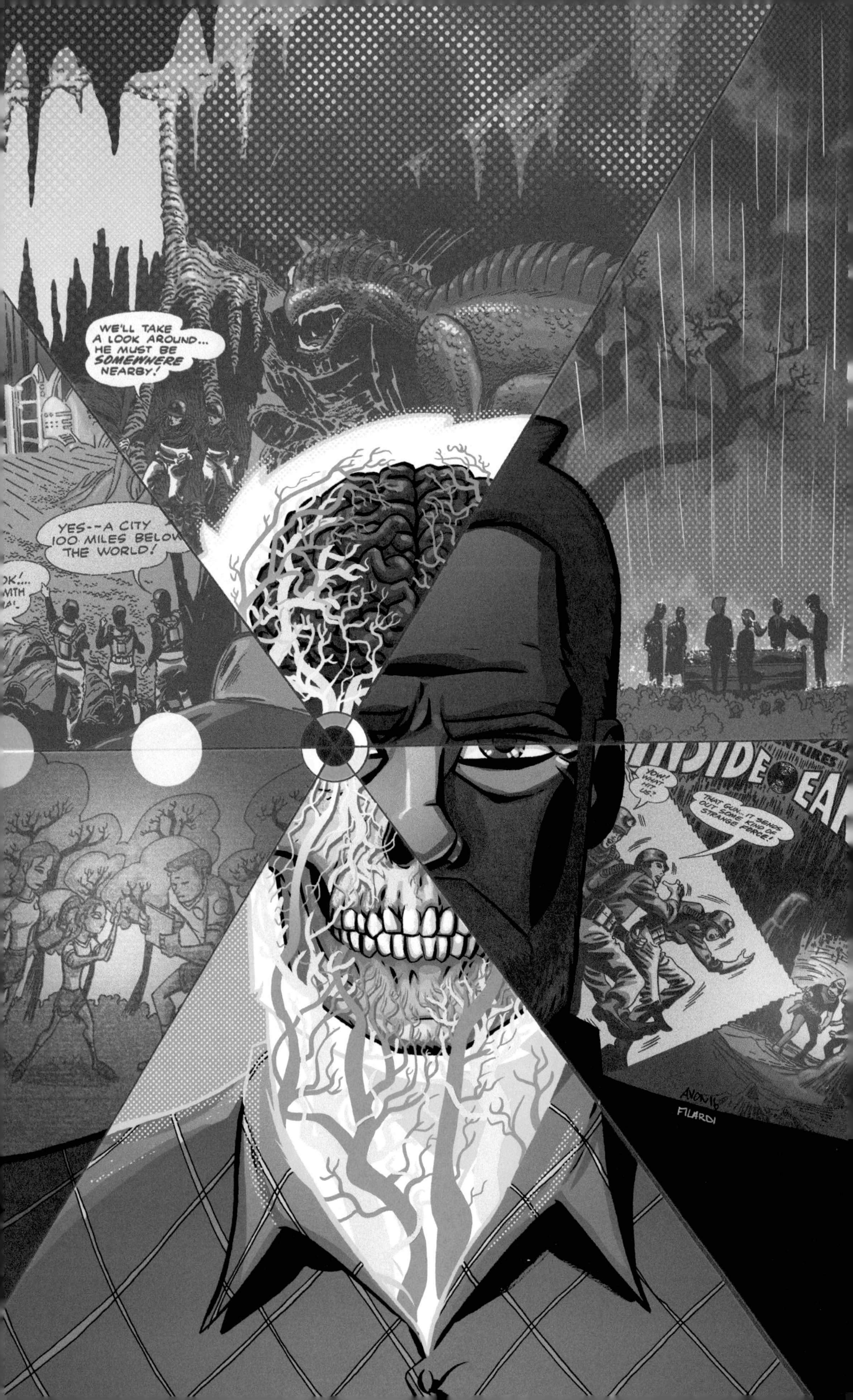
WE'LL TAKE A LOOK AROUND... HE MUST BE SOMEWHERE NEARBY!
YES--A CITY 100 MILES BELOW THE WORLD!
YOW! WHAT HIT US?
THAT GUN... IT SENDS OUT SOME KIND OF STRANGE FORCE!
AVON '16
FILARDI

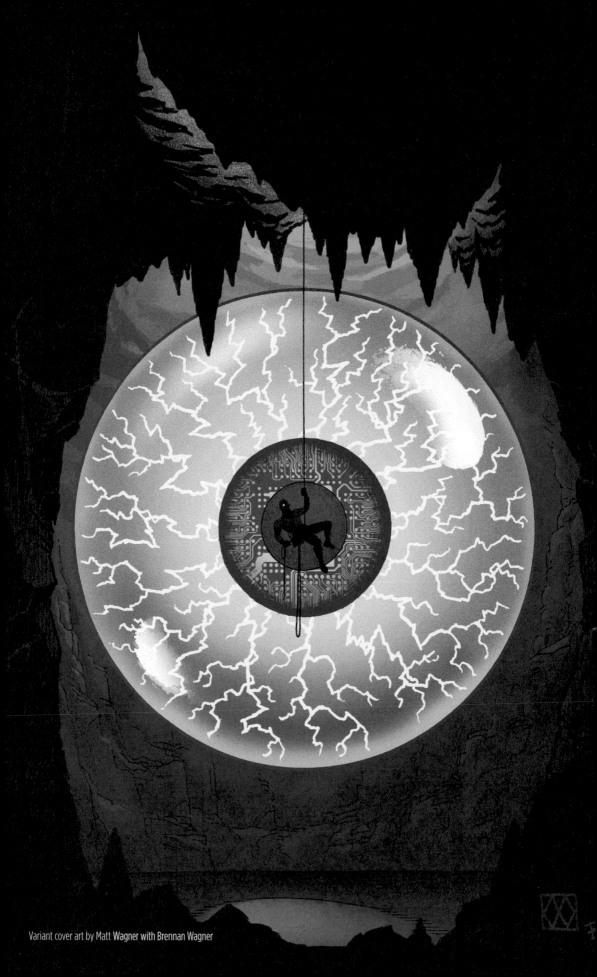

Variant cover art by Matt Wagner with Brennan Wagner

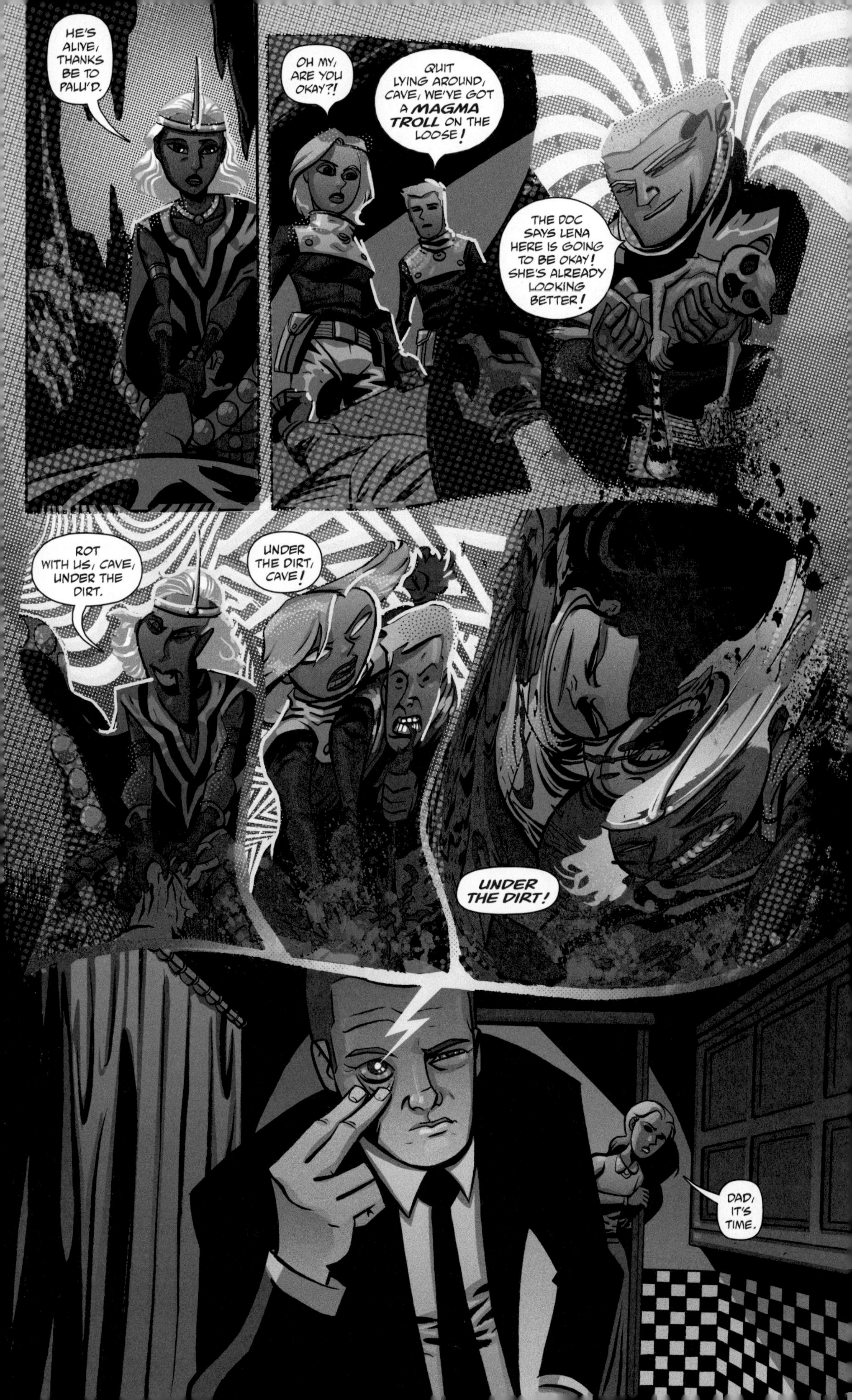
HE'S ALIVE, THANKS BE TO PALU'D.
OH MY, ARE YOU OKAY?!
QUIT LYING AROUND, CAVE, WE'VE GOT A MAGMA TROLL ON THE LOOSE!
THE DOC SAYS LENA HERE IS GOING TO BE OKAY! SHE'S ALREADY LOOKING BETTER!
ROT WITH US, CAVE, UNDER THE DIRT.
UNDER THE DIRT, CAVE!
UNDER THE DIRT!
DAD, IT'S TIME.

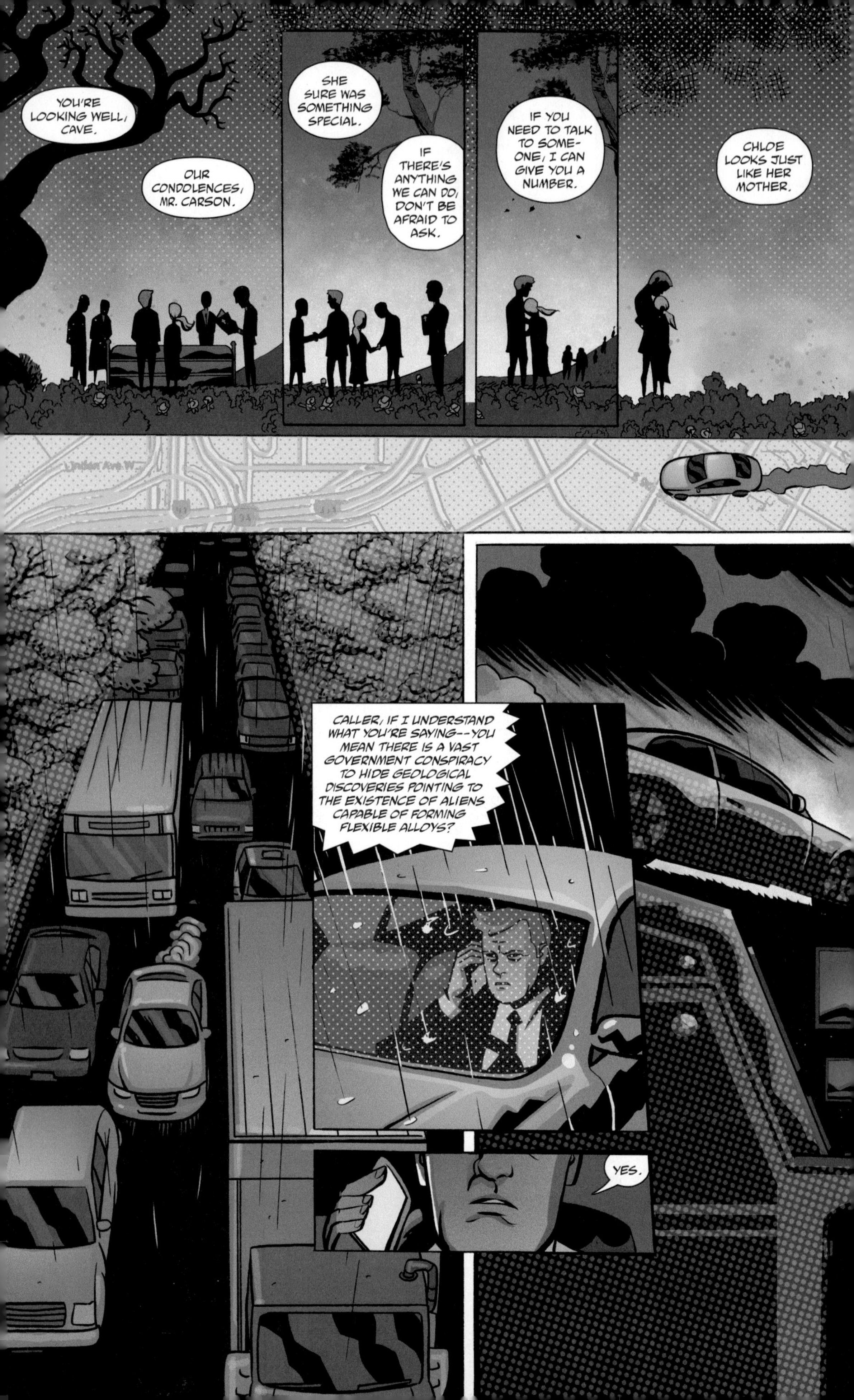
YOU'RE LOOKING WELL, CAVE.
OUR CONDOLENCES, MR. CARSON.
SHE SURE WAS SOMETHING SPECIAL.
IF THERE'S ANYTHING WE CAN DO, DON'T BE AFRAID TO ASK.
IF YOU NEED TO TALK TO SOME-ONE, I CAN GIVE YOU A NUMBER.
CHLOE LOOKS JUST LIKE HER MOTHER.
CALLER, IF I UNDERSTAND WHAT YOU'RE SAYING--YOU MEAN THERE IS A VAST GOVERNMENT CONSPIRACY TO HIDE GEOLOGICAL DISCOVERIES POINTING TO THE EXISTENCE OF ALIENS CAPABLE OF FORMING FLEXIBLE ALLOYS?
YES.

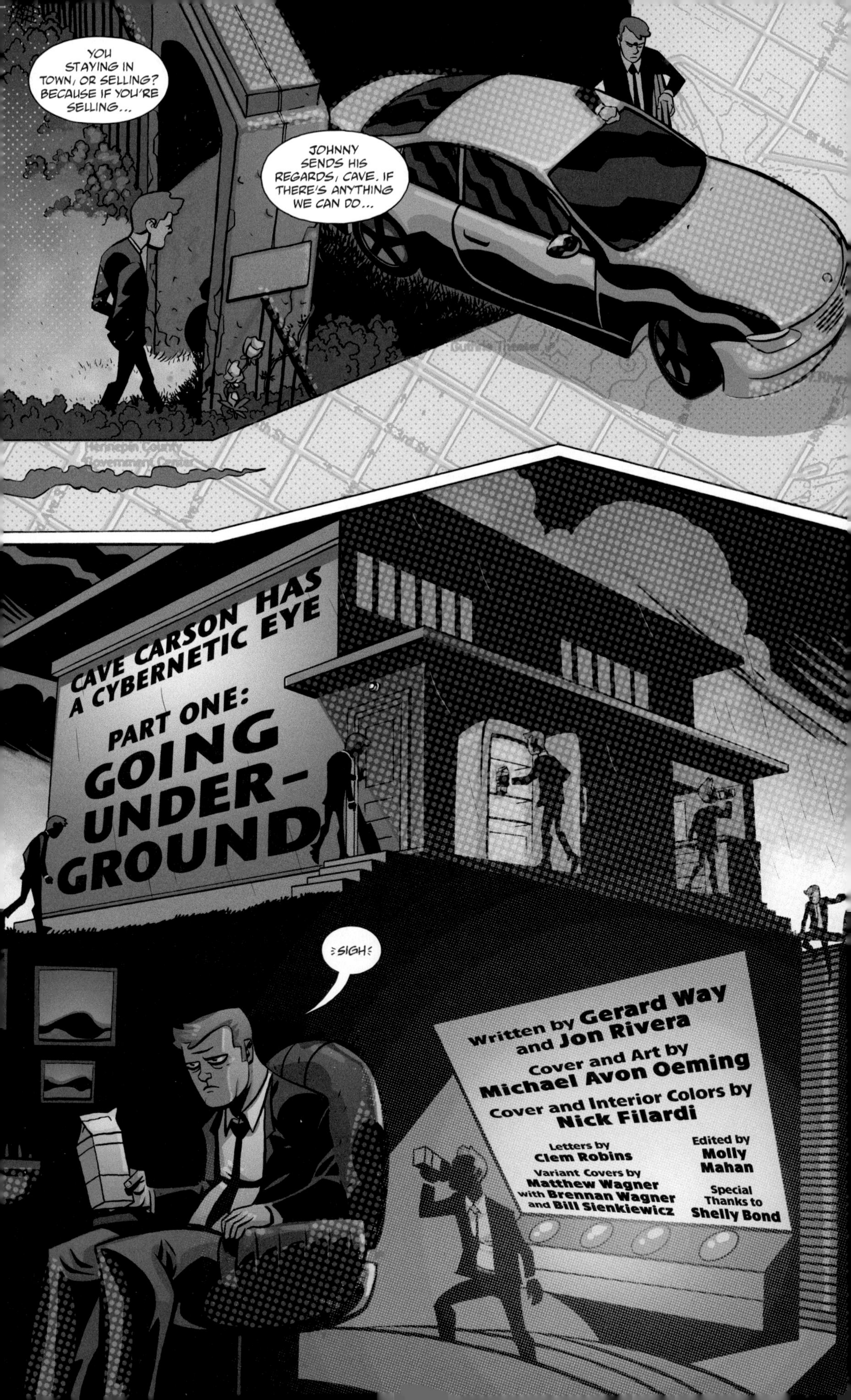
YOU STAYING IN TOWN, OR SELLING? BECAUSE IF YOU'RE SELLING...
JOHNNY SENDS HIS REGARDS, CAVE. IF THERE'S ANYTHING WE CAN DO...
CAVE CARSON HAS A CYBERNETIC EYE
PART ONE: GOING UNDER-GROUND
SIGH
Written by Gerard Way and Jon Rivera
Cover and Art by Michael Avon Oeming
Cover and Interior Colors by Nick Filardi
Letters by Clem Robins
Variant Covers by Matthew Wagner with Brennan Wagner and Bill Sienkiewicz
Edited by Molly Mahan
Special Thanks to Shelly Bond

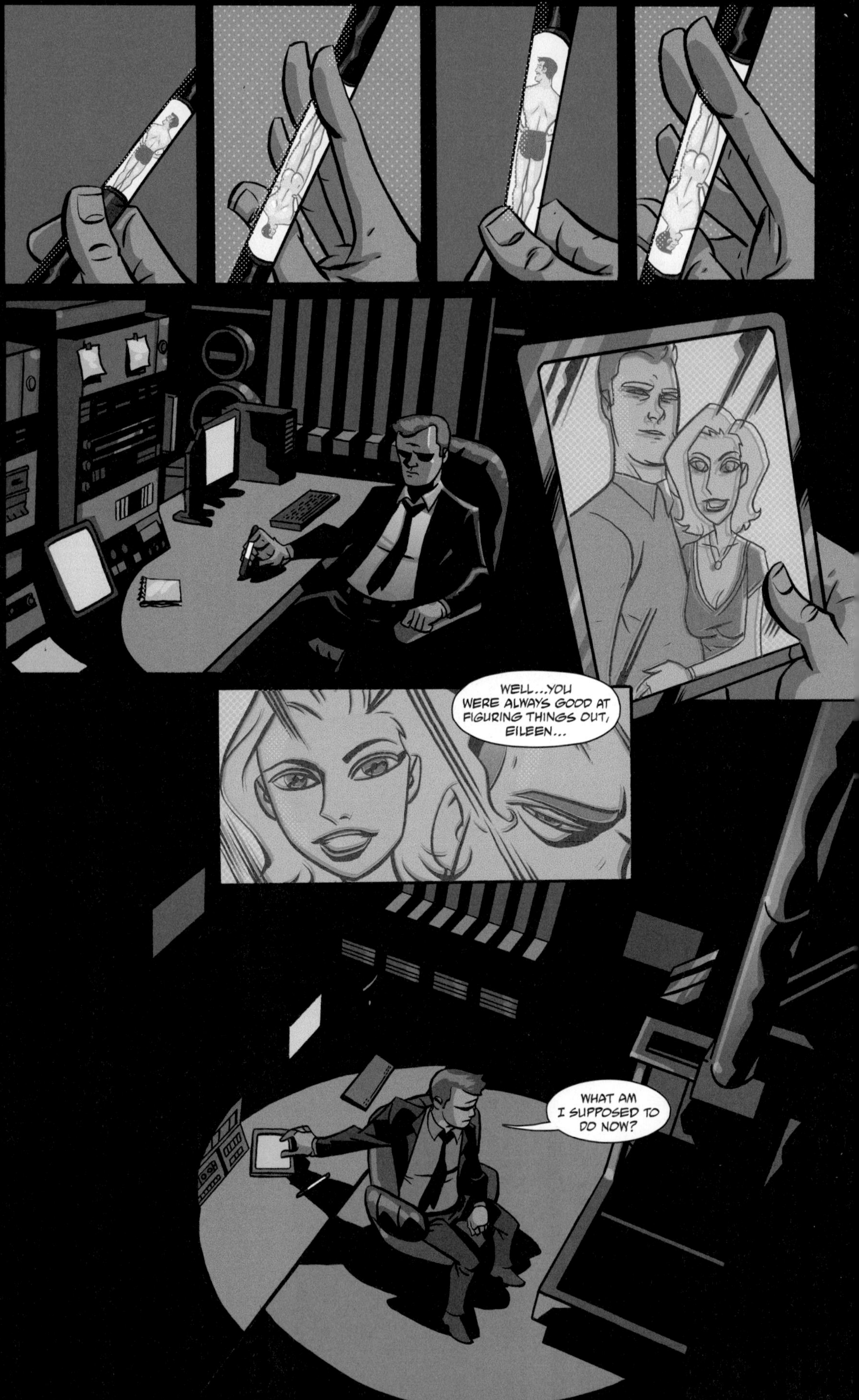
WELL...YOU WERE ALWAYS GOOD AT FIGURING THINGS OUT, EILEEN...
WHAT AM I SUPPOSED TO DO NOW?

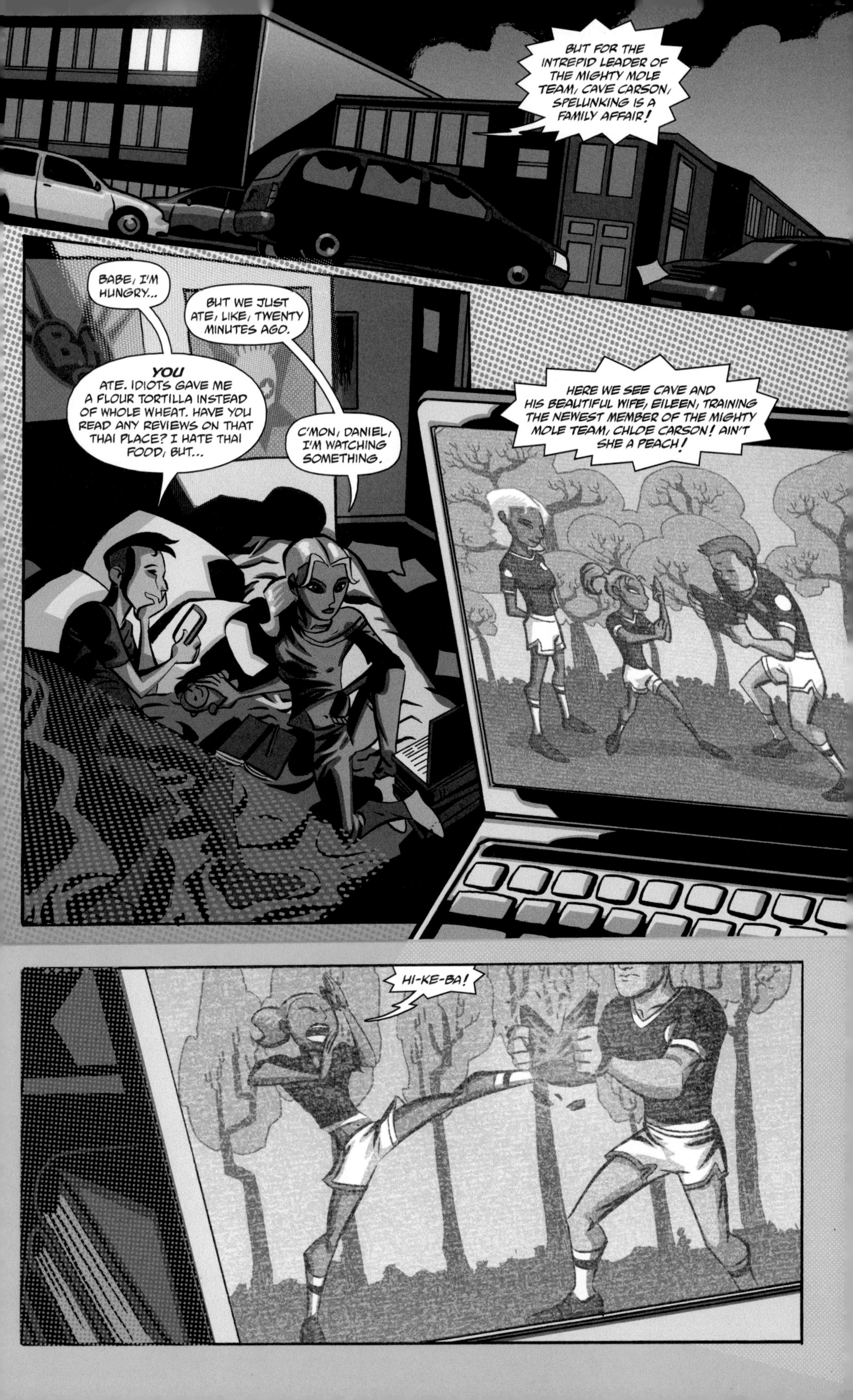
BUT FOR THE INTREPID LEADER OF THE MIGHTY MOLE TEAM, CAVE CARSON, SPELUNKING IS A FAMILY AFFAIR!
BABE, I'M HUNGRY...
BUT WE JUST ATE, LIKE, TWENTY MINUTES AGO.
YOU ATE. IDIOTS GAVE ME A FLOUR TORTILLA INSTEAD OF WHOLE WHEAT. HAVE YOU READ ANY REVIEWS ON THAT THAI PLACE? I HATE THAI FOOD, BUT...
C'MON, DANIEL, I'M WATCHING SOMETHING.
HERE WE SEE CAVE AND HIS BEAUTIFUL WIFE, EILEEN, TRAINING THE NEWEST MEMBER OF THE MIGHTY MOLE TEAM, CHLOE CARSON! AIN'T SHE A PEACH!
HI-KE-BA!

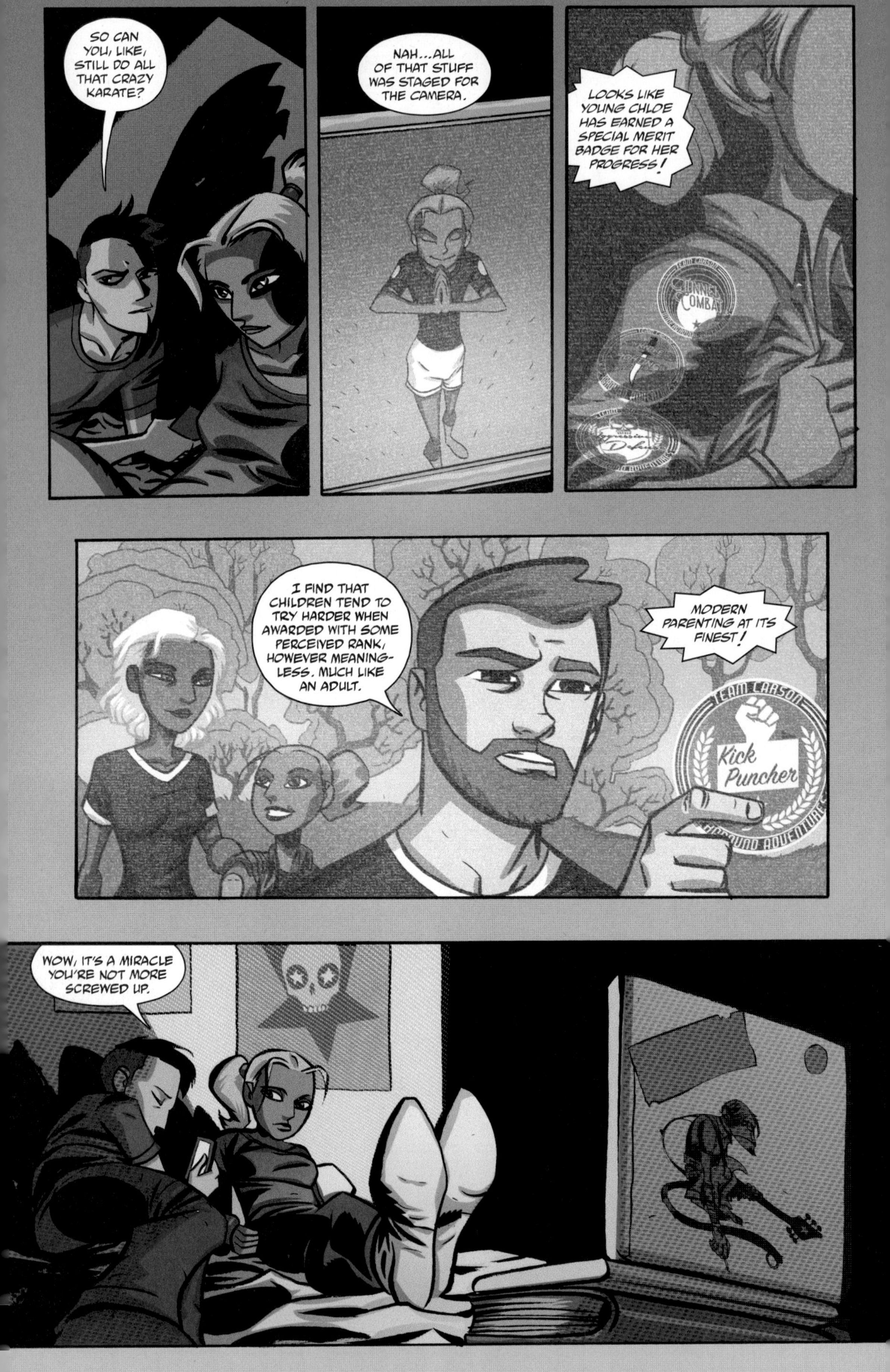
SO CAN YOU, LIKE, STILL DO ALL THAT CRAZY KARATE?
NAH...ALL OF THAT STUFF WAS STAGED FOR THE CAMERA.
LOOKS LIKE YOUNG CHLOE HAS EARNED A SPECIAL MERIT BADGE FOR HER PROGRESS!
I FIND THAT CHILDREN TEND TO TRY HARDER WHEN AWARDED WITH SOME PERCEIVED RANK, HOWEVER MEANING-LESS. MUCH LIKE AN ADULT.
MODERN PARENTING AT ITS FINEST!
TEAM CARSON
Kick Puncher
WOW, IT'S A MIRACLE YOU'RE NOT MORE SCREWED UP.

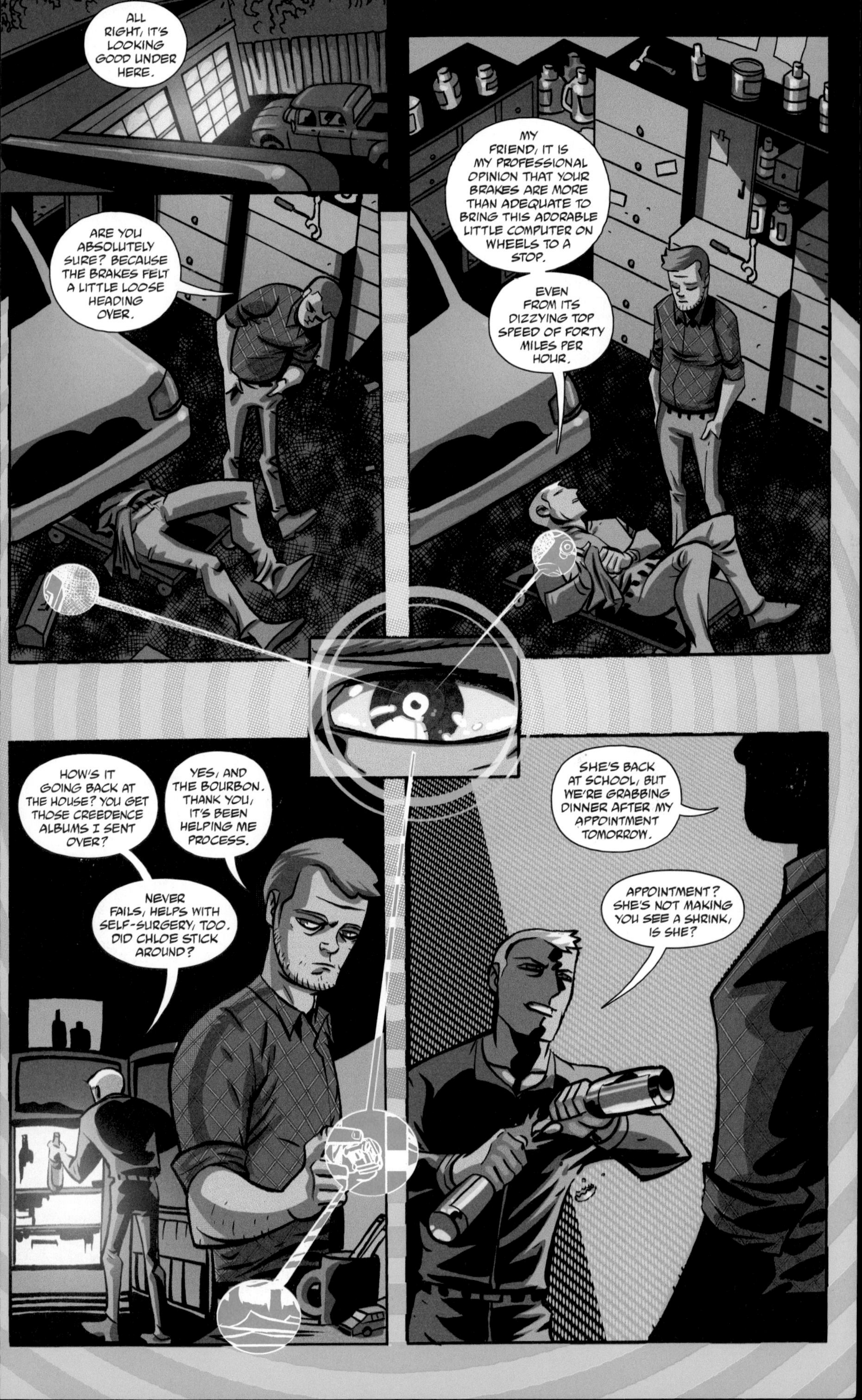

ALL RIGHT, IT'S LOOKING GOOD UNDER HERE.
ARE YOU ABSOLUTELY SURE? BECAUSE THE BRAKES FELT A LITTLE LOOSE HEADING OVER.
MY FRIEND, IT IS MY PROFESSIONAL OPINION THAT YOUR BRAKES ARE MORE THAN ADEQUATE TO BRING THIS ADORABLE LITTLE COMPUTER ON WHEELS TO A STOP.
EVEN FROM ITS DIZZYING TOP SPEED OF FORTY MILES PER HOUR.
HOW'S IT GOING BACK AT THE HOUSE? YOU GET THOSE CREEDENCE ALBUMS I SENT OVER?
YES, AND THE BOURBON. THANK YOU, IT'S BEEN HELPING ME PROCESS.
NEVER FAILS, HELPS WITH SELF-SURGERY, TOO. DID CHLOE STICK AROUND?
SHE'S BACK AT SCHOOL, BUT WE'RE GRABBING DINNER AFTER MY APPOINTMENT TOMORROW.
APPOINTMENT? SHE'S NOT MAKING YOU SEE A SHRINK, IS SHE?

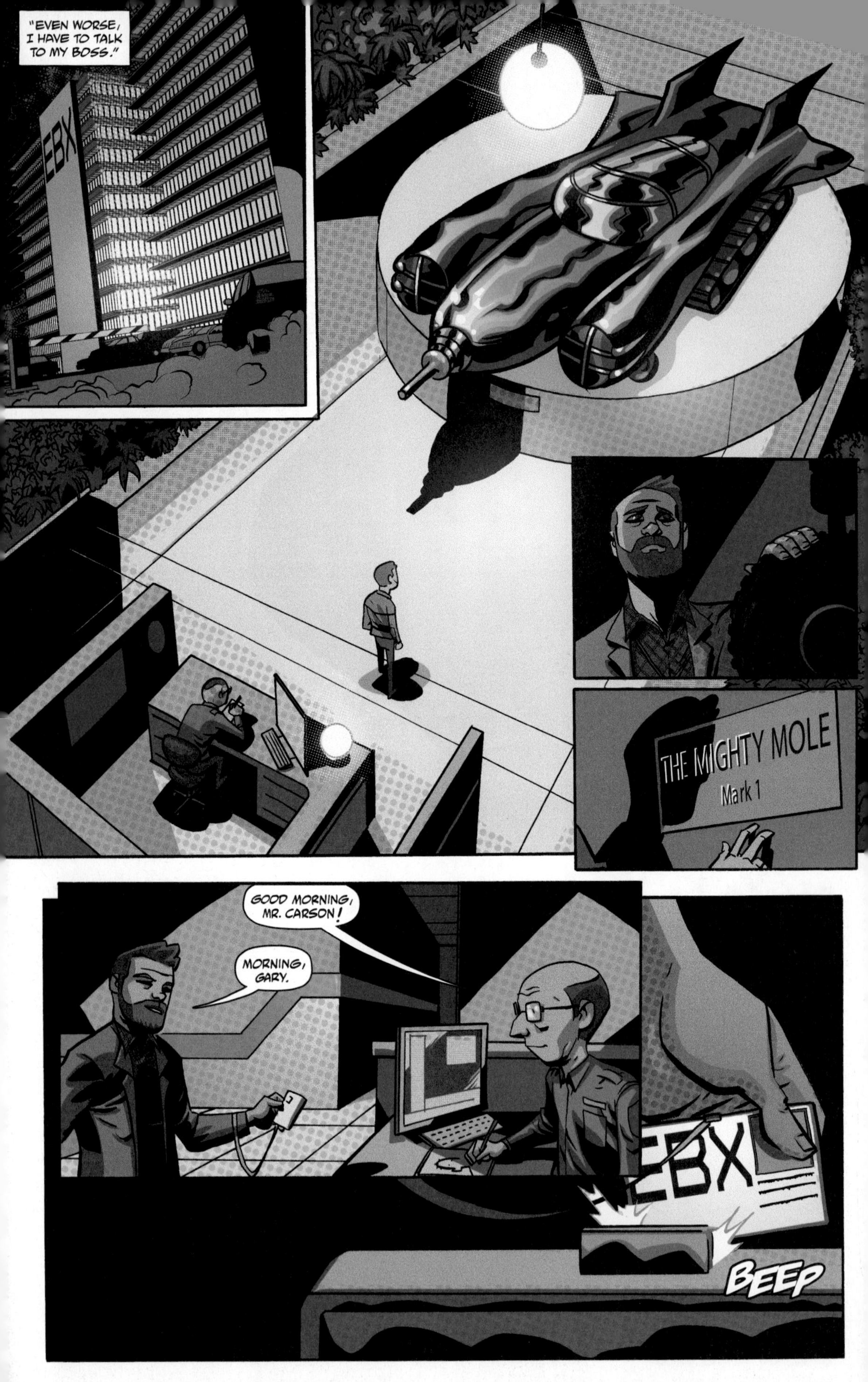

"EVEN WORSE, I HAVE TO TALK TO MY BOSS."
EBX
THE MIGHTY MOLE
Mark 1
GOOD MORNING, MR. CARSON!
MORNING, GARY.
EBX
BEEP

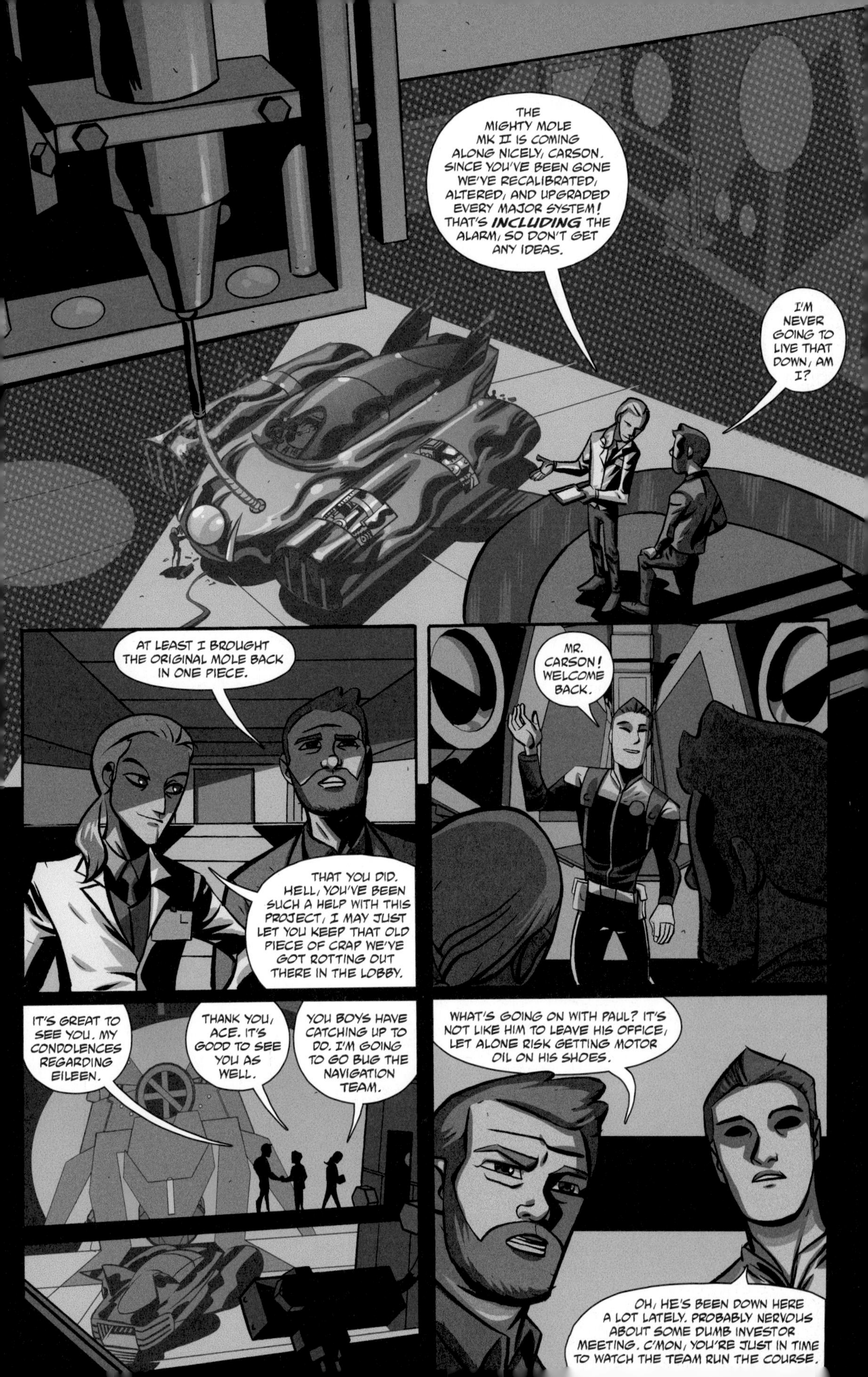
THE MIGHTY MOLE MK II IS COMING ALONG NICELY, CARSON. SINCE YOU'VE BEEN GONE WE'VE RECALIBRATED, ALTERED, AND UPGRADED EVERY MAJOR SYSTEM! THAT'S INCLUDING THE ALARM, SO DON'T GET ANY IDEAS.
I'M NEVER GOING TO LIVE THAT DOWN, AM I?
AT LEAST I BROUGHT THE ORIGINAL MOLE BACK IN ONE PIECE.
THAT YOU DID. HELL, YOU'VE BEEN SUCH A HELP WITH THIS PROJECT, I MAY JUST LET YOU KEEP THAT OLD PIECE OF CRAP WE'VE GOT ROTTING OUT THERE IN THE LOBBY.
MR. CARSON! WELCOME BACK.
IT'S GREAT TO SEE YOU. MY CONDOLENCES REGARDING EILEEN.
THANK YOU, ACE. IT'S GOOD TO SEE YOU AS WELL.
YOU BOYS HAVE CATCHING UP TO DO. I'M GOING TO GO BUG THE NAVIGATION TEAM.
WHAT'S GOING ON WITH PAUL? IT'S NOT LIKE HIM TO LEAVE HIS OFFICE, LET ALONE RISK GETTING MOTOR OIL ON HIS SHOES.
OH, HE'S BEEN DOWN HERE A LOT LATELY. PROBABLY NERVOUS ABOUT SOME DUMB INVESTOR MEETING. C'MON, YOU'RE JUST IN TIME TO WATCH THE TEAM RUN THE COURSE.

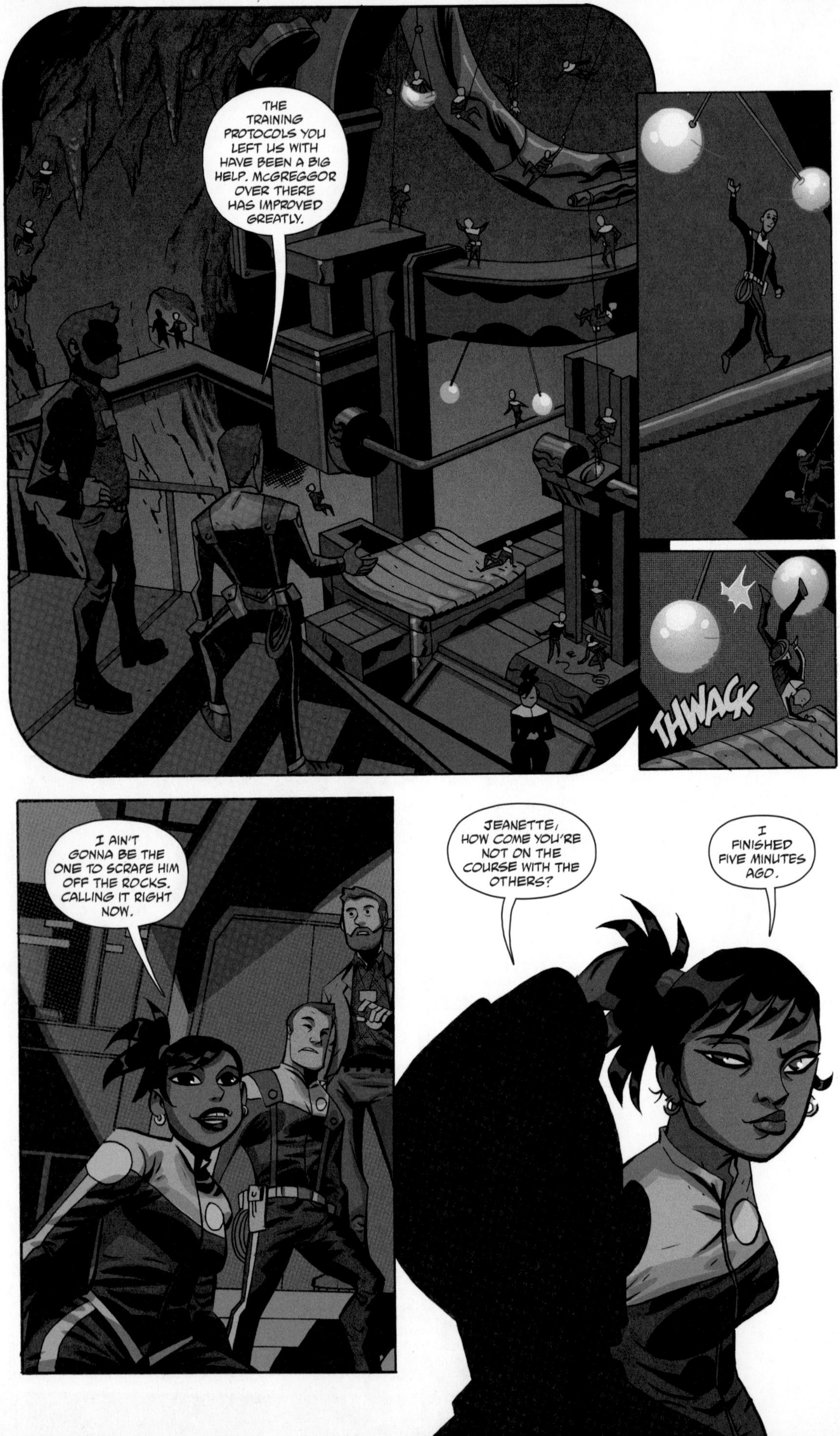
THE TRAINING PROTOCOLS YOU LEFT US WITH HAVE BEEN A BIG HELP. McGREGGOR OVER THERE HAS IMPROVED GREATLY.
THWACK
I AIN'T GONNA BE THE ONE TO SCRAPE HIM OFF THE ROCKS. CALLING IT RIGHT NOW.
JEANETTE, HOW COME YOU'RE NOT ON THE COURSE WITH THE OTHERS?
I FINISHED FIVE MINUTES AGO.

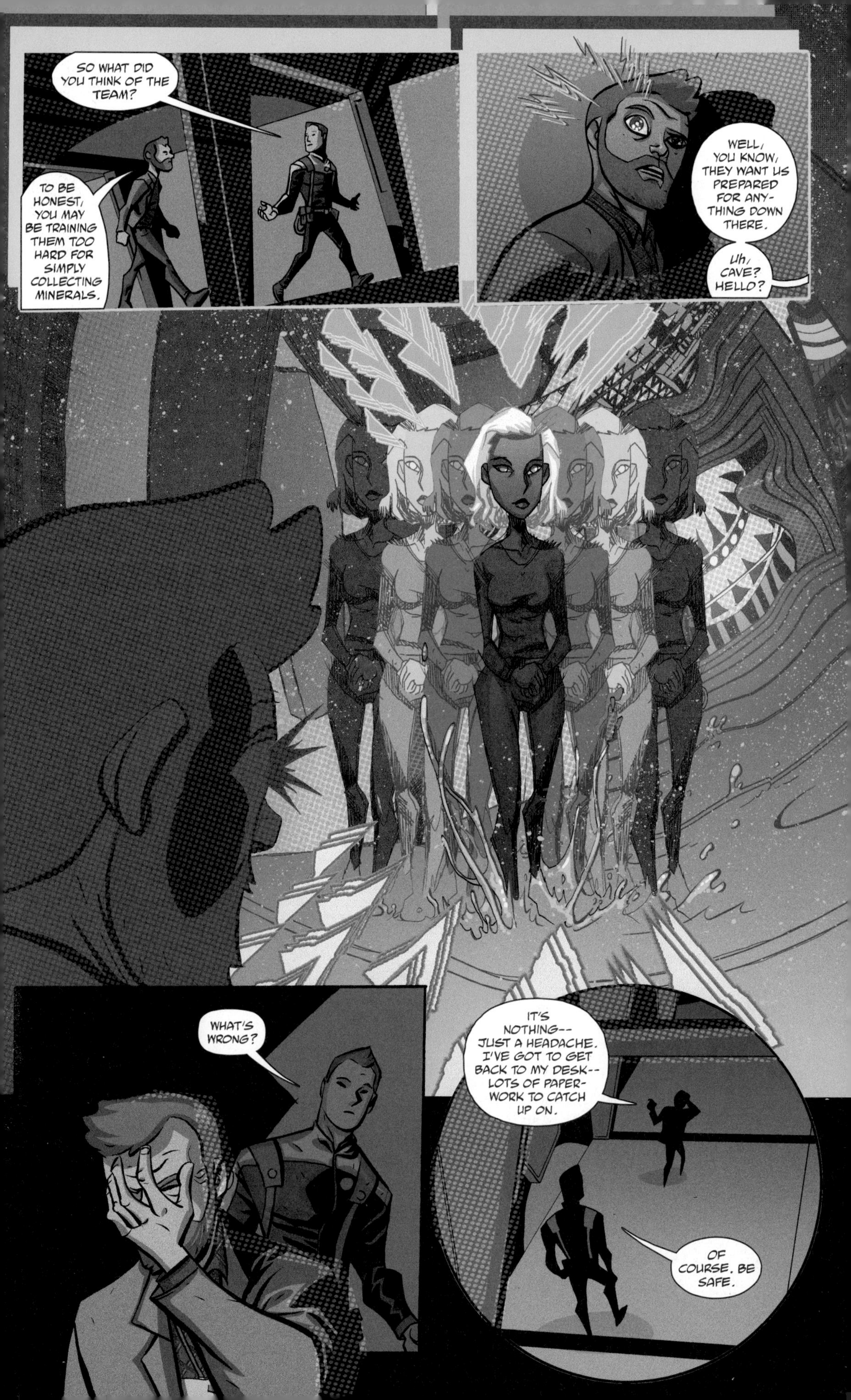
SO WHAT DID YOU THINK OF THE TEAM?
TO BE HONEST, YOU MAY BE TRAINING THEM TOO HARD FOR SIMPLY COLLECTING MINERALS.
WELL, YOU KNOW, THEY WANT US PREPARED FOR ANY-THING DOWN THERE.
Uh, CAVE? HELLO?
WHAT'S WRONG?
IT'S NOTHING-- JUST A HEADACHE. I'VE GOT TO GET BACK TO MY DESK-- LOTS OF PAPER-WORK TO CATCH UP ON.
OF COURSE. BE SAFE.

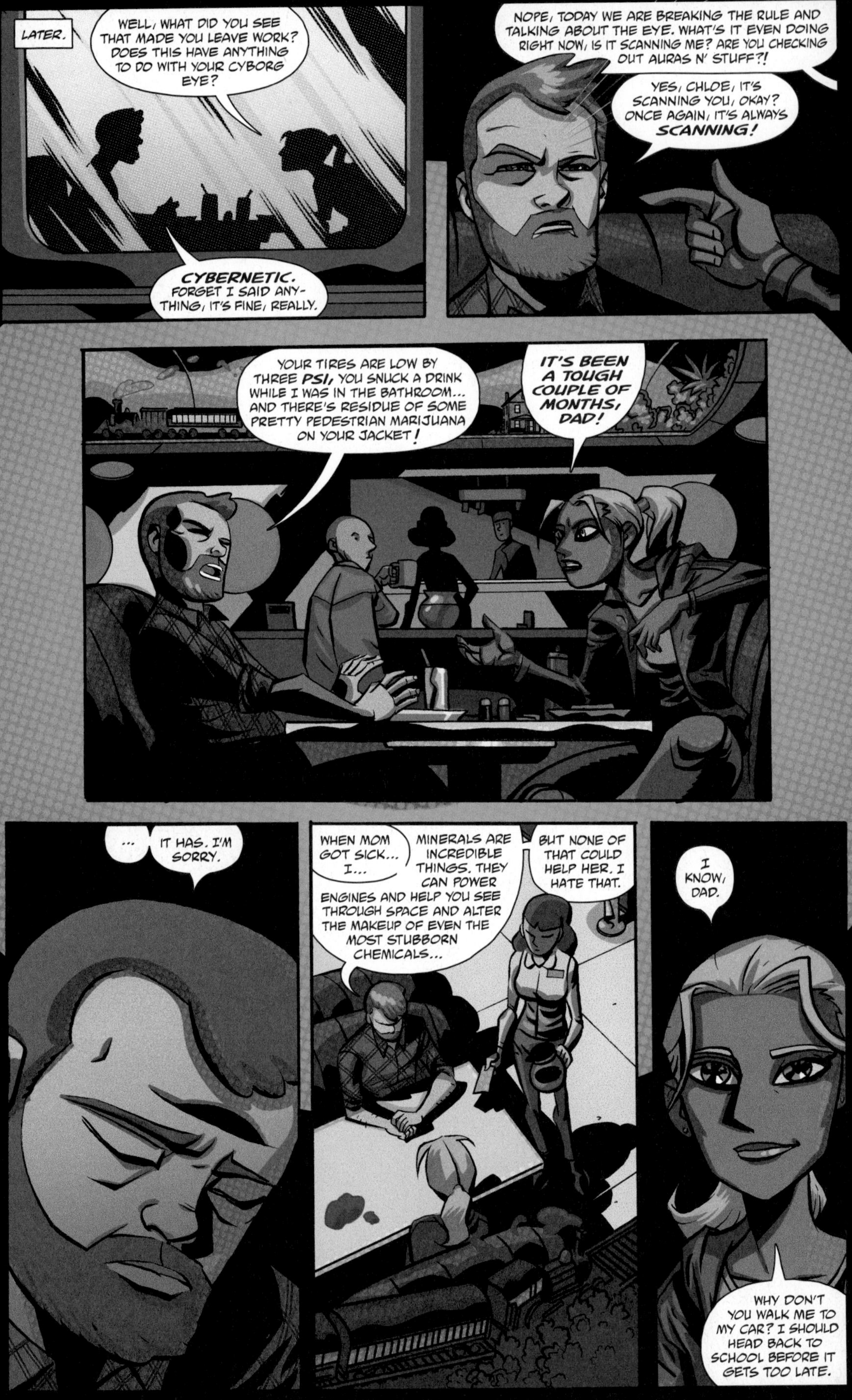
LATER.
WELL, WHAT DID YOU SEE THAT MADE YOU LEAVE WORK? DOES THIS HAVE ANYTHING TO DO WITH YOUR CYBORG EYE?
CYBERNETIC. FORGET I SAID ANYTHING, IT'S FINE, REALLY.
NOPE, TODAY WE ARE BREAKING THE RULE AND TALKING ABOUT THE EYE. WHAT'S IT EVEN DOING RIGHT NOW, IS IT SCANNING ME? ARE YOU CHECKING OUT AURAS N' STUFF?!
YES, CHLOE, IT'S SCANNING YOU, OKAY? ONCE AGAIN, IT'S ALWAYS SCANNING!
YOUR TIRES ARE LOW BY THREE PSI, YOU SNUCK A DRINK WHILE I WAS IN THE BATHROOM... AND THERE'S RESIDUE OF SOME PRETTY PEDESTRIAN MARIJUANA ON YOUR JACKET!
IT'S BEEN A TOUGH COUPLE OF MONTHS, DAD!
...
IT HAS. I'M SORRY.
WHEN MOM GOT SICK... I...
MINERALS ARE INCREDIBLE THINGS. THEY CAN POWER ENGINES AND HELP YOU SEE THROUGH SPACE AND ALTER THE MAKEUP OF EVEN THE MOST STUBBORN CHEMICALS...
BUT NONE OF THAT COULD HELP HER. I HATE THAT.
I KNOW, DAD.
WHY DON'T YOU WALK ME TO MY CAR? I SHOULD HEAD BACK TO SCHOOL BEFORE IT GETS TOO LATE.

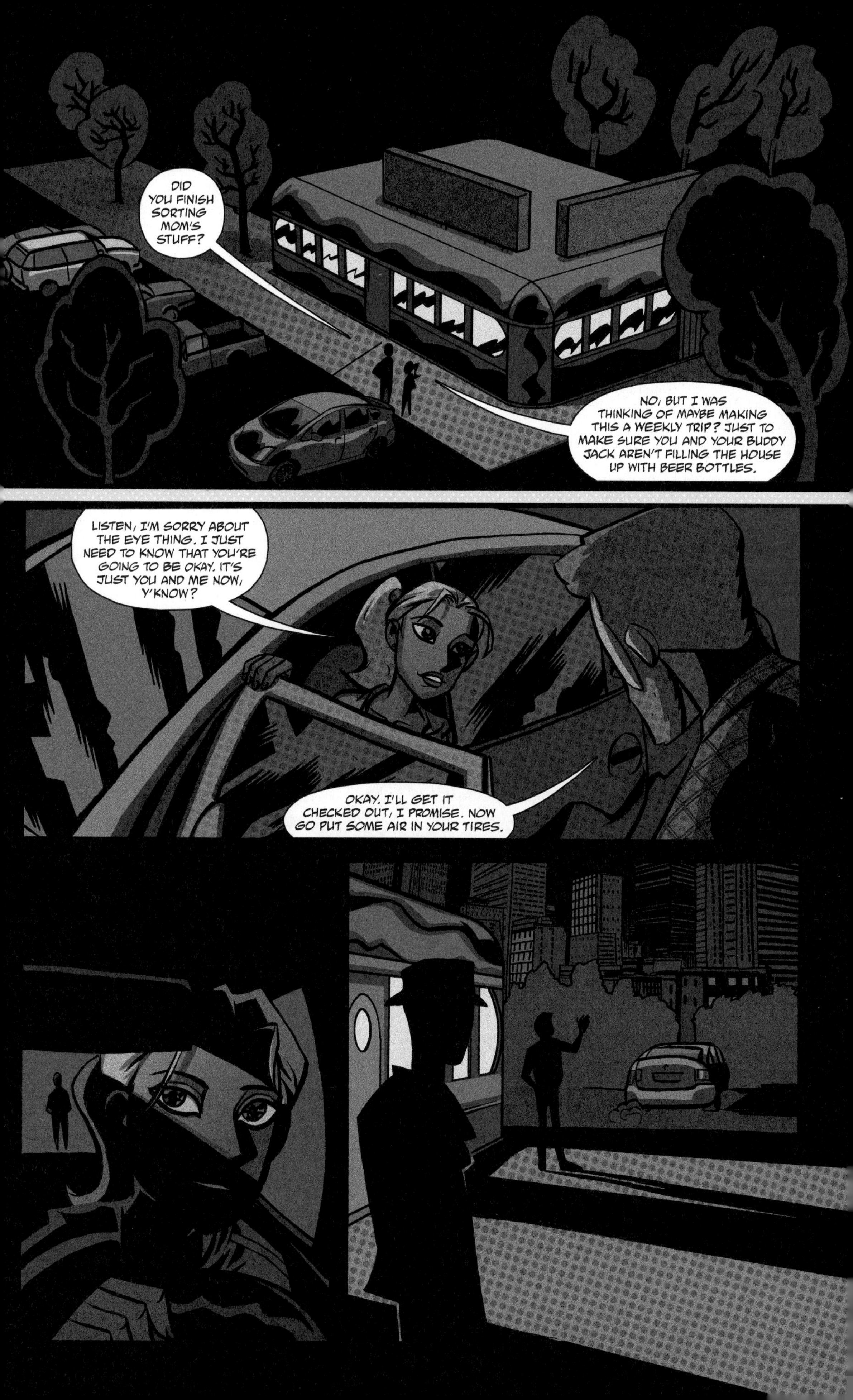
DID YOU FINISH SORTING MOM'S STUFF?
NO, BUT I WAS THINKING OF MAYBE MAKING THIS A WEEKLY TRIP? JUST TO MAKE SURE YOU AND YOUR BUDDY JACK AREN'T FILLING THE HOUSE UP WITH BEER BOTTLES.
LISTEN, I'M SORRY ABOUT THE EYE THING. I JUST NEED TO KNOW THAT YOU'RE GOING TO BE OKAY. IT'S JUST YOU AND ME NOW, Y'KNOW?
OKAY. I'LL GET IT CHECKED OUT, I PROMISE. NOW GO PUT SOME AIR IN YOUR TIRES.

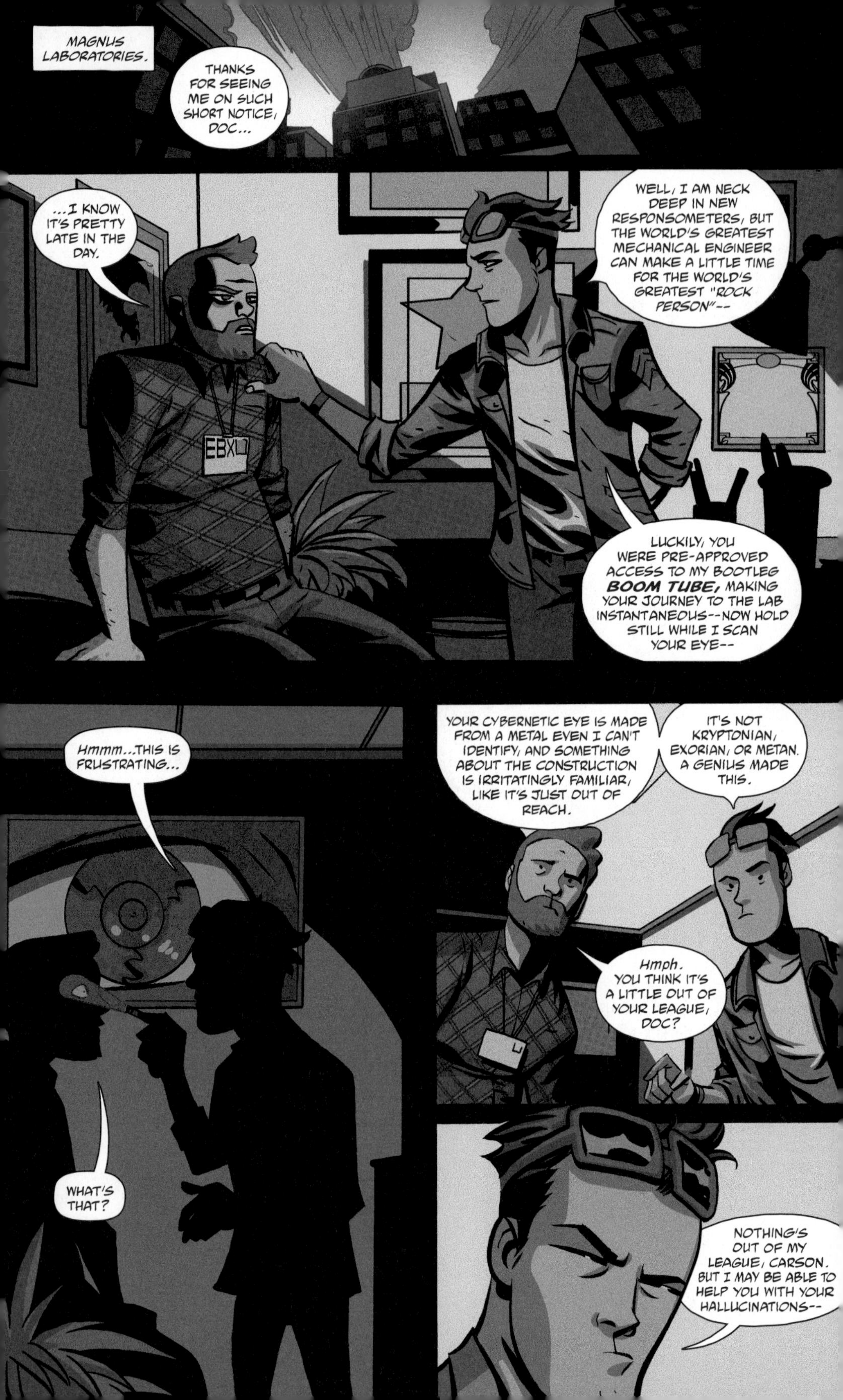
MAGNUS LABORATORIES.
THANKS FOR SEEING ME ON SUCH SHORT NOTICE, DOC...
...I KNOW IT'S PRETTY LATE IN THE DAY.
WELL, I AM NECK DEEP IN NEW RESPONSOMETERS, BUT THE WORLD'S GREATEST MECHANICAL ENGINEER CAN MAKE A LITTLE TIME FOR THE WORLD'S GREATEST "ROCK PERSON"--
LUCKILY, YOU WERE PRE-APPROVED ACCESS TO MY BOOTLEG BOOM TUBE, MAKING YOUR JOURNEY TO THE LAB INSTANTANEOUS--NOW HOLD STILL WHILE I SCAN YOUR EYE--
EBXL
Hmmm...THIS IS FRUSTRATING...
WHAT'S THAT?
YOUR CYBERNETIC EYE IS MADE FROM A METAL EVEN I CAN'T IDENTIFY, AND SOMETHING ABOUT THE CONSTRUCTION IS IRRITATINGLY FAMILIAR, LIKE IT'S JUST OUT OF REACH.
IT'S NOT KRYPTONIAN, EXORIAN, OR METAN. A GENIUS MADE THIS.
Hmph. YOU THINK IT'S A LITTLE OUT OF YOUR LEAGUE, DOC?
NOTHING'S OUT OF MY LEAGUE, CARSON. BUT I MAY BE ABLE TO HELP YOU WITH YOUR HALLUCINATIONS--

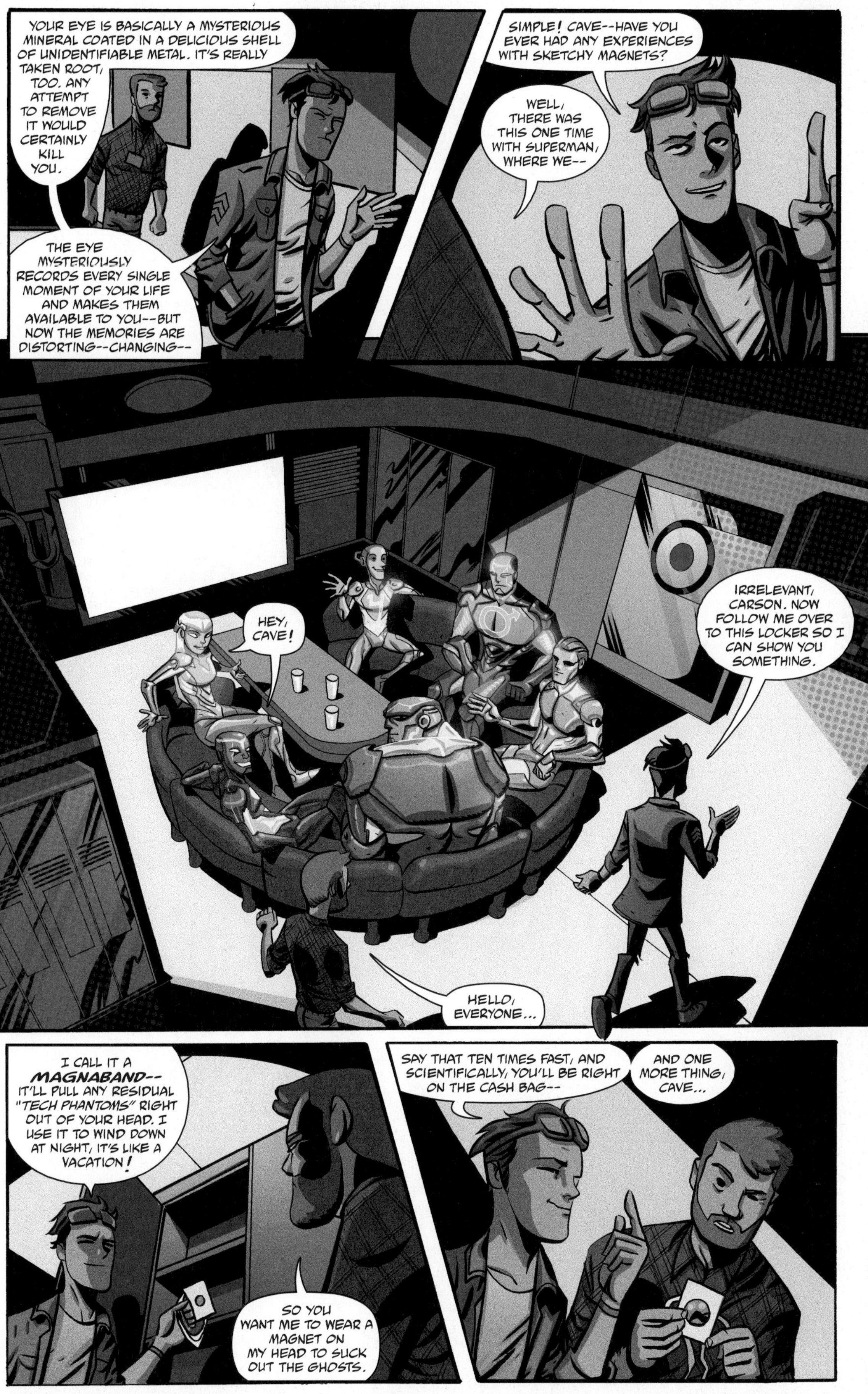
YOUR EYE IS BASICALLY A MYSTERIOUS MINERAL COATED IN A DELICIOUS SHELL OF UNIDENTIFIABLE METAL. IT'S REALLY TAKEN ROOT, TOO. ANY ATTEMPT TO REMOVE IT WOULD CERTAINLY KILL YOU.
THE EYE MYSTERIOUSLY RECORDS EVERY SINGLE MOMENT OF YOUR LIFE AND MAKES THEM AVAILABLE TO YOU--BUT NOW THE MEMORIES ARE DISTORTING--CHANGING--
SIMPLE! CAVE--HAVE YOU EVER HAD ANY EXPERIENCES WITH SKETCHY MAGNETS?
WELL, THERE WAS THIS ONE TIME WITH SUPERMAN, WHERE WE--
HEY, CAVE!
IRRELEVANT, CARSON. NOW FOLLOW ME OVER TO THIS LOCKER SO I CAN SHOW YOU SOMETHING.
HELLO, EVERYONE...
I CALL IT A MAGNABAND--IT'LL PULL ANY RESIDUAL "TECH PHANTOMS" RIGHT OUT OF YOUR HEAD. I USE IT TO WIND DOWN AT NIGHT, IT'S LIKE A VACATION!
SO YOU WANT ME TO WEAR A MAGNET ON MY HEAD TO SUCK OUT THE GHOSTS.
SAY THAT TEN TIMES FAST, AND SCIENTIFICALLY, YOU'LL BE RIGHT ON THE CASH BAG--
AND ONE MORE THING, CAVE...

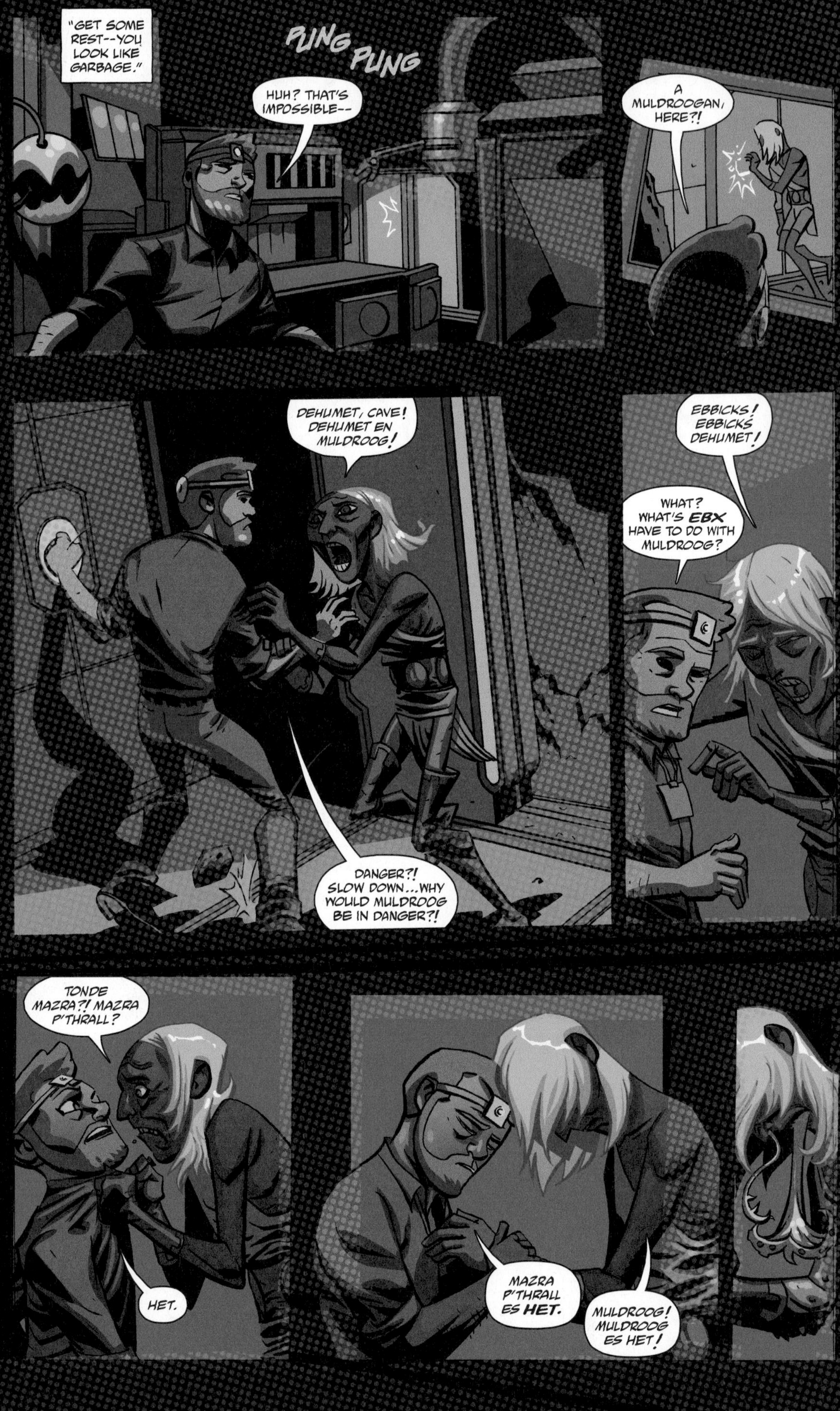
"GET SOME REST--YOU LOOK LIKE GARBAGE."
PUNG PUNG
HUH? THAT'S IMPOSSIBLE--
A MULDROOGAN, HERE?!
DEHUMET, CAVE! DEHUMET EN MULDROOG!
DANGER?! SLOW DOWN...WHY WOULD MULDROOG BE IN DANGER?!
EBBICKS! EBBICKS DEHUMET!
WHAT? WHAT'S EBX HAVE TO DO WITH MULDROOG?
TONDE MAZRA?! MAZRA P'THRALL?
HET.
MAZRA P'THRALL ES HET.
MULDROOG! MULDROOG ES HET!

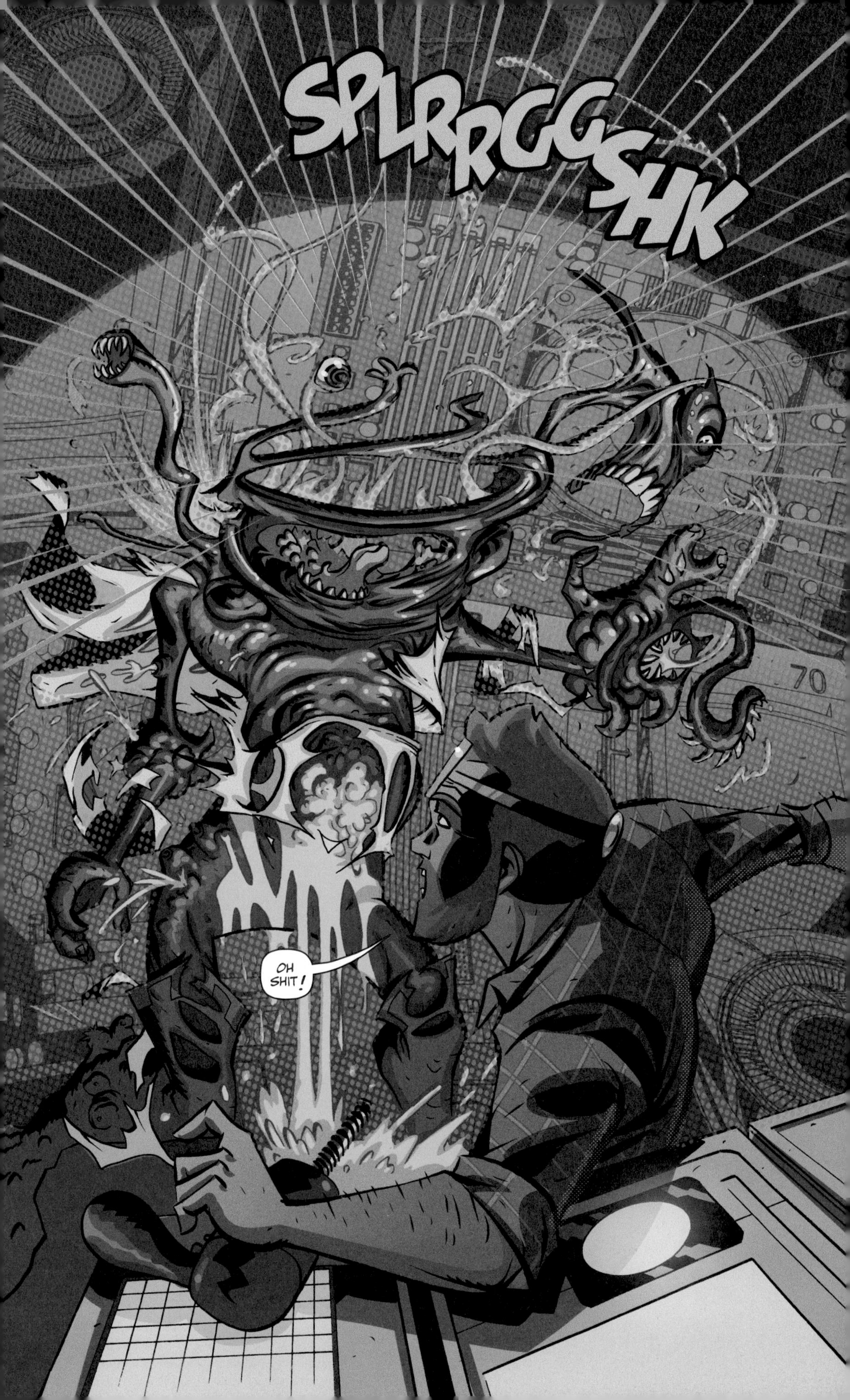
SPLRRGGSHK
70
OH SHIT!

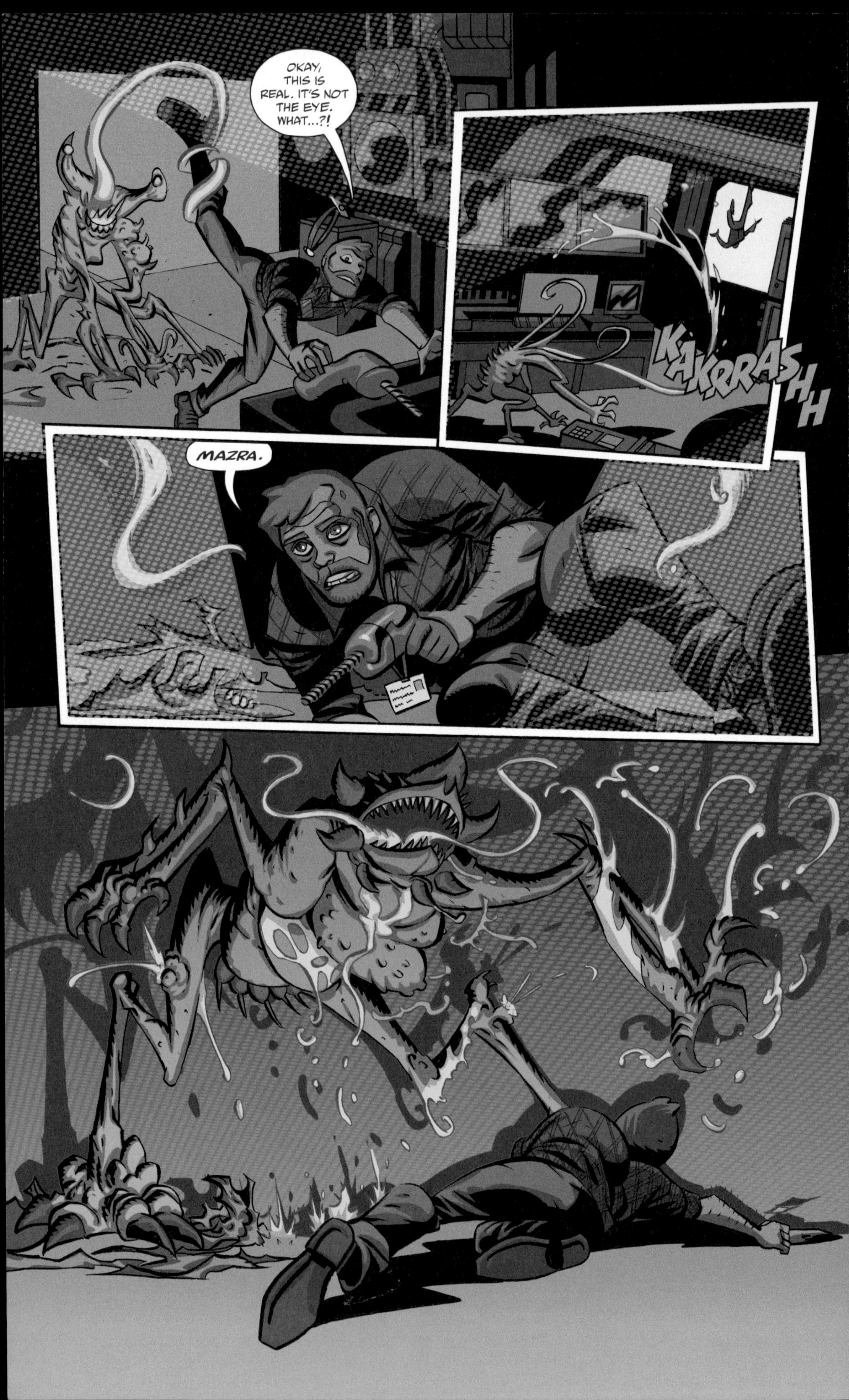
OKAY, THIS IS REAL. IT'S NOT THE EYE. WHAT...?!
KAKERASHHH
MAZRA.

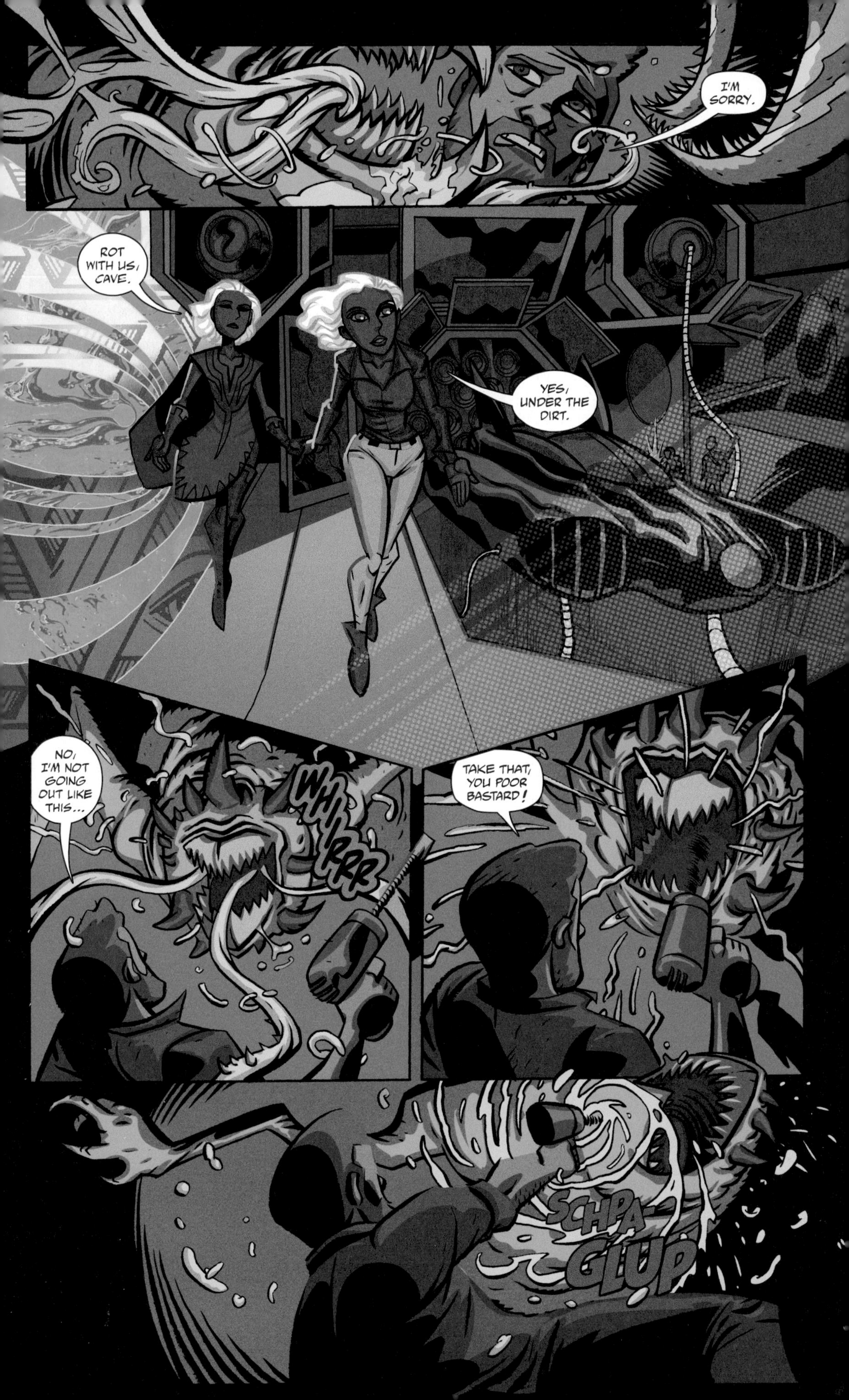
I'M SORRY.
ROT WITH US, CAVE.
YES, UNDER THE DIRT.
NO, I'M NOT GOING OUT LIKE THIS...
WHIRRR
TAKE THAT, YOU POOR BASTARD!
SCHPA-GLUP

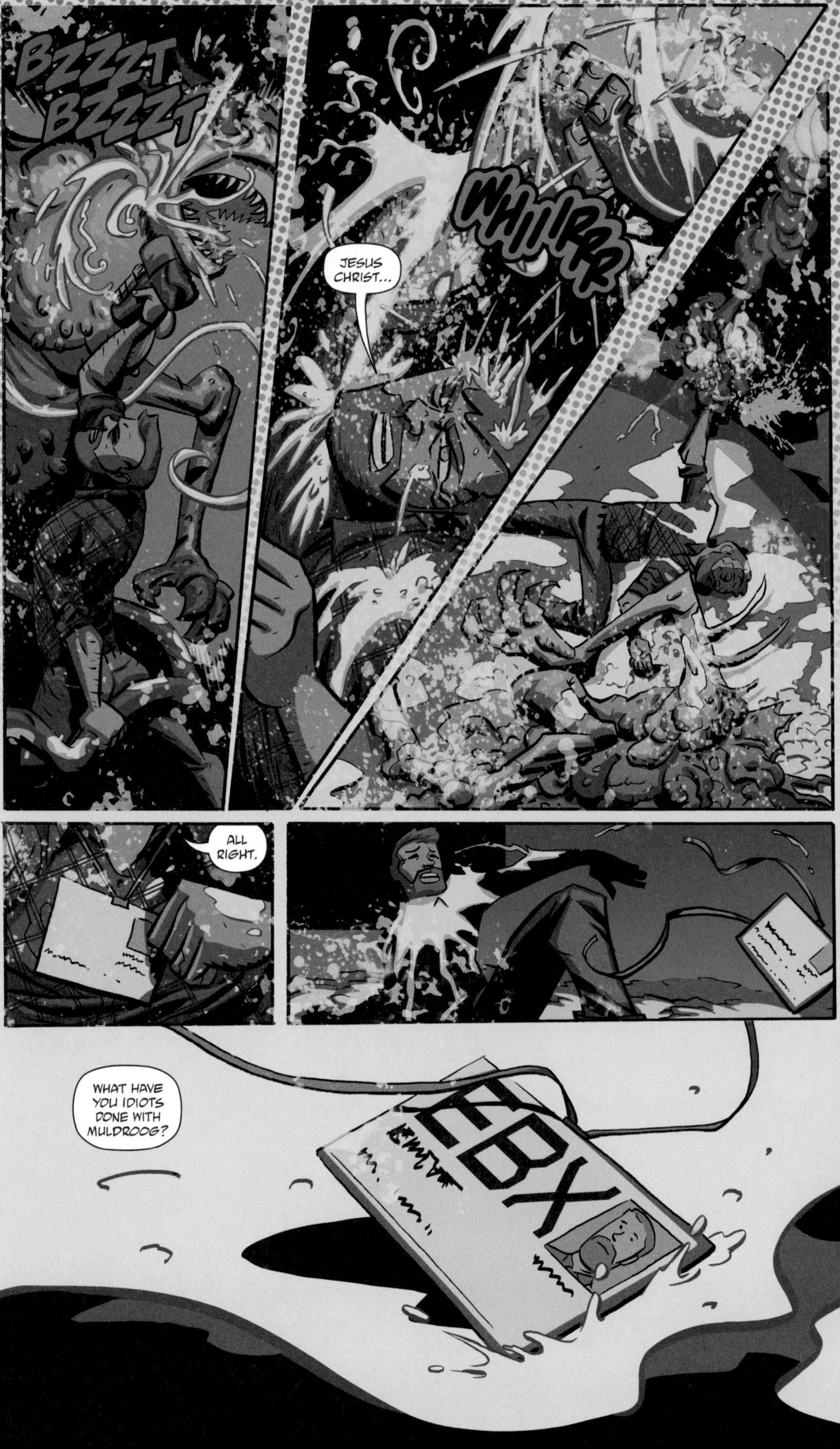
BZZZZT
BZZZZT
WHURRR
JESUS CHRIST...
ALL RIGHT.
WHAT HAVE YOU IDIOTS DONE WITH MULDROOG?
FBX

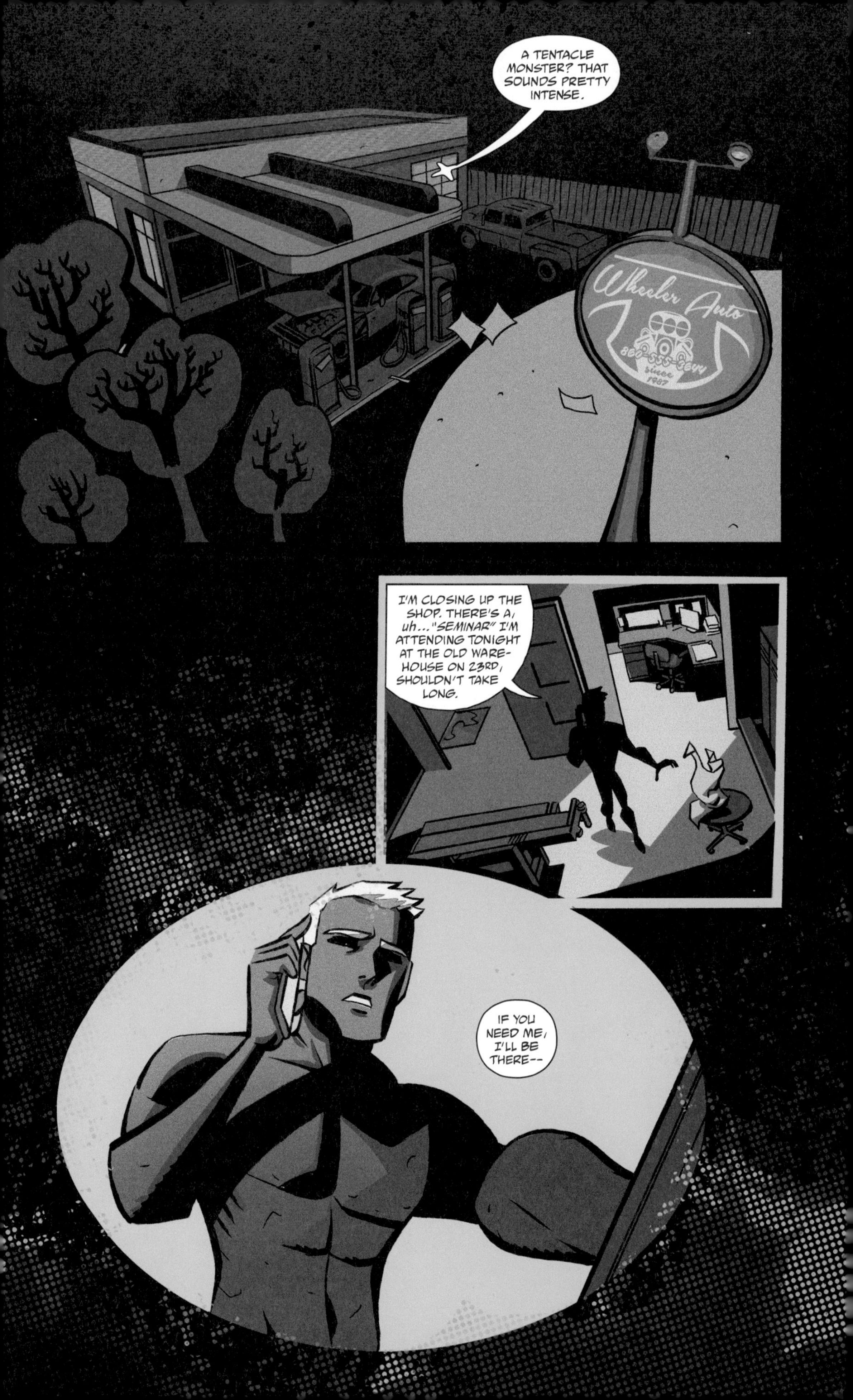
A TENTACLE MONSTER? THAT SOUNDS PRETTY INTENSE.
Wheeler Auto
I'M CLOSING UP THE SHOP. THERE'S A, uh... "SEMINAR" I'M ATTENDING TONIGHT AT THE OLD WAREHOUSE ON 23RD, SHOULDN'T TAKE LONG.
IF YOU NEED ME, I'LL BE THERE--

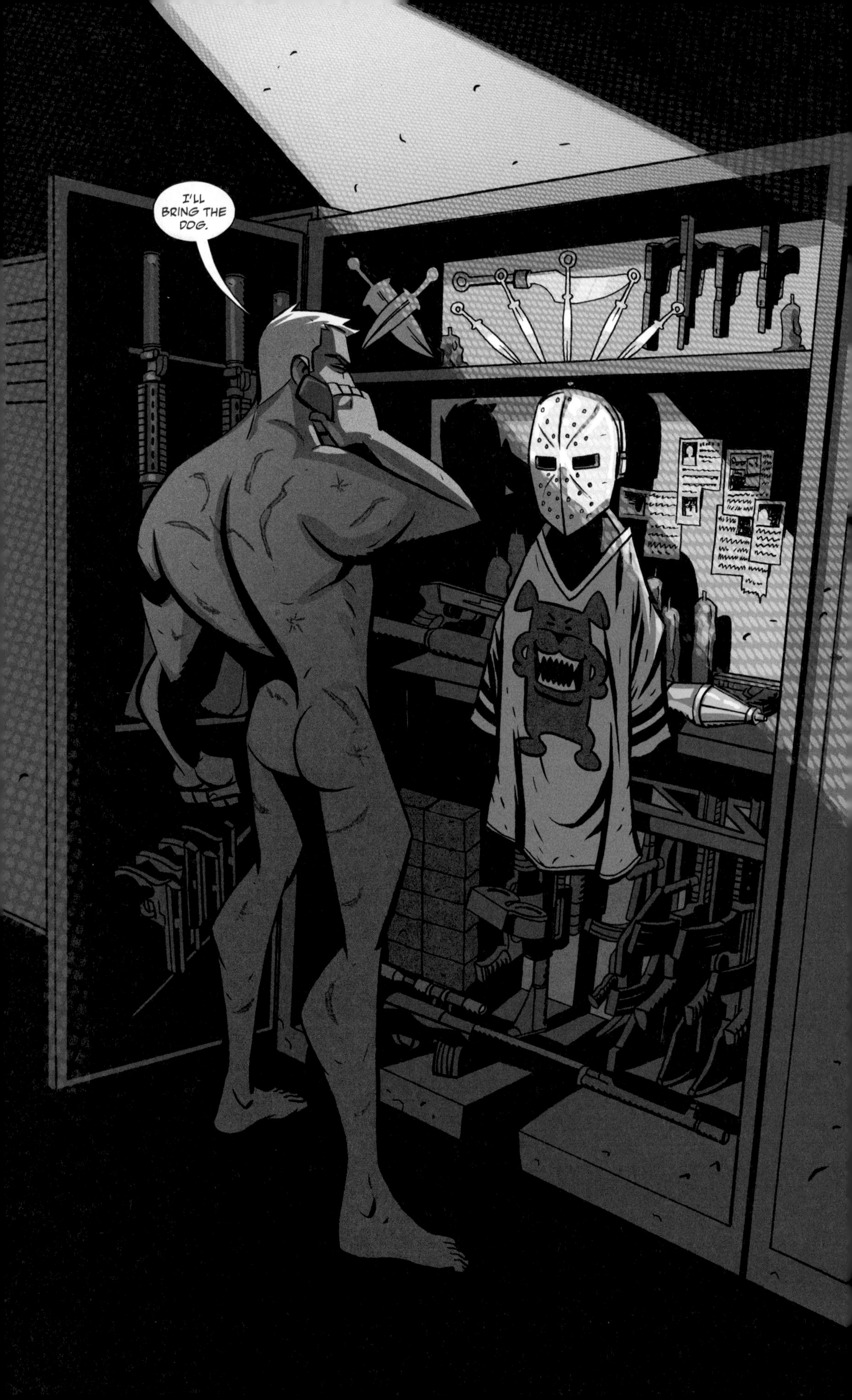
I'LL BRING THE DOG.

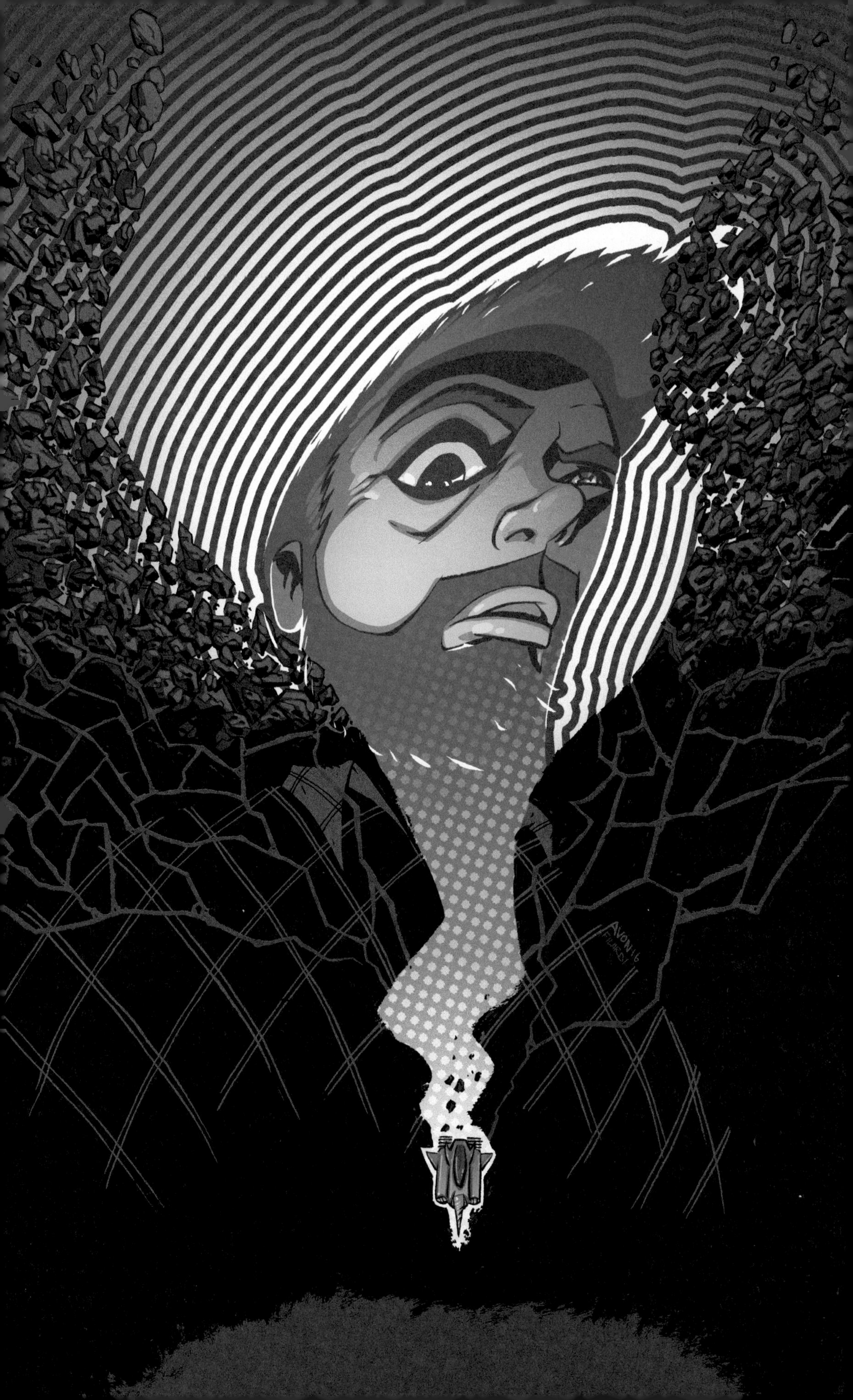

Variant cover art by Matt Taylor

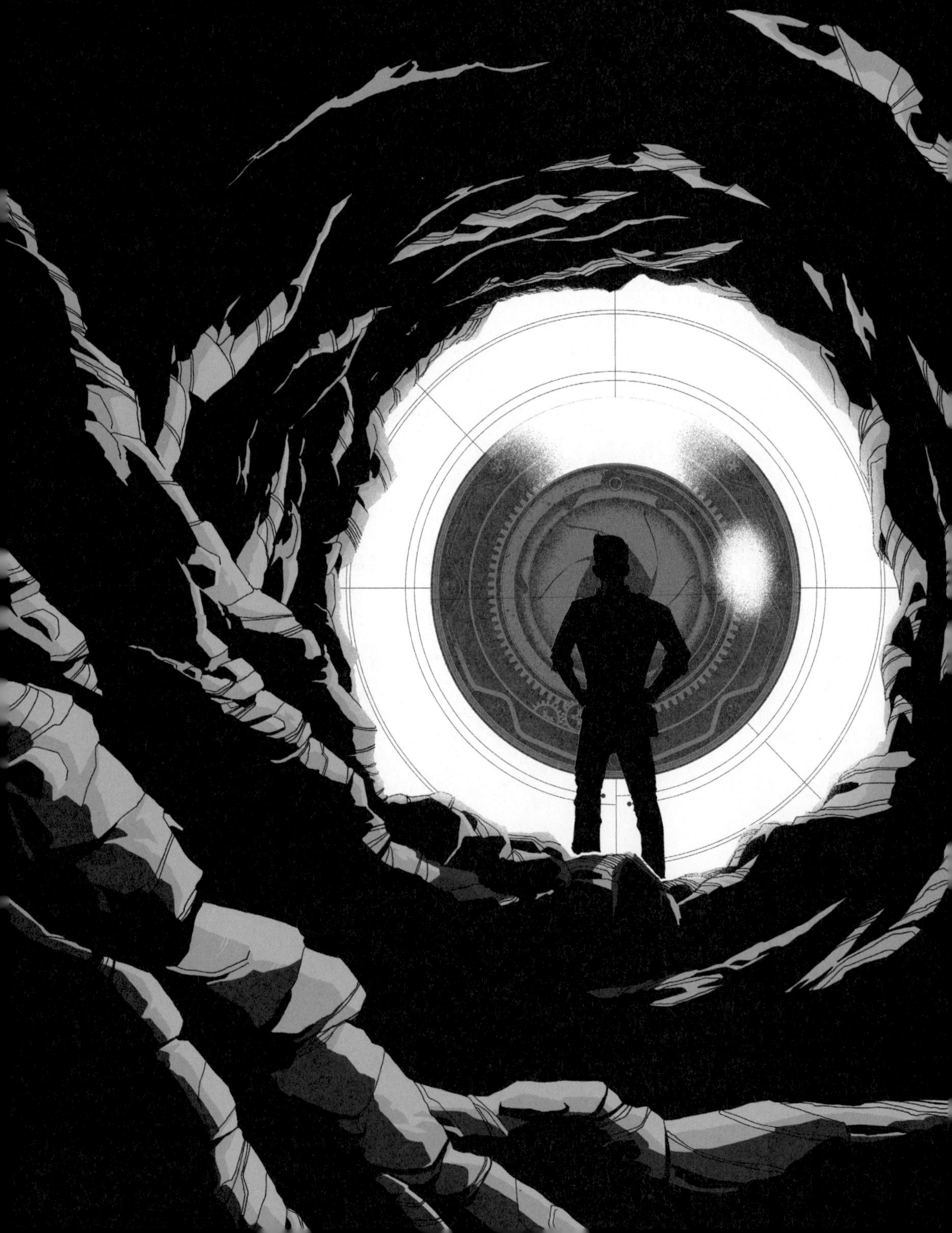

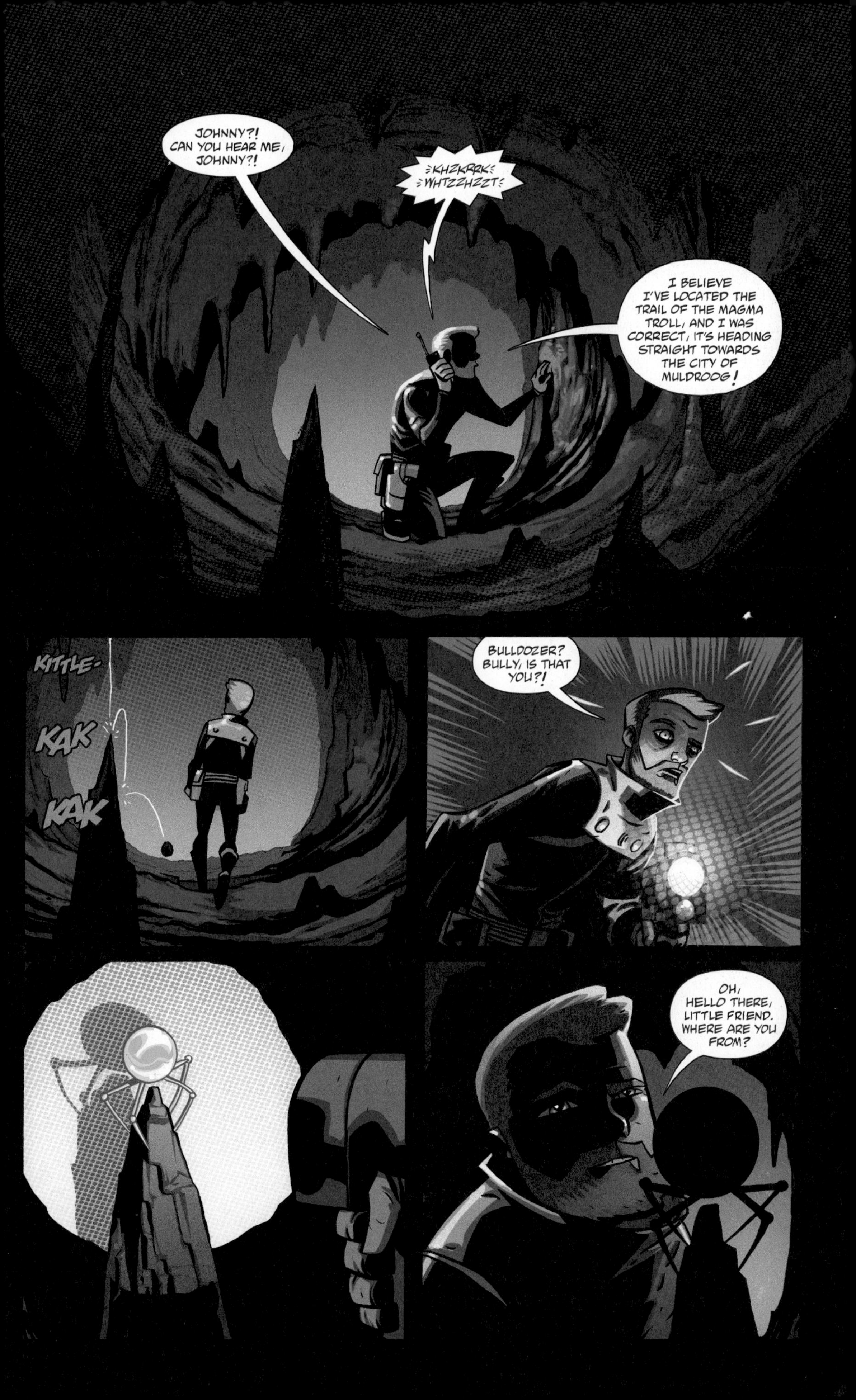
JOHNNY?! CAN YOU HEAR ME, JOHNNY?!
KHZKRRK WHTZZHZZT
I BELIEVE I'VE LOCATED THE TRAIL OF THE MAGMA TROLL, AND I WAS CORRECT, IT'S HEADING STRAIGHT TOWARDS THE CITY OF MULDROOG!
KITTLE-
KAK
KAK
BULLDOZER? BULLY, IS THAT YOU?!
OH, HELLO THERE, LITTLE FRIEND. WHERE ARE YOU FROM?

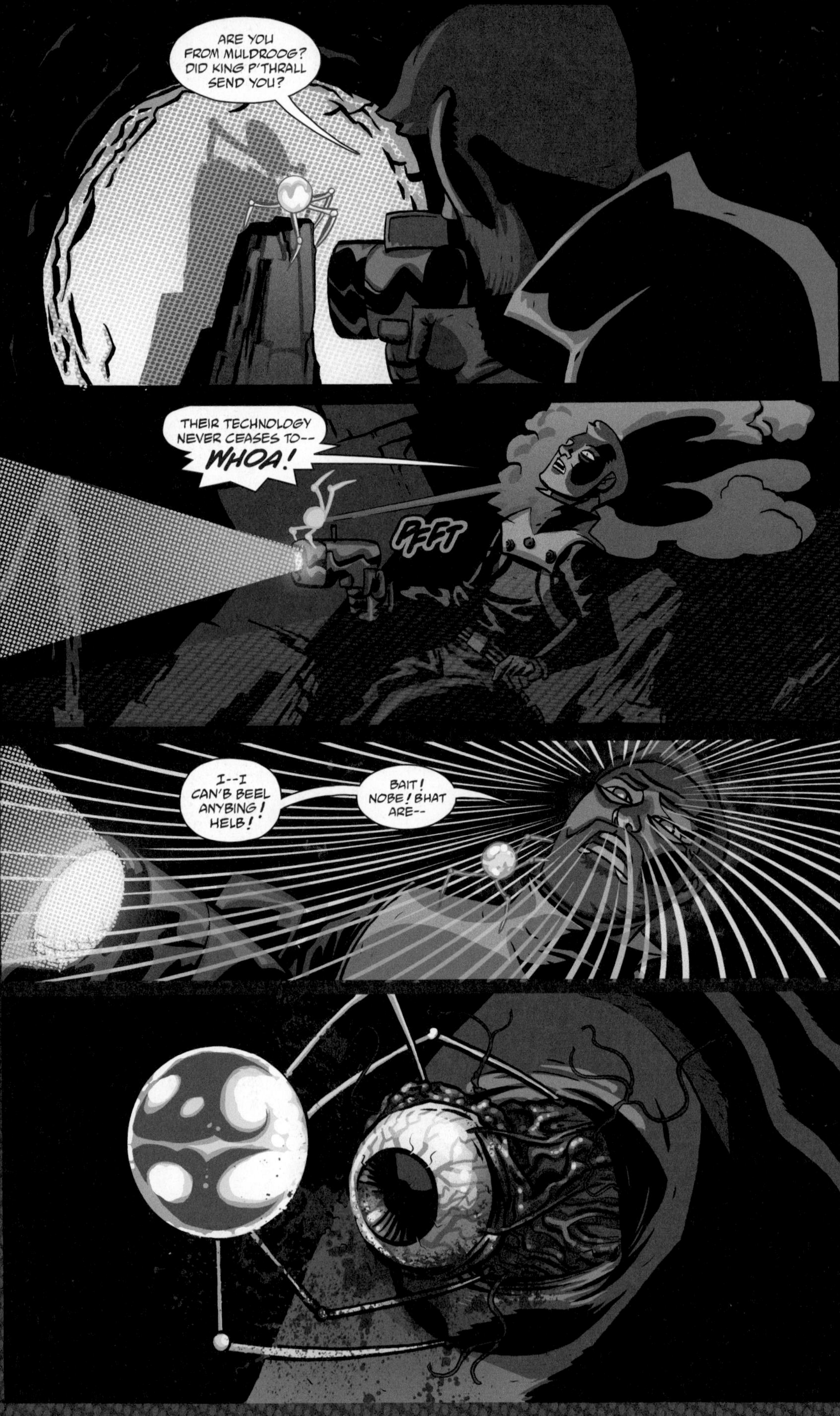
ARE YOU FROM MULDROOG? DID KING P'THRALL SEND YOU?
THEIR TECHNOLOGY NEVER CEASES TO-- WHOA!
PFFT
I--I CAN'B BEEL ANYBING! HELB!
BAIT! NOBE! BHAT ARE--

Cave Carson Has a Cybernetic Eye

HEADACHES

Written by **GERARD WAY & JON RIVERA**
Art & Cover by **MICHAEL AVON OEMING**
Variant Cover by **MATT TAYLOR**
Interior & Cover Colors by **NICK FILARDI**
Letters by **CLEM ROBINS**
Edited by **MOLLY MAHAN**

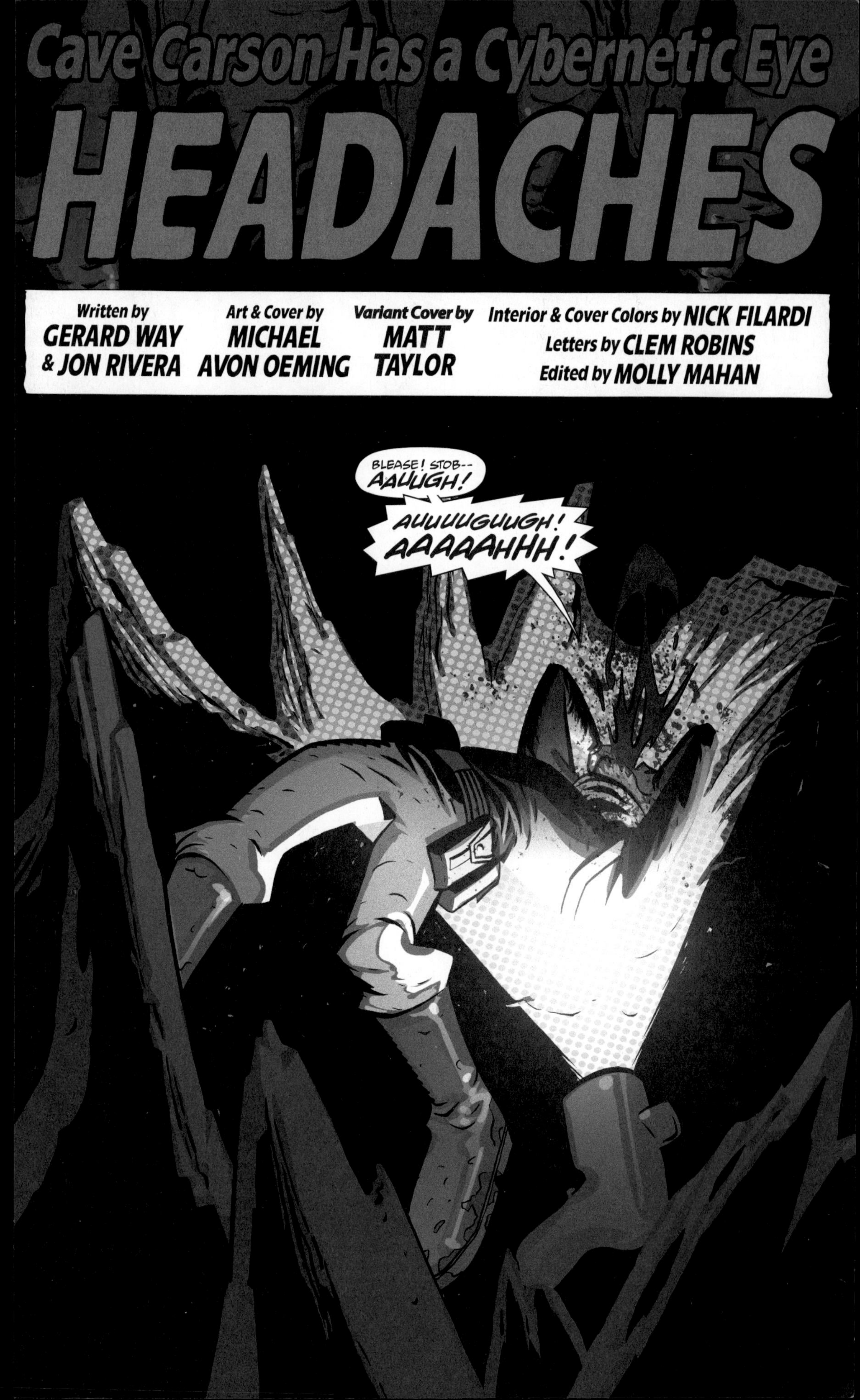
BLEASE! STOB-- AAUUGH!
AUUUUGUUGH! AAAAAHHH!

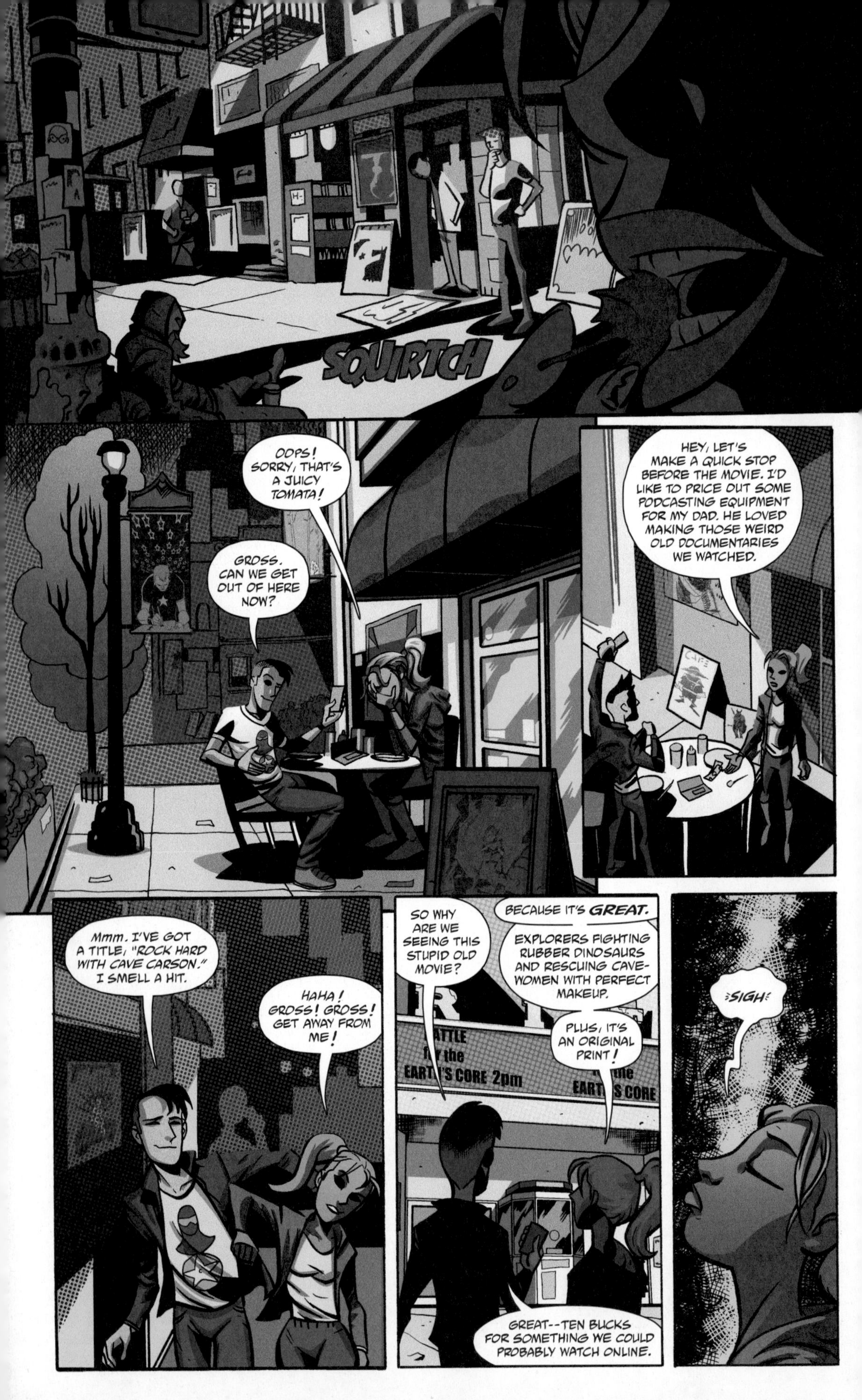
SQUIRTCH
OOPS! SORRY, THAT'S A JUICY TOMATA!
GROSS. CAN WE GET OUT OF HERE NOW?
HEY, LET'S MAKE A QUICK STOP BEFORE THE MOVIE. I'D LIKE TO PRICE OUT SOME PODCASTING EQUIPMENT FOR MY DAD. HE LOVED MAKING THOSE WEIRD OLD DOCUMENTARIES WE WATCHED.
CAFE
Mmm. I'VE GOT A TITLE; "ROCK HARD WITH CAVE CARSON." I SMELL A HIT.
HAHA! GROSS! GROSS! GET AWAY FROM ME!
SO WHY ARE WE SEEING THIS STUPID OLD MOVIE?
BECAUSE IT'S GREAT.
EXPLORERS FIGHTING RUBBER DINOSAURS AND RESCUING CAVE-WOMEN WITH PERFECT MAKEUP.
PLUS, IT'S AN ORIGINAL PRINT!
EARTH'S CORE 2pm
GREAT--TEN BUCKS FOR SOMETHING WE COULD PROBABLY WATCH ONLINE.
SIGH

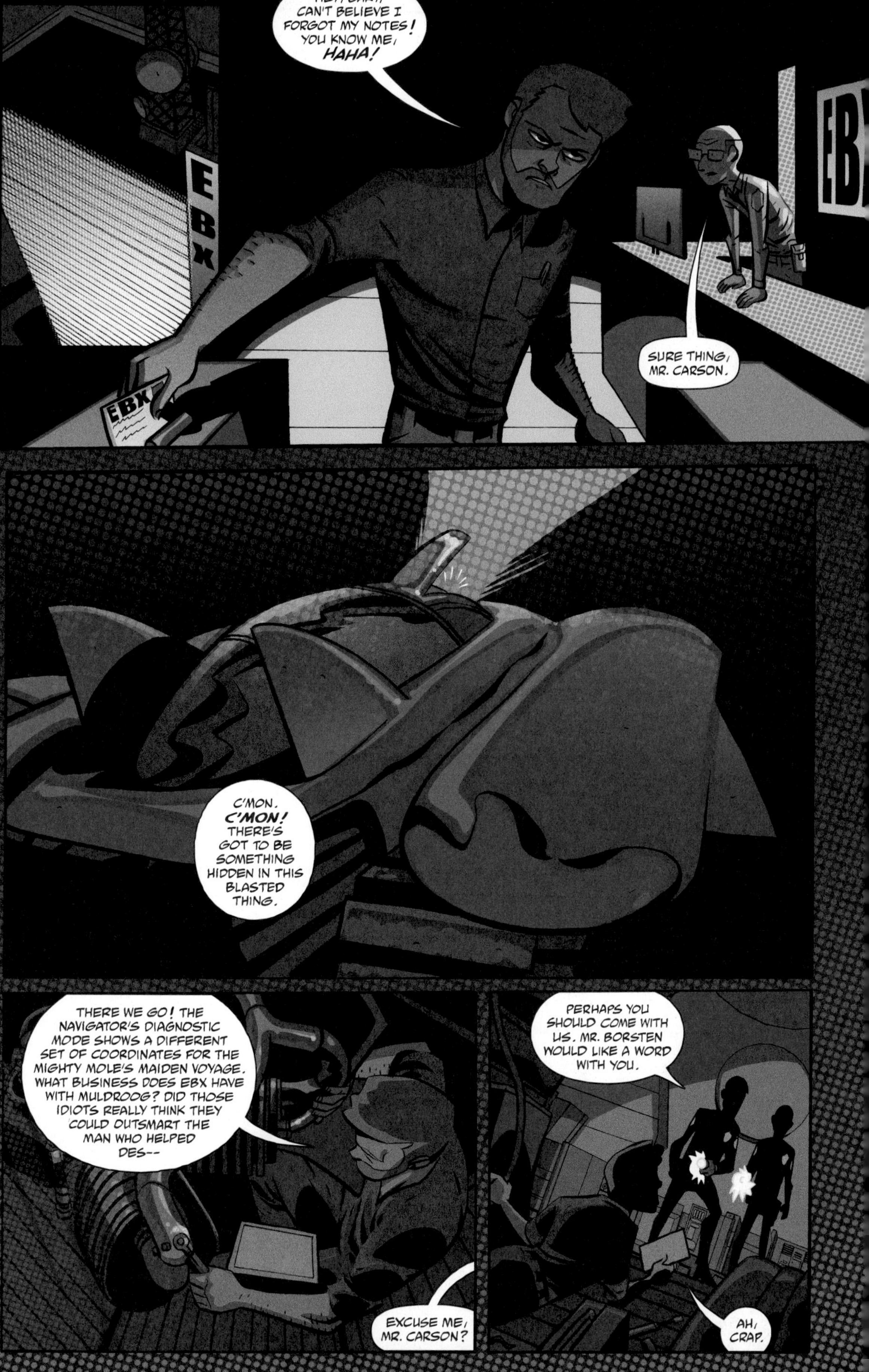
HEY, GARY, CAN'T BELIEVE I FORGOT MY NOTES! YOU KNOW ME, HAHA!
EBX
EBX
EBX
SURE THING, MR. CARSON.
C'MON. C'MON! THERE'S GOT TO BE SOMETHING HIDDEN IN THIS BLASTED THING.
THERE WE GO! THE NAVIGATOR'S DIAGNOSTIC MODE SHOWS A DIFFERENT SET OF COORDINATES FOR THE MIGHTY MOLE'S MAIDEN VOYAGE. WHAT BUSINESS DOES EBX HAVE WITH MULDROOG? DID THOSE IDIOTS REALLY THINK THEY COULD OUTSMART THE MAN WHO HELPED DES--
EXCUSE ME, MR. CARSON?
PERHAPS YOU SHOULD COME WITH US. MR. BORSTEN WOULD LIKE A WORD WITH YOU.
AH, CRAP.

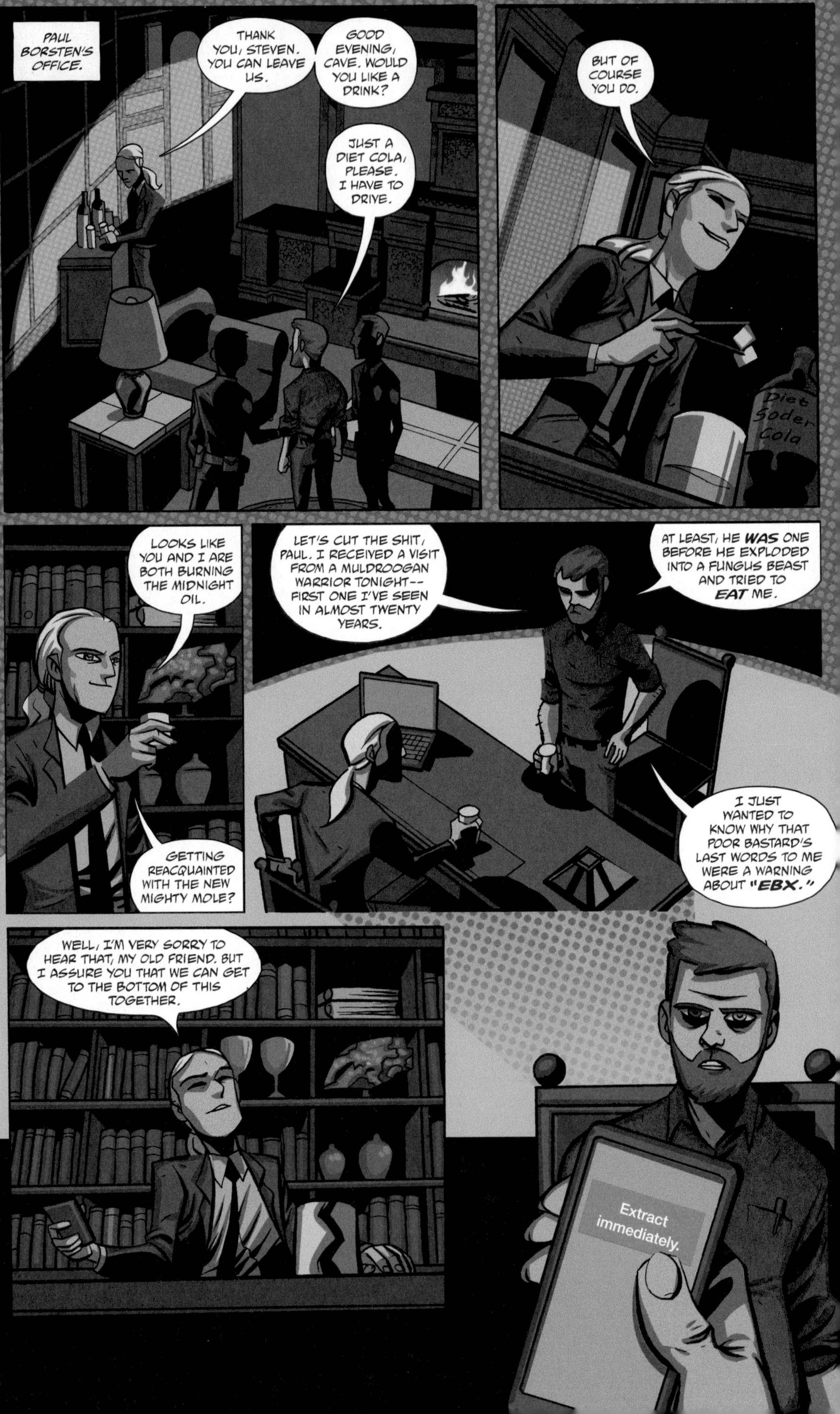
PAUL BORSTEN'S OFFICE.
THANK YOU, STEVEN. YOU CAN LEAVE US.
GOOD EVENING, CAVE. WOULD YOU LIKE A DRINK?
JUST A DIET COLA, PLEASE. I HAVE TO DRIVE.
BUT OF COURSE YOU DO.
Diet Soder Cola
LOOKS LIKE YOU AND I ARE BOTH BURNING THE MIDNIGHT OIL.
GETTING REACQUAINTED WITH THE NEW MIGHTY MOLE?
LET'S CUT THE SHIT, PAUL. I RECEIVED A VISIT FROM A MULDROOGAN WARRIOR TONIGHT-- FIRST ONE I'VE SEEN IN ALMOST TWENTY YEARS.
AT LEAST, HE **WAS** ONE BEFORE HE EXPLODED INTO A FUNGUS BEAST AND TRIED TO **EAT** ME.
I JUST WANTED TO KNOW WHY THAT POOR BASTARD'S LAST WORDS TO ME WERE A WARNING ABOUT **"EBX."**
WELL, I'M VERY SORRY TO HEAR THAT, MY OLD FRIEND. BUT I ASSURE YOU THAT WE CAN GET TO THE BOTTOM OF THIS TOGETHER.
Extract immediately.

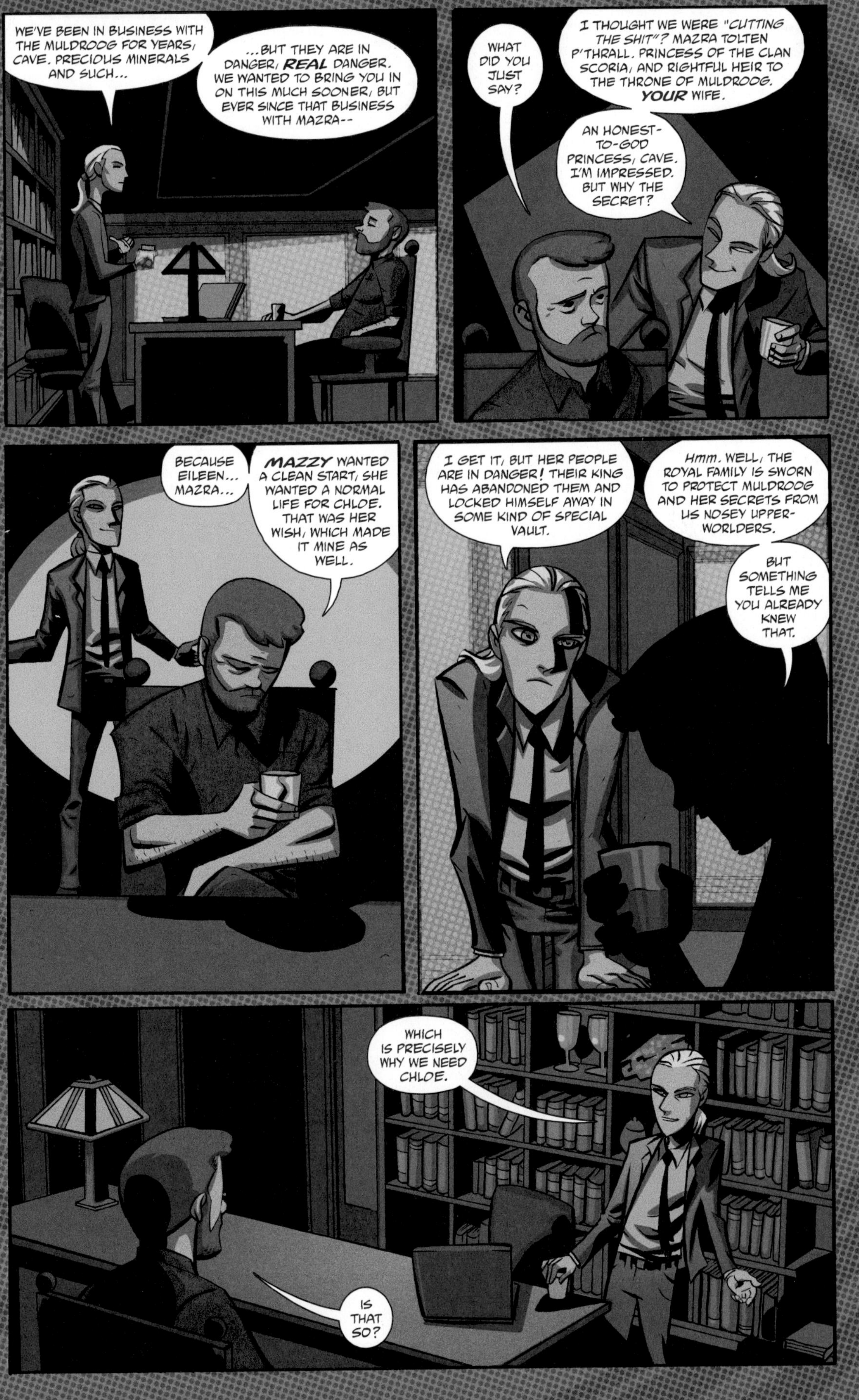
WE'VE BEEN IN BUSINESS WITH THE MULDROOG FOR YEARS, CAVE. PRECIOUS MINERALS AND SUCH...
...BUT THEY ARE IN DANGER, REAL DANGER. WE WANTED TO BRING YOU IN ON THIS MUCH SOONER, BUT EVER SINCE THAT BUSINESS WITH MAZRA--
WHAT DID YOU JUST SAY?
I THOUGHT WE WERE "CUTTING THE SHIT"? MAZRA TOLTEN P'THRALL. PRINCESS OF THE CLAN SCORIA, AND RIGHTFUL HEIR TO THE THRONE OF MULDROOG. YOUR WIFE.
AN HONEST-TO-GOD PRINCESS, CAVE. I'M IMPRESSED. BUT WHY THE SECRET?
BECAUSE EILEEN... MAZRA...
MAZZY WANTED A CLEAN START, SHE WANTED A NORMAL LIFE FOR CHLOE. THAT WAS HER WISH, WHICH MADE IT MINE AS WELL.
I GET IT, BUT HER PEOPLE ARE IN DANGER! THEIR KING HAS ABANDONED THEM AND LOCKED HIMSELF AWAY IN SOME KIND OF SPECIAL VAULT.
Hmm. WELL, THE ROYAL FAMILY IS SWORN TO PROTECT MULDROOG AND HER SECRETS FROM US NOSEY UPPER-WORLDERS.
BUT SOMETHING TELLS ME YOU ALREADY KNEW THAT.
WHICH IS PRECISELY WHY WE NEED CHLOE.
IS THAT SO?

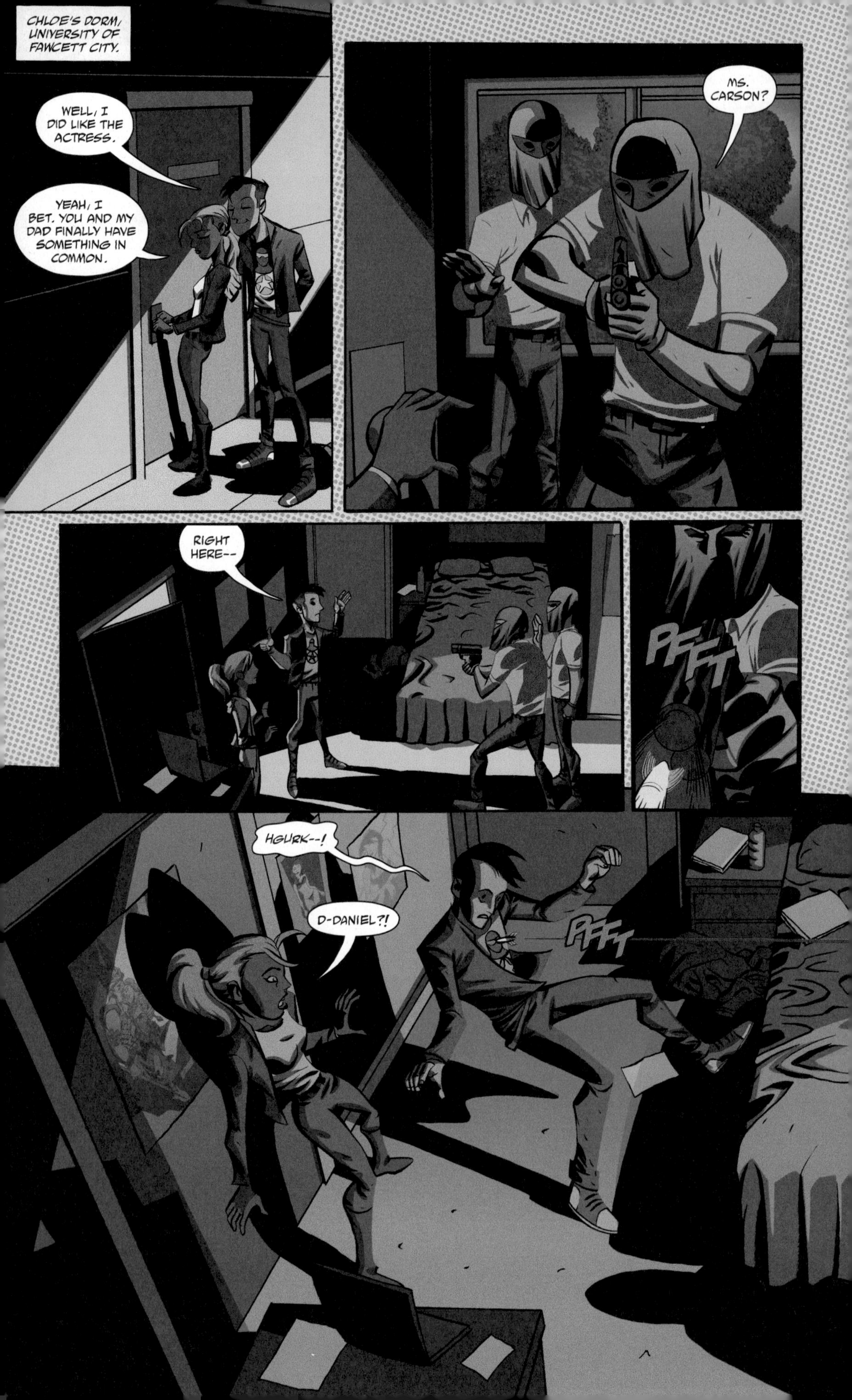
CHLOE'S DORM, UNIVERSITY OF FAWCETT CITY.
WELL, I DID LIKE THE ACTRESS.
YEAH, I BET. YOU AND MY DAD FINALLY HAVE SOMETHING IN COMMON.
MS. CARSON?
RIGHT HERE--
PFFT
HGURK--!
D-DANIEL?!
PFFT

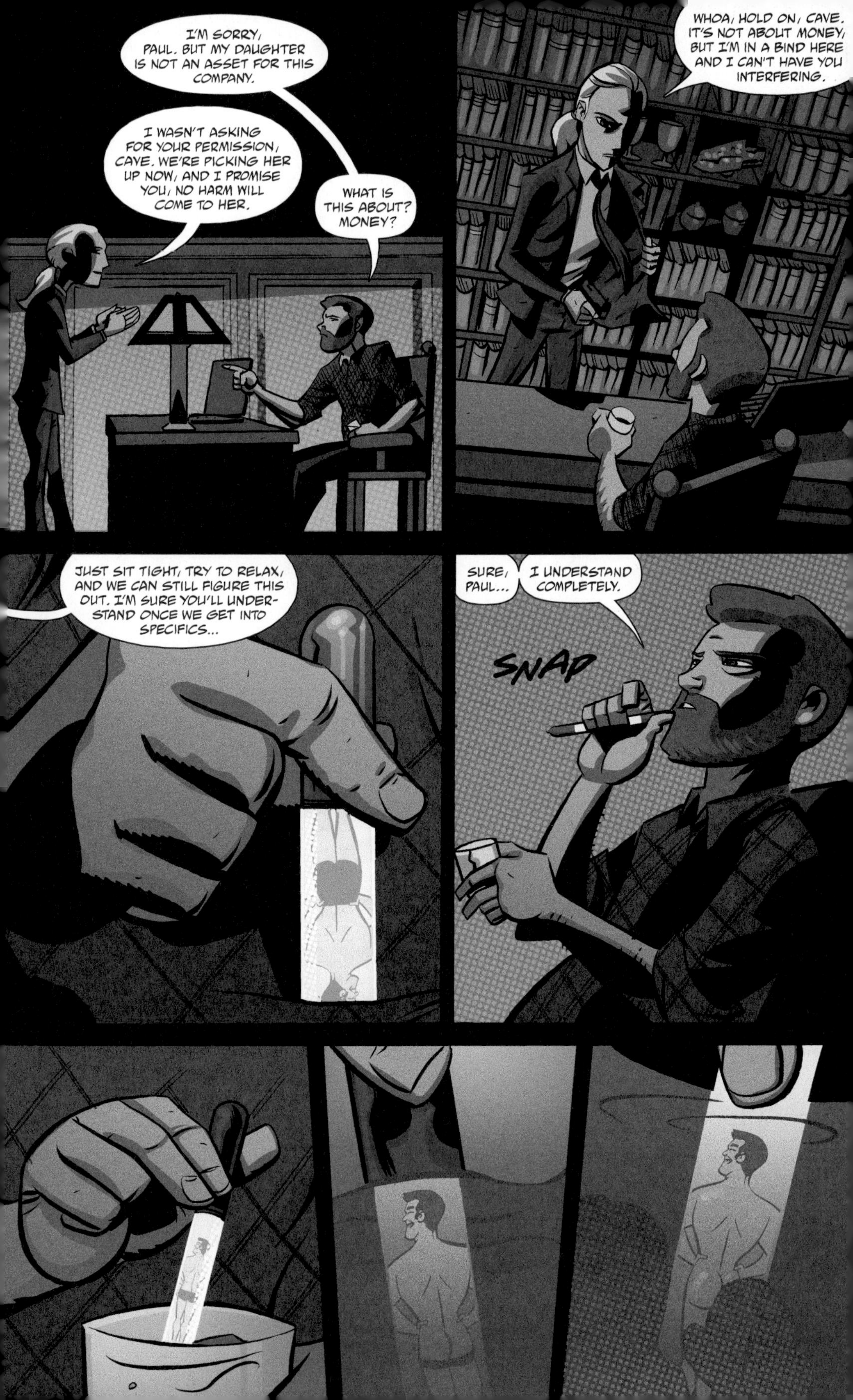
I'M SORRY, PAUL. BUT MY DAUGHTER IS NOT AN ASSET FOR THIS COMPANY.
I WASN'T ASKING FOR YOUR PERMISSION, CAVE. WE'RE PICKING HER UP NOW, AND I PROMISE YOU, NO HARM WILL COME TO HER.
WHAT IS THIS ABOUT? MONEY?
WHOA, HOLD ON, CAVE. IT'S NOT ABOUT MONEY, BUT I'M IN A BIND HERE AND I CAN'T HAVE YOU INTERFERING.
JUST SIT TIGHT, TRY TO RELAX, AND WE CAN STILL FIGURE THIS OUT. I'M SURE YOU'LL UNDER-STAND ONCE WE GET INTO SPECIFICS...
SURE, PAUL...
I UNDERSTAND COMPLETELY.
SNAP

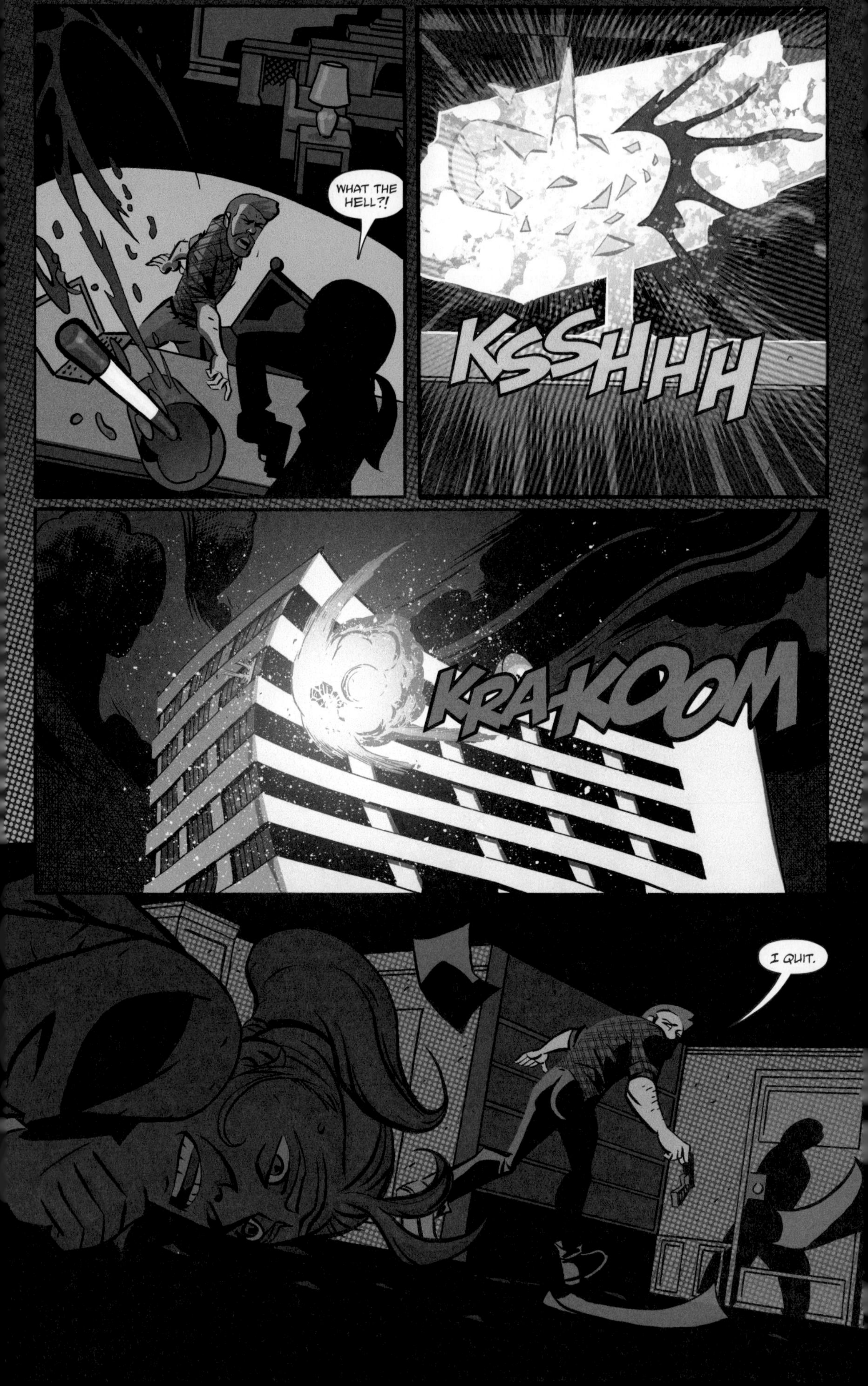
WHAT THE HELL?!
KSSHHH
KRA-KOOM
I QUIT.

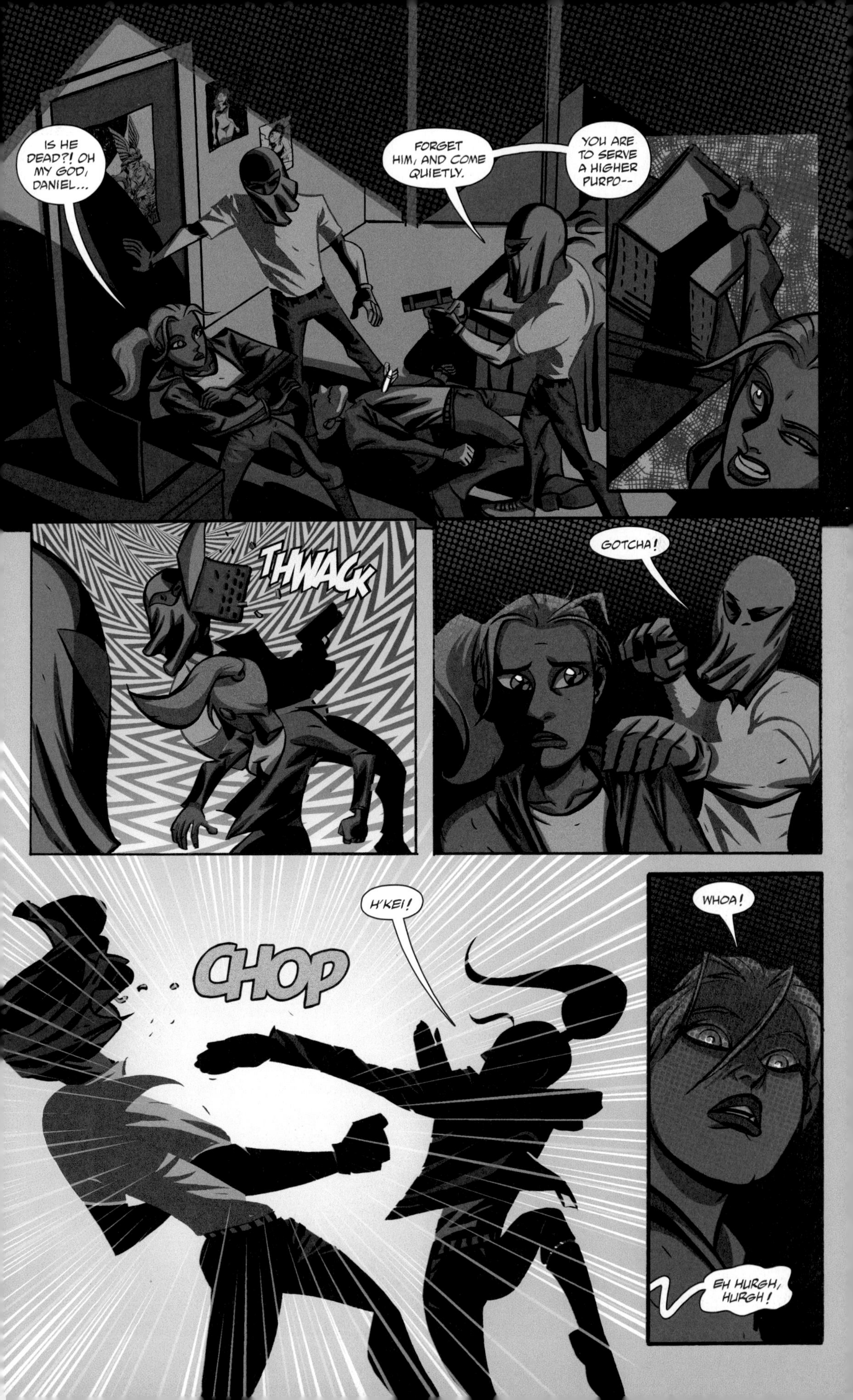
IS HE DEAD?! OH MY GOD, DANIEL...
FORGET HIM, AND COME QUIETLY.
YOU ARE TO SERVE A HIGHER PURPO--
THWACK
GOTCHA!
CHOP
H'KEI!
WHOA!
EH HURGH, HURGH!

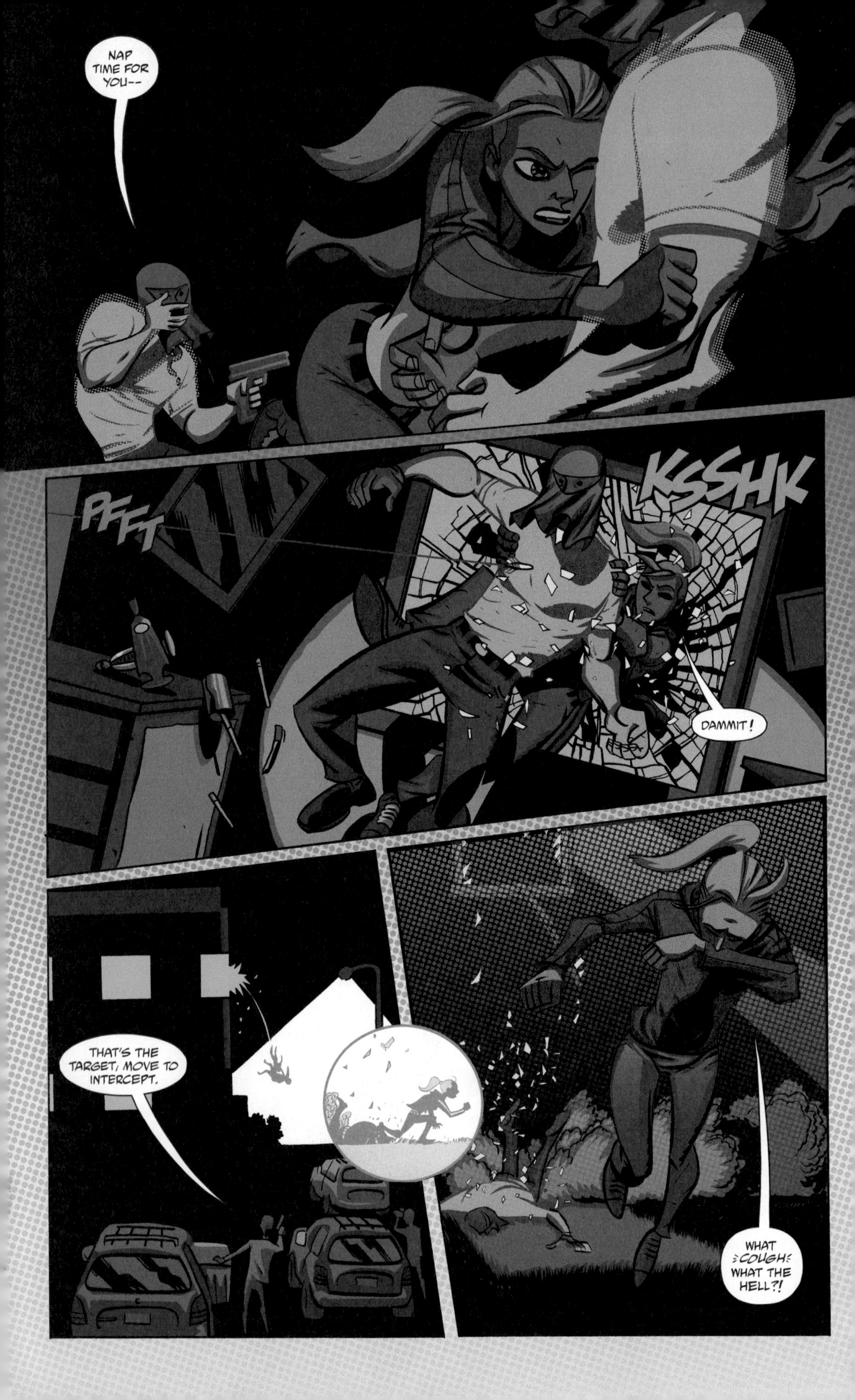
NAP TIME FOR YOU--
PFFFT
KSSHK
DAMMIT!
THAT'S THE TARGET, MOVE TO INTERCEPT.
WHAT *COUGH* WHAT THE HELL?!

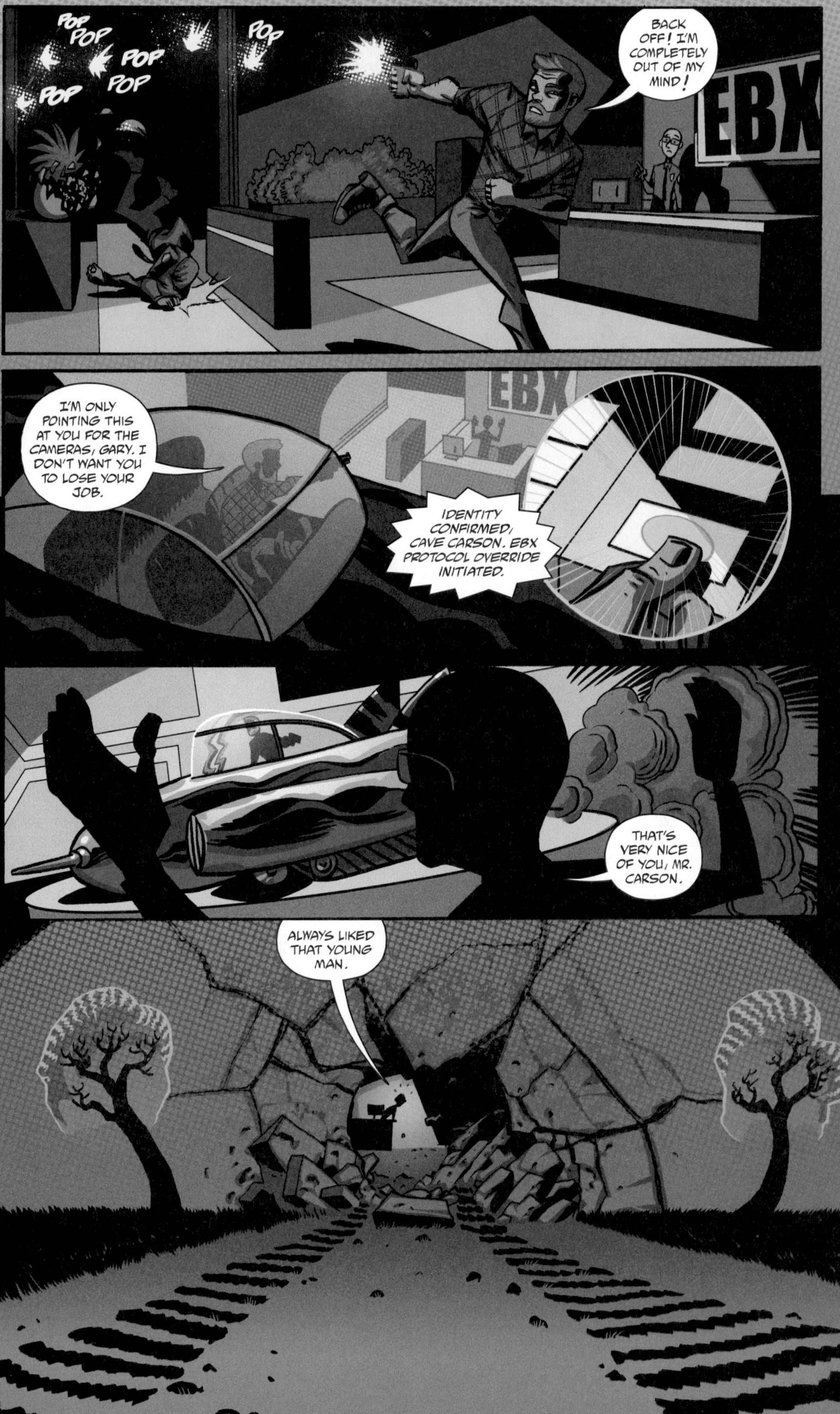
POP
POP
POP
POP
POP
POP
BACK OFF! I'M COMPLETELY OUT OF MY MIND!
EBX
EBX
I'M ONLY POINTING THIS AT YOU FOR THE CAMERAS, GARY. I DON'T WANT YOU TO LOSE YOUR JOB.
IDENTITY CONFIRMED, CAVE CARSON. EBX PROTOCOL OVERRIDE INITIATED.
THAT'S VERY NICE OF YOU, MR. CARSON.
ALWAYS LIKED THAT YOUNG MAN.

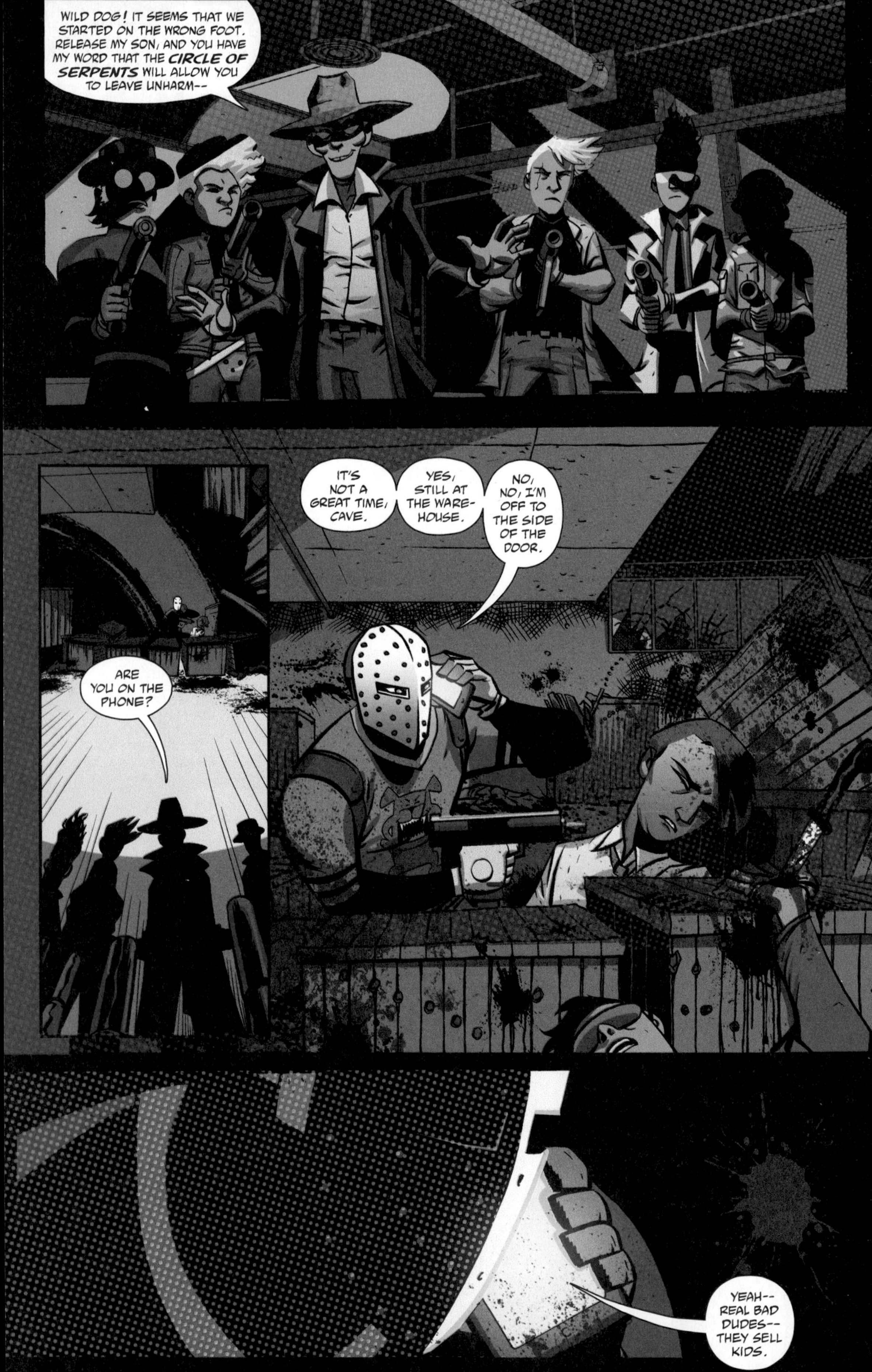
WILD DOG! IT SEEMS THAT WE STARTED ON THE WRONG FOOT. RELEASE MY SON, AND YOU HAVE MY WORD THAT THE CIRCLE OF SERPENTS WILL ALLOW YOU TO LEAVE UNHARM--
ARE YOU ON THE PHONE?
IT'S NOT A GREAT TIME, CAVE.
YES, STILL AT THE WARE-HOUSE.
NO, NO, I'M OFF TO THE SIDE OF THE DOOR.
YEAH-- REAL BAD DUDES-- THEY SELL KIDS.

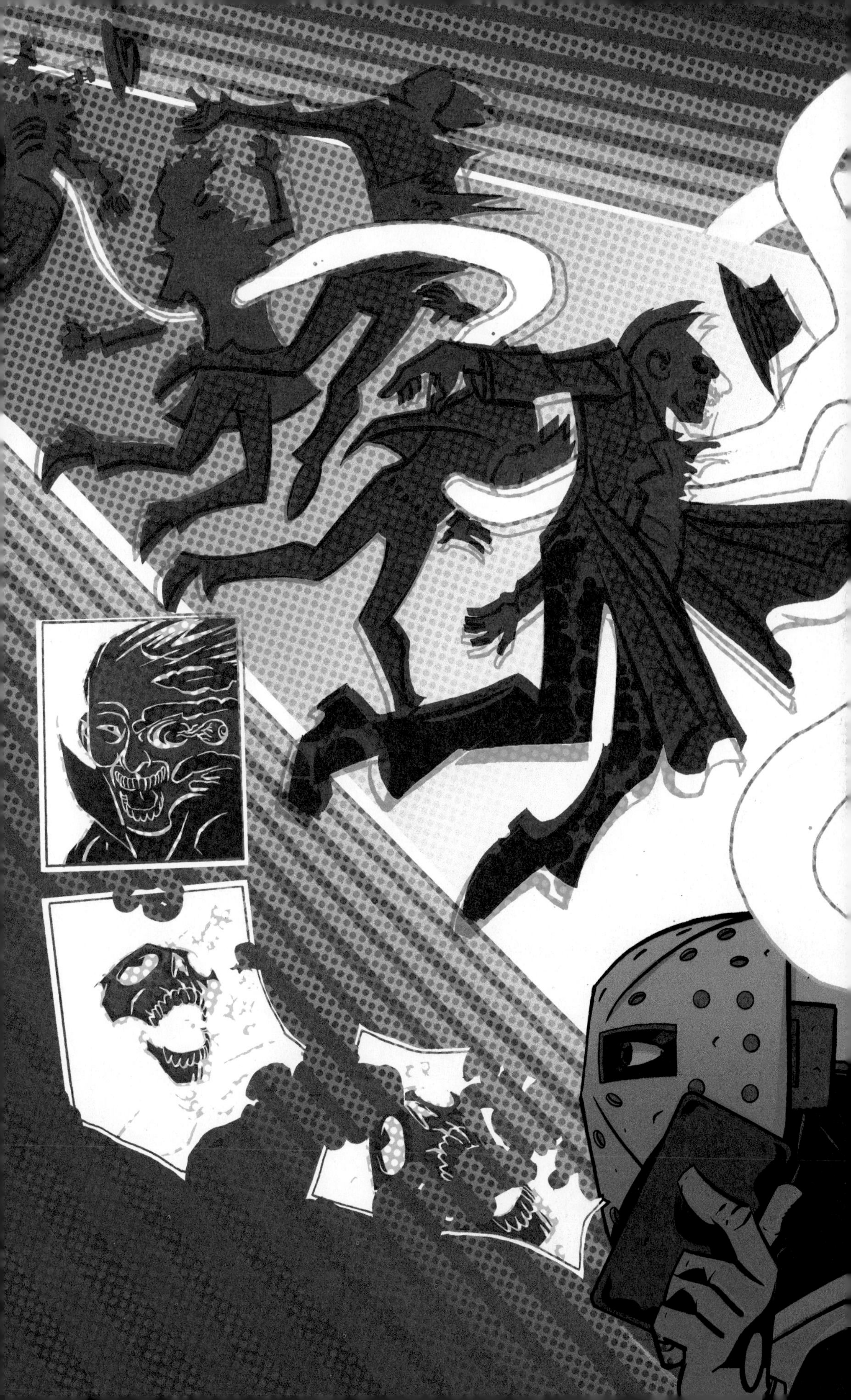

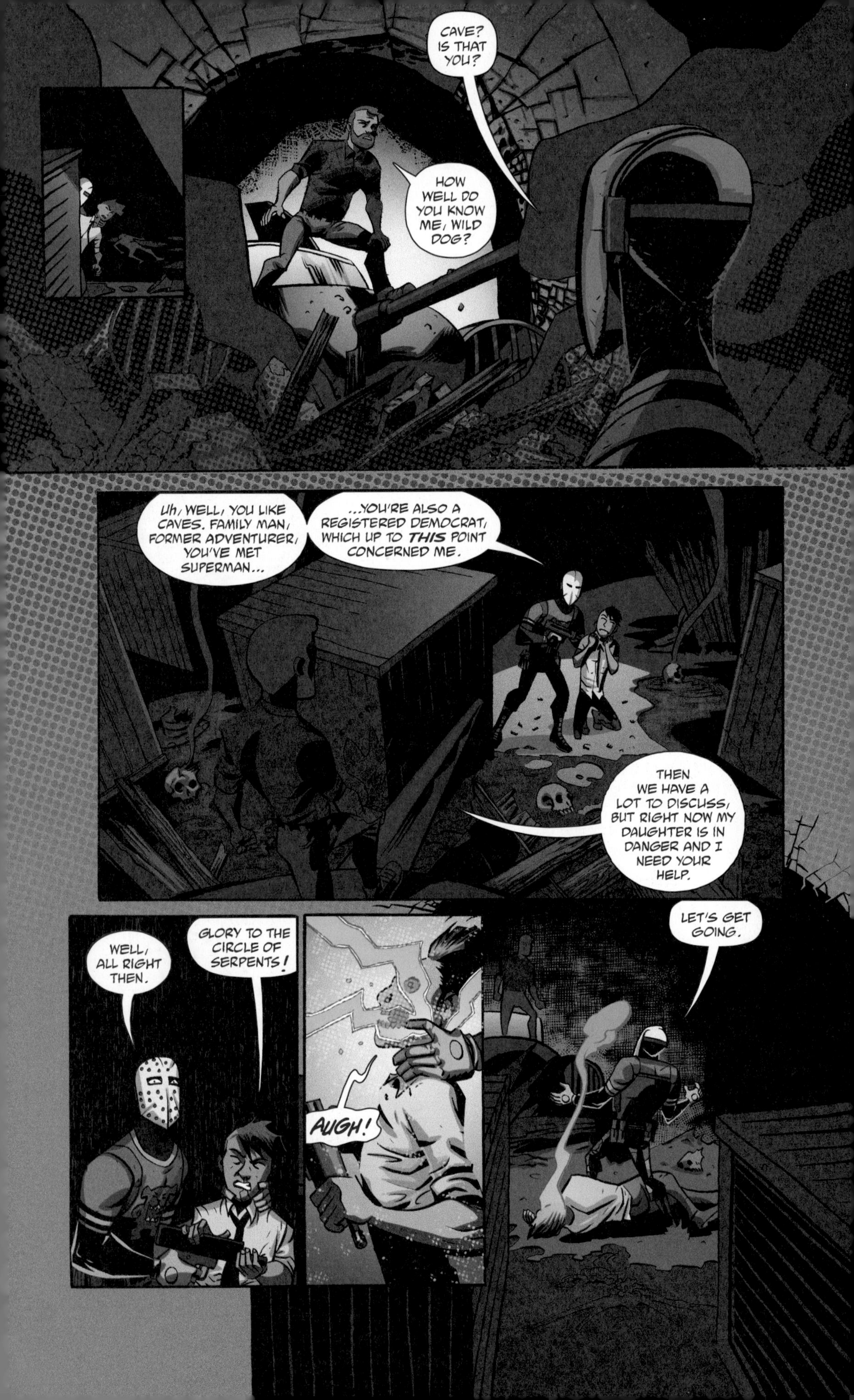
CAVE? IS THAT YOU?
HOW WELL DO YOU KNOW ME, WILD DOG?
UH, WELL, YOU LIKE CAVES. FAMILY MAN, FORMER ADVENTURER, YOU'VE MET SUPERMAN...
...YOU'RE ALSO A REGISTERED DEMOCRAT, WHICH UP TO THIS POINT CONCERNED ME.
THEN WE HAVE A LOT TO DISCUSS, BUT RIGHT NOW MY DAUGHTER IS IN DANGER AND I NEED YOUR HELP.
WELL, ALL RIGHT THEN.
GLORY TO THE CIRCLE OF SERPENTS!
AUGH!
LET'S GET GOING.

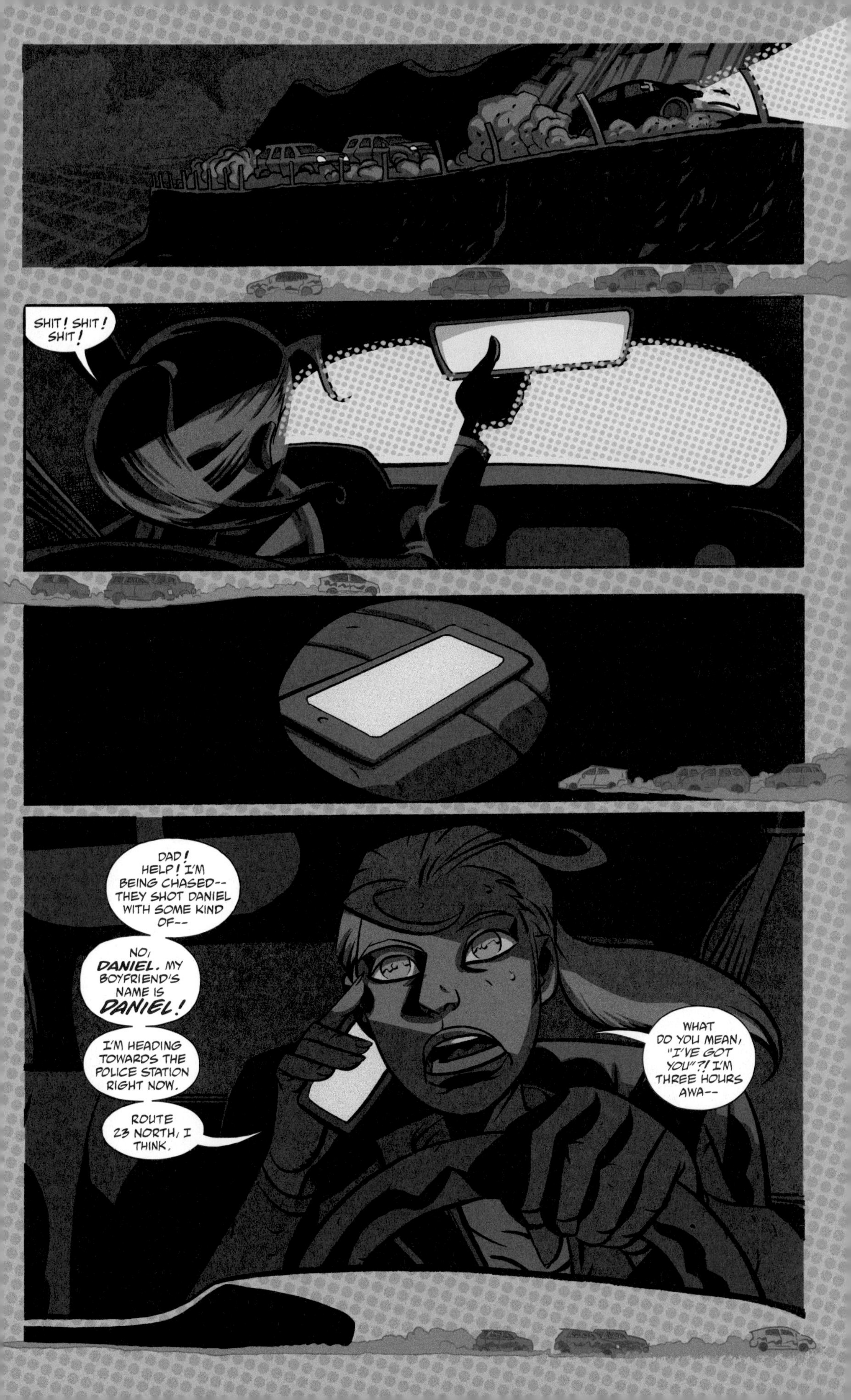
SHIT! SHIT! SHIT!
DAD! HELP! I'M BEING CHASED-- THEY SHOT DANIEL WITH SOME KIND OF--
NO, DANIEL. MY BOYFRIEND'S NAME IS DANIEL!
I'M HEADING TOWARDS THE POLICE STATION RIGHT NOW.
ROUTE 23 NORTH, I THINK.
WHAT DO YOU MEAN, "I'VE GOT YOU"?! I'M THREE HOURS AWA--

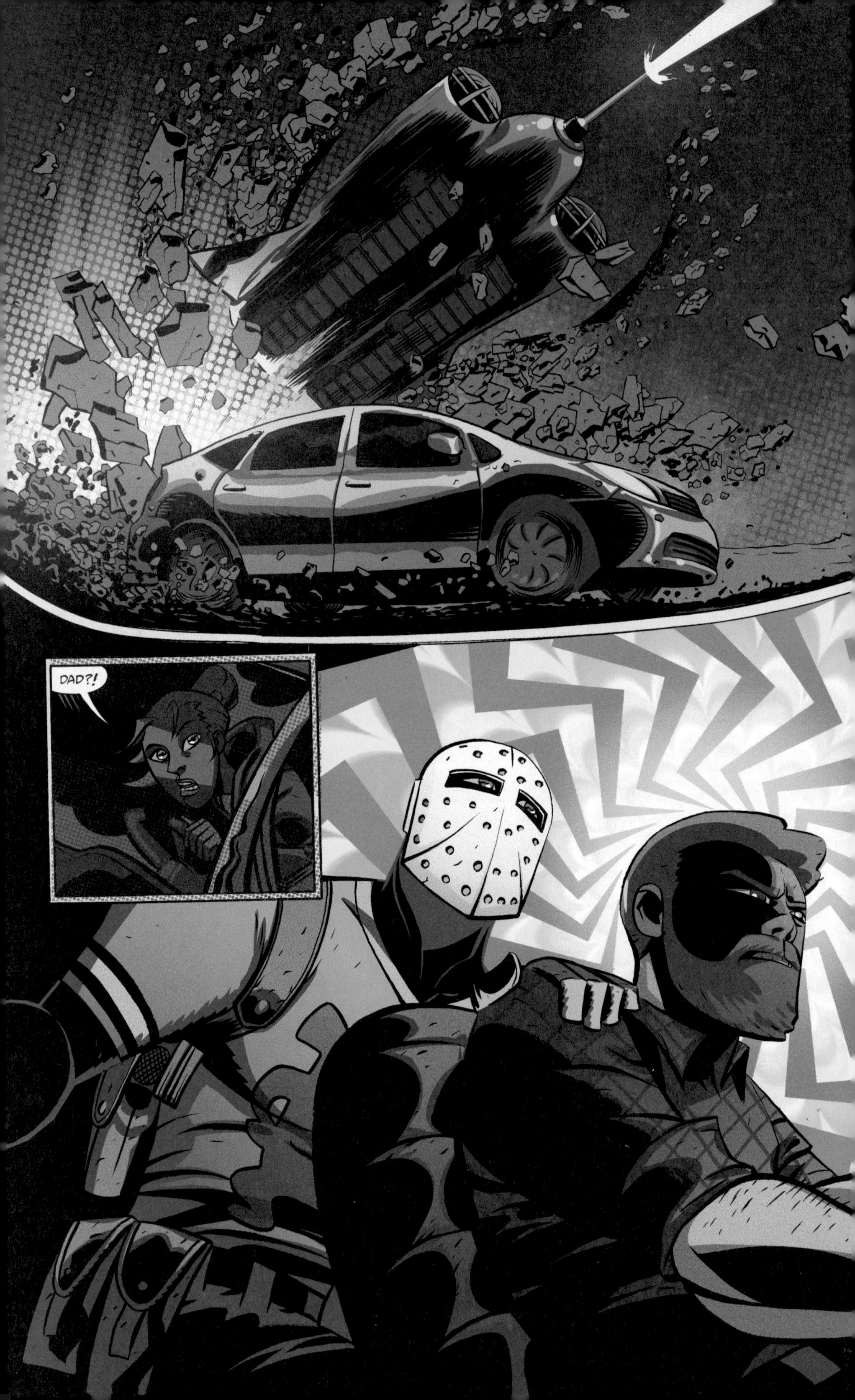
DAD?!

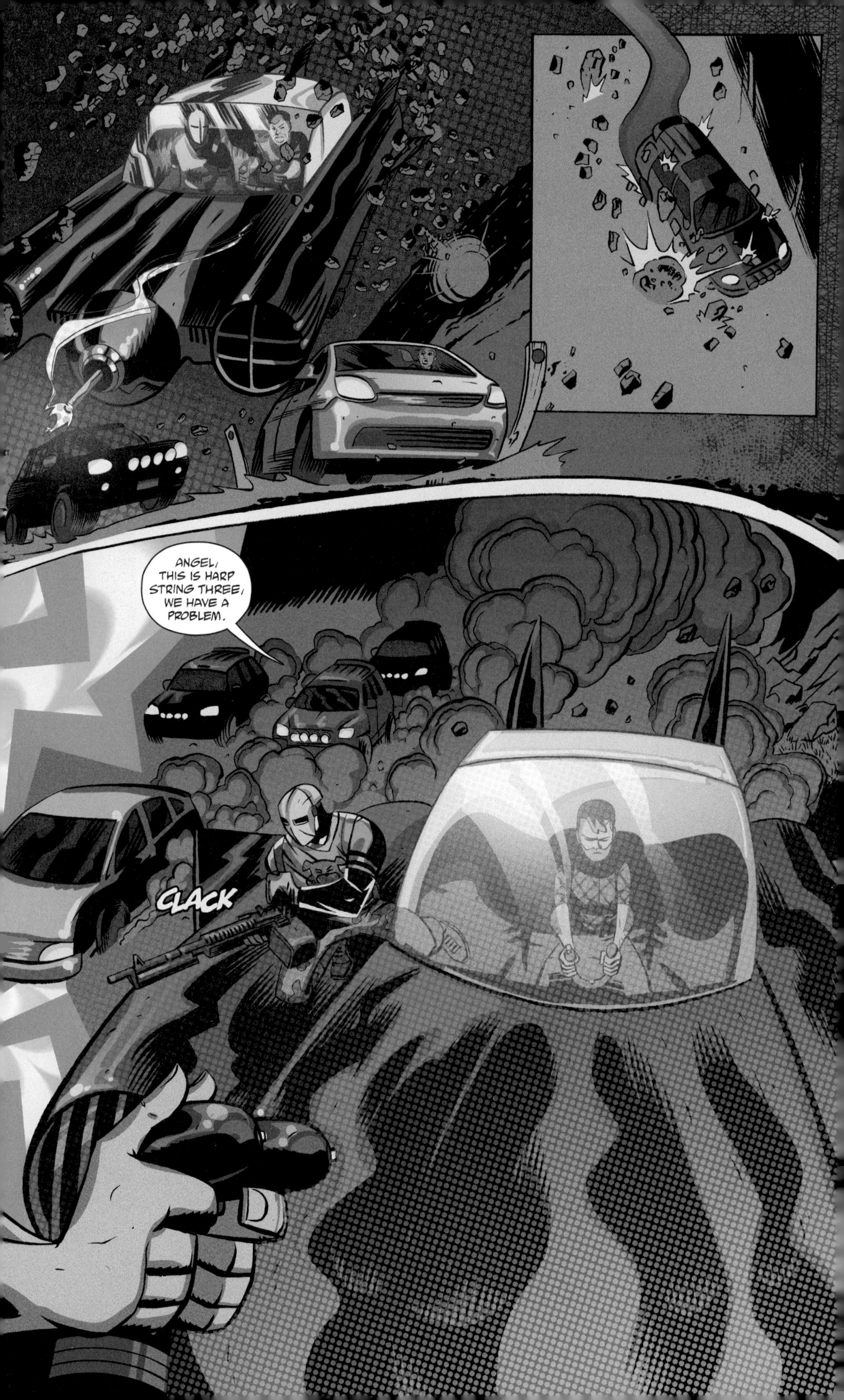
ANGEL, THIS IS HARP STRING THREE, WE HAVE A PROBLEM.
CLACK

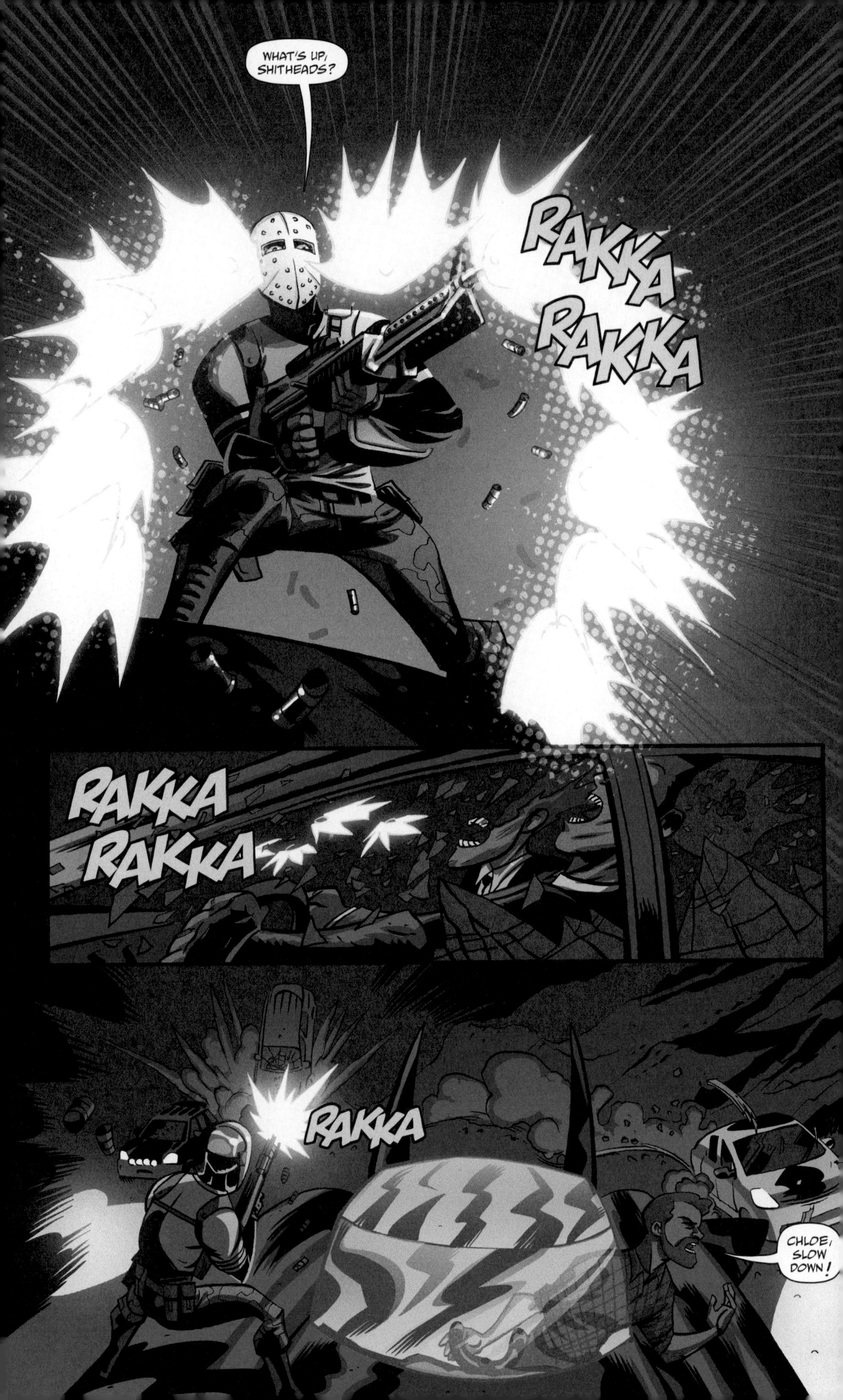
WHAT'S UP, SHITHEADS?
RAKKA RAKKA
RAKKA RAKKA
RAKKA
CHLOE, SLOW DOWN!

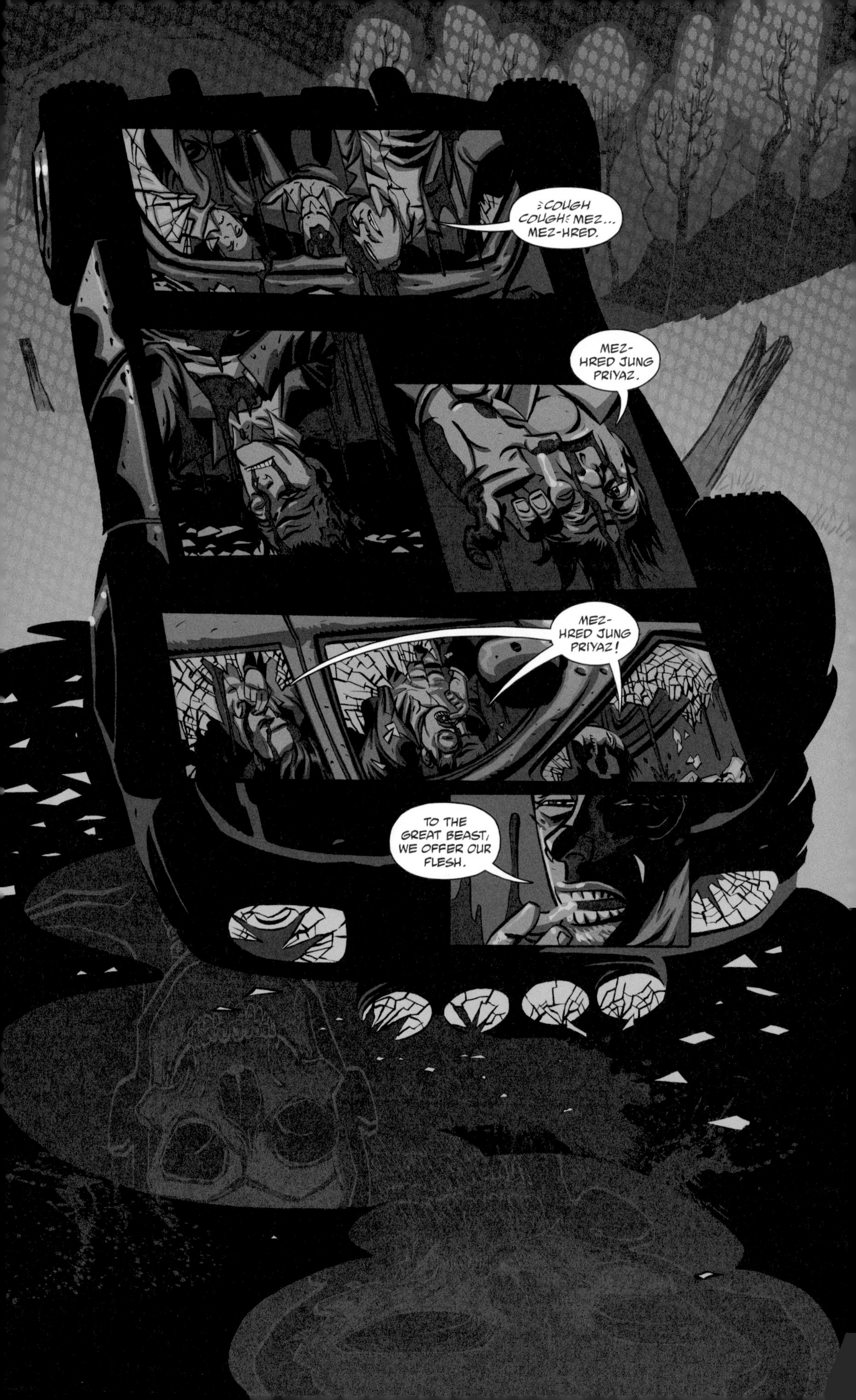

COUGH COUGH MEZ... MEZ-HRED.
MEZ-HRED JUNG PRIYAZ.
MEZ-HRED JUNG PRIYAZ!
TO THE GREAT BEAST, WE OFFER OUR FLESH.

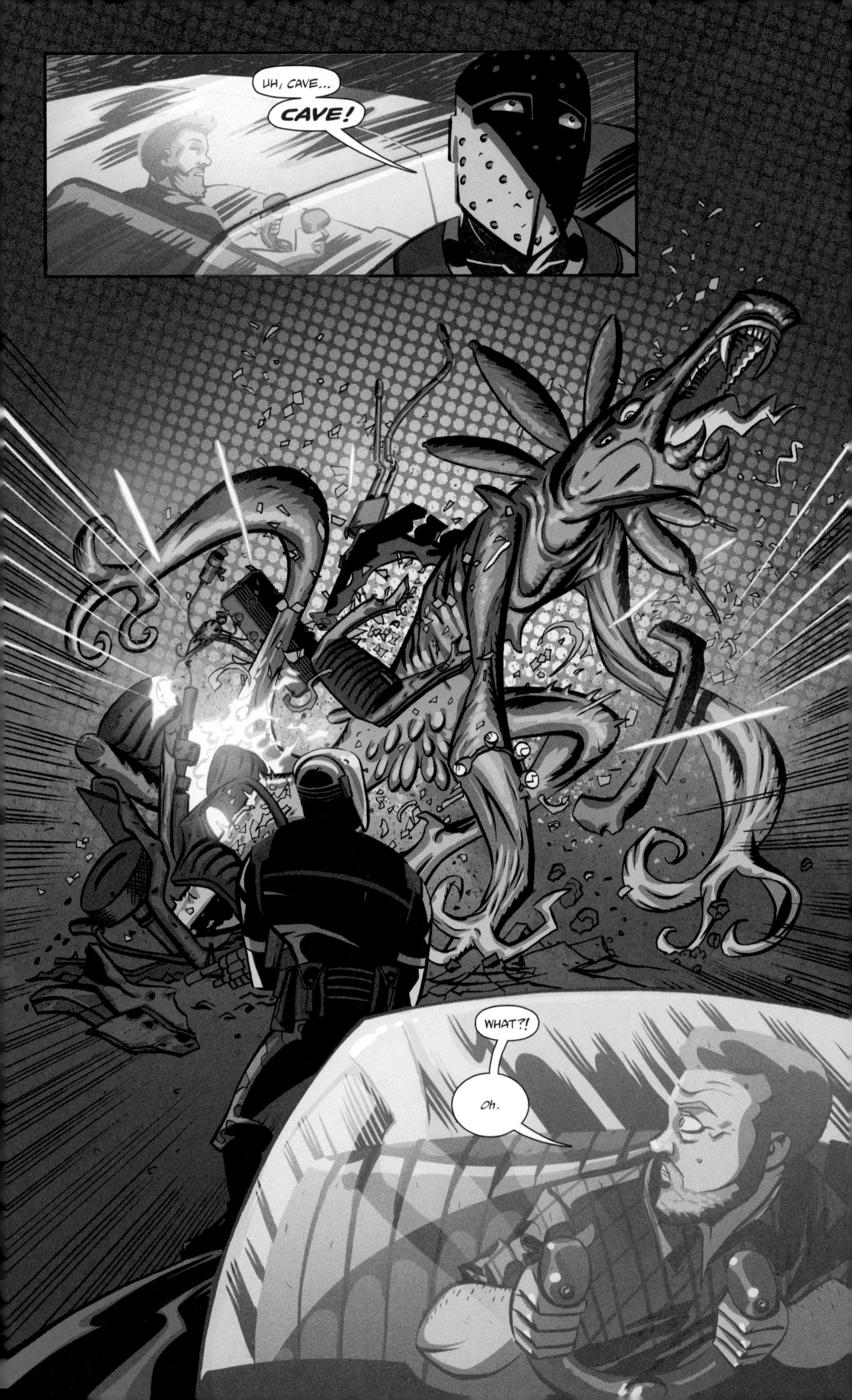
UH, CAVE...
CAVE!
WHAT?!
Oh.

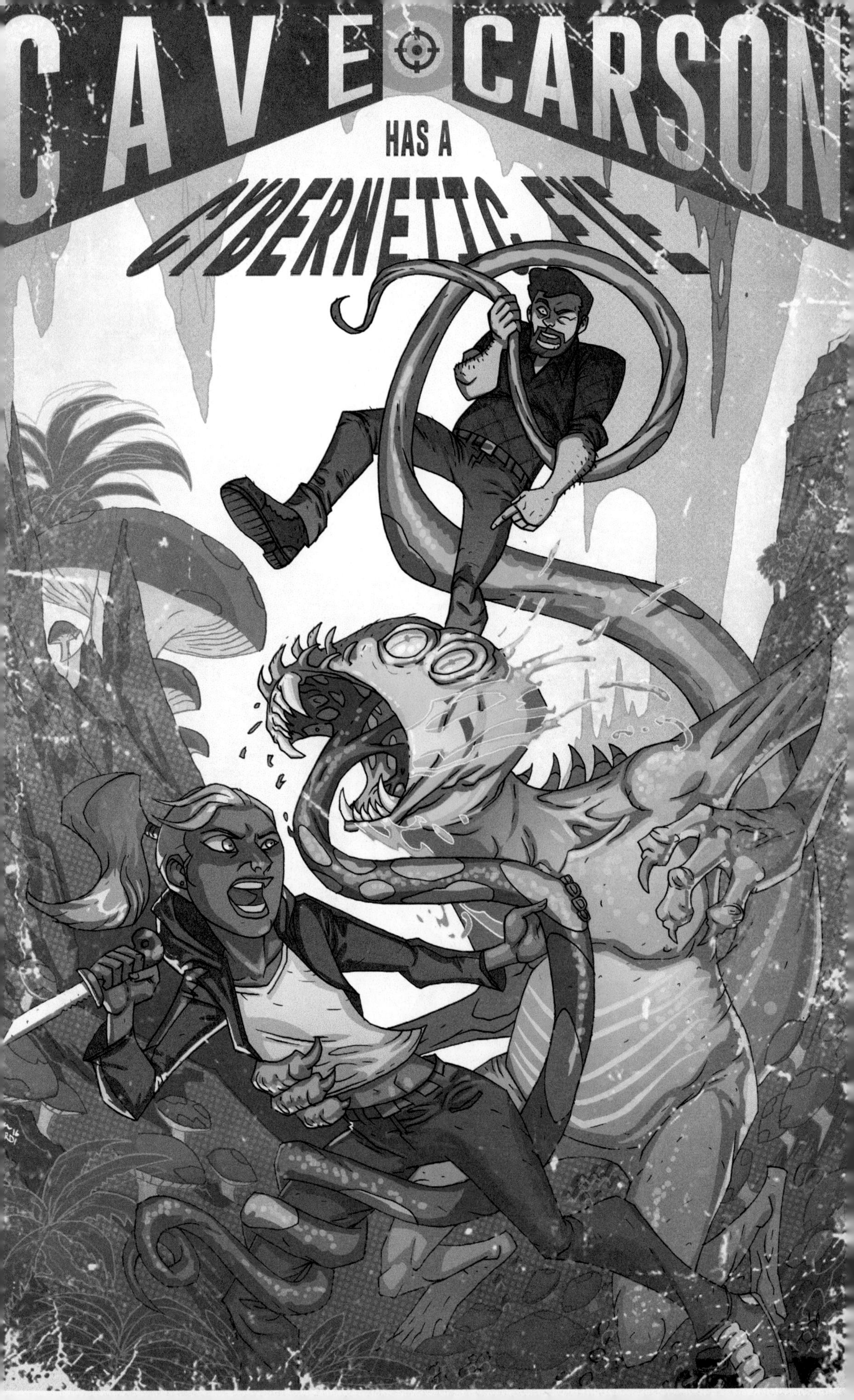
CAVE CARSON
HAS A
CYBERNETIC EYE

Variant cover art by Paul Rentler

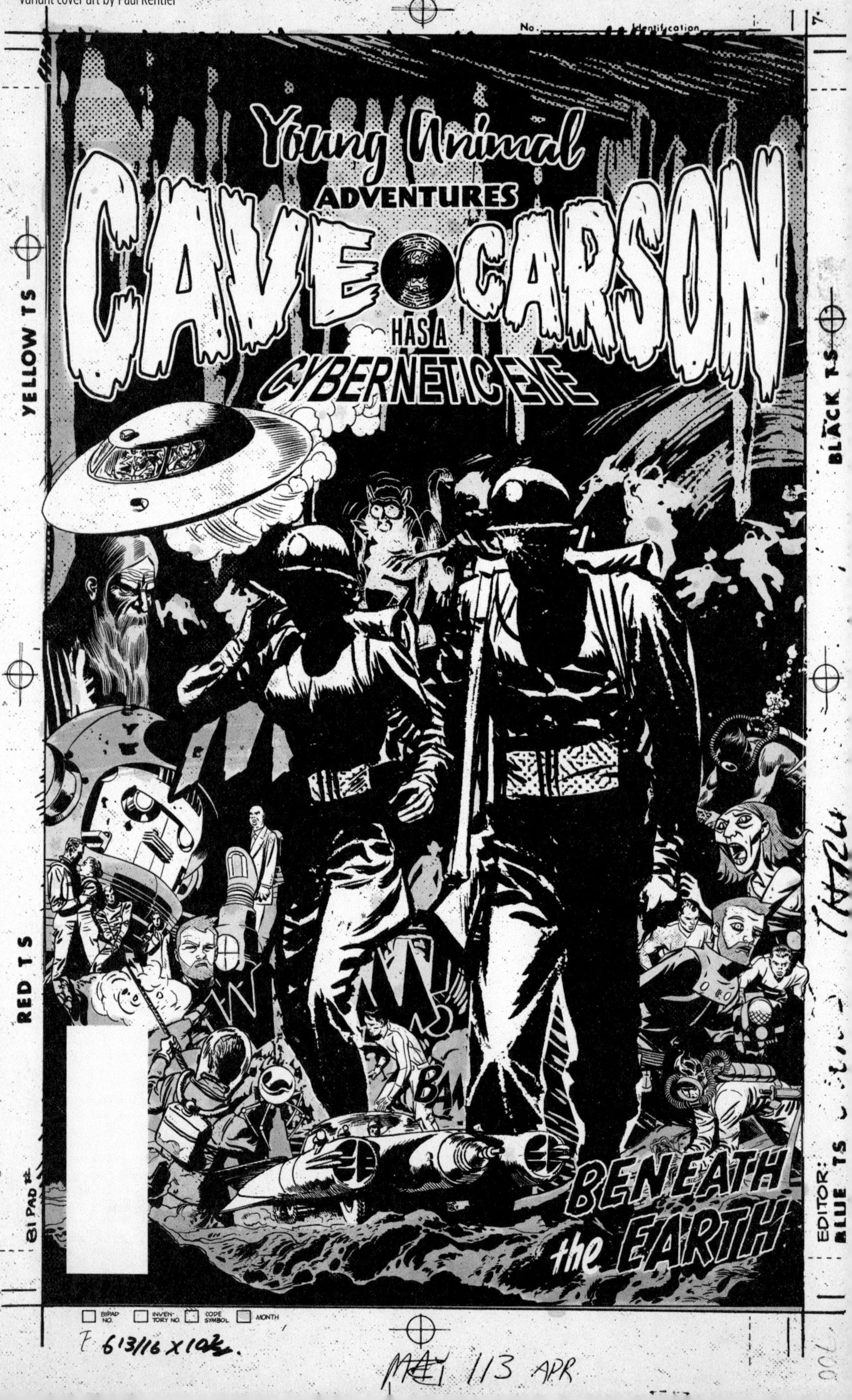

No.
Identification
Young Animal
ADVENTURES
CAVE CARSON
HAS A
CYBERNETIC EYE
BENEATH the EARTH
YELLOW TS
RED TS
BLACK TS
EDITOR:
BLUE TS
BIPAD NO.
INVEN-TORY NO.
CODE SYMBOL
MONTH

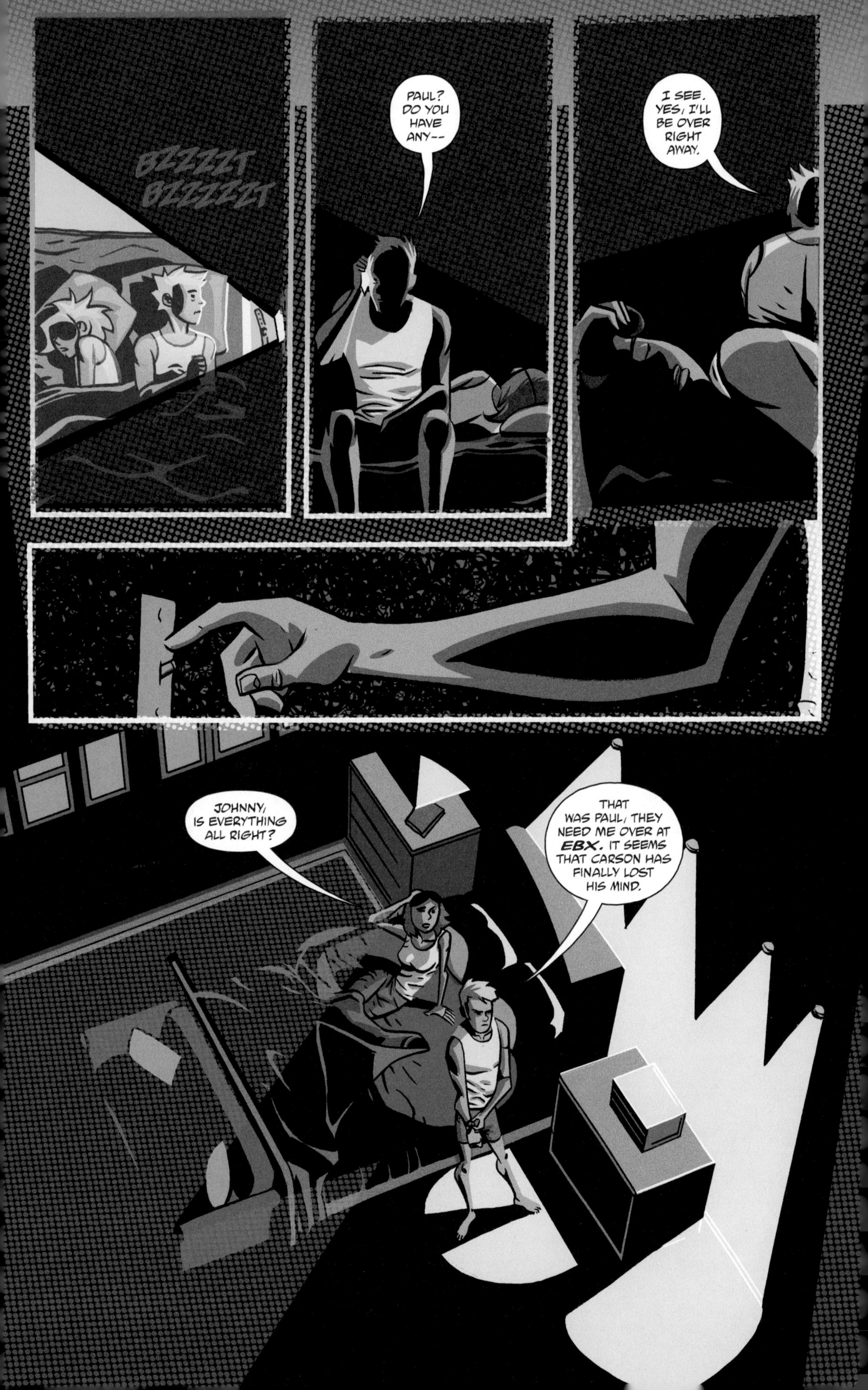
BZZZZZT
BZZZZZT
PAUL? DO YOU HAVE ANY--
I SEE. YES, I'LL BE OVER RIGHT AWAY.
JOHNNY, IS EVERYTHING ALL RIGHT?
THAT WAS PAUL, THEY NEED ME OVER AT EBX. IT SEEMS THAT CARSON HAS FINALLY LOST HIS MIND.

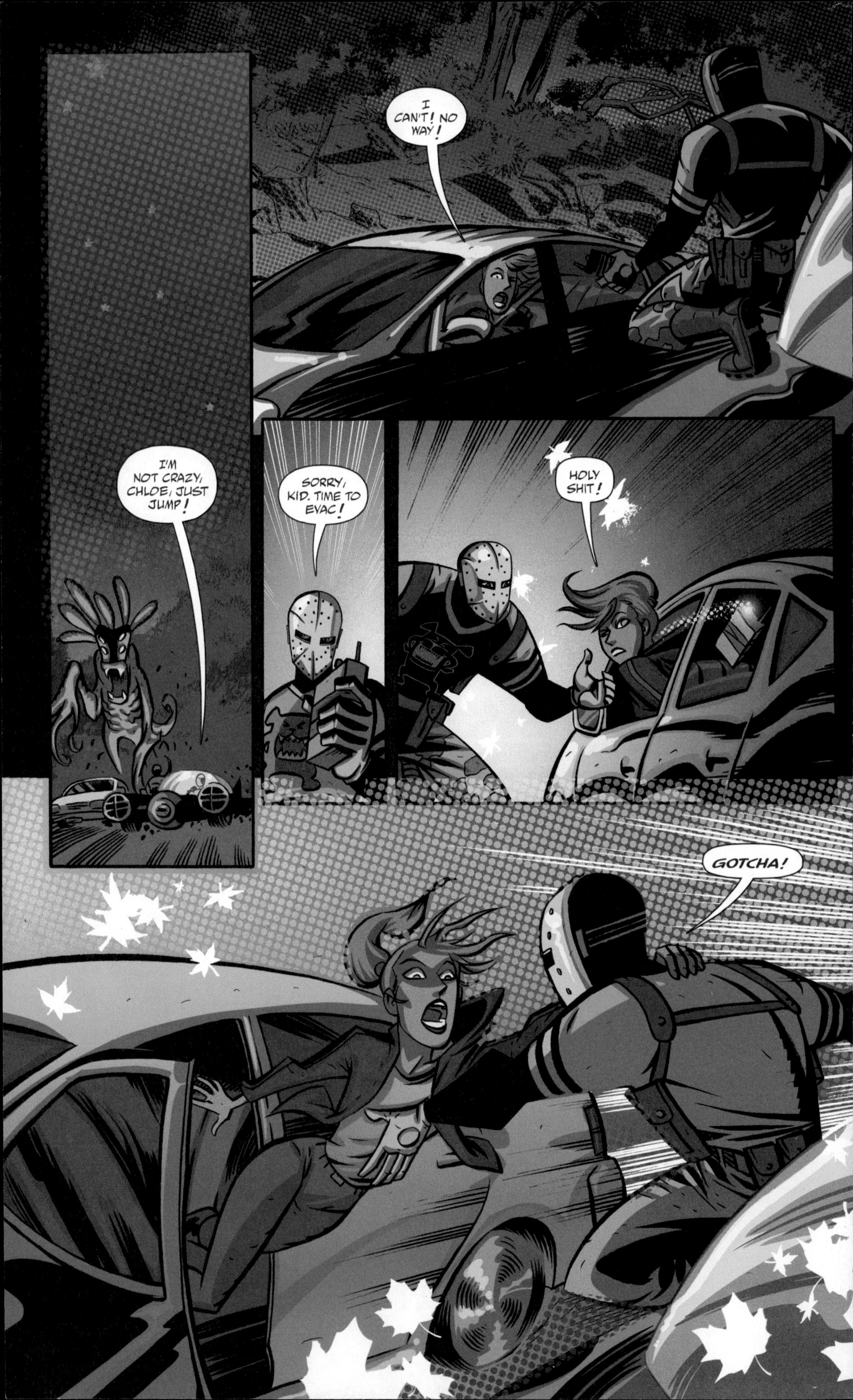
I CAN'T! NO WAY!
I'M NOT CRAZY, CHLOE, JUST JUMP!
SORRY, KID. TIME TO EVAC!
HOLY SHIT!
GOTCHA!

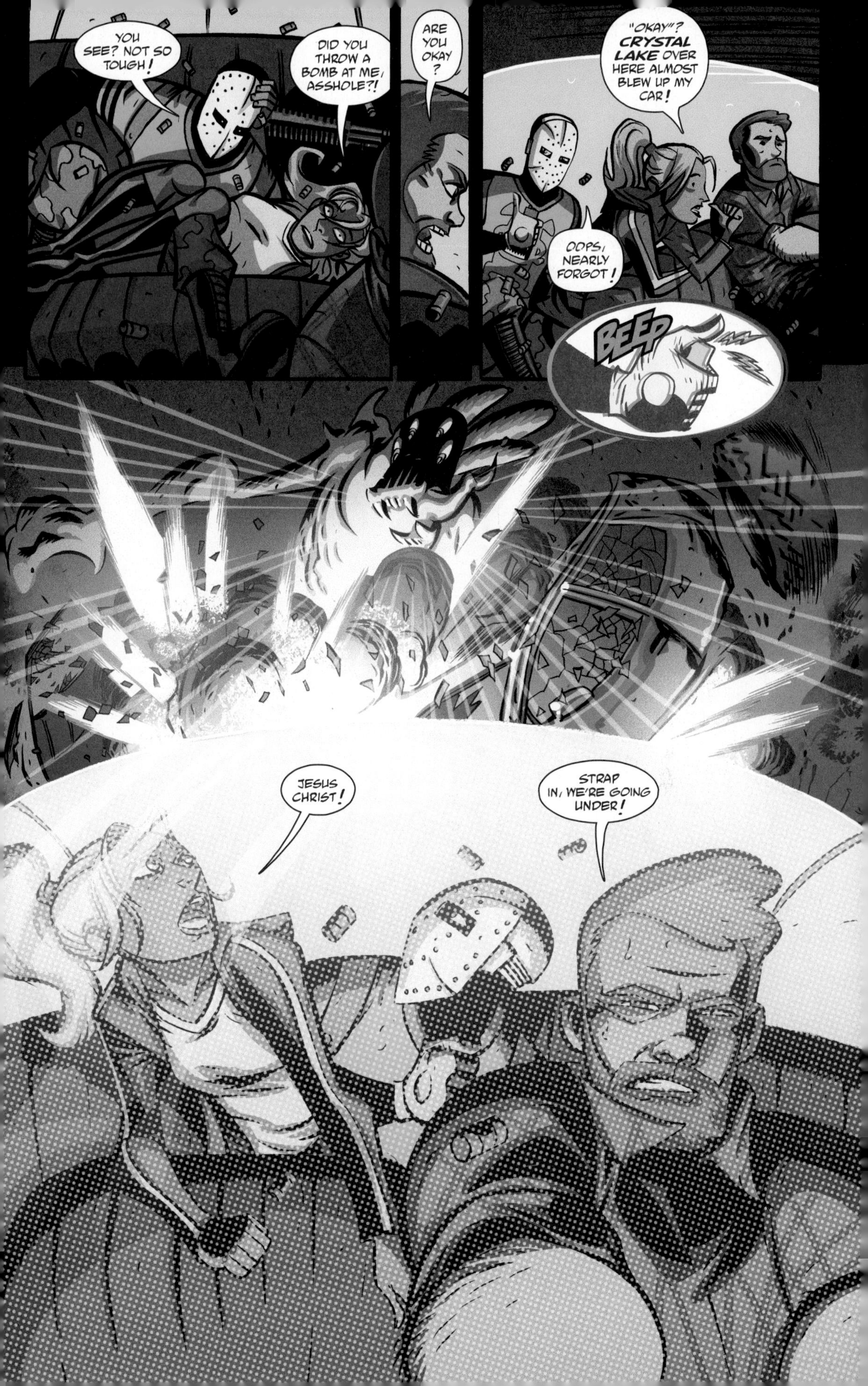
YOU SEE? NOT SO TOUGH!
DID YOU THROW A BOMB AT ME, ASSHOLE?!
ARE YOU OKAY?
"OKAY"? CRYSTAL LAKE OVER HERE ALMOST BLEW UP MY CAR!
OOPS, NEARLY FORGOT!
BEEP
JESUS CHRIST!
STRAP IN, WE'RE GOING UNDER!

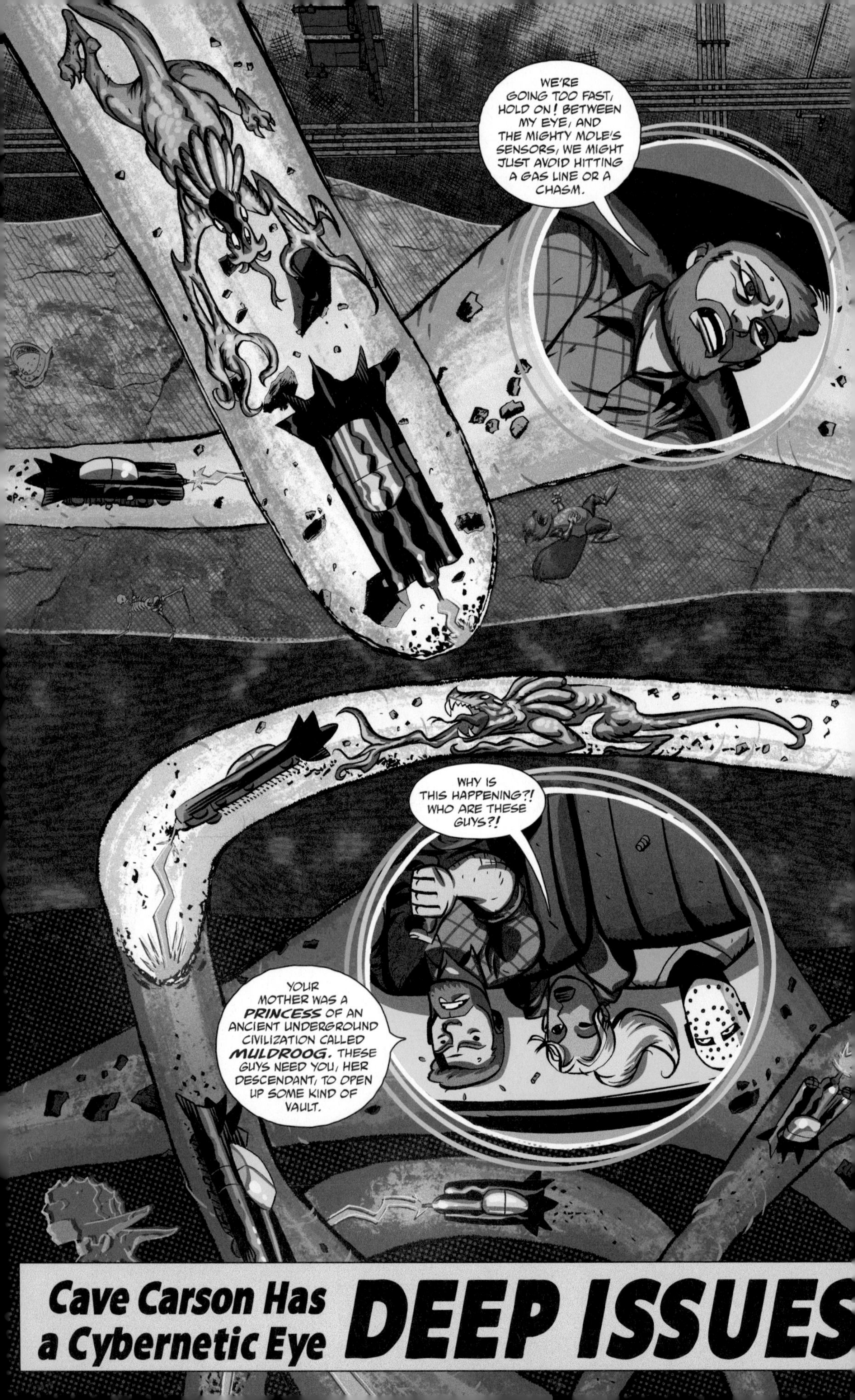
WE'RE GOING TOO FAST, HOLD ON! BETWEEN MY EYE, AND THE MIGHTY MOLE'S SENSORS, WE MIGHT JUST AVOID HITTING A GAS LINE OR A CHASM.
WHY IS THIS HAPPENING?! WHO ARE THESE GUYS?!
YOUR MOTHER WAS A PRINCESS OF AN ANCIENT UNDERGROUND CIVILIZATION CALLED MULDROOG. THESE GUYS NEED YOU, HER DESCENDANT, TO OPEN UP SOME KIND OF VAULT.
Cave Carson Has a Cybernetic Eye
DEEP ISSUES

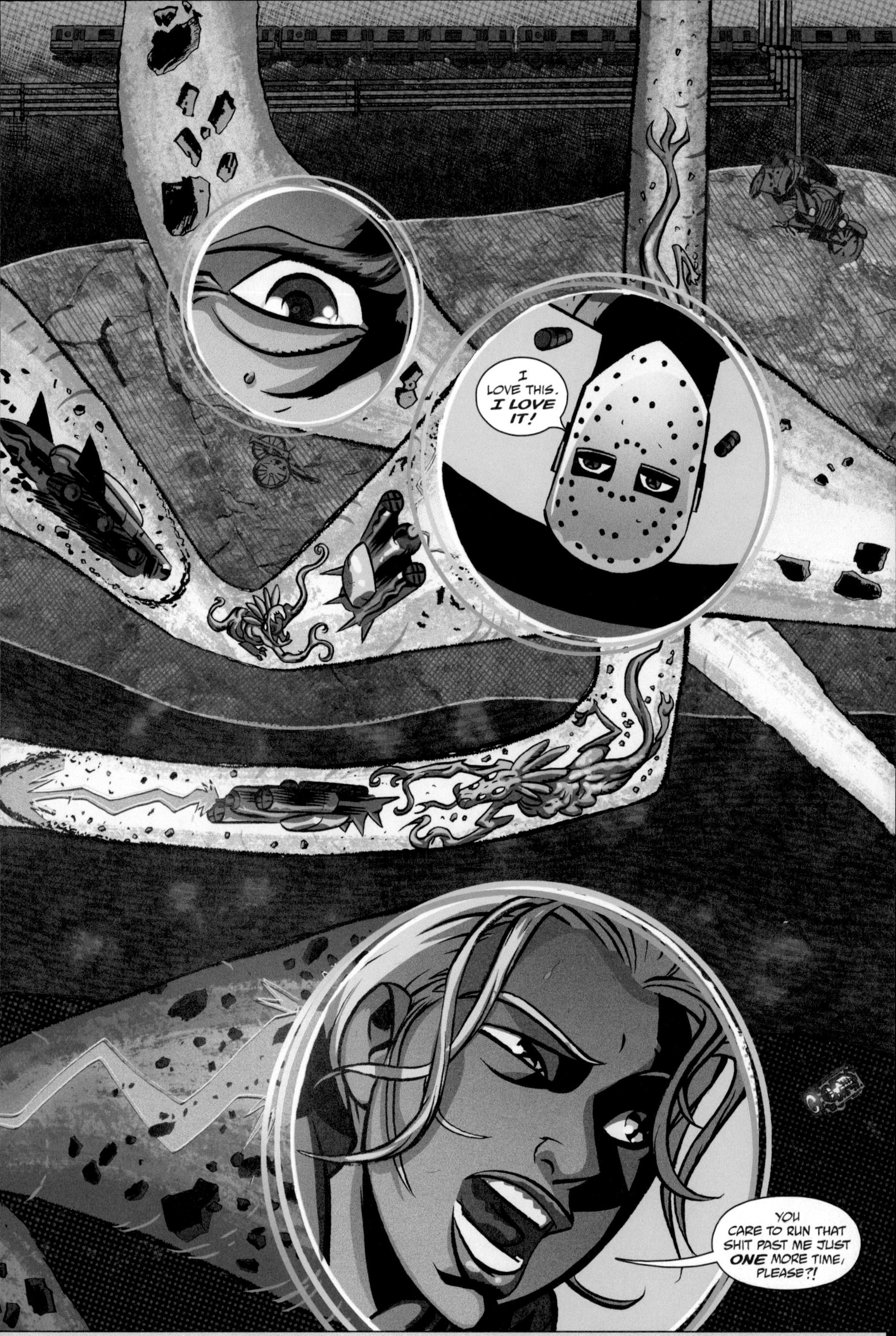
I LOVE THIS. I LOVE IT!
YOU CARE TO RUN THAT SHIT PAST ME JUST ONE MORE TIME, PLEASE?!

Written by
GERARD WAY & JON RIVERA

Art by
MICHAEL AVON OEMING

Colors by NICK FILARDI **Letters by CLEM ROBINS**
Cover by MICHAEL AVON OEMING and NICK FILARDI
Variant Cover by PAUL RENTLER **Edited by MOLLY MAHAN**

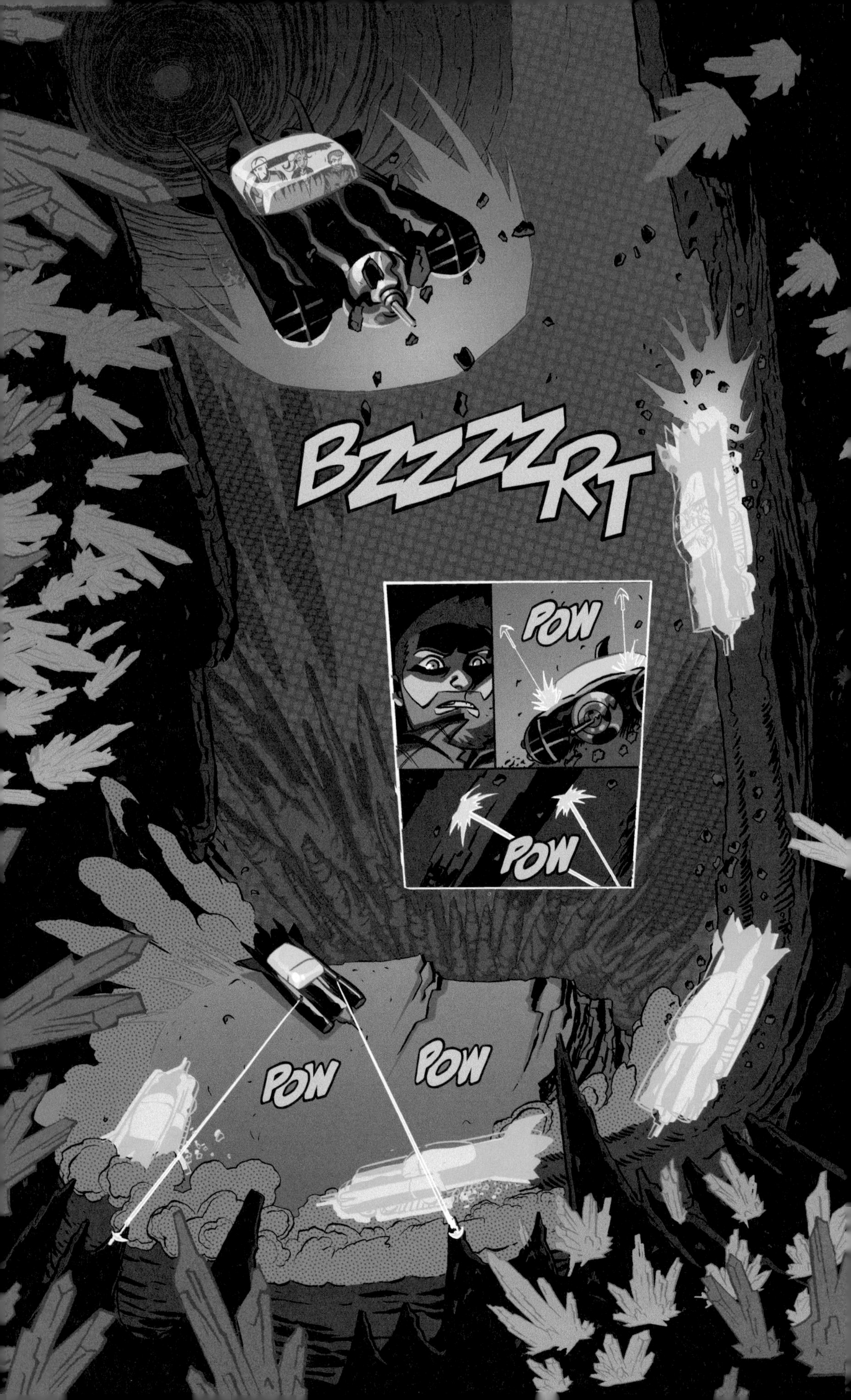
BZZZZRT
POW
POW
POW
POW

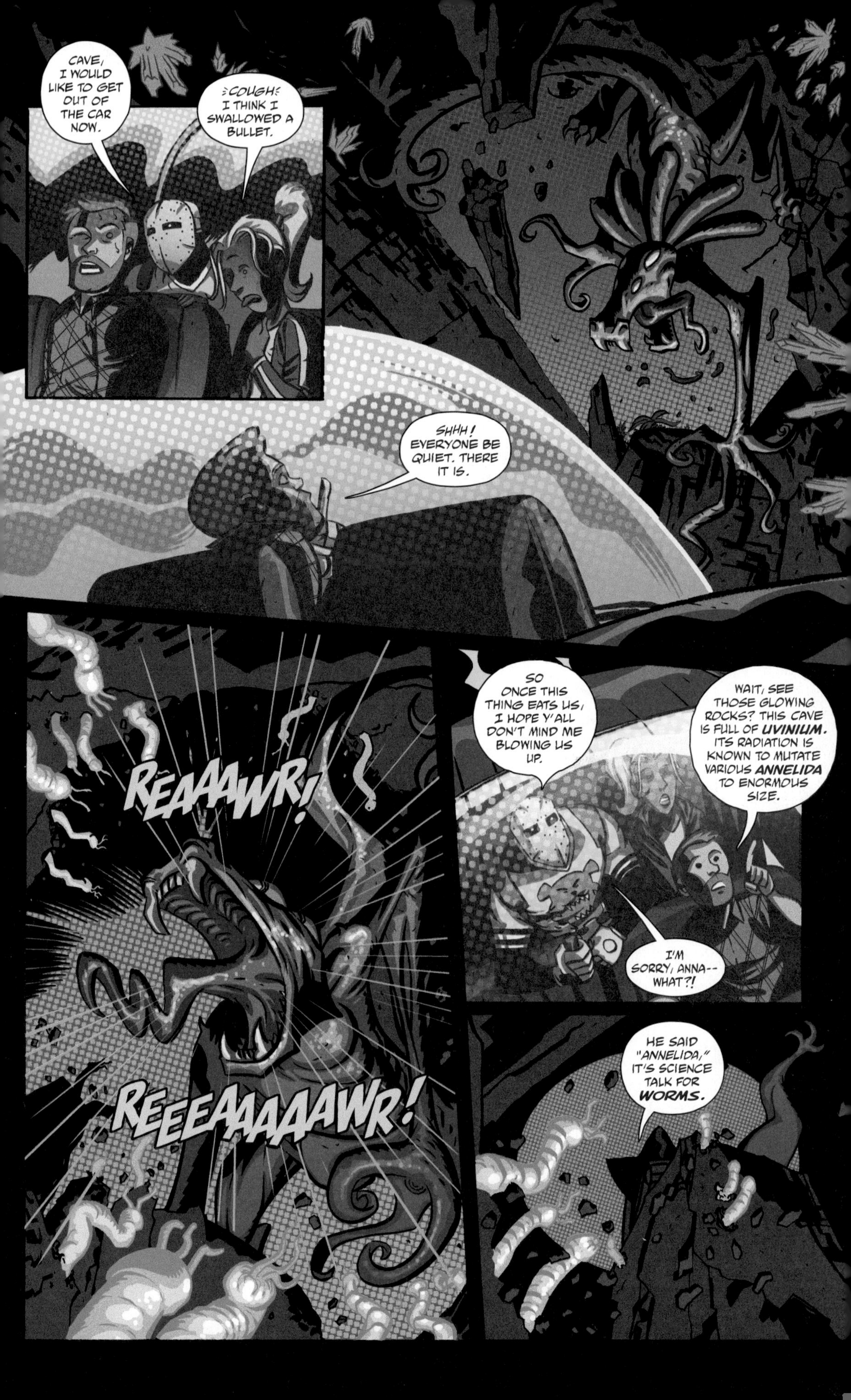
CAVE, I WOULD LIKE TO GET OUT OF THE CAR NOW.
COUGH I THINK I SWALLOWED A BULLET.
SHHH! EVERYONE BE QUIET. THERE IT IS.
REAAAWR!
REEEAAAAAAWR!
SO ONCE THIS THING EATS US, I HOPE Y'ALL DON'T MIND ME BLOWING US UP.
WAIT, SEE THOSE GLOWING ROCKS? THIS CAVE IS FULL OF UVINIUM. ITS RADIATION IS KNOWN TO MUTATE VARIOUS ANNELIDA TO ENORMOUS SIZE.
I'M SORRY, ANNA-- WHAT?!
HE SAID "ANNELIDA," IT'S SCIENCE TALK FOR WORMS.

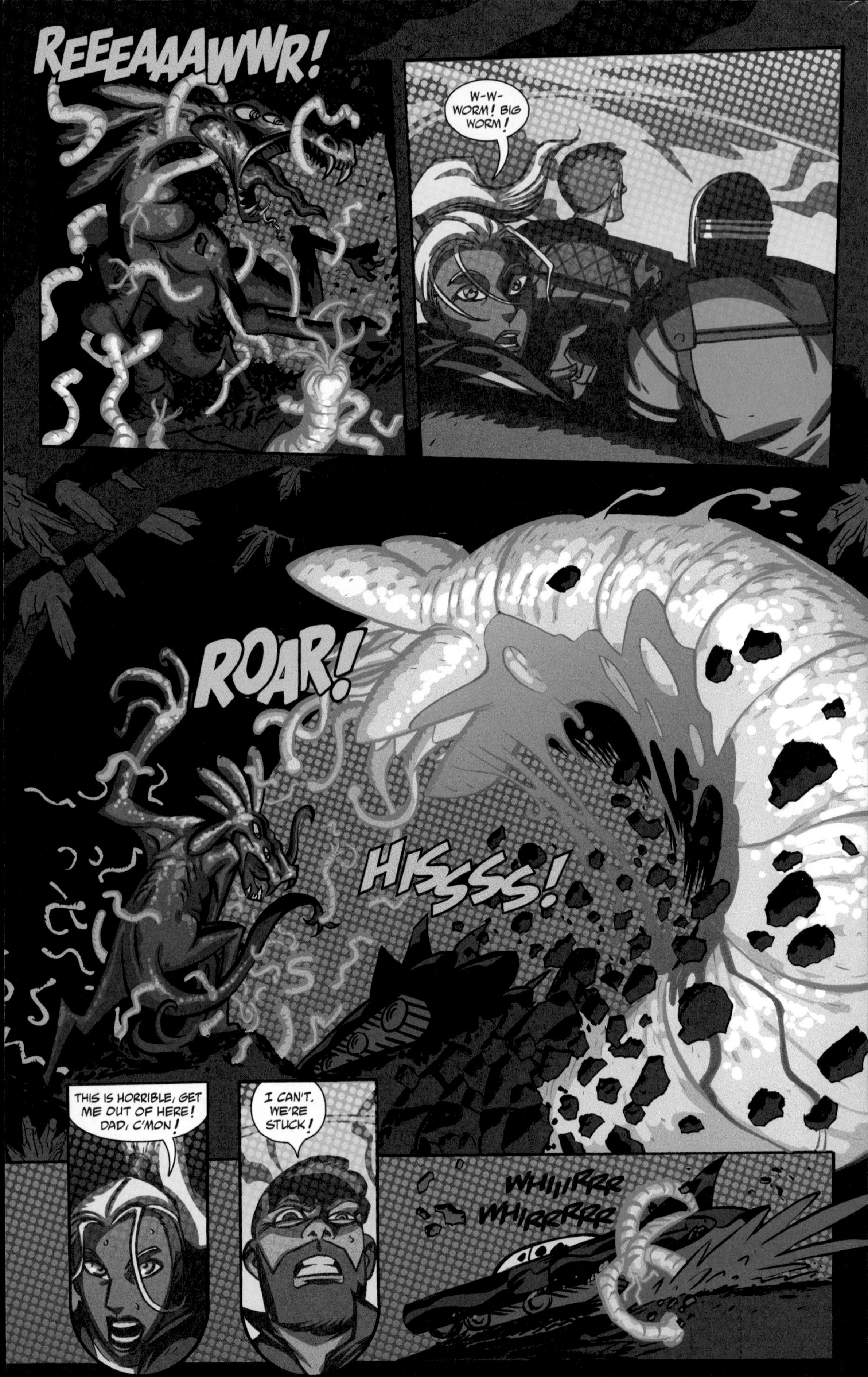
REEEAAAAWWR!
W-W-WORM! BIG WORM!
ROAR!
HISSSSS!
THIS IS HORRIBLE, GET ME OUT OF HERE! DAD, C'MON!
I CAN'T. WE'RE STUCK!
WHIIIRRR WHIRRRRR

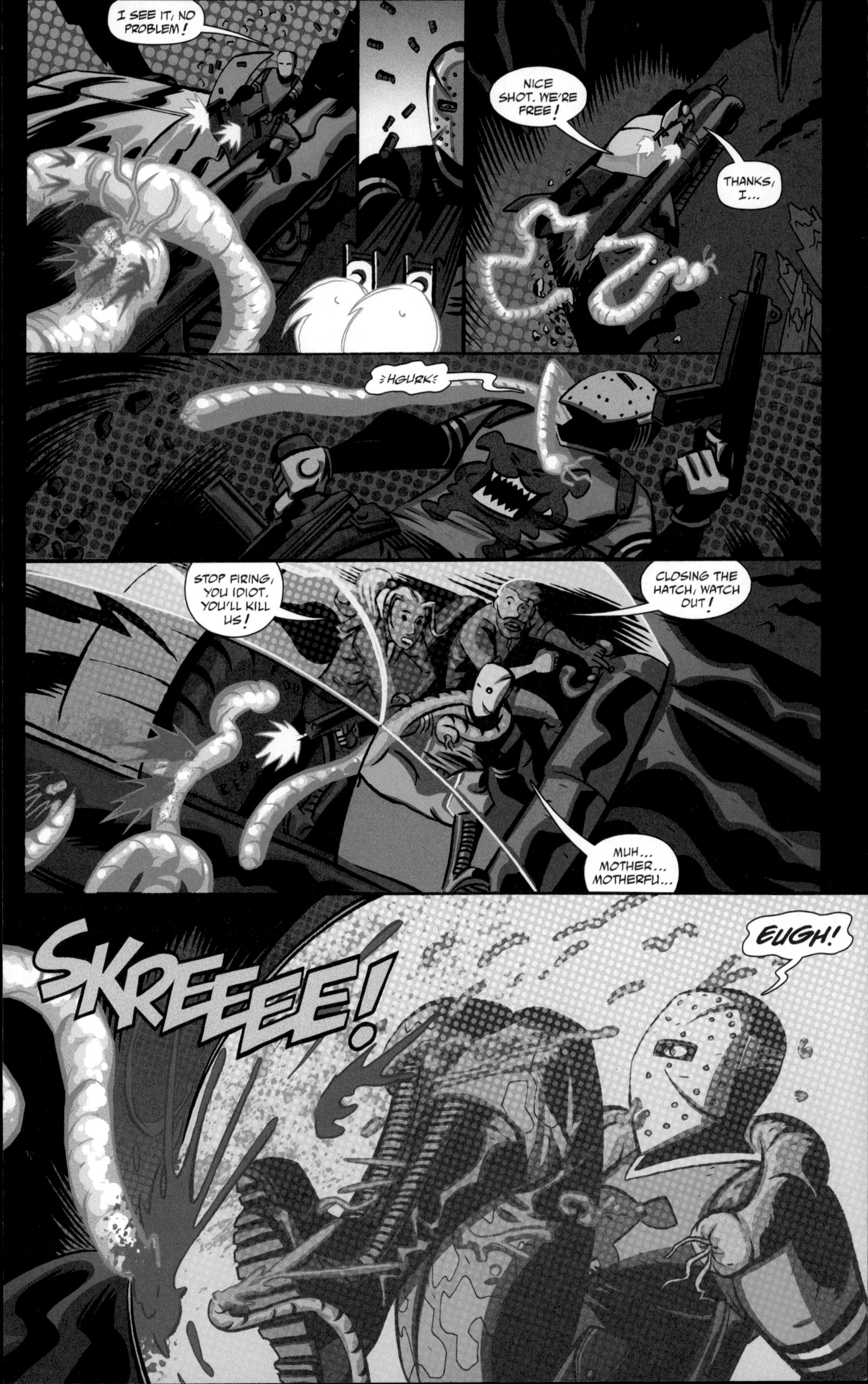
I SEE IT, NO PROBLEM!
NICE SHOT. WE'RE FREE!
THANKS, I...
HGURK
STOP FIRING, YOU IDIOT. YOU'LL KILL US!
CLOSING THE HATCH, WATCH OUT!
MUH... MOTHER... MOTHERFU...
SKREEEEE!
EUGH!

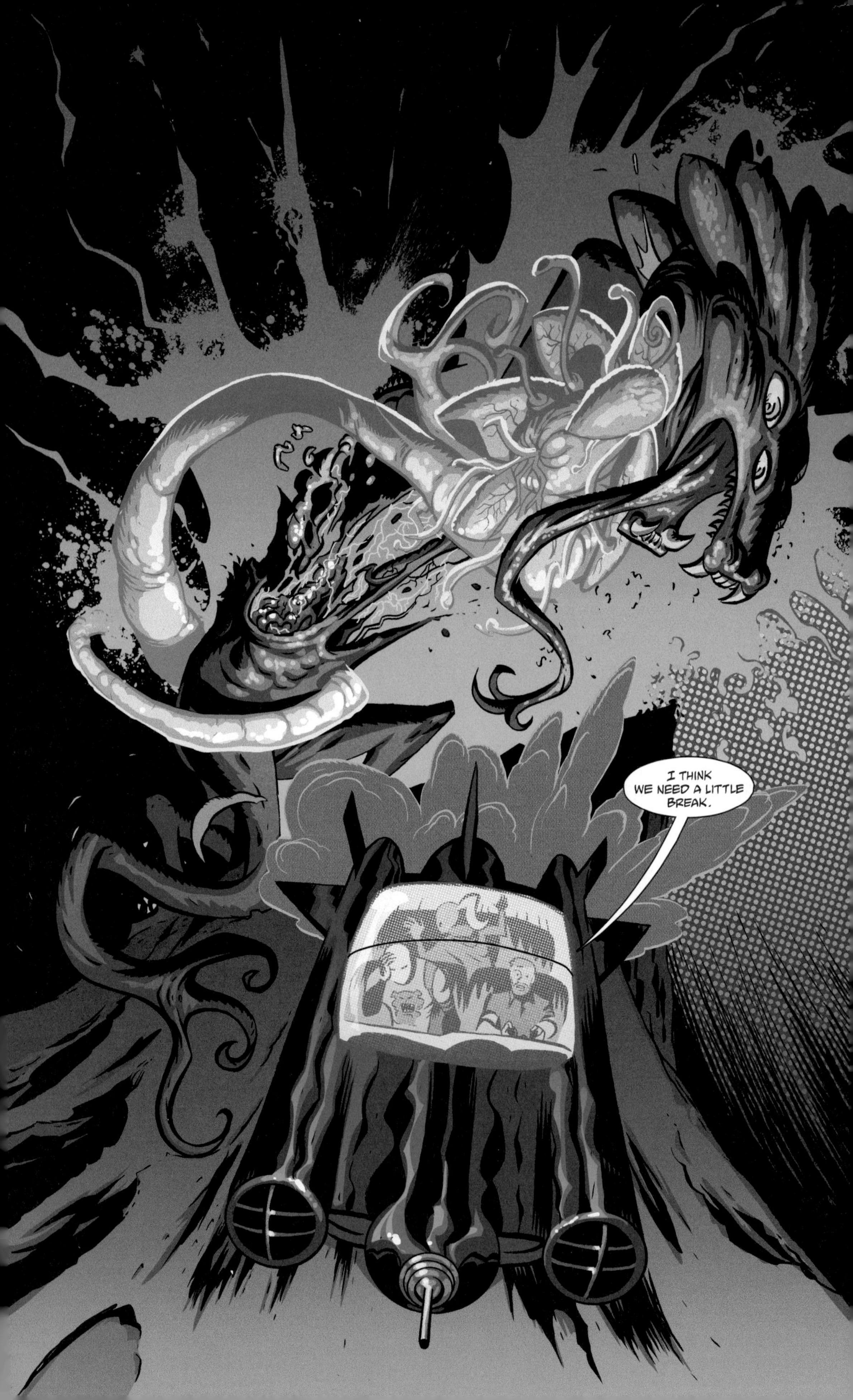
I THINK WE NEED A LITTLE BREAK.

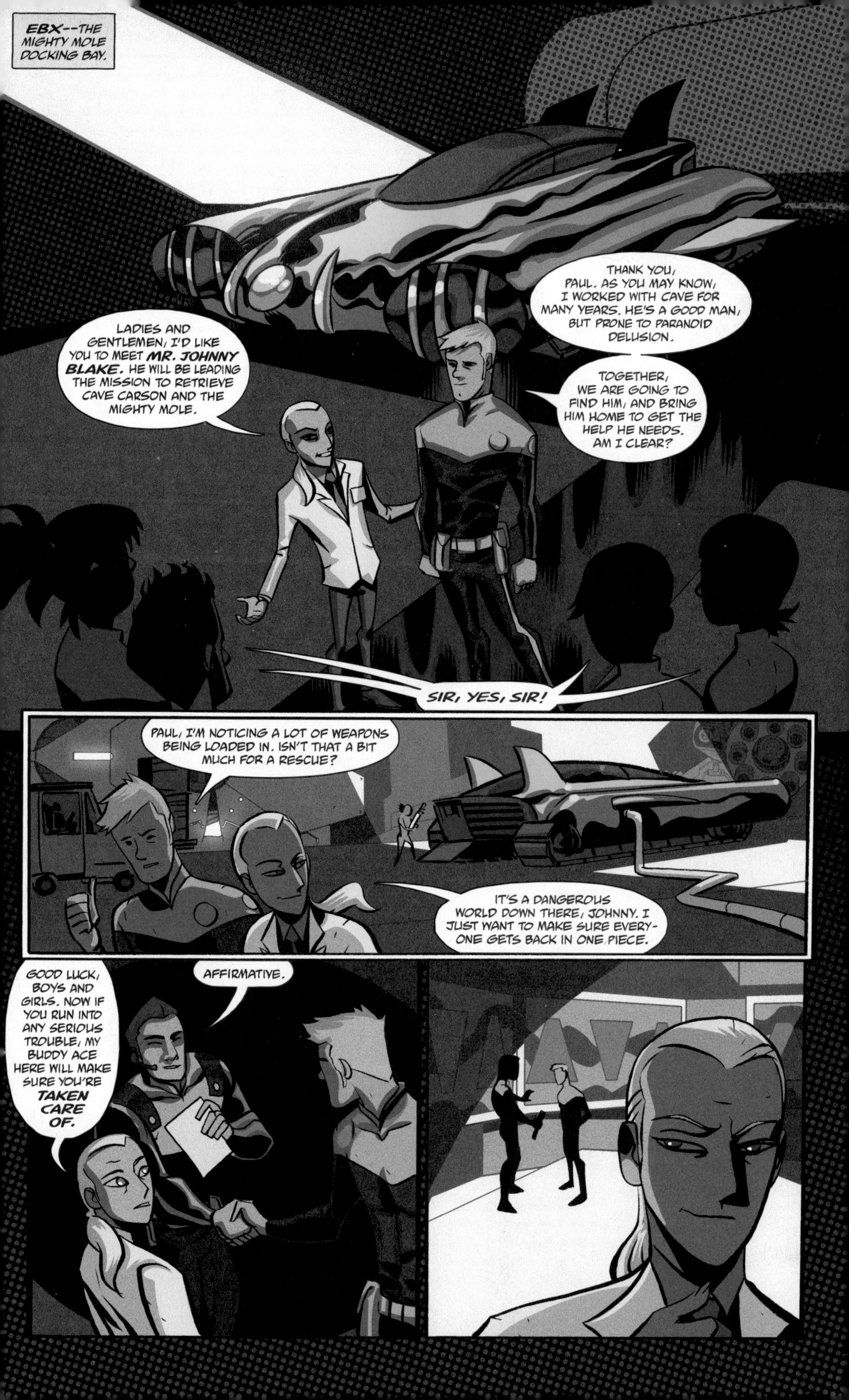
EBX--THE MIGHTY MOLE DOCKING BAY.
LADIES AND GENTLEMEN, I'D LIKE YOU TO MEET MR. JOHNNY BLAKE. HE WILL BE LEADING THE MISSION TO RETRIEVE CAVE CARSON AND THE MIGHTY MOLE.
THANK YOU, PAUL. AS YOU MAY KNOW, I WORKED WITH CAVE FOR MANY YEARS. HE'S A GOOD MAN, BUT PRONE TO PARANOID DELUSION.
TOGETHER, WE ARE GOING TO FIND HIM, AND BRING HIM HOME TO GET THE HELP HE NEEDS. AM I CLEAR?
SIR, YES, SIR!
PAUL, I'M NOTICING A LOT OF WEAPONS BEING LOADED IN. ISN'T THAT A BIT MUCH FOR A RESCUE?
IT'S A DANGEROUS WORLD DOWN THERE, JOHNNY. I JUST WANT TO MAKE SURE EVERY-ONE GETS BACK IN ONE PIECE.
GOOD LUCK, BOYS AND GIRLS. NOW IF YOU RUN INTO ANY SERIOUS TROUBLE, MY BUDDY ACE HERE WILL MAKE SURE YOU'RE TAKEN CARE OF.
AFFIRMATIVE.

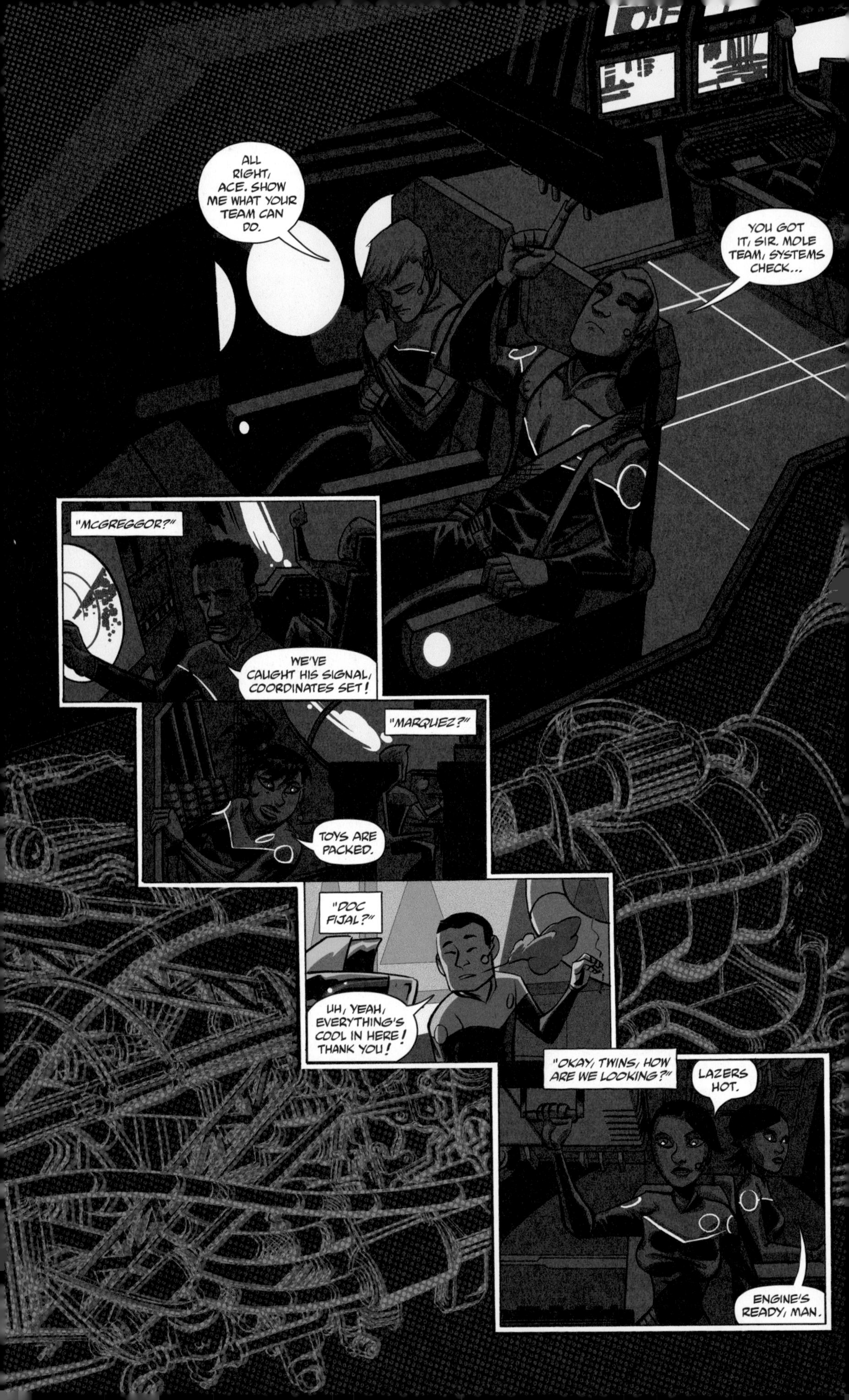
ALL RIGHT, ACE. SHOW ME WHAT YOUR TEAM CAN DO.
YOU GOT IT, SIR. MOLE TEAM, SYSTEMS CHECK...
"MCGREGGOR?"
WE'VE CAUGHT HIS SIGNAL, COORDINATES SET!
"MARQUEZ?"
TOYS ARE PACKED.
"DOC FIJAL?"
UH, YEAH, EVERYTHING'S COOL IN HERE! THANK YOU!
"OKAY, TWINS, HOW ARE WE LOOKING?"
LAZERS HOT.
ENGINE'S READY, MAN.

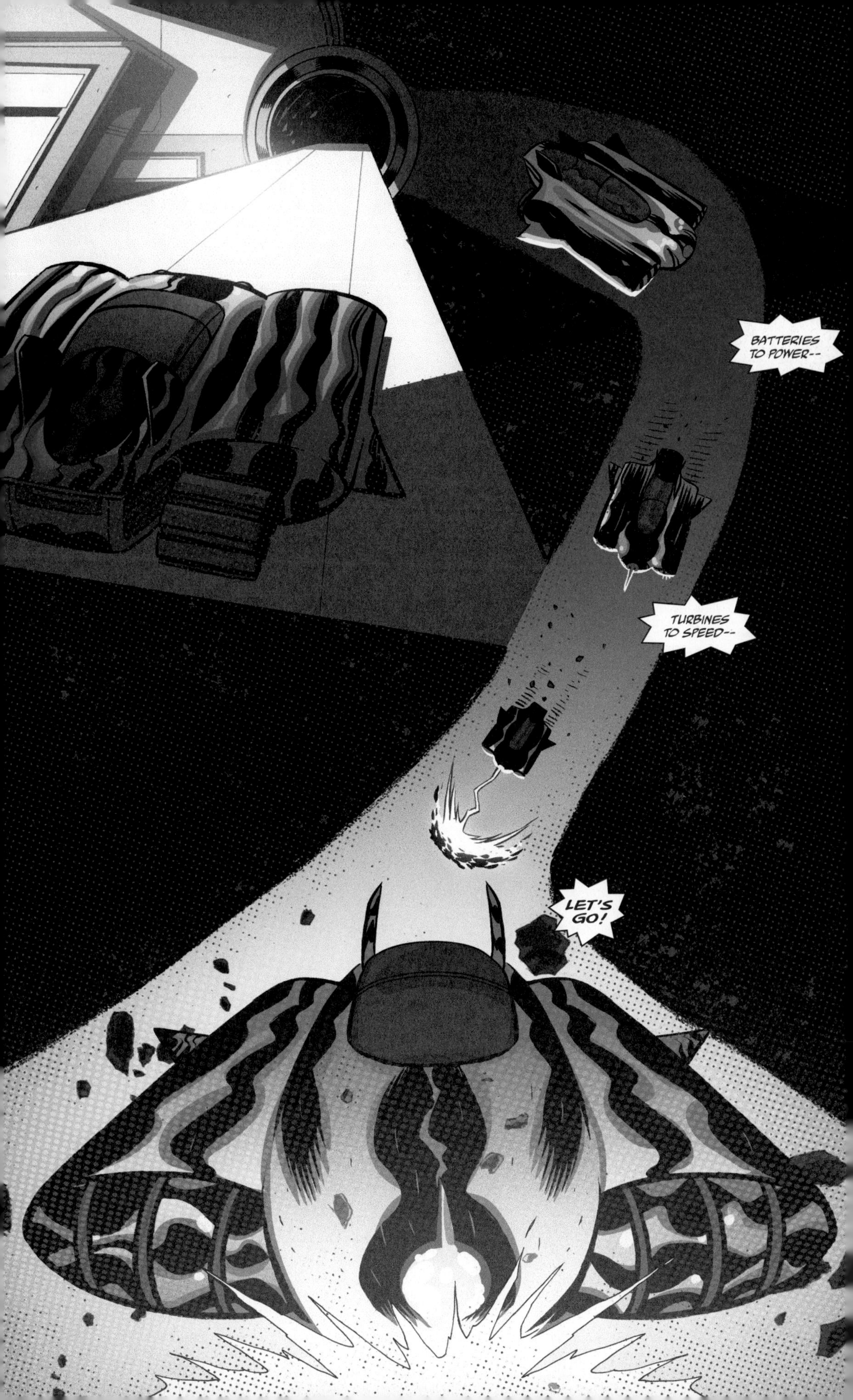
BATTERIES TO POWER--
TURBINES TO SPEED--
LET'S GO!

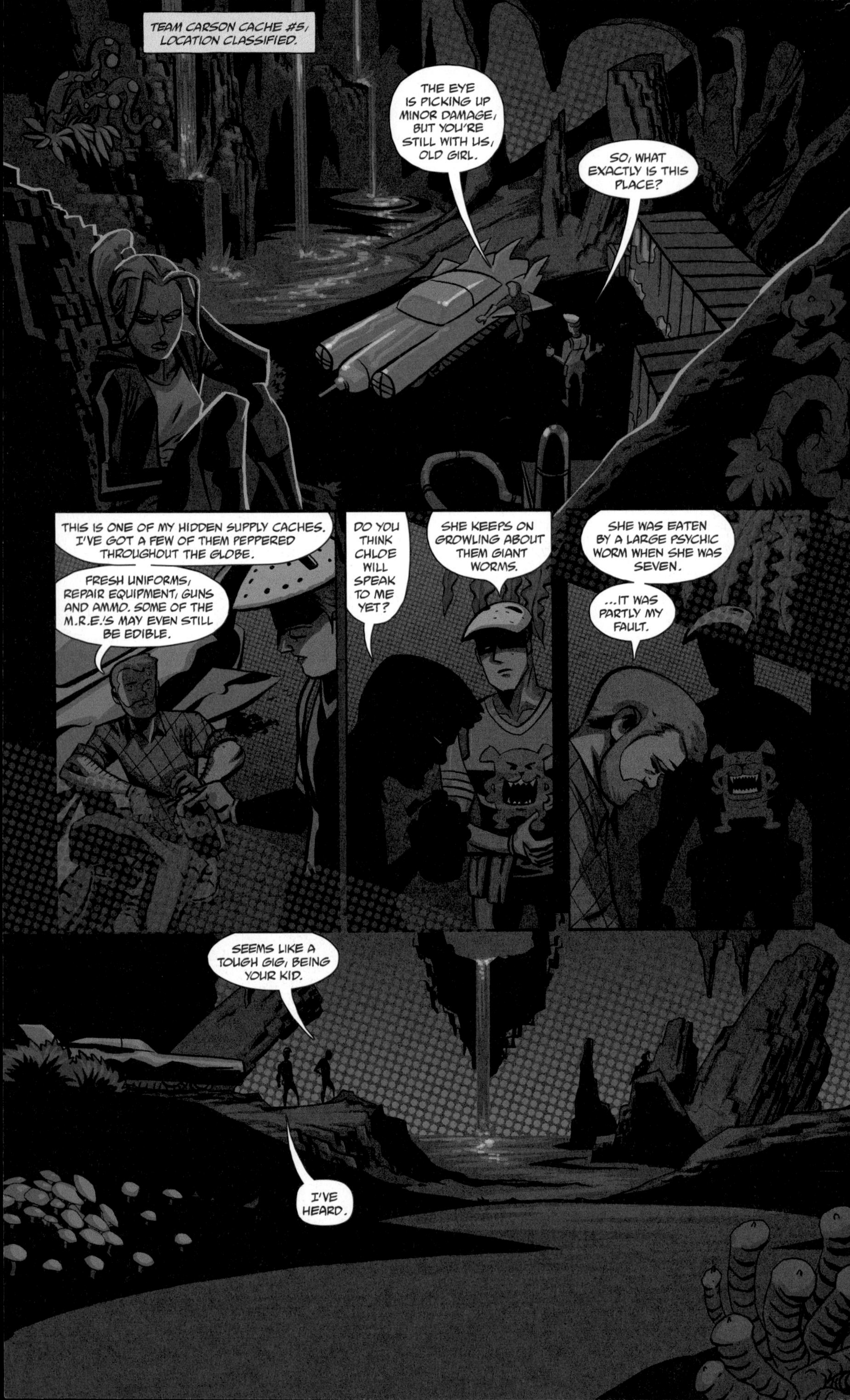
TEAM CARSON CACHE #5, LOCATION CLASSIFIED.
THE EYE IS PICKING UP MINOR DAMAGE, BUT YOU'RE STILL WITH US, OLD GIRL.
SO, WHAT EXACTLY IS THIS PLACE?
THIS IS ONE OF MY HIDDEN SUPPLY CACHES. I'VE GOT A FEW OF THEM PEPPERED THROUGHOUT THE GLOBE.
FRESH UNIFORMS, REPAIR EQUIPMENT, GUNS AND AMMO. SOME OF THE M.R.E.'S MAY EVEN STILL BE EDIBLE.
DO YOU THINK CHLOE WILL SPEAK TO ME YET?
SHE KEEPS ON GROWLING ABOUT THEM GIANT WORMS.
SHE WAS EATEN BY A LARGE PSYCHIC WORM WHEN SHE WAS SEVEN.
...IT WAS PARTLY MY FAULT.
SEEMS LIKE A TOUGH GIG, BEING YOUR KID.
I'VE HEARD.

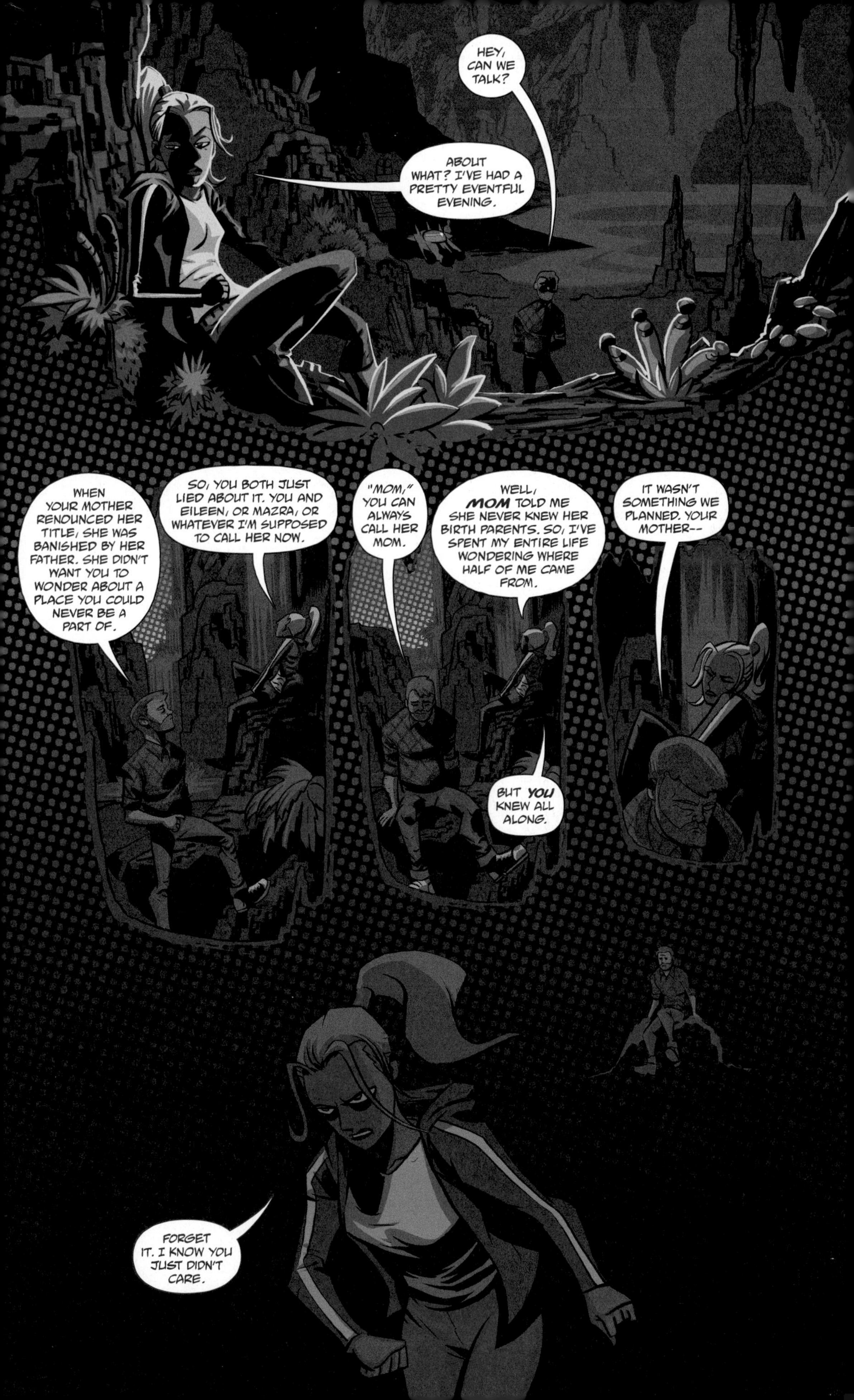
HEY, CAN WE TALK?
ABOUT WHAT? I'VE HAD A PRETTY EVENTFUL EVENING.
WHEN YOUR MOTHER RENOUNCED HER TITLE, SHE WAS BANISHED BY HER FATHER. SHE DIDN'T WANT YOU TO WONDER ABOUT A PLACE YOU COULD NEVER BE A PART OF.
SO, YOU BOTH JUST LIED ABOUT IT. YOU AND EILEEN, OR MAZRA, OR WHATEVER I'M SUPPOSED TO CALL HER NOW.
"MOM," YOU CAN ALWAYS CALL HER MOM.
WELL, **MOM** TOLD ME SHE NEVER KNEW HER BIRTH PARENTS. SO, I'VE SPENT MY ENTIRE LIFE WONDERING WHERE HALF OF ME CAME FROM.
BUT ***YOU*** KNEW ALL ALONG.
IT WASN'T SOMETHING WE PLANNED. YOUR MOTHER--
FORGET IT. I KNOW YOU JUST DIDN'T CARE.

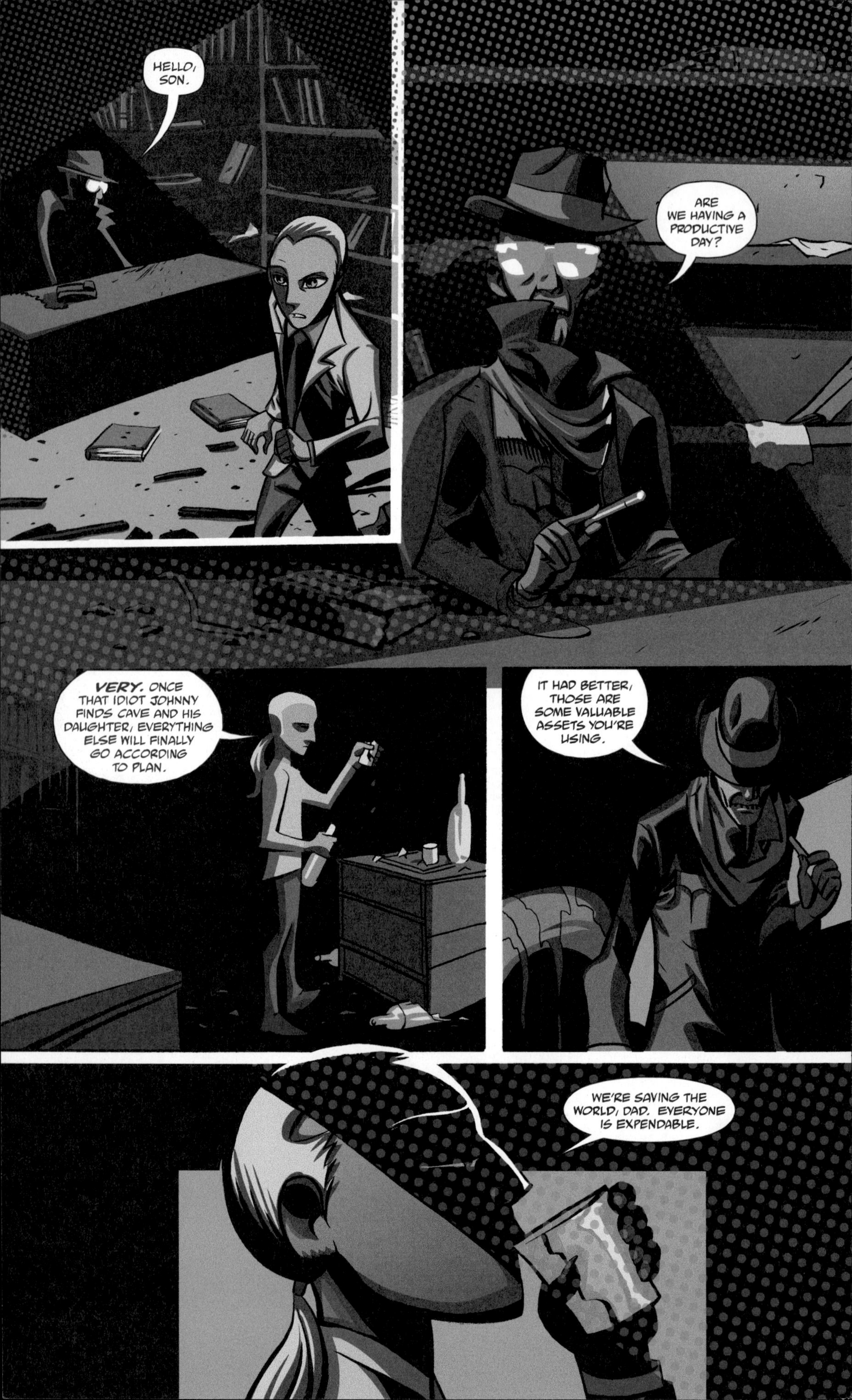
HELLO, SON.
ARE WE HAVING A PRODUCTIVE DAY?
VERY. ONCE THAT IDIOT JOHNNY FINDS CAVE AND HIS DAUGHTER, EVERYTHING ELSE WILL FINALLY GO ACCORDING TO PLAN.
IT HAD BETTER, THOSE ARE SOME VALUABLE ASSETS YOU'RE USING.
WE'RE SAVING THE WORLD, DAD. EVERYONE IS EXPENDABLE.

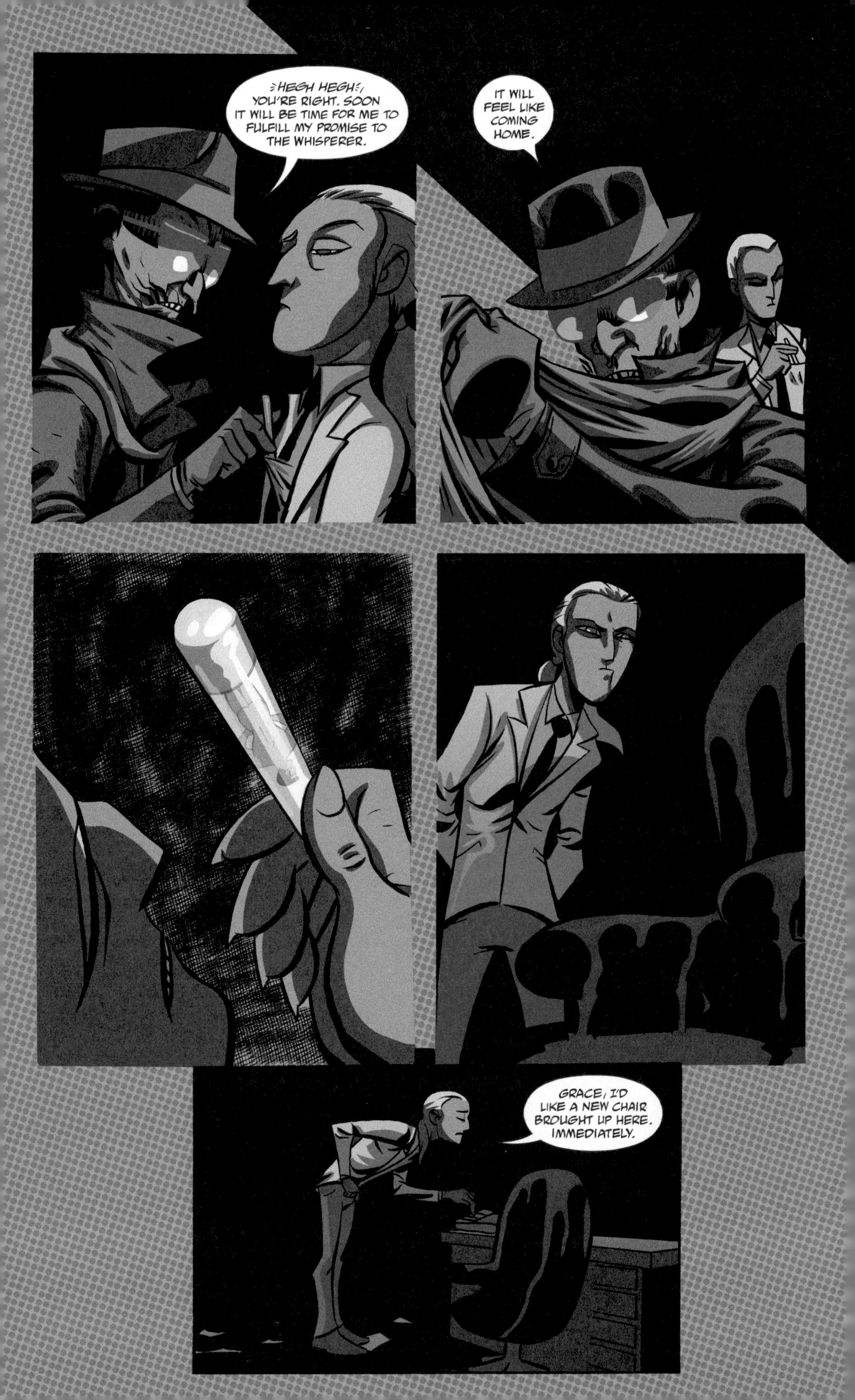
HEGH HEGH. YOU'RE RIGHT. SOON IT WILL BE TIME FOR ME TO FULFILL MY PROMISE TO THE WHISPERER.
IT WILL FEEL LIKE COMING HOME.
GRACE, I'D LIKE A NEW CHAIR BROUGHT UP HERE. IMMEDIATELY.

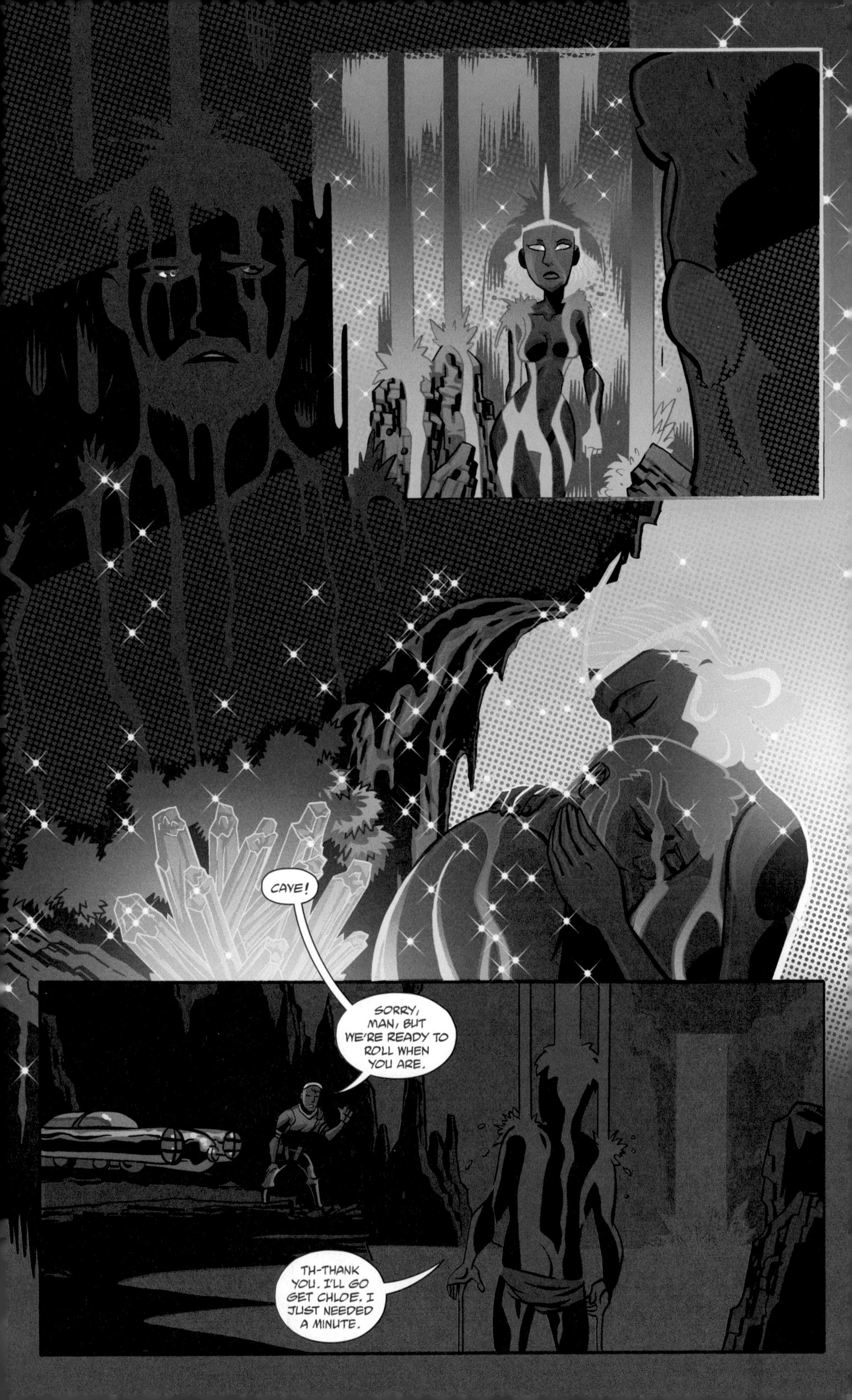
CAVE!
SORRY, MAN, BUT WE'RE READY TO ROLL WHEN YOU ARE.
TH-THANK YOU. I'LL GO GET CHLOE. I JUST NEEDED A MINUTE.

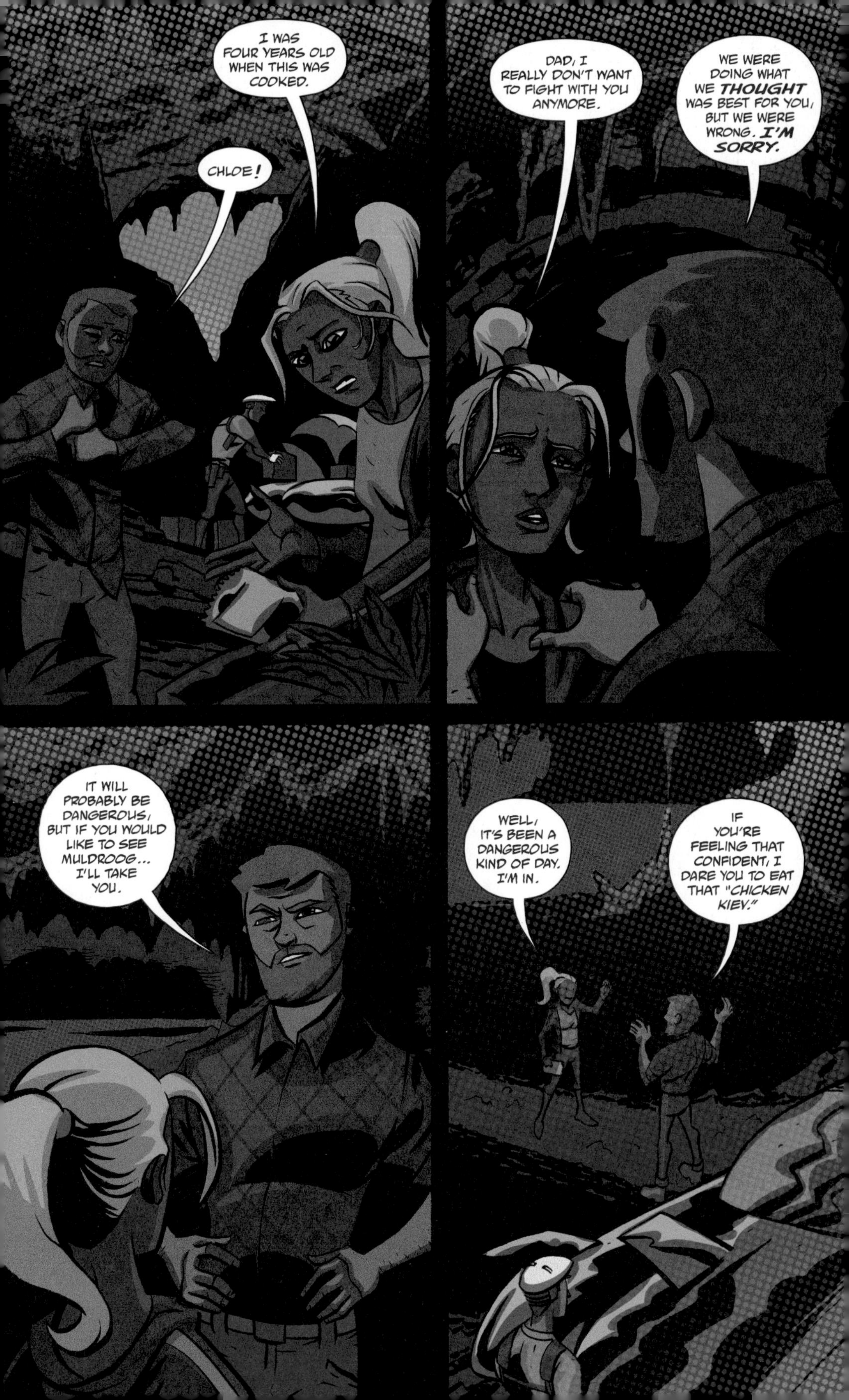
I WAS FOUR YEARS OLD WHEN THIS WAS COOKED.
CHLOE!
DAD, I REALLY DON'T WANT TO FIGHT WITH YOU ANYMORE.
WE WERE DOING WHAT WE THOUGHT WAS BEST FOR YOU, BUT WE WERE WRONG. I'M SORRY.
IT WILL PROBABLY BE DANGEROUS, BUT IF YOU WOULD LIKE TO SEE MULDROOG... I'LL TAKE YOU.
WELL, IT'S BEEN A DANGEROUS KIND OF DAY. I'M IN.
IF YOU'RE FEELING THAT CONFIDENT, I DARE YOU TO EAT THAT "CHICKEN KIEV."

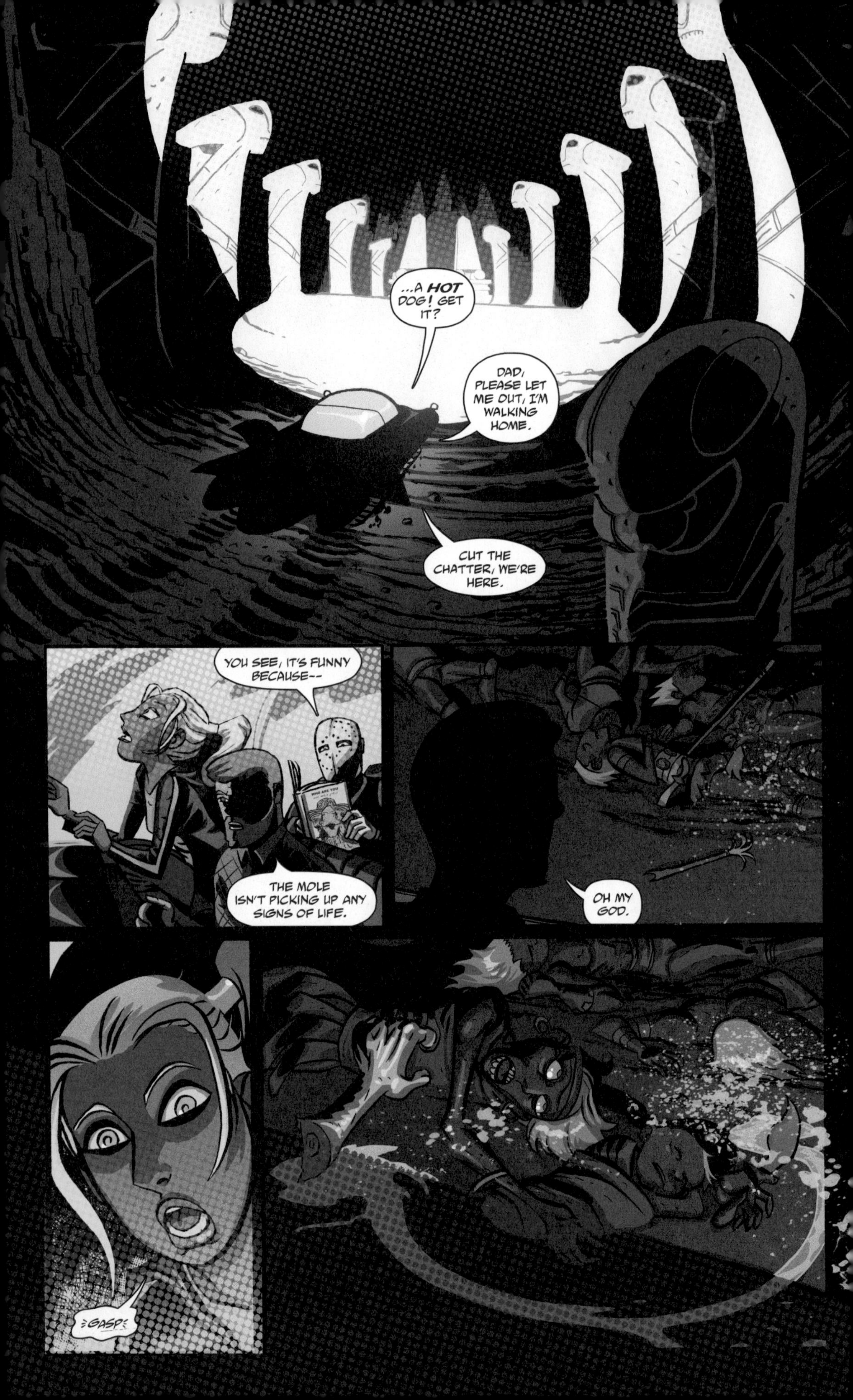
...A HOT DOG! GET IT?
DAD, PLEASE LET ME OUT, I'M WALKING HOME.
CUT THE CHATTER, WE'RE HERE.
YOU SEE, IT'S FUNNY BECAUSE--
THE MOLE ISN'T PICKING UP ANY SIGNS OF LIFE.
OH MY GOD.
GASP

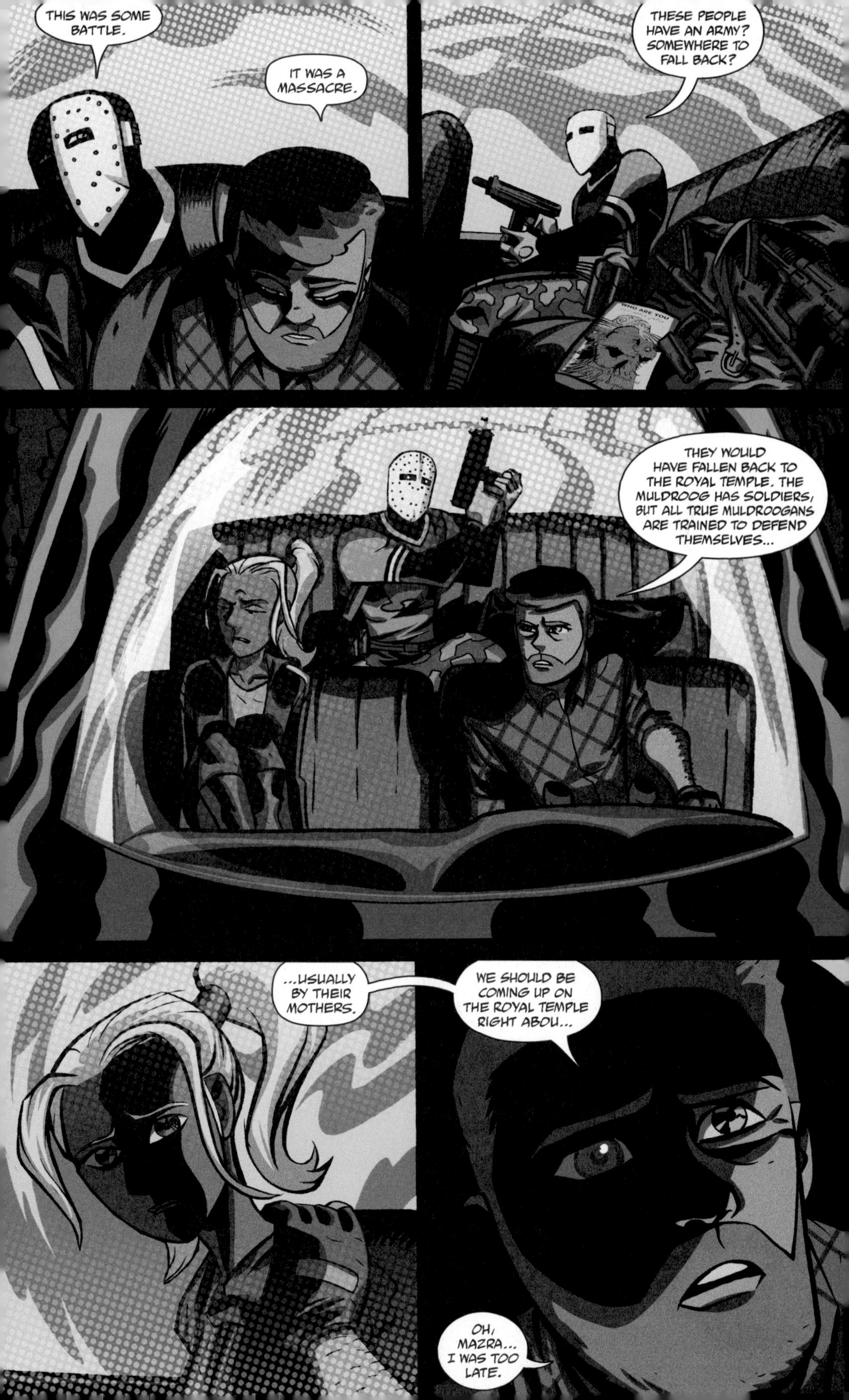
THIS WAS SOME BATTLE.
IT WAS A MASSACRE.
THESE PEOPLE HAVE AN ARMY? SOMEWHERE TO FALL BACK?
WHO ARE YOU
THEY WOULD HAVE FALLEN BACK TO THE ROYAL TEMPLE. THE MULDROOG HAS SOLDIERS, BUT ALL TRUE MULDROOGANS ARE TRAINED TO DEFEND THEMSELVES...
...USUALLY BY THEIR MOTHERS.
WE SHOULD BE COMING UP ON THE ROYAL TEMPLE RIGHT ABOU...
OH, MAZRA... I WAS TOO LATE.

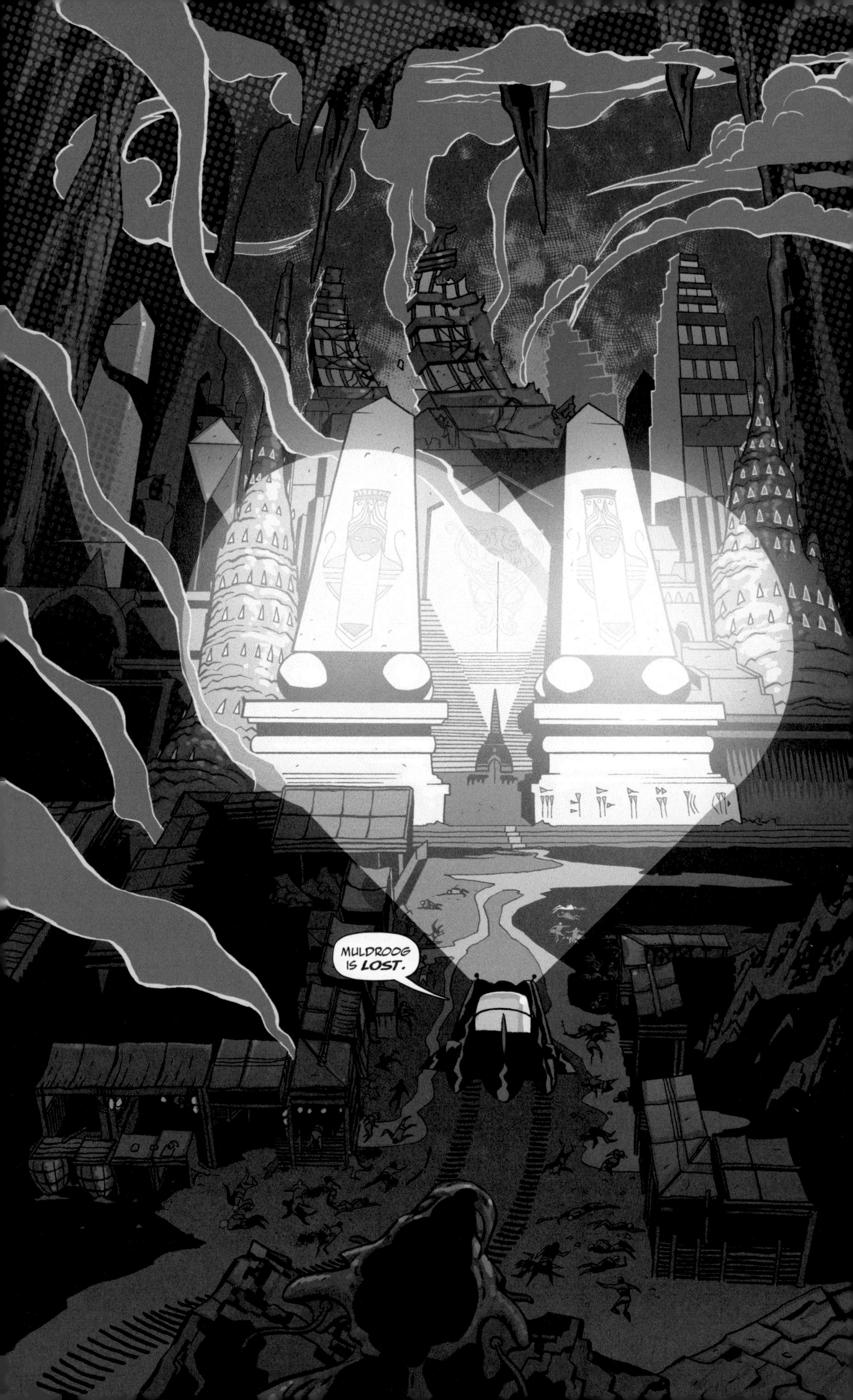
MULDROOG IS LOST.

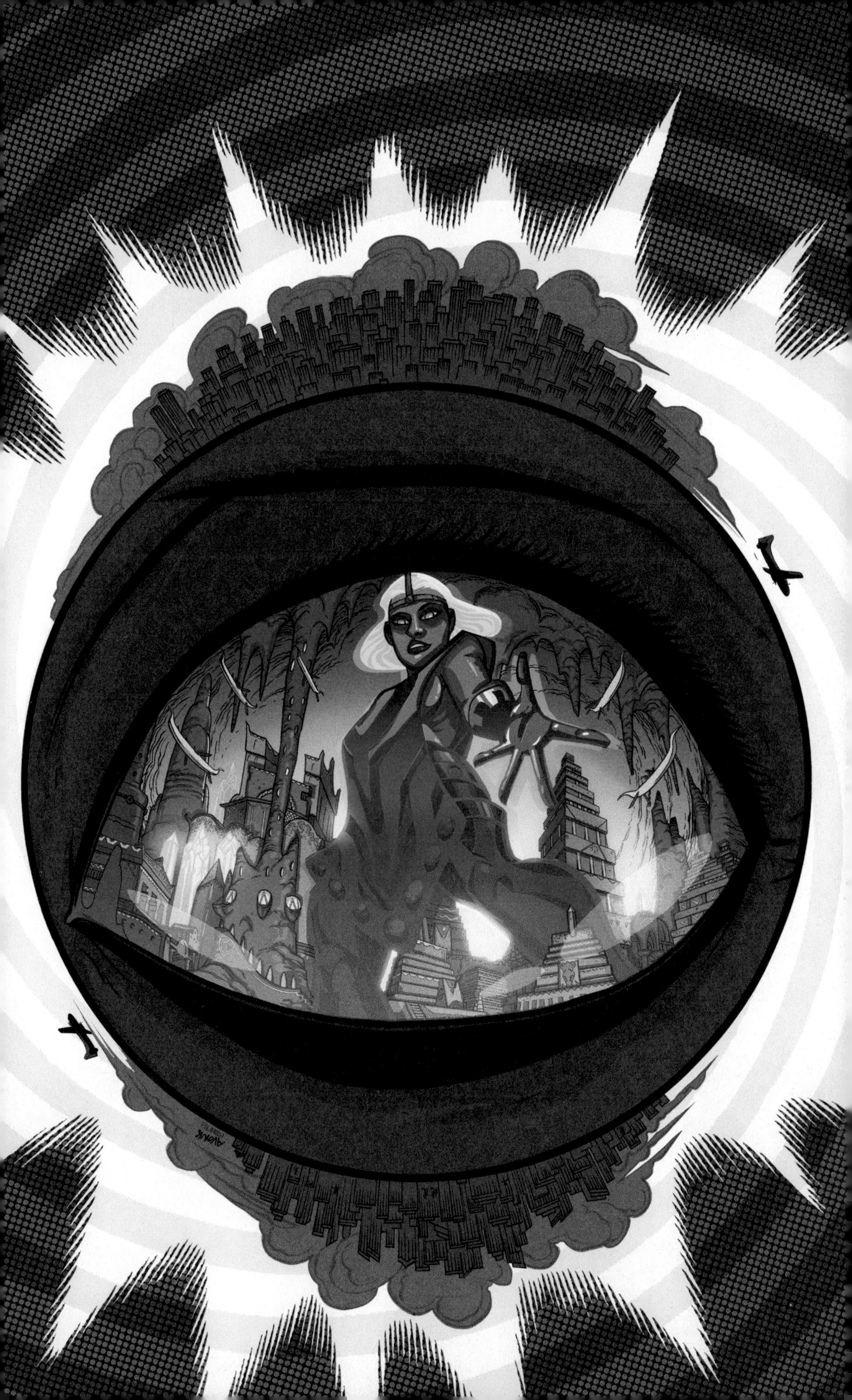

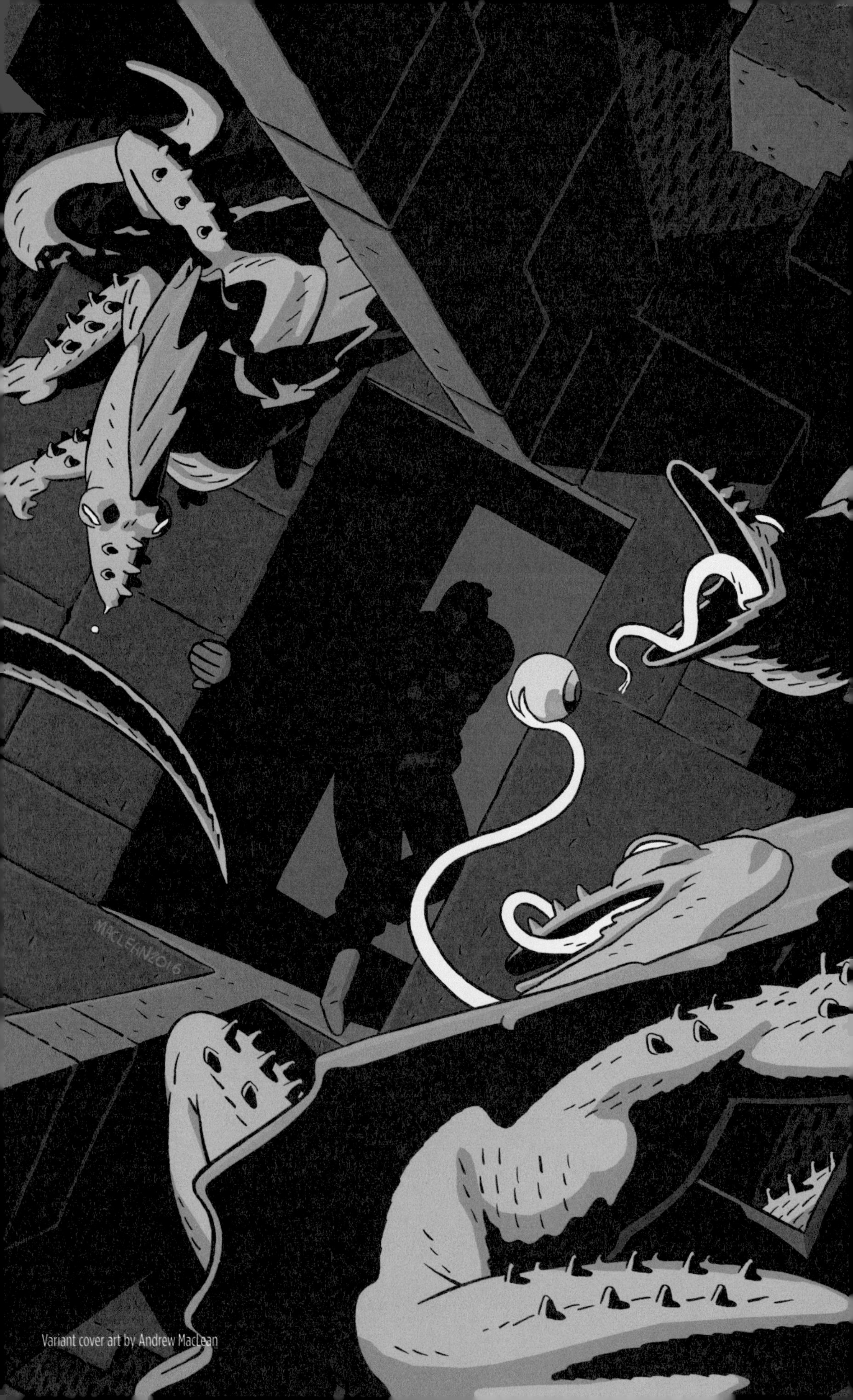

Variant cover art by Andrew MacLean

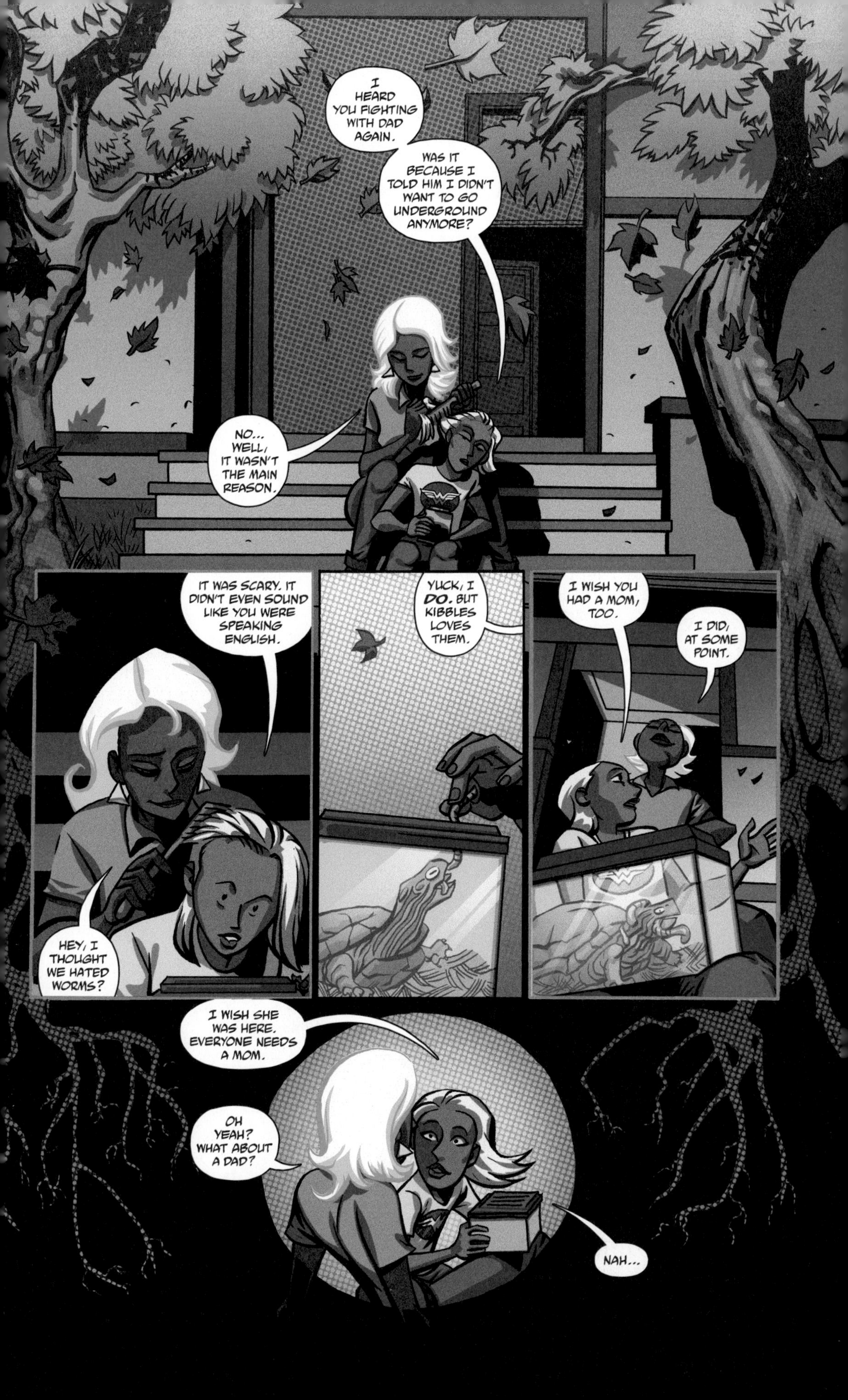
I HEARD YOU FIGHTING WITH DAD AGAIN.
WAS IT BECAUSE I TOLD HIM I DIDN'T WANT TO GO UNDERGROUND ANYMORE?
NO... WELL, IT WASN'T THE MAIN REASON.
IT WAS SCARY. IT DIDN'T EVEN SOUND LIKE YOU WERE SPEAKING ENGLISH.
HEY, I THOUGHT WE HATED WORMS?
YUCK, I DO. BUT KIBBLES LOVES THEM.
I WISH YOU HAD A MOM, TOO.
I DID, AT SOME POINT.
I WISH SHE WAS HERE. EVERYONE NEEDS A MOM.
OH YEAH? WHAT ABOUT A DAD?
NAH...

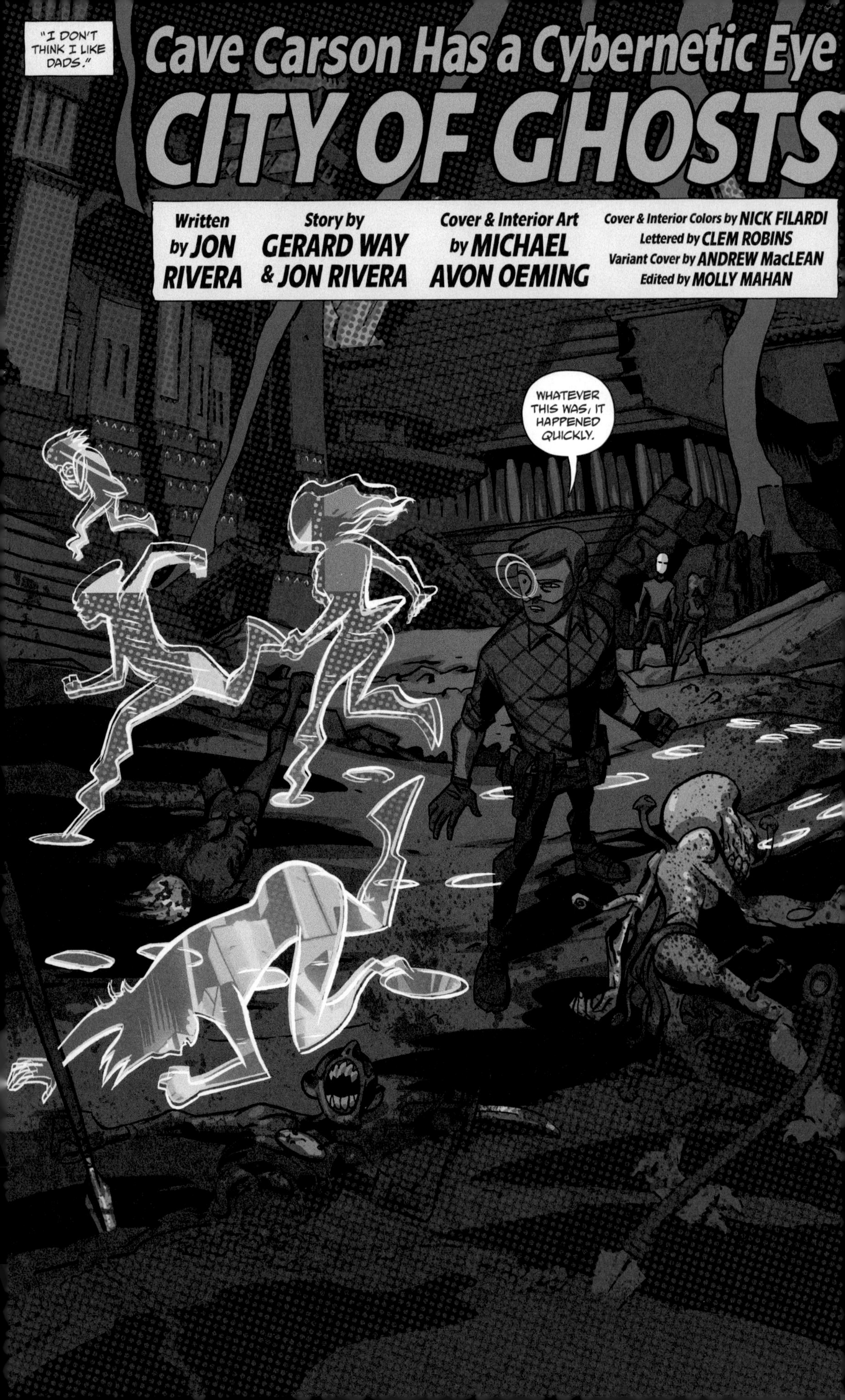
"I DON'T THINK I LIKE DADS."
Cave Carson Has a Cybernetic Eye
CITY OF GHOSTS
Written by JON RIVERA
Story by GERARD WAY & JON RIVERA
Cover & Interior Art by MICHAEL AVON OEMING
Cover & Interior Colors by NICK FILARDI
Lettered by CLEM ROBINS
Variant Cover by ANDREW MacLEAN
Edited by MOLLY MAHAN
WHATEVER THIS WAS, IT HAPPENED QUICKLY.

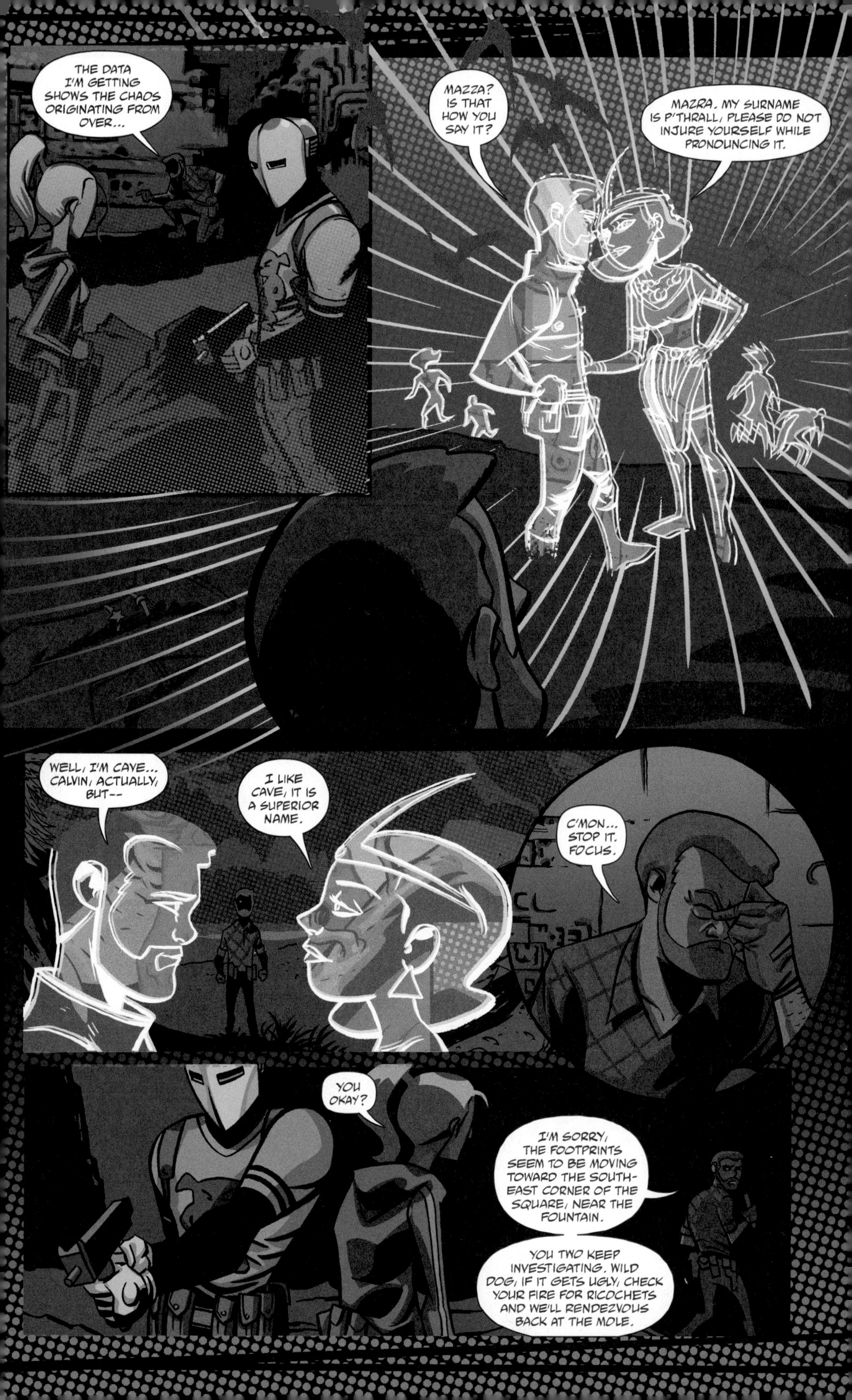
THE DATA I'M GETTING SHOWS THE CHAOS ORIGINATING FROM OVER...
MAZZA? IS THAT HOW YOU SAY IT?
MAZRA. MY SURNAME IS P'THRALL, PLEASE DO NOT INJURE YOURSELF WHILE PRONOUNCING IT.
WELL, I'M CAVE... CALVIN, ACTUALLY, BUT--
I LIKE CAVE, IT IS A SUPERIOR NAME.
C'MON... STOP IT. FOCUS.
YOU OKAY?
I'M SORRY, THE FOOTPRINTS SEEM TO BE MOVING TOWARD THE SOUTH-EAST CORNER OF THE SQUARE, NEAR THE FOUNTAIN.
YOU TWO KEEP INVESTIGATING. WILD DOG, IF IT GETS UGLY, CHECK YOUR FIRE FOR RICOCHETS AND WE'LL RENDEZVOUS BACK AT THE MOLE.

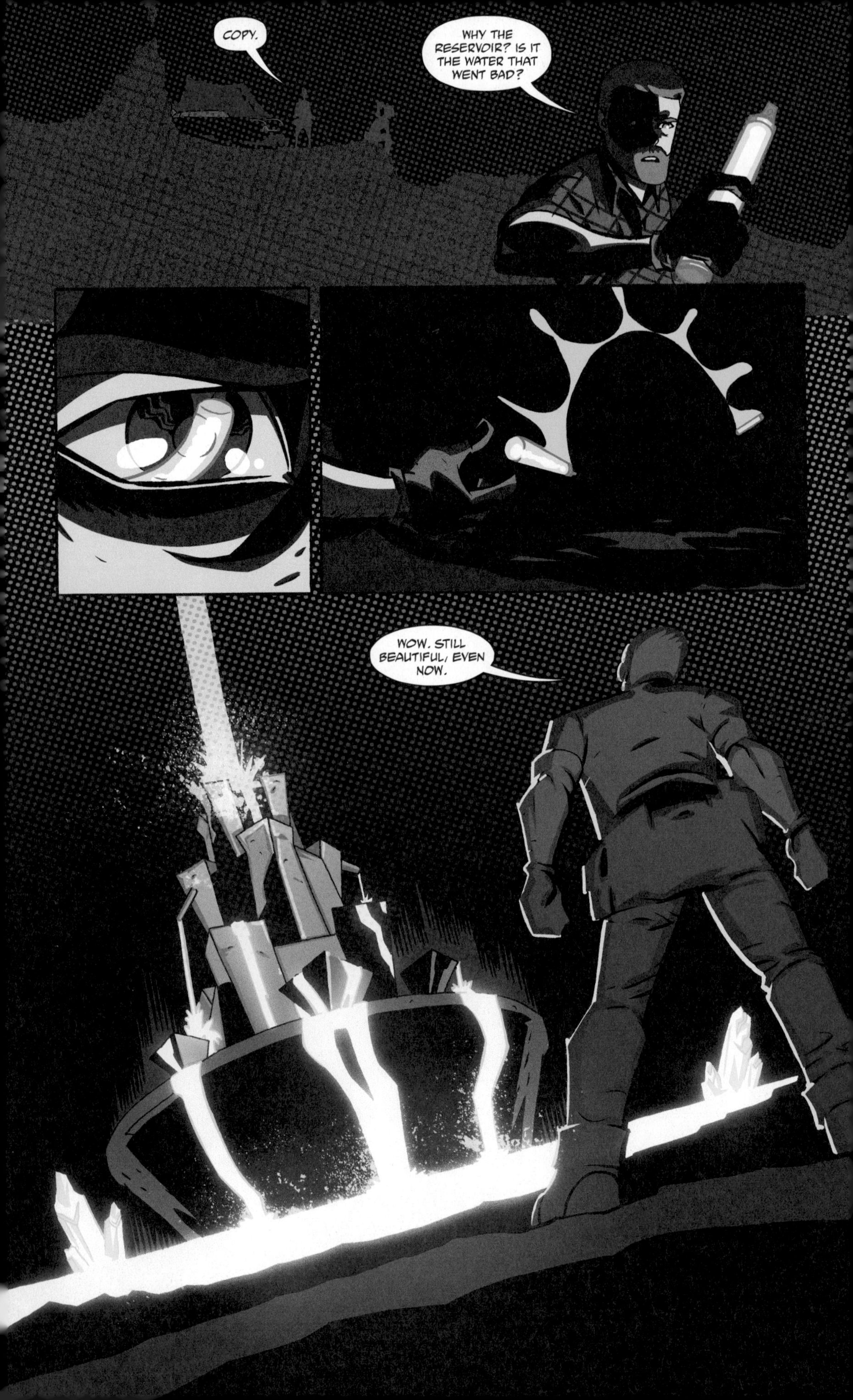
COPY.
WHY THE RESERVOIR? IS IT THE WATER THAT WENT BAD?
WOW. STILL BEAUTIFUL, EVEN NOW.

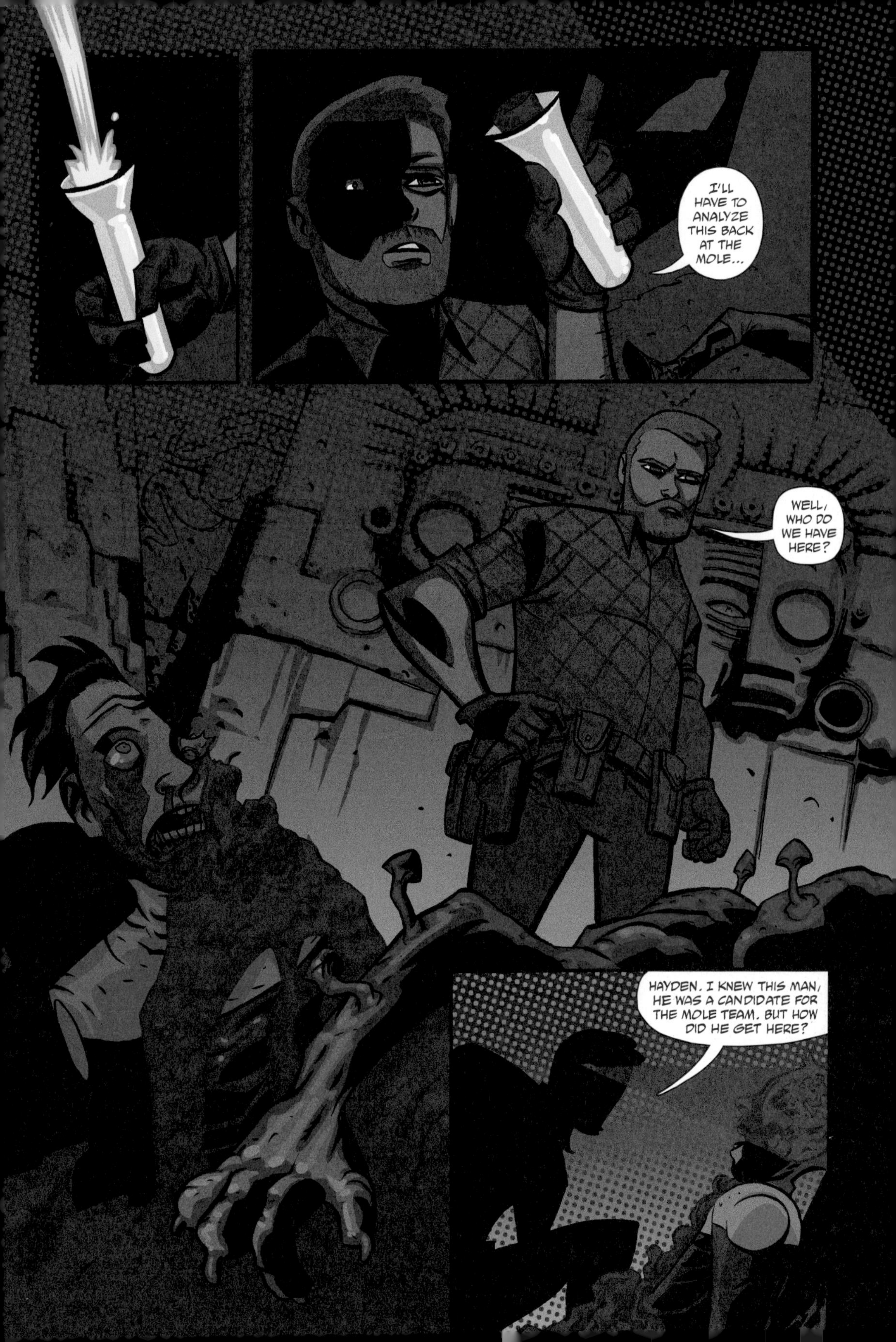
I'LL HAVE TO ANALYZE THIS BACK AT THE MOLE...
WELL, WHO DO WE HAVE HERE?
HAYDEN. I KNEW THIS MAN, HE WAS A CANDIDATE FOR THE MOLE TEAM. BUT HOW DID HE GET HERE?

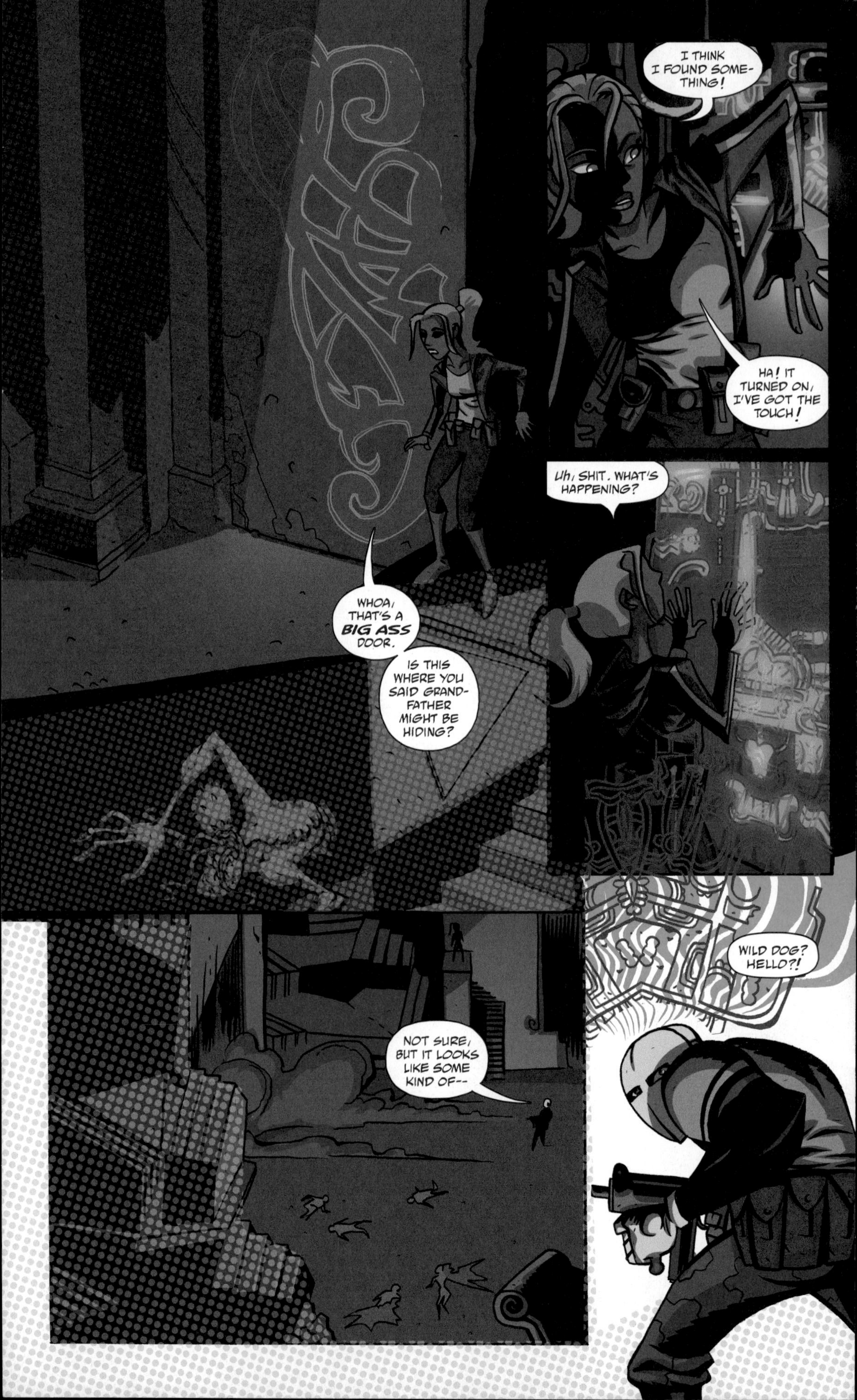
I THINK I FOUND SOME-THING!
HA! IT TURNED ON, I'VE GOT THE TOUCH!
WHOA, THAT'S A BIG ASS DOOR.
IS THIS WHERE YOU SAID GRAND-FATHER MIGHT BE HIDING?
Uh, SHIT. WHAT'S HAPPENING?
NOT SURE, BUT IT LOOKS LIKE SOME KIND OF--
WILD DOG? HELLO?!

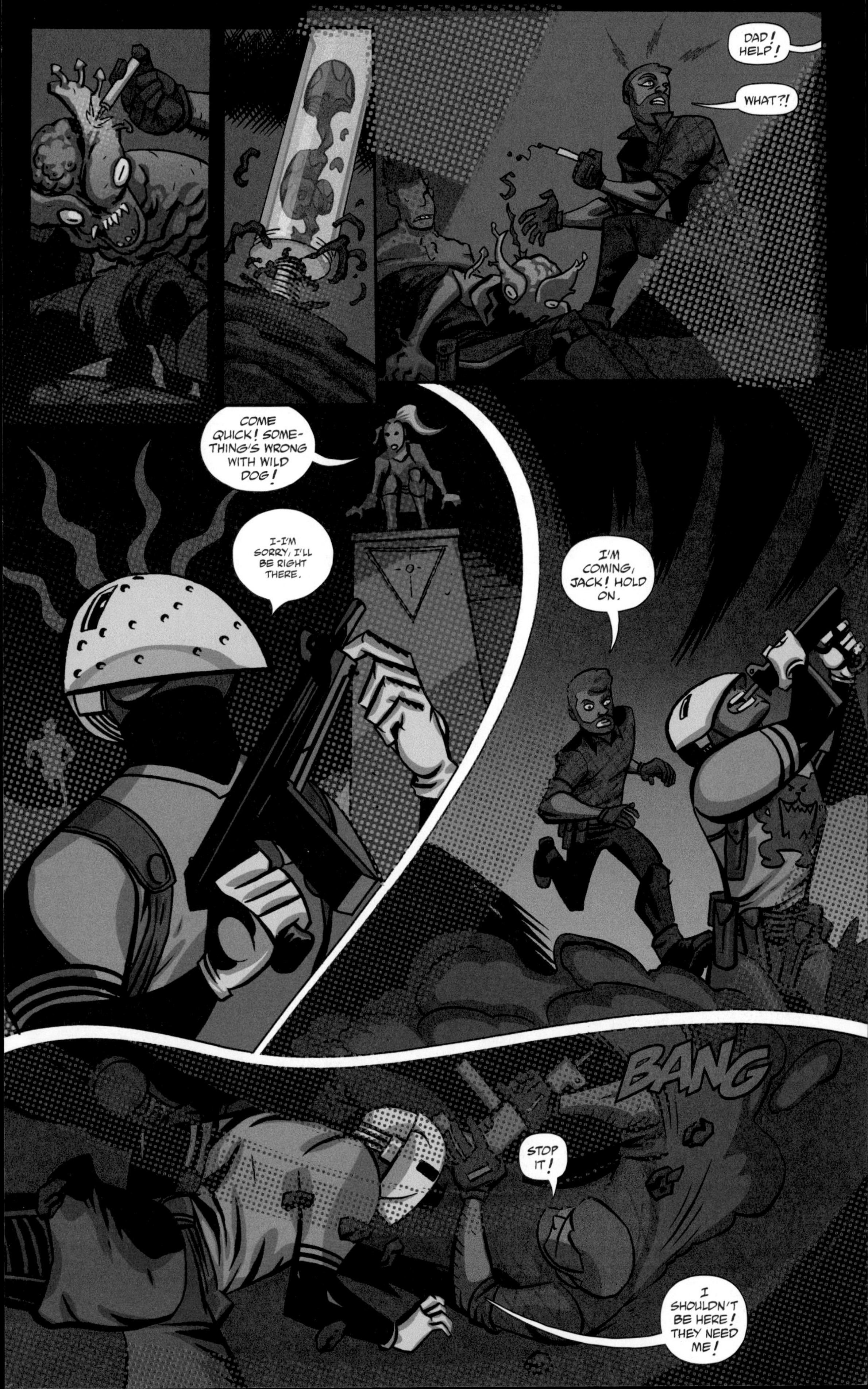

DAD! HELP!
WHAT?!
COME QUICK! SOME-THING'S WRONG WITH WILD DOG!
I-I'M SORRY, I'LL BE RIGHT THERE.
I'M COMING, JACK! HOLD ON.
BANG
STOP IT!
I SHOULDN'T BE HERE! THEY NEED ME!

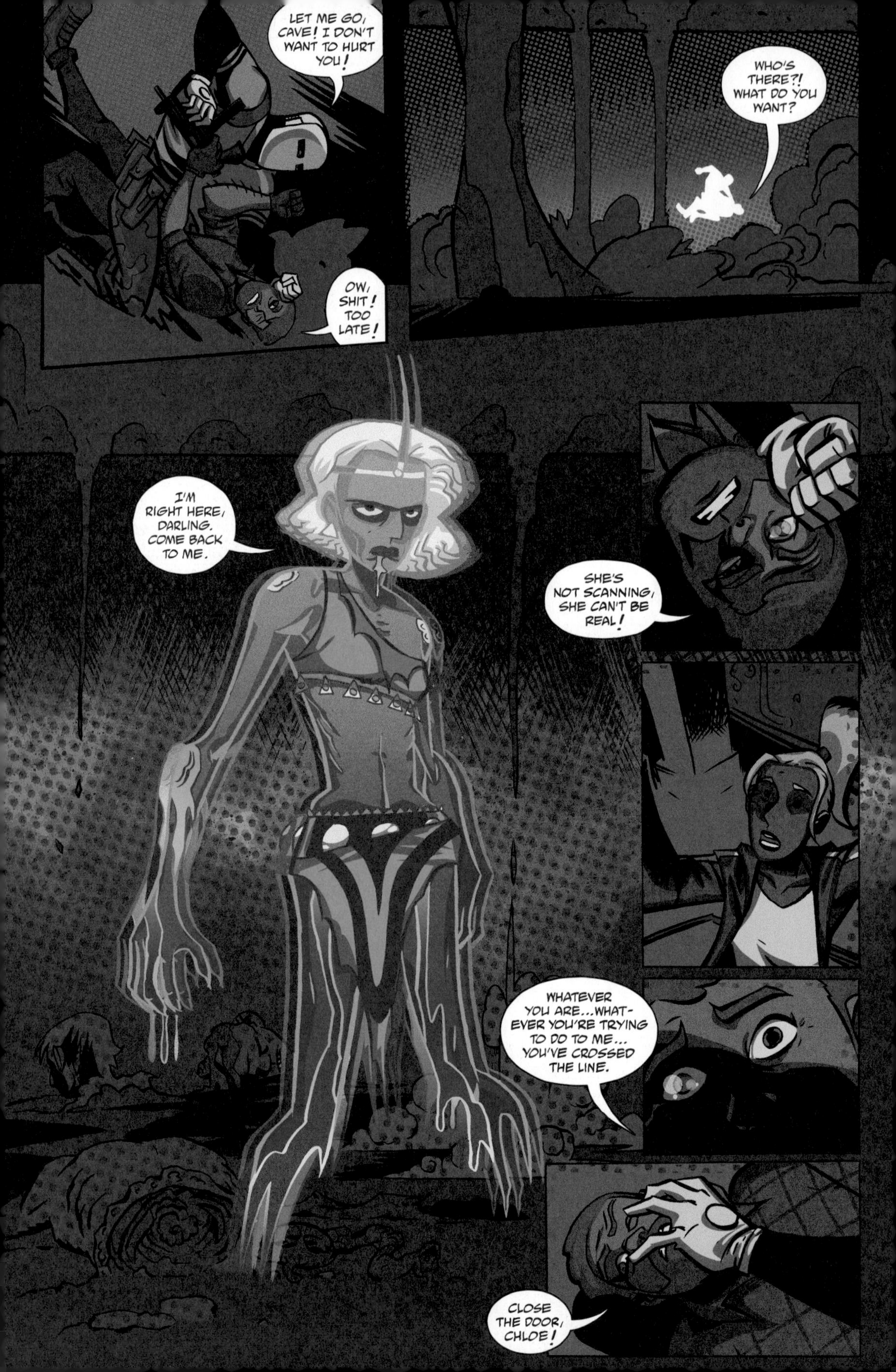
LET ME GO, CAVE! I DON'T WANT TO HURT YOU!
OW, SHIT! TOO LATE!
WHO'S THERE?! WHAT DO YOU WANT?
I'M RIGHT HERE, DARLING. COME BACK TO ME.
SHE'S NOT SCANNING, SHE CAN'T BE REAL!
WHATEVER YOU ARE...WHAT-EVER YOU'RE TRYING TO DO TO ME... YOU'VE CROSSED THE LINE.
CLOSE THE DOOR, CHLOE!

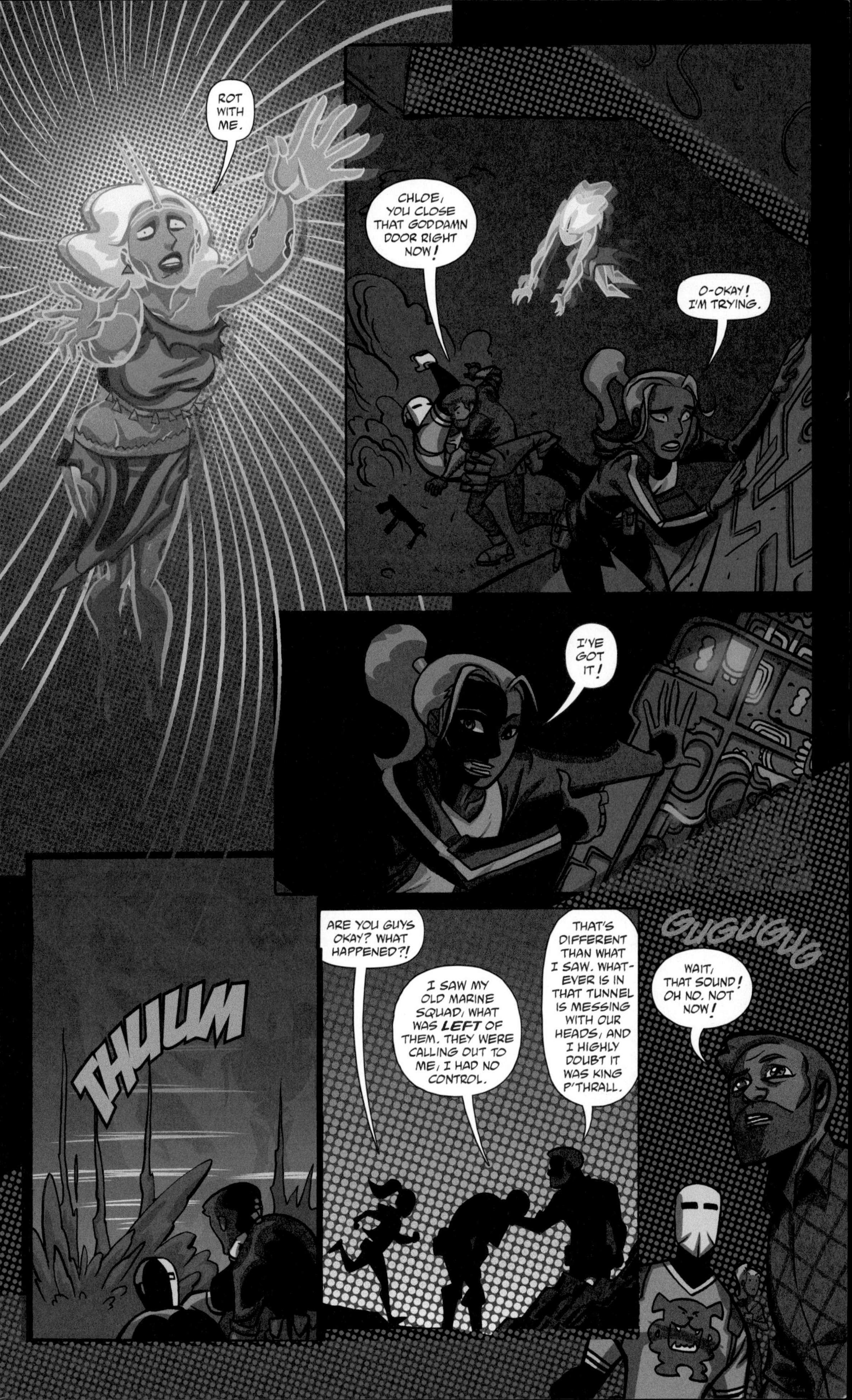
ROT WITH ME.
CHLOE, YOU CLOSE THAT GODDAMN DOOR RIGHT NOW!
O-OKAY! I'M TRYING.
I'VE GOT IT!
THUUM
ARE YOU GUYS OKAY? WHAT HAPPENED?!
I SAW MY OLD MARINE SQUAD, WHAT WAS LEFT OF THEM. THEY WERE CALLING OUT TO ME, I HAD NO CONTROL.
THAT'S DIFFERENT THAN WHAT I SAW. WHAT-EVER IS IN THAT TUNNEL IS MESSING WITH OUR HEADS, AND I HIGHLY DOUBT IT WAS KING P'THRALL.
GUGUGUG
WAIT, THAT SOUND! OH NO. NOT NOW!

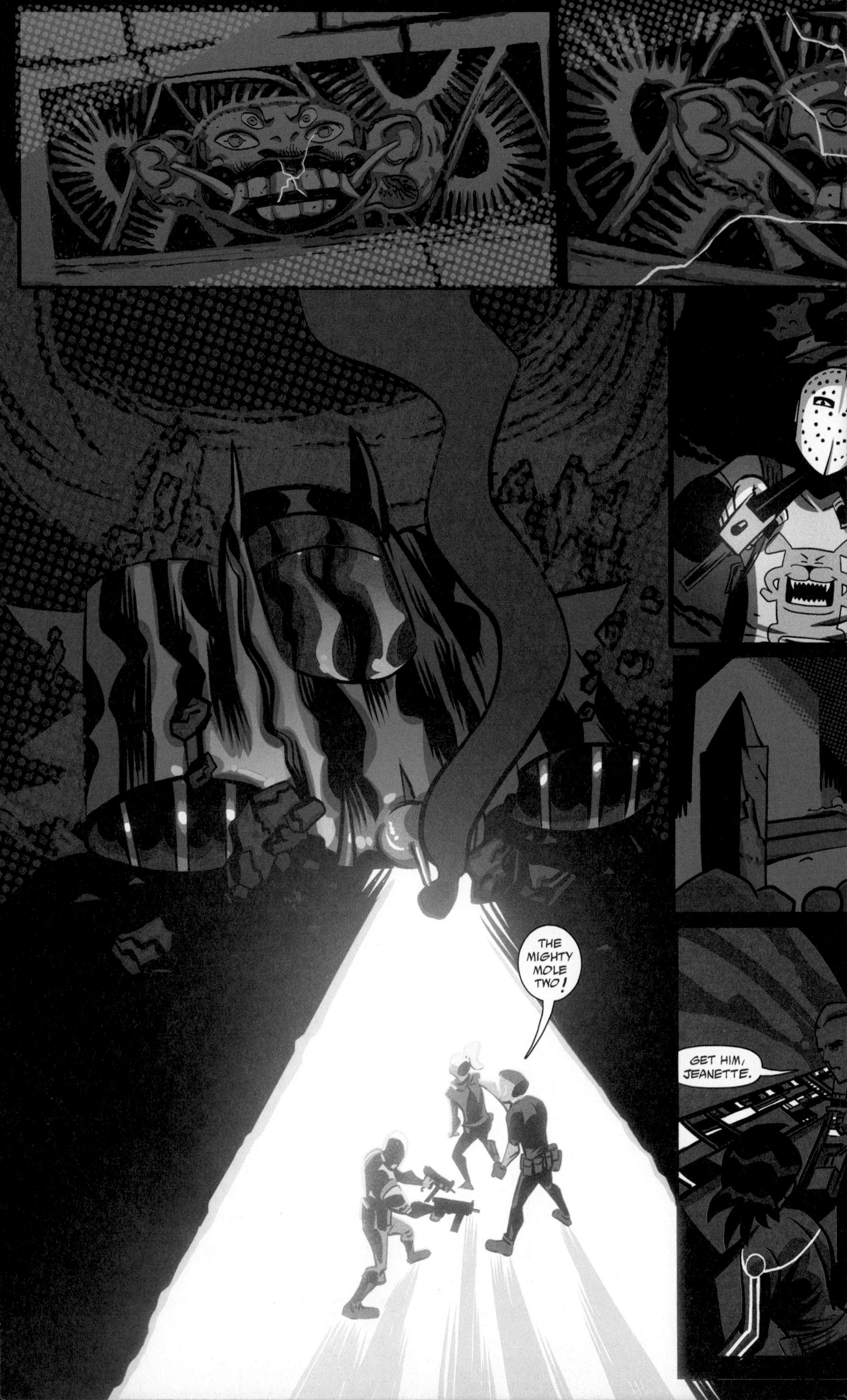
THE MIGHTY MOLE TWO!
GET HIM, JEANETTE.

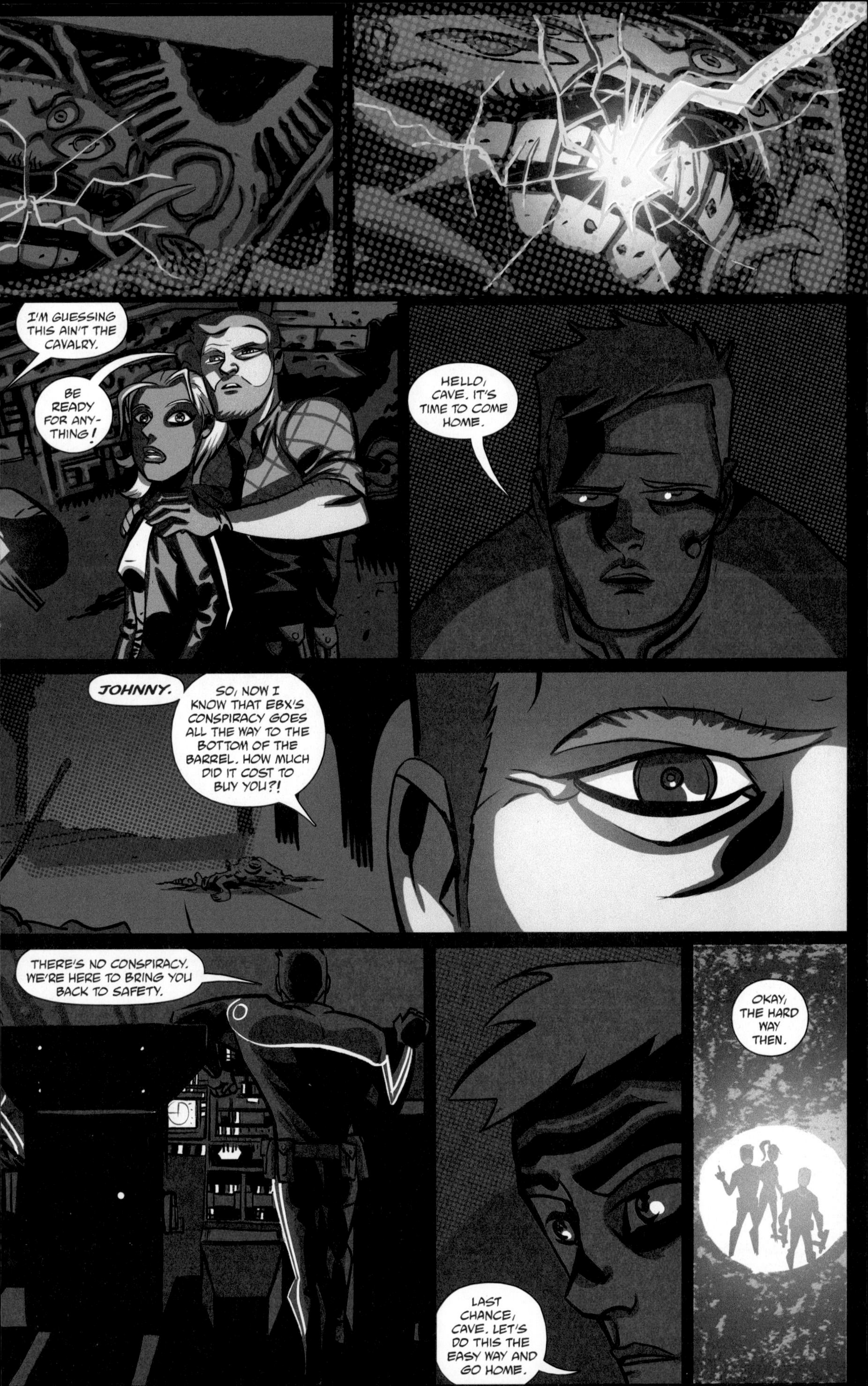

I'M GUESSING THIS AIN'T THE CAVALRY.
BE READY FOR ANY-THING!
HELLO, CAVE. IT'S TIME TO COME HOME.
JOHNNY.
SO, NOW I KNOW THAT EBX'S CONSPIRACY GOES ALL THE WAY TO THE BOTTOM OF THE BARREL. HOW MUCH DID IT COST TO BUY YOU?!
THERE'S NO CONSPIRACY. WE'RE HERE TO BRING YOU BACK TO SAFETY.
LAST CHANCE, CAVE. LET'S DO THIS THE EASY WAY AND GO HOME.
OKAY, THE HARD WAY THEN.

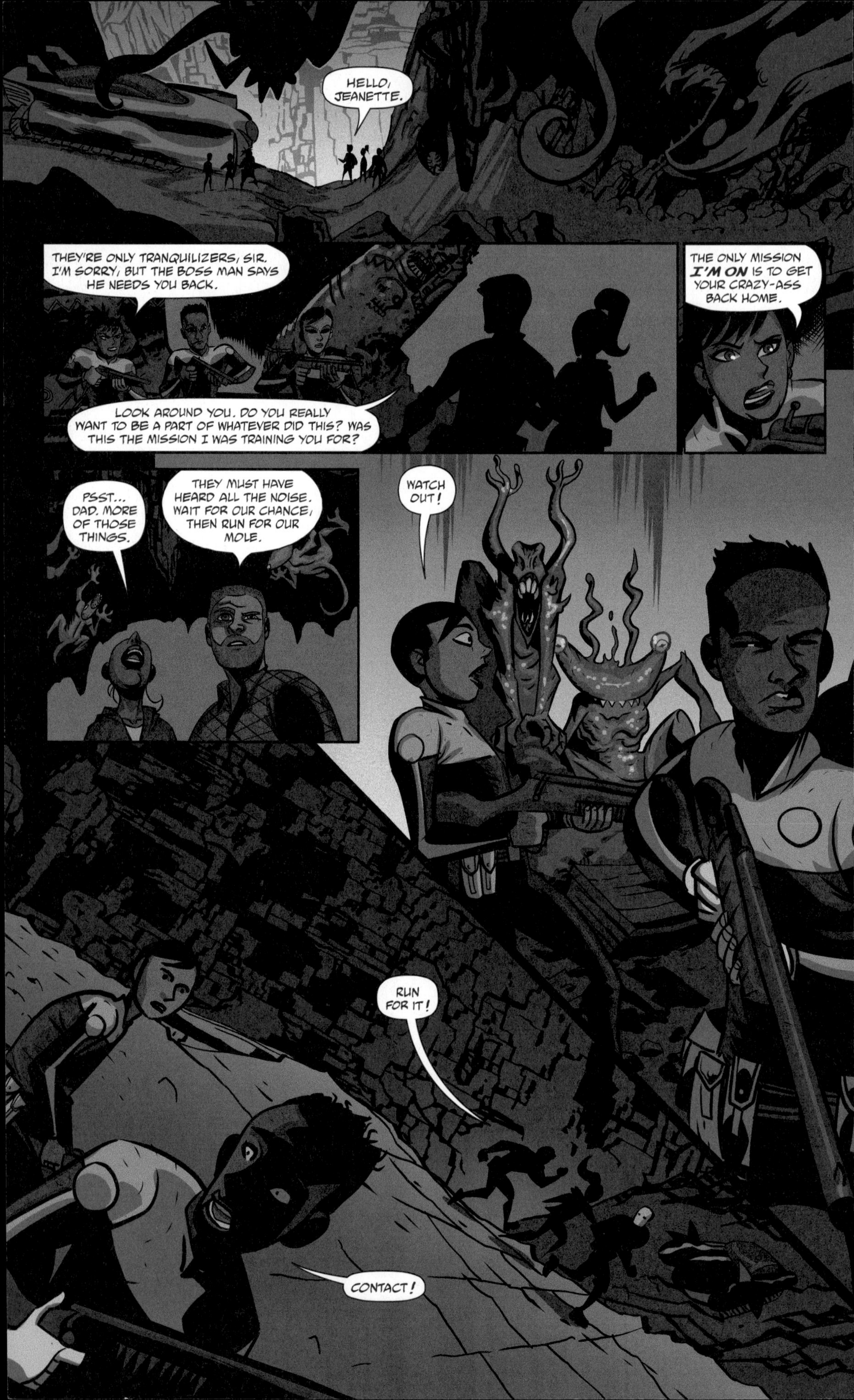
HELLO, JEANETTE.
THEY'RE ONLY TRANQUILIZERS, SIR. I'M SORRY, BUT THE BOSS MAN SAYS HE NEEDS YOU BACK.
LOOK AROUND YOU. DO YOU REALLY WANT TO BE A PART OF WHATEVER DID THIS? WAS THIS THE MISSION I WAS TRAINING YOU FOR?
THE ONLY MISSION I'M ON IS TO GET YOUR CRAZY-ASS BACK HOME.
PSST... DAD. MORE OF THOSE THINGS.
THEY MUST HAVE HEARD ALL THE NOISE. WAIT FOR OUR CHANCE, THEN RUN FOR OUR MOLE.
WATCH OUT!
RUN FOR IT!
CONTACT!

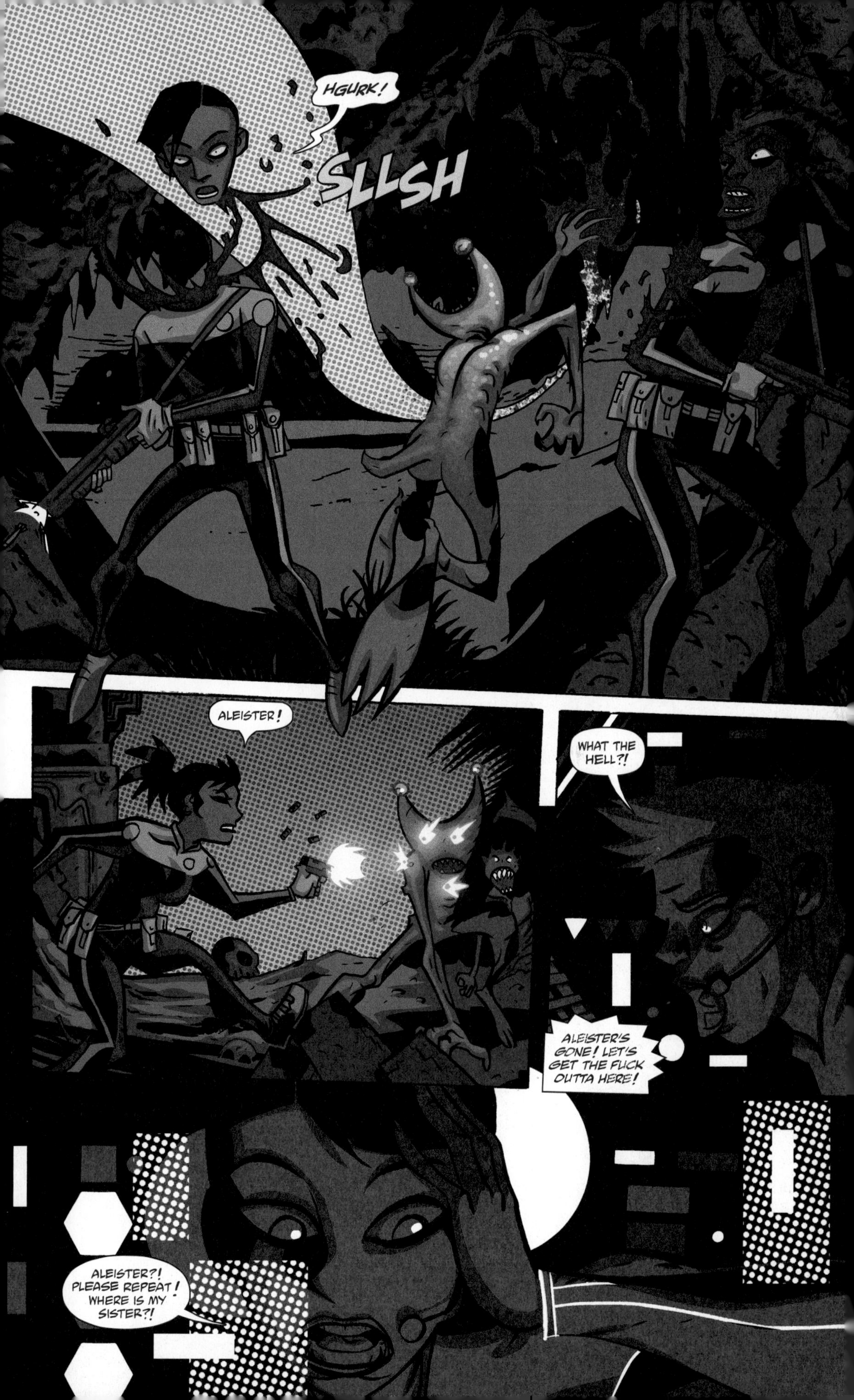
HGURK!
SLLSH
ALEISTER!
WHAT THE HELL?!
ALEISTER'S GONE! LET'S GET THE FUCK OUTTA HERE!
ALEISTER?! PLEASE REPEAT! WHERE IS MY SISTER?!

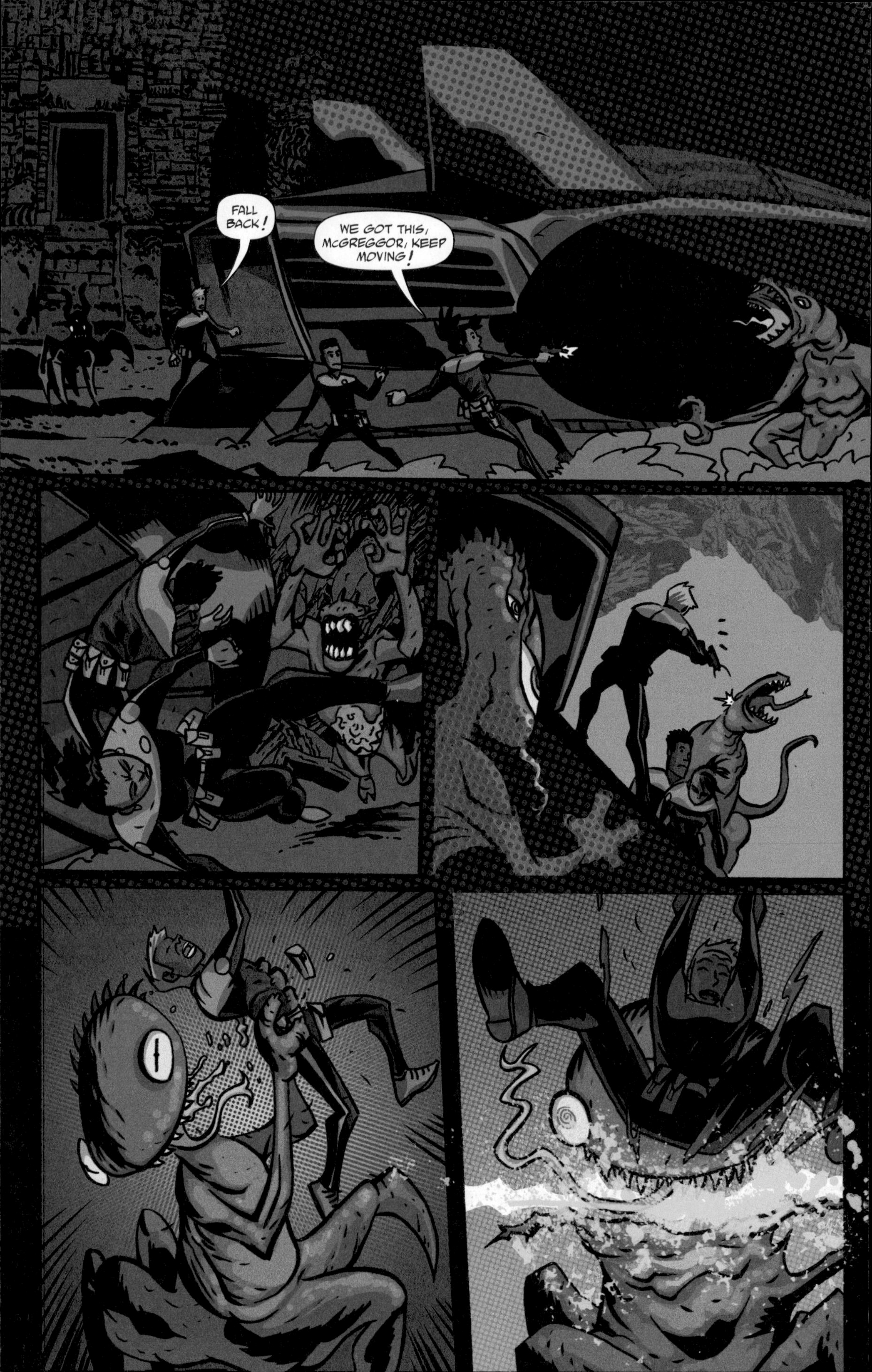
FALL BACK!
WE GOT THIS, McGREGGOR, KEEP MOVING!

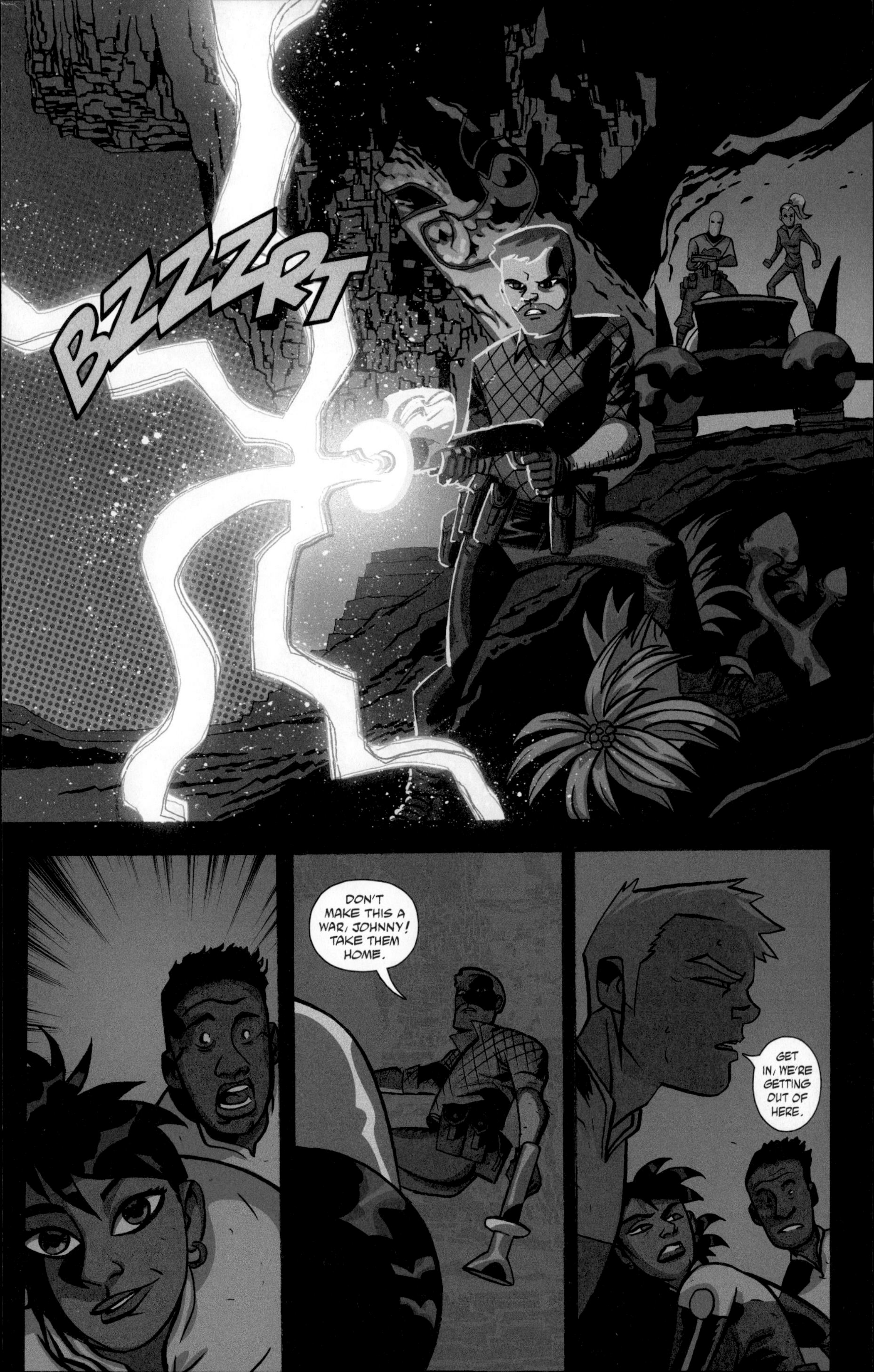
BZZZRT
DON'T MAKE THIS A WAR, JOHNNY! TAKE THEM HOME.
GET IN, WE'RE GETTING OUT OF HERE.

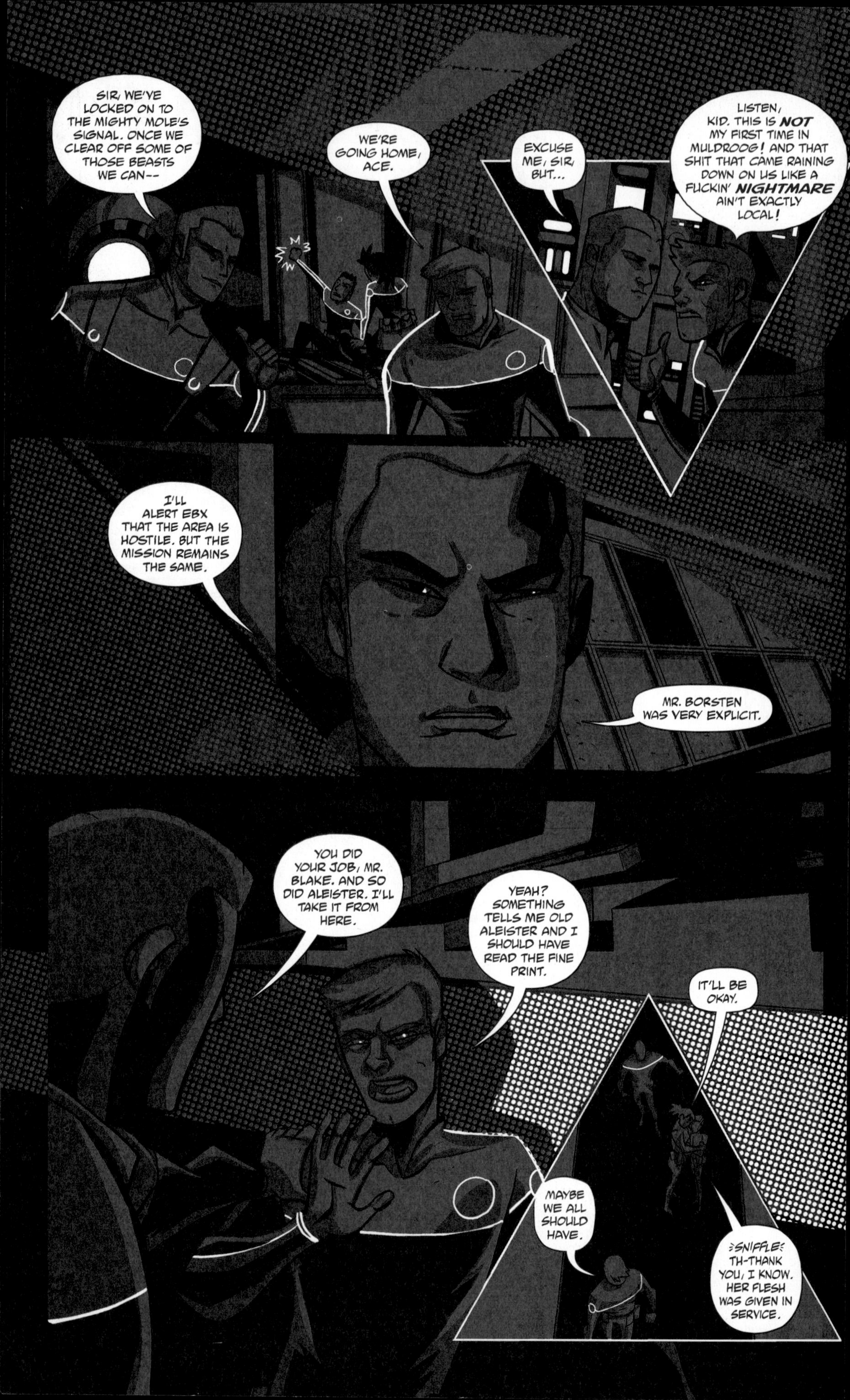
SIR, WE'VE LOCKED ON TO THE MIGHTY MOLE'S SIGNAL. ONCE WE CLEAR OFF SOME OF THOSE BEASTS WE CAN--
WE'RE GOING HOME, ACE.
EXCUSE ME, SIR, BUT...
LISTEN, KID. THIS IS **NOT** MY FIRST TIME IN MULDROOG! AND THAT SHIT THAT CAME RAINING DOWN ON US LIKE A FUCKIN' **NIGHTMARE** AIN'T EXACTLY LOCAL!
I'LL ALERT EBX THAT THE AREA IS HOSTILE. BUT THE MISSION REMAINS THE SAME.
MR. BORSTEN WAS VERY EXPLICIT.
YOU DID YOUR JOB, MR. BLAKE. AND SO DID ALEISTER. I'LL TAKE IT FROM HERE.
YEAH? SOMETHING TELLS ME OLD ALEISTER AND I SHOULD HAVE READ THE FINE PRINT.
IT'LL BE OKAY.
MAYBE WE ALL SHOULD HAVE.
SNIFFLE TH-THANK YOU, I KNOW. HER FLESH WAS GIVEN IN SERVICE.

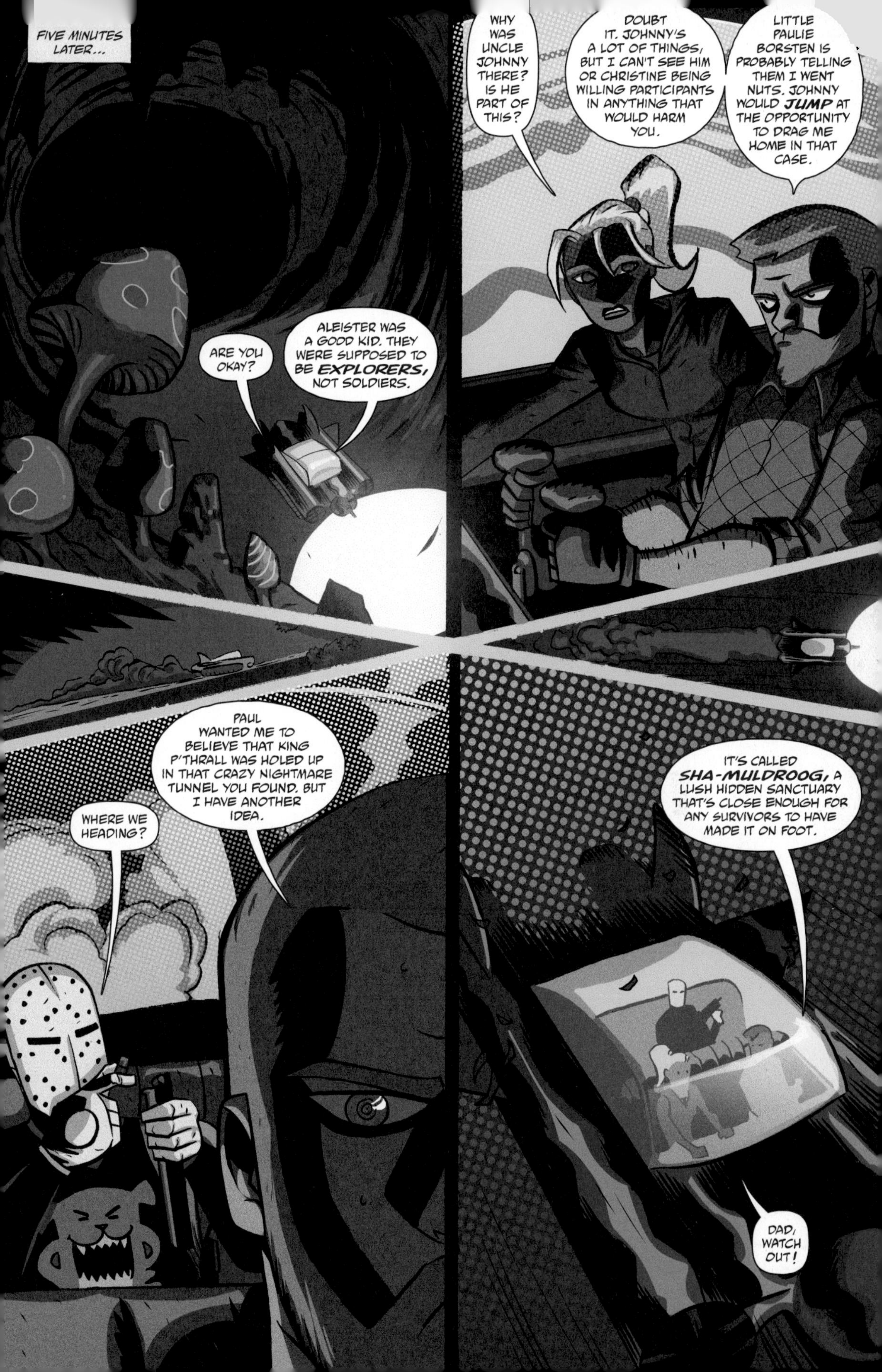
FIVE MINUTES LATER...
ARE YOU OKAY?
ALEISTER WAS A GOOD KID. THEY WERE SUPPOSED TO BE EXPLORERS, NOT SOLDIERS.
WHY WAS UNCLE JOHNNY THERE? IS HE PART OF THIS?
DOUBT IT. JOHNNY'S A LOT OF THINGS, BUT I CAN'T SEE HIM OR CHRISTINE BEING WILLING PARTICIPANTS IN ANYTHING THAT WOULD HARM YOU.
LITTLE PAULIE BORSTEN IS PROBABLY TELLING THEM I WENT NUTS. JOHNNY WOULD JUMP AT THE OPPORTUNITY TO DRAG ME HOME IN THAT CASE.
WHERE WE HEADING?
PAUL WANTED ME TO BELIEVE THAT KING P'THRALL WAS HOLED UP IN THAT CRAZY NIGHTMARE TUNNEL YOU FOUND. BUT I HAVE ANOTHER IDEA.
IT'S CALLED SHA-MULDROOG, A LUSH HIDDEN SANCTUARY THAT'S CLOSE ENOUGH FOR ANY SURVIVORS TO HAVE MADE IT ON FOOT.
DAD, WATCH OUT!

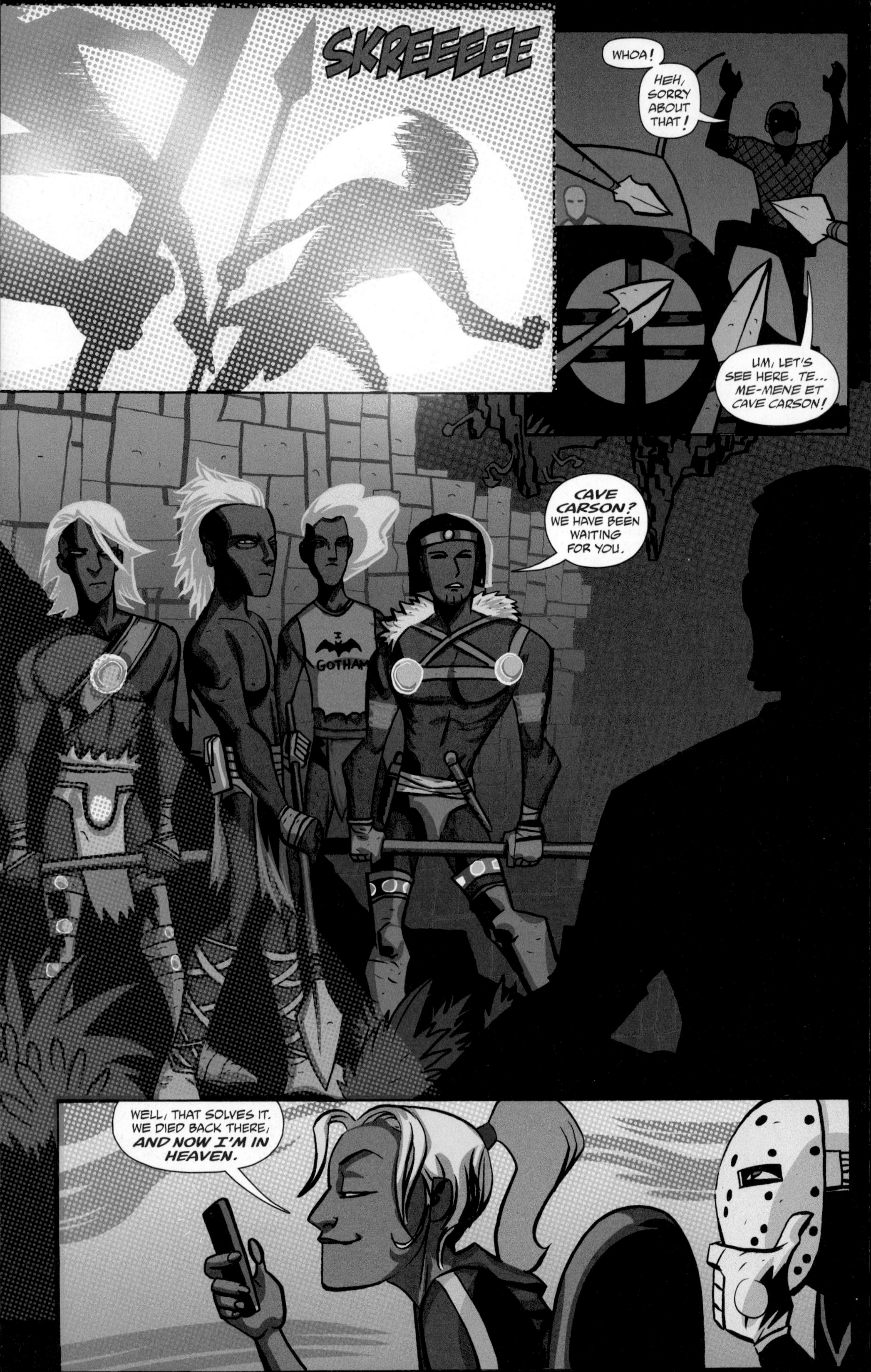
SKREEEEEE
WHOA!
HEH, SORRY ABOUT THAT!
UM, LET'S SEE HERE. TE... ME-MENE ET CAVE CARSON!
CAVE CARSON? WE HAVE BEEN WAITING FOR YOU.
GOTHAM
WELL, THAT SOLVES IT. WE DIED BACK THERE, AND NOW I'M IN HEAVEN.

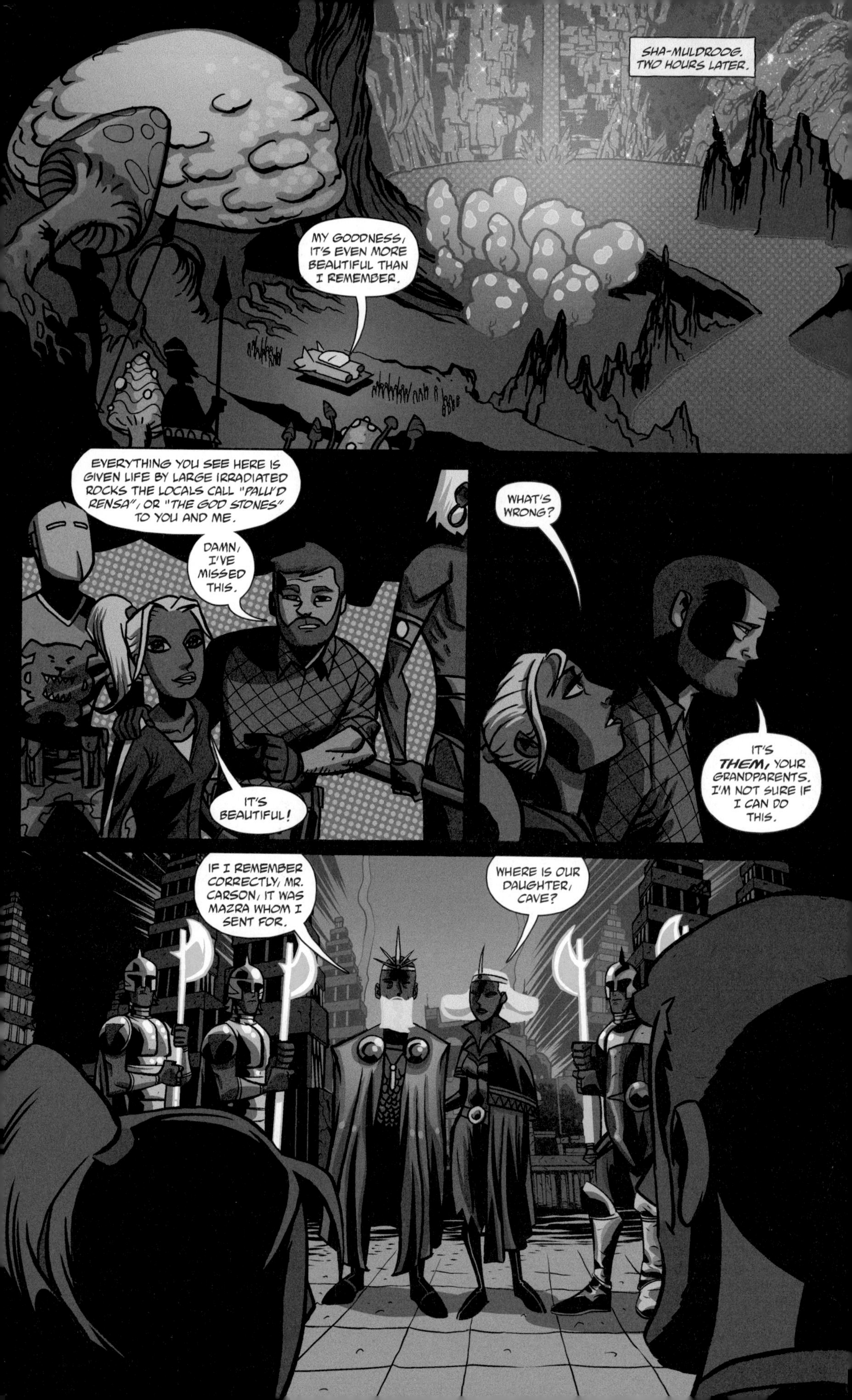
SHA-MULDROOG. TWO HOURS LATER.
MY GOODNESS, IT'S EVEN MORE BEAUTIFUL THAN I REMEMBER.
EVERYTHING YOU SEE HERE IS GIVEN LIFE BY LARGE IRRADIATED ROCKS THE LOCALS CALL "PALLI'D RENSA", OR "THE GOD STONES" TO YOU AND ME.
DAMN, I'VE MISSED THIS.
IT'S BEAUTIFUL!
WHAT'S WRONG?
IT'S THEM, YOUR GRANDPARENTS. I'M NOT SURE IF I CAN DO THIS.
IF I REMEMBER CORRECTLY, MR. CARSON, IT WAS MAZRA WHOM I SENT FOR.
WHERE IS OUR DAUGHTER, CAVE?

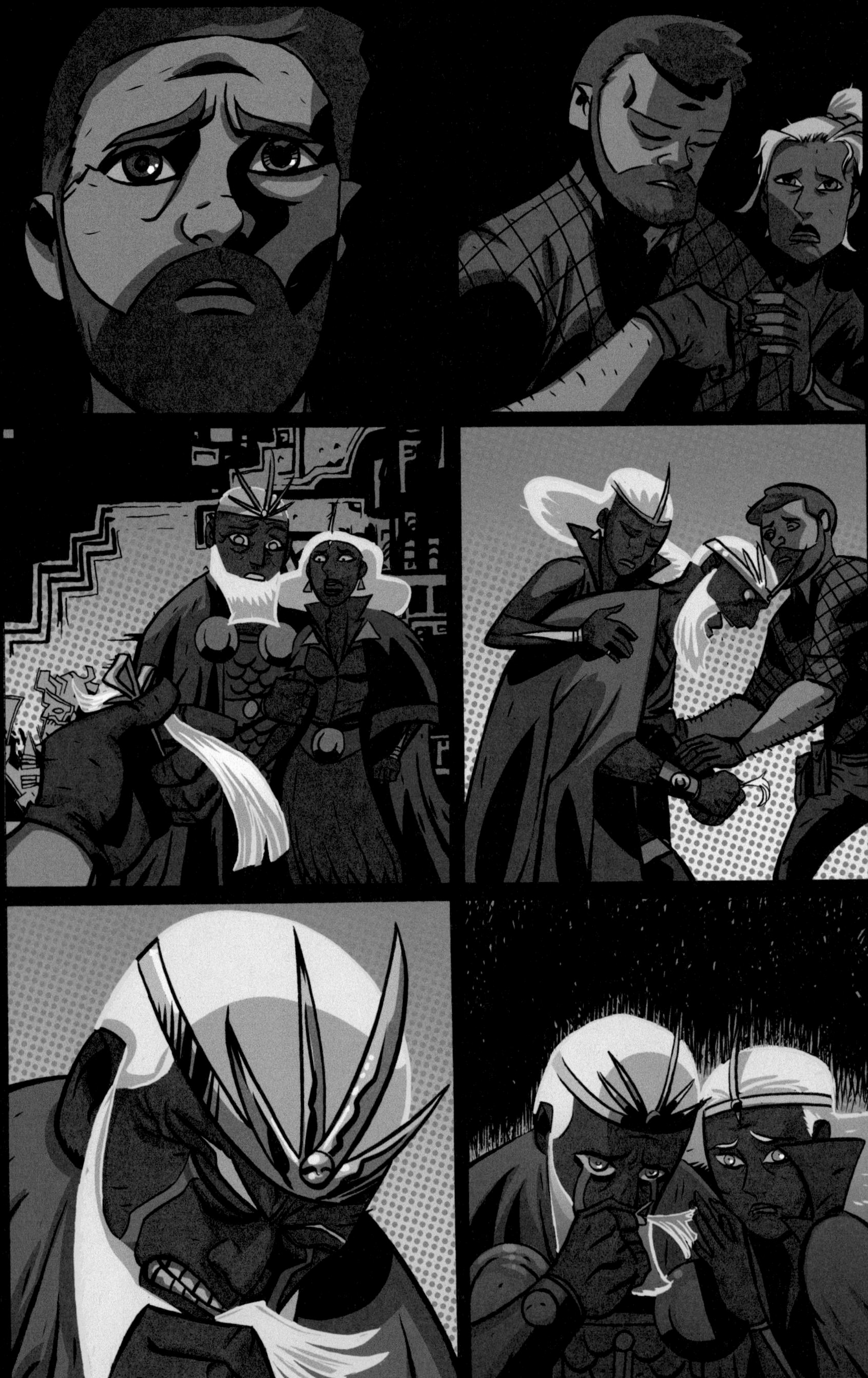

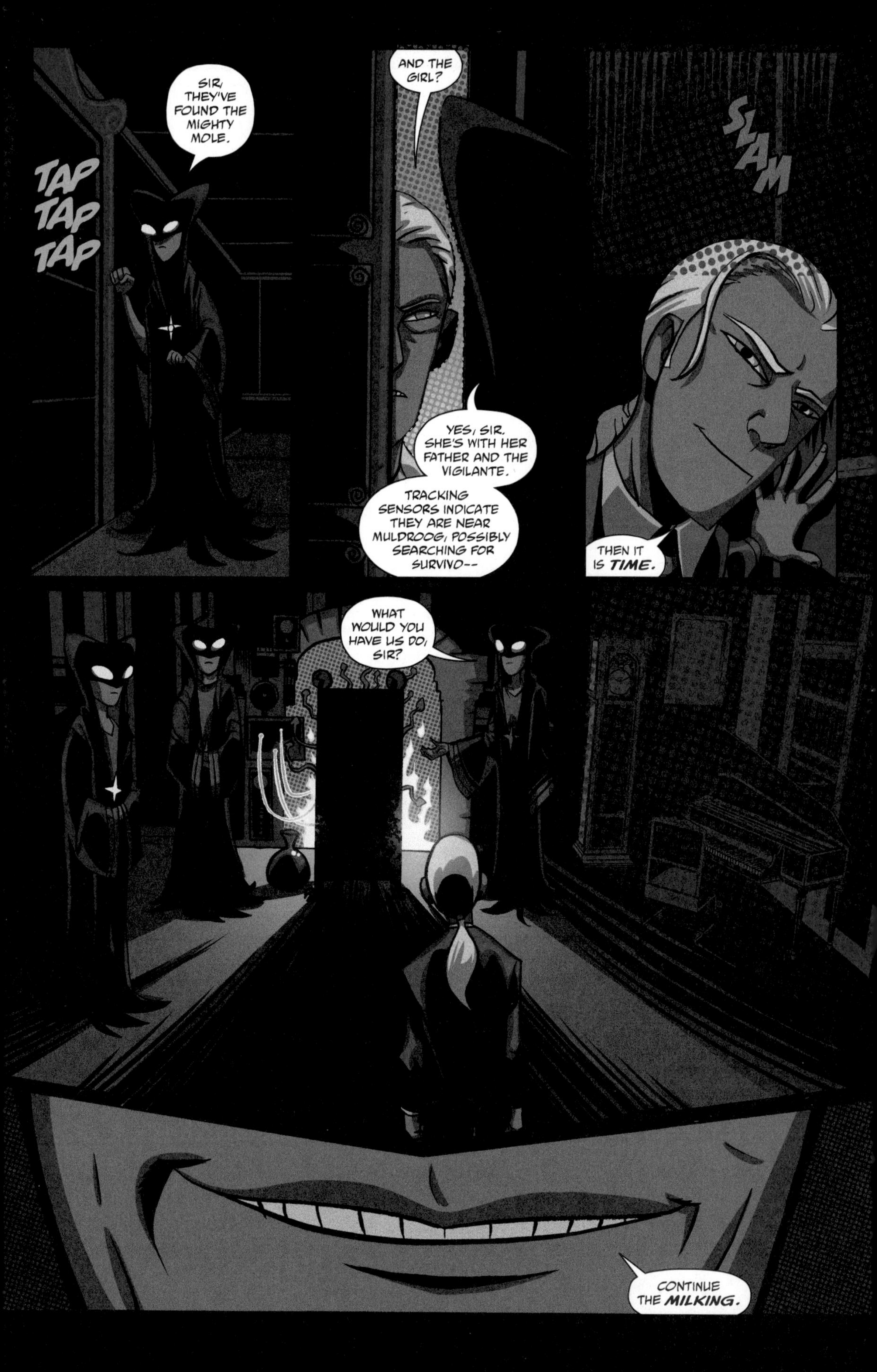
SIR, THEY'VE FOUND THE MIGHTY MOLE.
TAP TAP TAP
AND THE GIRL?
YES, SIR. SHE'S WITH HER FATHER AND THE VIGILANTE.
TRACKING SENSORS INDICATE THEY ARE NEAR MULDROOG, POSSIBLY SEARCHING FOR SURVIVO--
SLAM
THEN IT IS TIME.
WHAT WOULD YOU HAVE US DO, SIR?
CONTINUE THE MILKING.

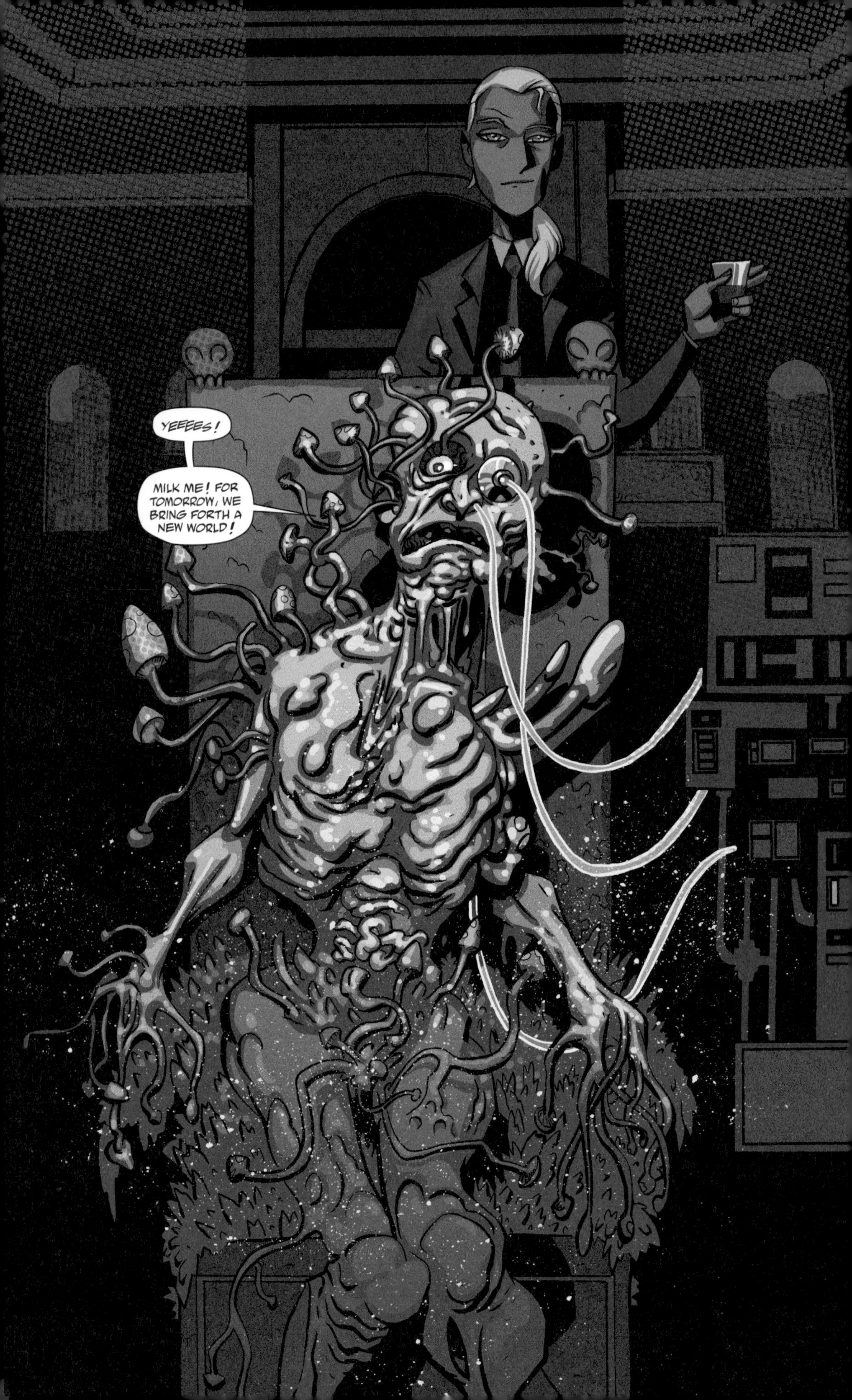
YEEEEES!
MILK ME! FOR TOMORROW, WE BRING FORTH A NEW WORLD!

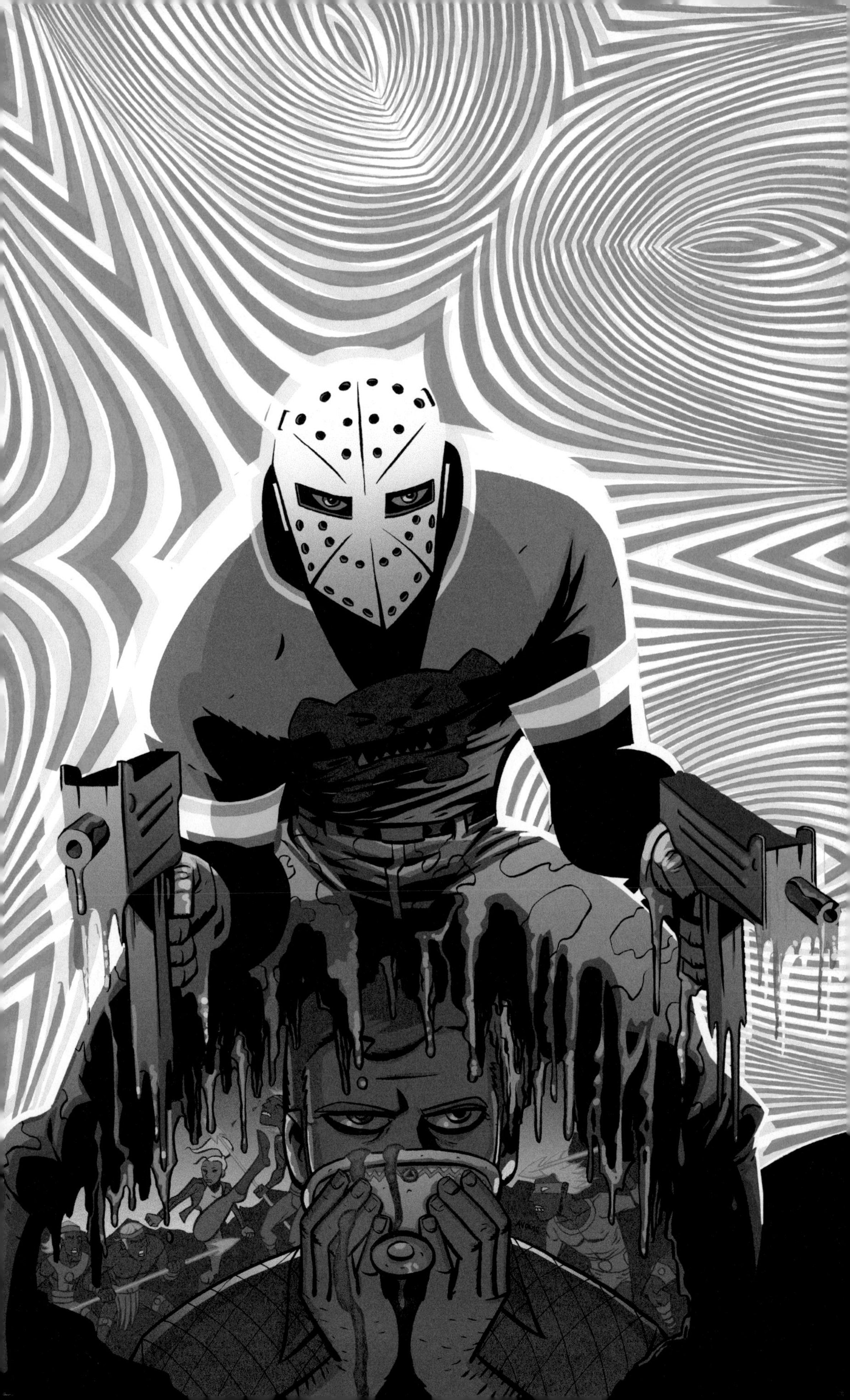

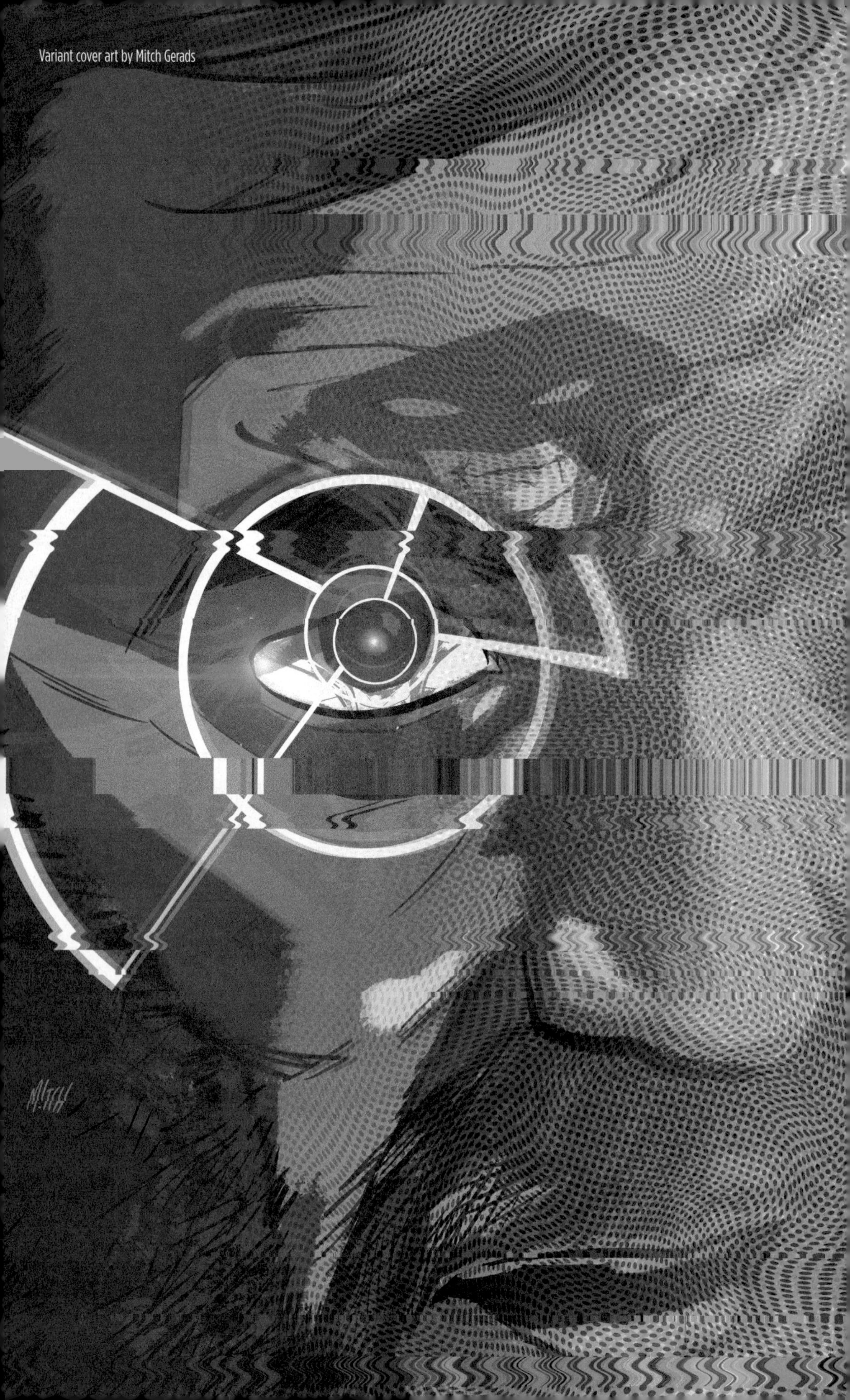

Variant cover art by Mitch Gerads

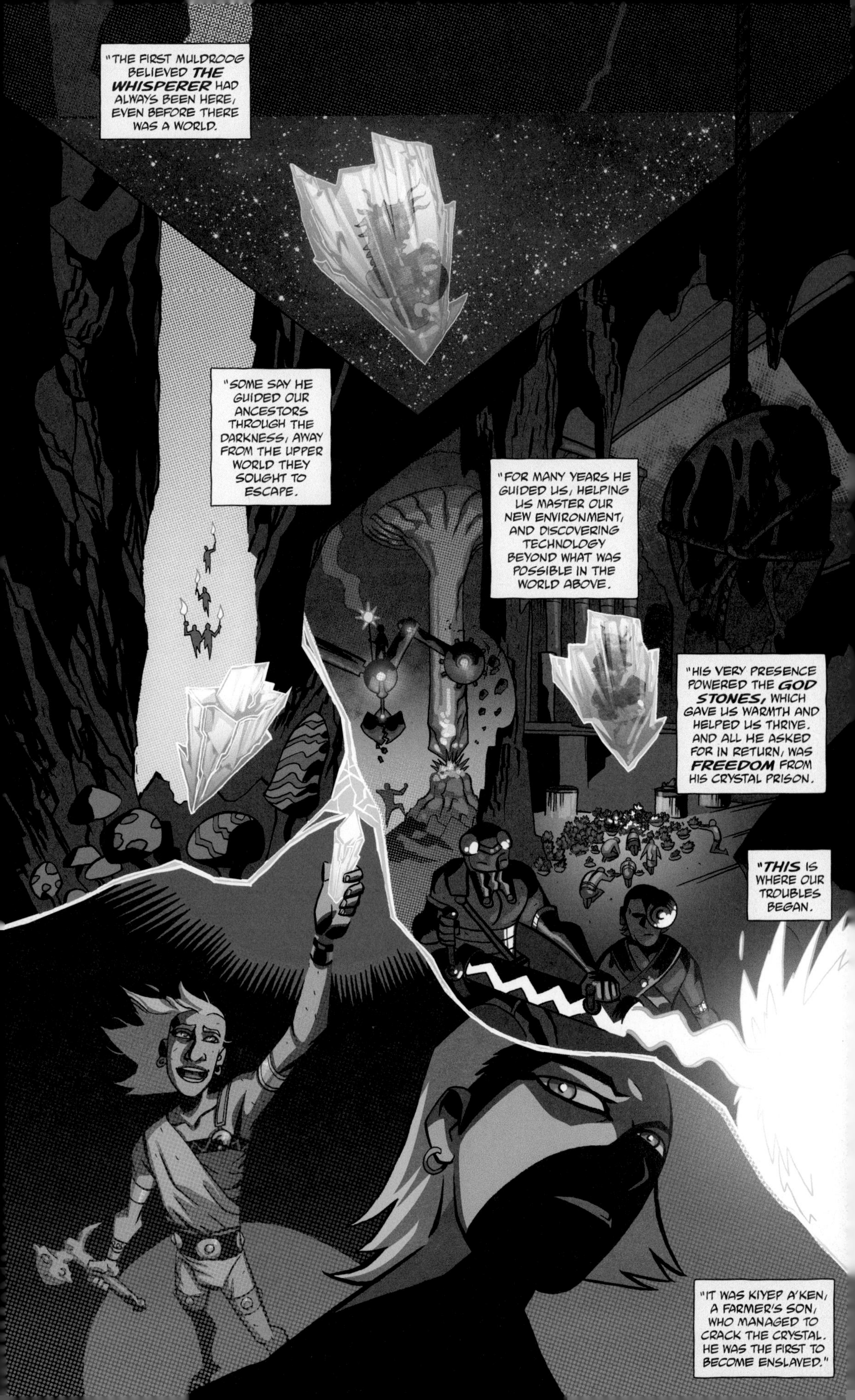
"THE FIRST MULDROOG BELIEVED THE WHISPERER HAD ALWAYS BEEN HERE, EVEN BEFORE THERE WAS A WORLD.
"SOME SAY HE GUIDED OUR ANCESTORS THROUGH THE DARKNESS, AWAY FROM THE UPPER WORLD THEY SOUGHT TO ESCAPE.
"FOR MANY YEARS HE GUIDED US, HELPING US MASTER OUR NEW ENVIRONMENT, AND DISCOVERING TECHNOLOGY BEYOND WHAT WAS POSSIBLE IN THE WORLD ABOVE.
"HIS VERY PRESENCE POWERED THE GOD STONES, WHICH GAVE US WARMTH AND HELPED US THRIVE. AND ALL HE ASKED FOR IN RETURN, WAS FREEDOM FROM HIS CRYSTAL PRISON.
"THIS IS WHERE OUR TROUBLES BEGAN.
"IT WAS KIYEP A'KEN, A FARMER'S SON, WHO MANAGED TO CRACK THE CRYSTAL. HE WAS THE FIRST TO BECOME ENSLAVED."

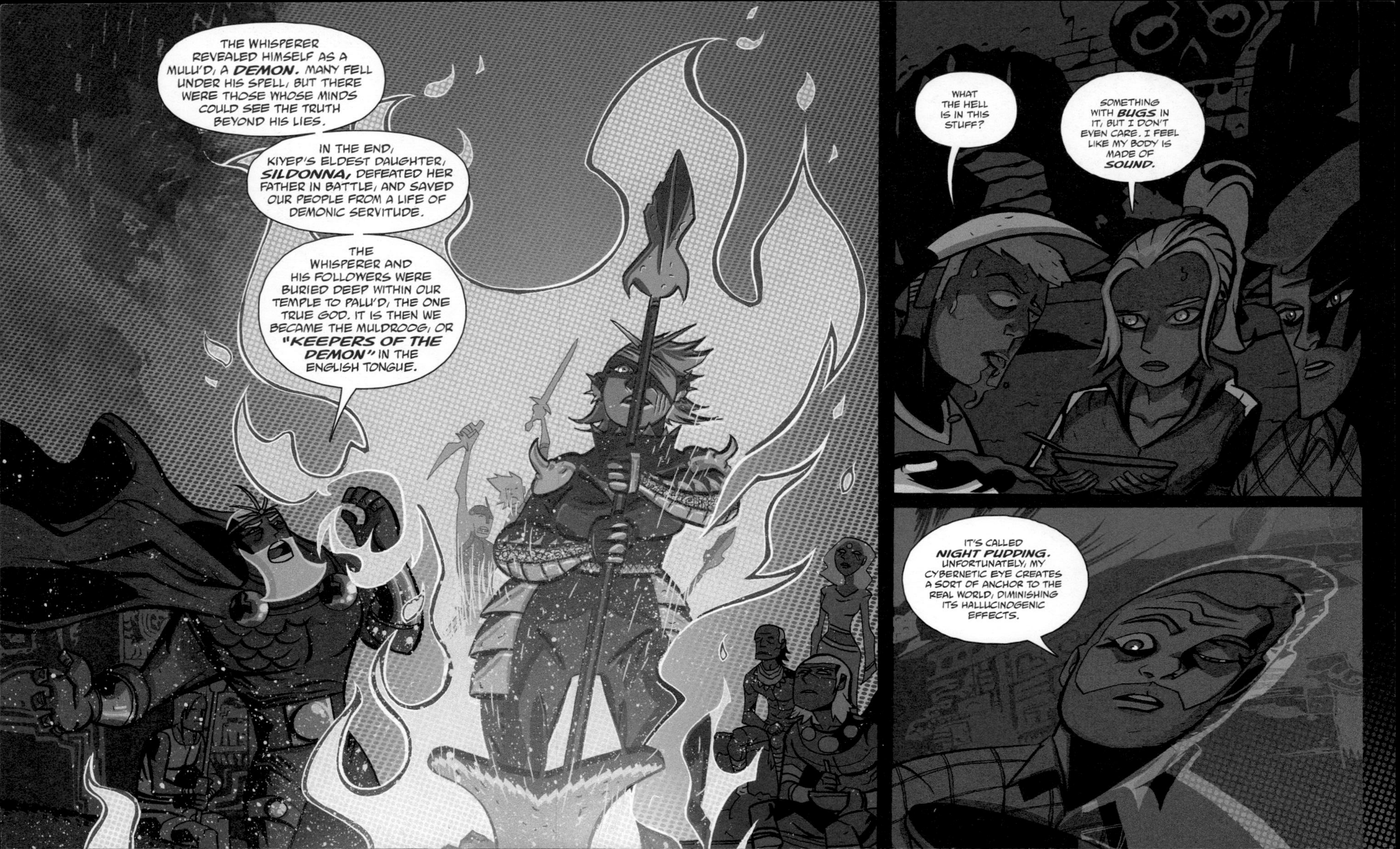
THE WHISPERER REVEALED HIMSELF AS A MULU'D, A **DEMON.** MANY FELL UNDER HIS SPELL, BUT THERE WERE THOSE WHOSE MINDS COULD SEE THE TRUTH BEYOND HIS LIES.
IN THE END, KIYEP'S ELDEST DAUGHTER, **SILDONNA,** DEFEATED HER FATHER IN BATTLE, AND SAVED OUR PEOPLE FROM A LIFE OF DEMONIC SERVITUDE.
THE WHISPERER AND HIS FOLLOWERS WERE BURIED DEEP WITHIN OUR TEMPLE TO PALU'D, THE ONE TRUE GOD. IT IS THEN WE BECAME THE MULDROOG, OR **"KEEPERS OF THE DEMON"** IN THE ENGLISH TONGUE.
WHAT THE HELL IS IN THIS STUFF?
SOMETHING WITH **BUGS** IN IT, BUT I DON'T EVEN CARE. I FEEL LIKE MY BODY IS MADE OF **SOUND.**
IT'S CALLED **NIGHT PUDDING.** UNFORTUNATELY, MY CYBERNETIC EYE CREATES A SORT OF ANCHOR TO THE REAL WORLD, DIMINISHING ITS HALLUCINOGENIC EFFECTS.

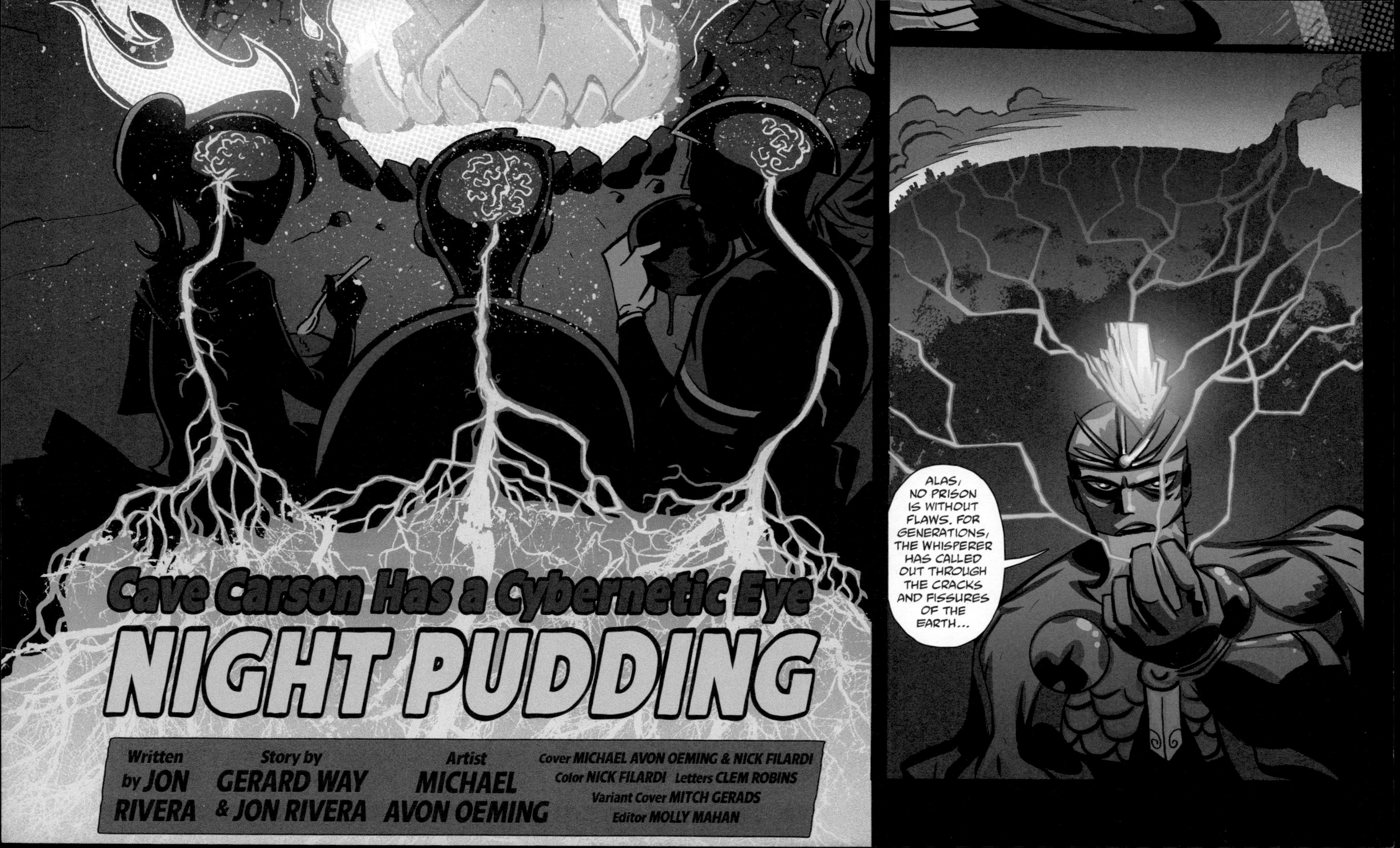
Cave Carson Has a Cybernetic Eye
NIGHT PUDDING
Written by JON RIVERA
Story by GERARD WAY & JON RIVERA
Artist MICHAEL AVON OEMING
Cover MICHAEL AVON OEMING & NICK FILARDI
Color NICK FILARDI Letters CLEM ROBINS
Variant Cover MITCH GERADS
Editor MOLLY MAHAN
ALAS, NO PRISON IS WITHOUT FLAWS. FOR GENERATIONS, THE WHISPERER HAS CALLED OUT THROUGH THE CRACKS AND FISSURES OF THE EARTH...

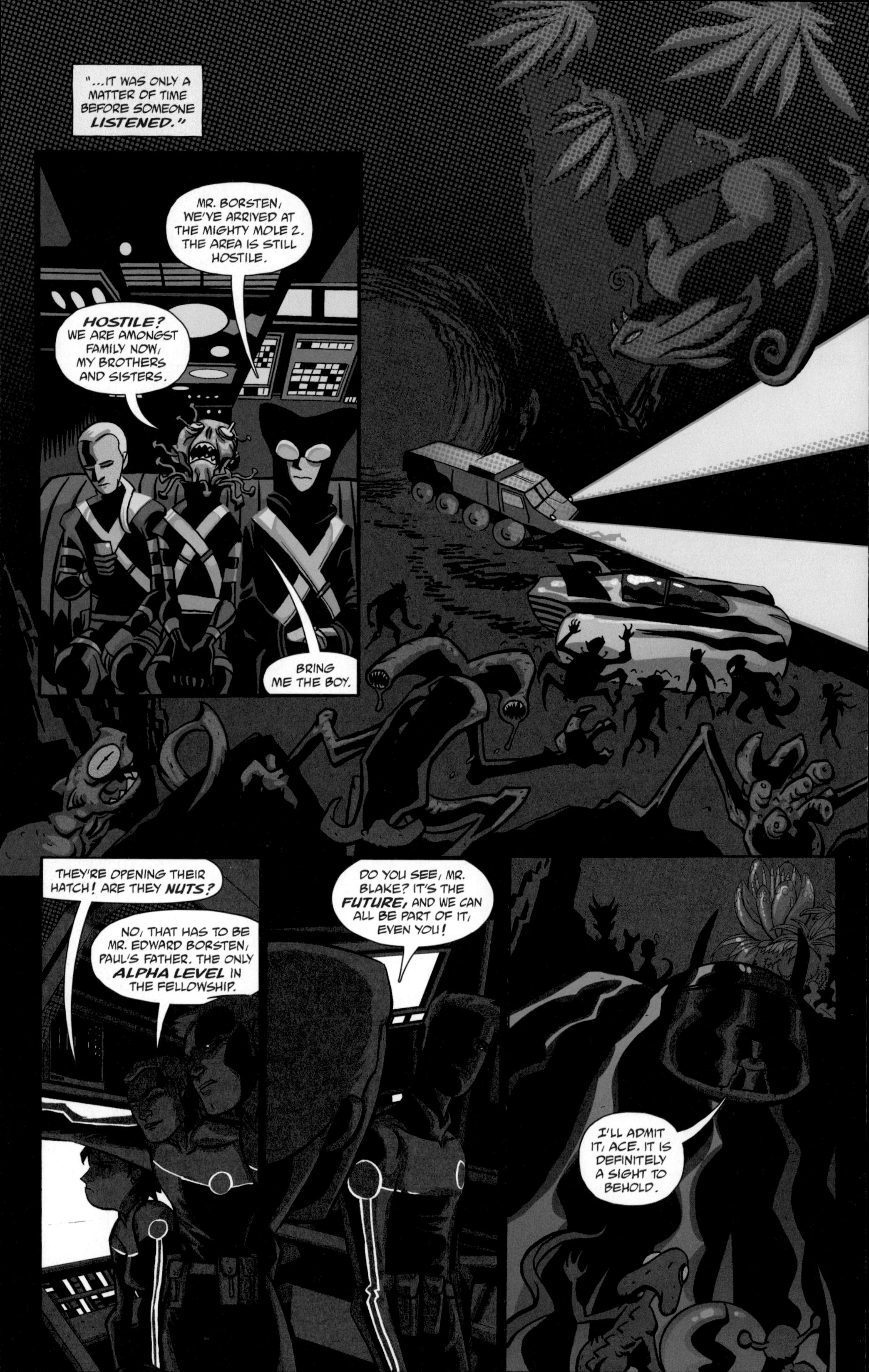
"...IT WAS ONLY A MATTER OF TIME BEFORE SOMEONE LISTENED."
MR. BORSTEN, WE'VE ARRIVED AT THE MIGHTY MOLE 2. THE AREA IS STILL HOSTILE.
HOSTILE? WE ARE AMONGST FAMILY NOW, MY BROTHERS AND SISTERS.
BRING ME THE BOY.
THEY'RE OPENING THEIR HATCH! ARE THEY NUTS?
NO, THAT HAS TO BE MR. EDWARD BORSTEN, PAUL'S FATHER. THE ONLY ALPHA LEVEL IN THE FELLOWSHIP.
DO YOU SEE, MR. BLAKE? IT'S THE FUTURE, AND WE CAN ALL BE PART OF IT, EVEN YOU!
I'LL ADMIT IT, ACE. IT IS DEFINITELY A SIGHT TO BEHOLD.

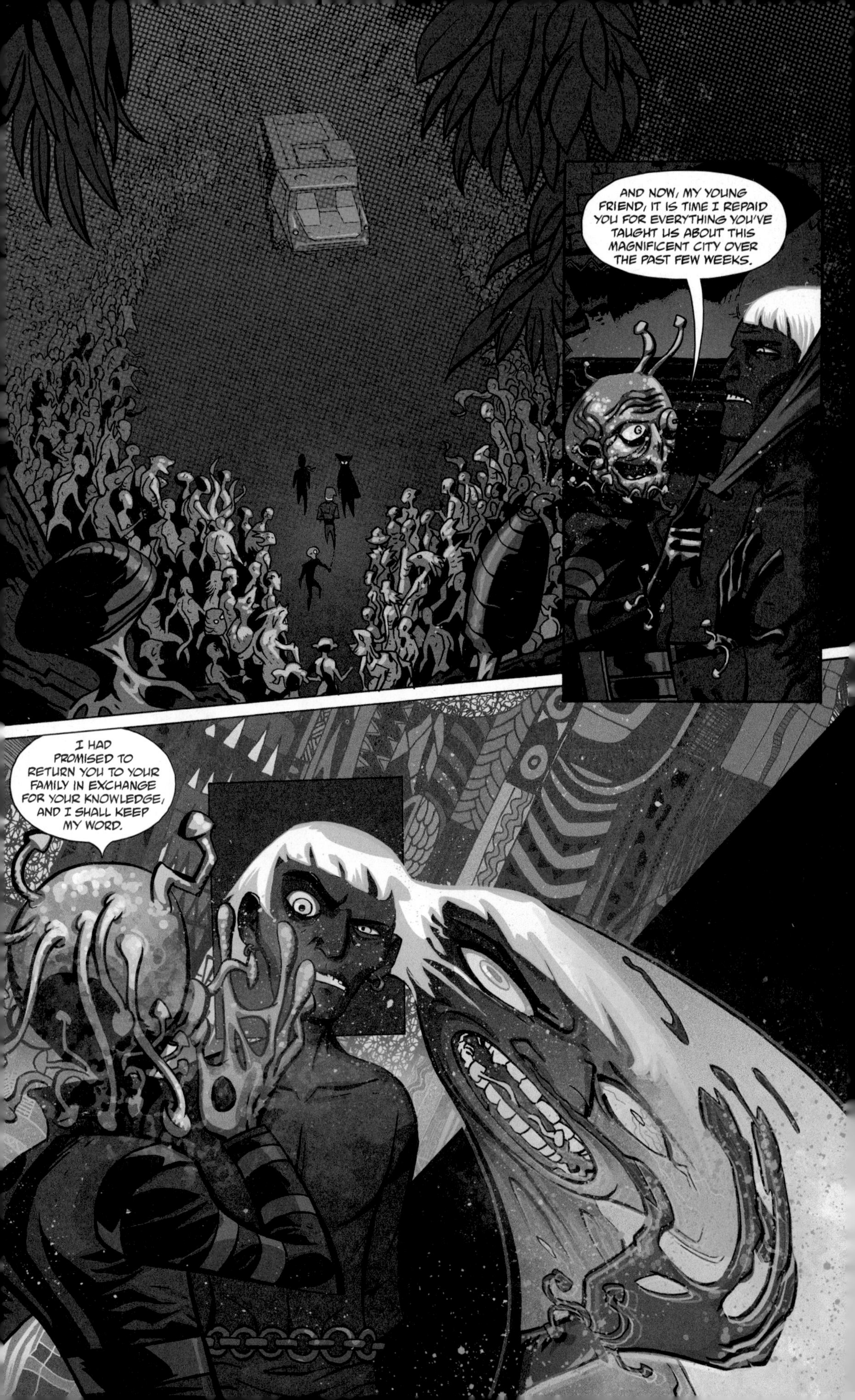
AND NOW, MY YOUNG FRIEND, IT IS TIME I REPAID YOU FOR EVERYTHING YOU'VE TAUGHT US ABOUT THIS MAGNIFICENT CITY OVER THE PAST FEW WEEKS.
I HAD PROMISED TO RETURN YOU TO YOUR FAMILY IN EXCHANGE FOR YOUR KNOWLEDGE, AND I SHALL KEEP MY WORD.

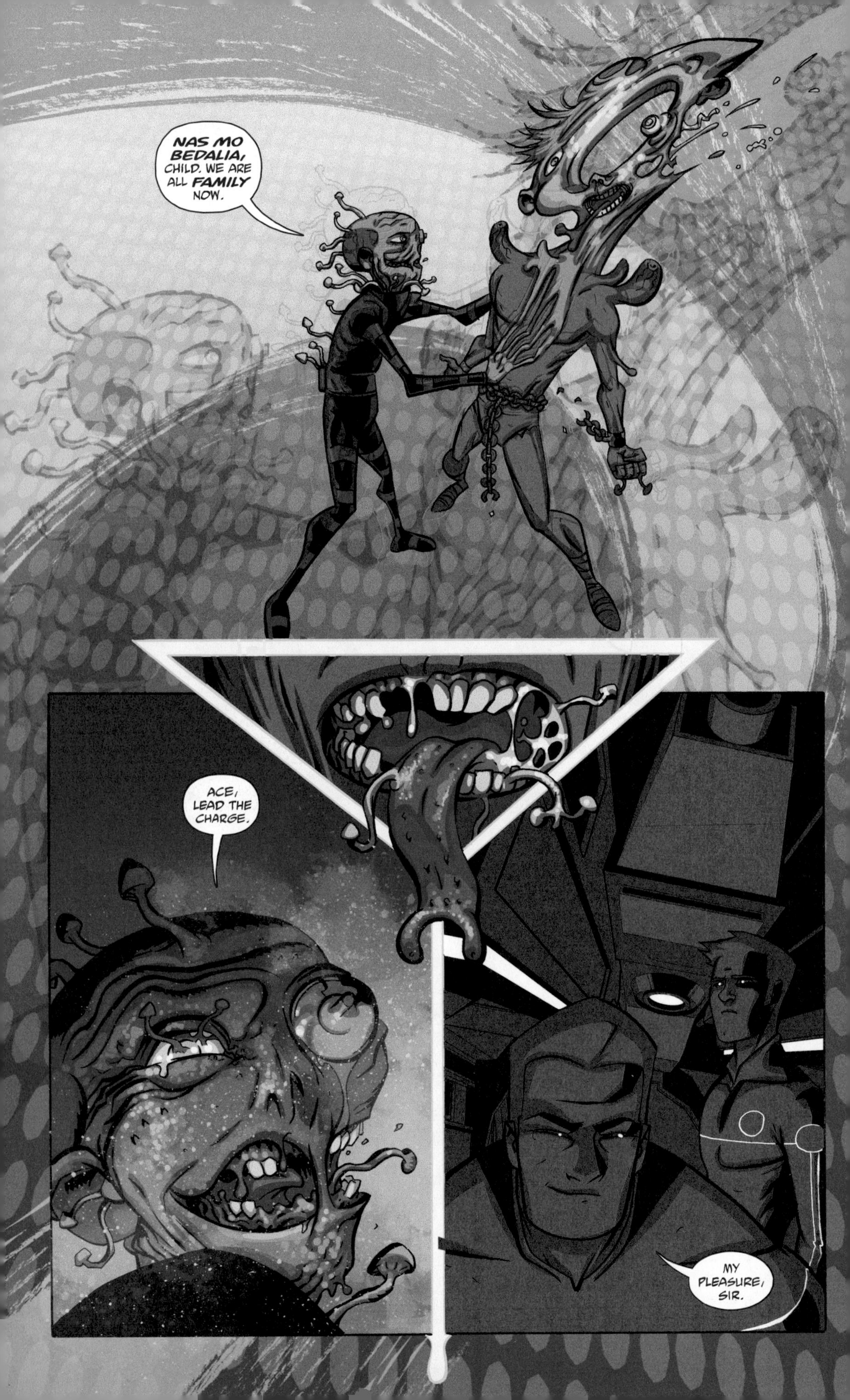
NAS MO BEDALIA, CHILD. WE ARE ALL FAMILY NOW.
ACE, LEAD THE CHARGE.
MY PLEASURE, SIR.

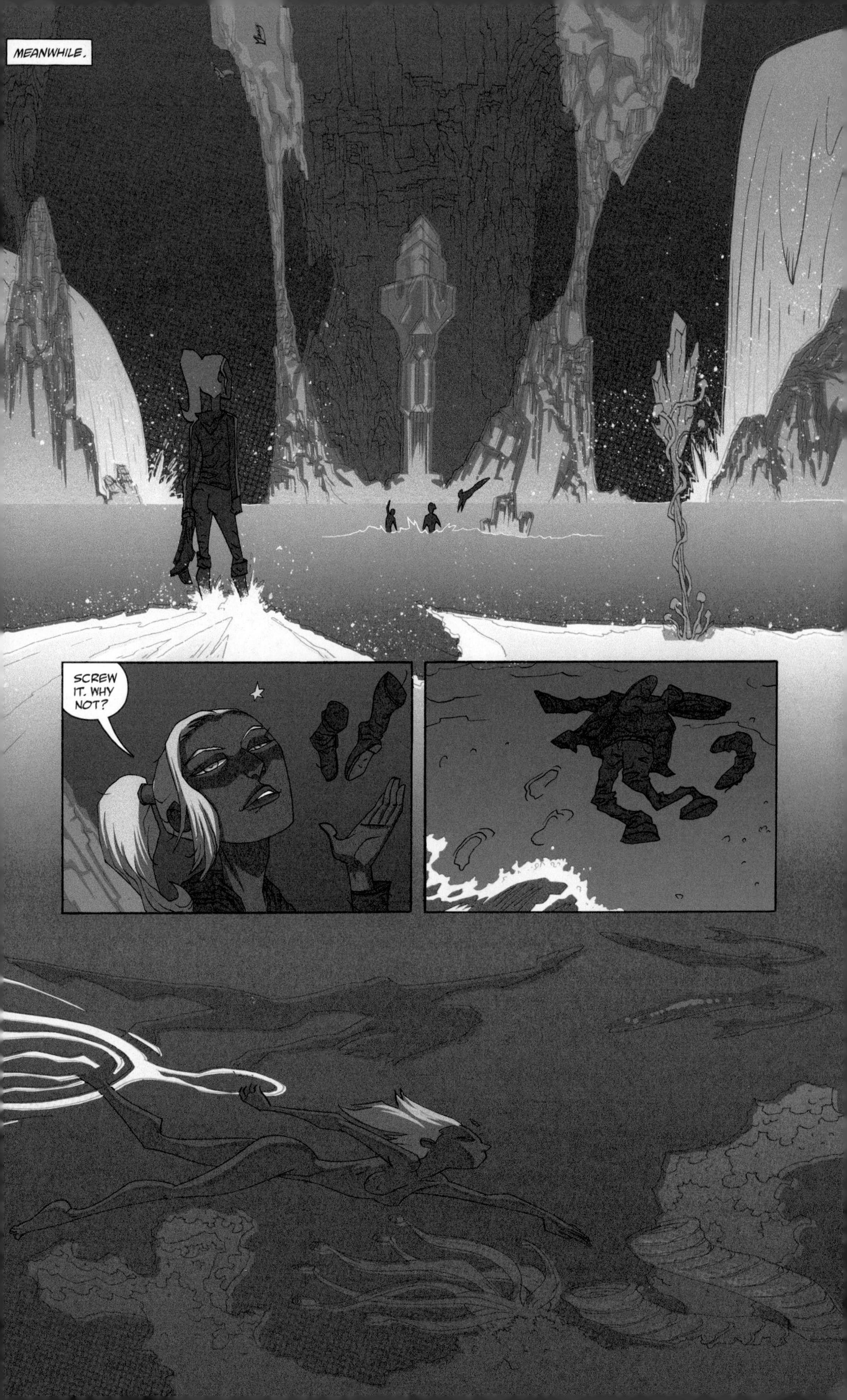
MEANWHILE.
SCREW IT. WHY NOT?

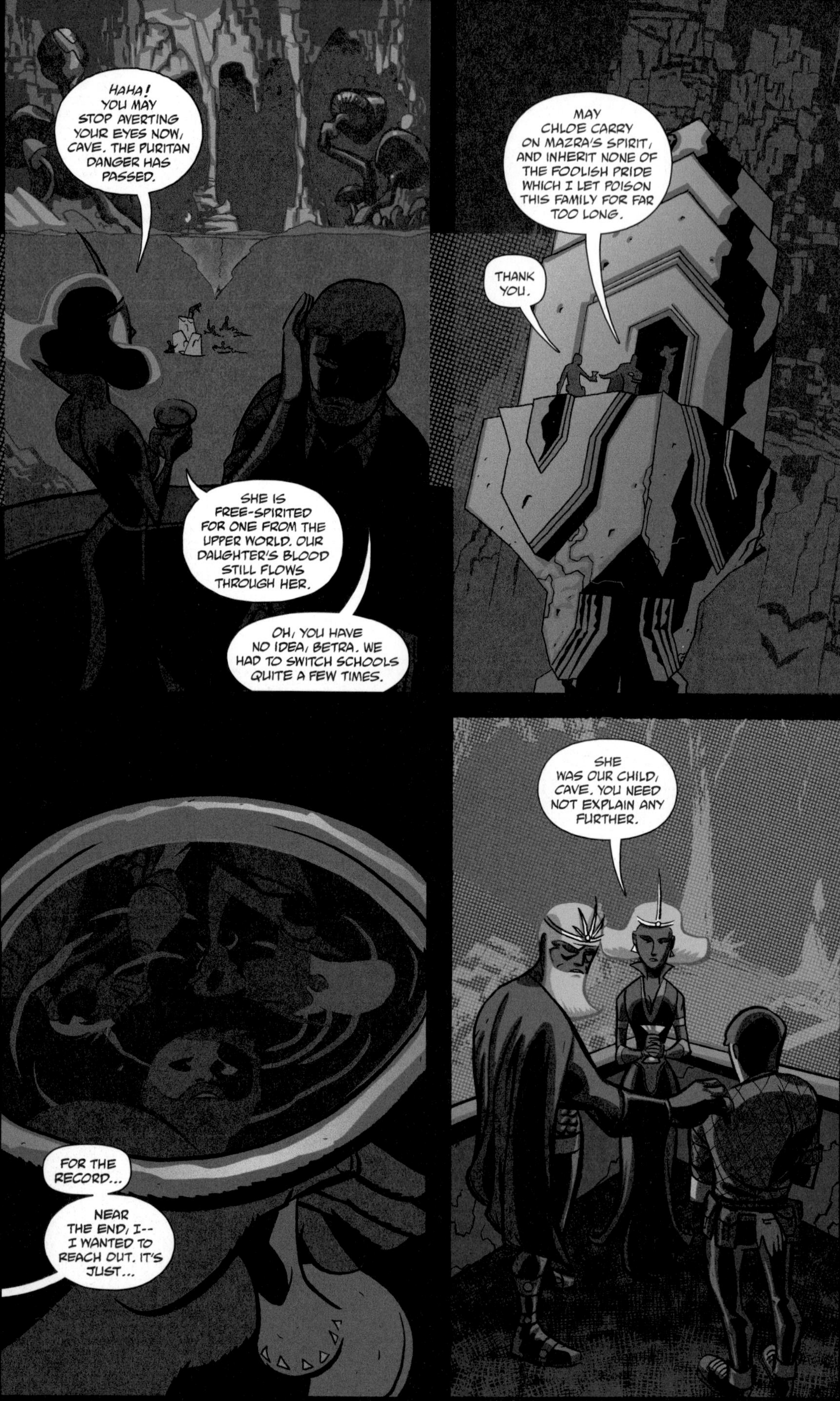
HAHA! YOU MAY STOP AVERTING YOUR EYES NOW, CAVE. THE PURITAN DANGER HAS PASSED.
SHE IS FREE-SPIRITED FOR ONE FROM THE UPPER WORLD. OUR DAUGHTER'S BLOOD STILL FLOWS THROUGH HER.
OH, YOU HAVE NO IDEA, BETRA. WE HAD TO SWITCH SCHOOLS QUITE A FEW TIMES.
MAY CHLOE CARRY ON MAZRA'S SPIRIT, AND INHERIT NONE OF THE FOOLISH PRIDE WHICH I LET POISON THIS FAMILY FOR FAR TOO LONG.
THANK YOU.
FOR THE RECORD...
NEAR THE END, I-- I WANTED TO REACH OUT. IT'S JUST...
SHE WAS OUR CHILD, CAVE. YOU NEED NOT EXPLAIN ANY FURTHER.

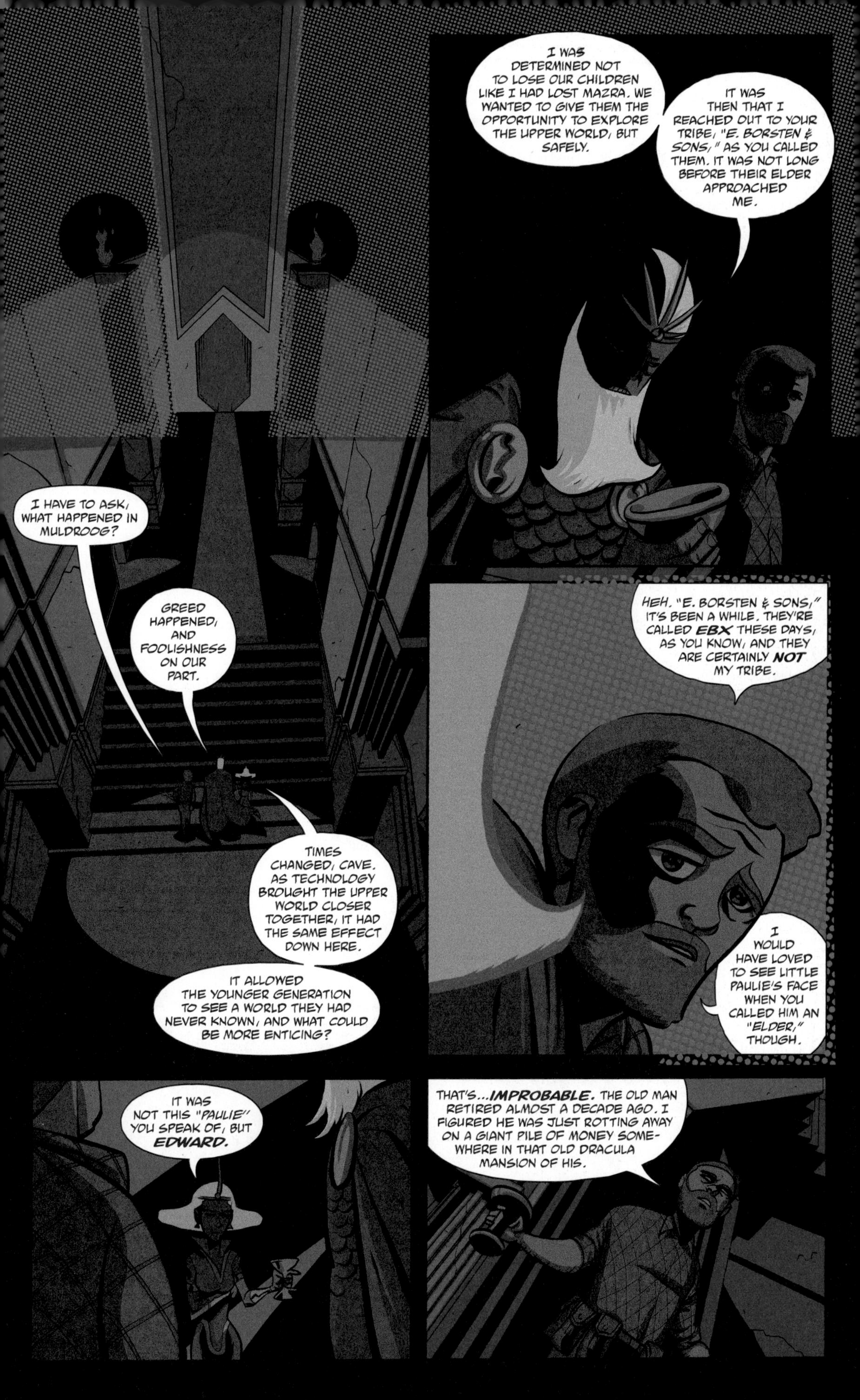
I WAS DETERMINED NOT TO LOSE OUR CHILDREN LIKE I HAD LOST MAZRA. WE WANTED TO GIVE THEM THE OPPORTUNITY TO EXPLORE THE UPPER WORLD, BUT SAFELY.
IT WAS THEN THAT I REACHED OUT TO YOUR TRIBE, "E. BORSTEN & SONS," AS YOU CALLED THEM. IT WAS NOT LONG BEFORE THEIR ELDER APPROACHED ME.
I HAVE TO ASK, WHAT HAPPENED IN MULDROOG?
GREED HAPPENED, AND FOOLISHNESS ON OUR PART.
TIMES CHANGED, CAVE. AS TECHNOLOGY BROUGHT THE UPPER WORLD CLOSER TOGETHER, IT HAD THE SAME EFFECT DOWN HERE.
IT ALLOWED THE YOUNGER GENERATION TO SEE A WORLD THEY HAD NEVER KNOWN, AND WHAT COULD BE MORE ENTICING?
HEH. "E. BORSTEN & SONS," IT'S BEEN A WHILE. THEY'RE CALLED EBX THESE DAYS, AS YOU KNOW, AND THEY ARE CERTAINLY NOT MY TRIBE.
I WOULD HAVE LOVED TO SEE LITTLE PAULIE'S FACE WHEN YOU CALLED HIM AN "ELDER," THOUGH.
IT WAS NOT THIS "PAULIE" YOU SPEAK OF, BUT EDWARD.
THAT'S...IMPROBABLE. THE OLD MAN RETIRED ALMOST A DECADE AGO. I FIGURED HE WAS JUST ROTTING AWAY ON A GIANT PILE OF MONEY SOMEWHERE IN THAT OLD DRACULA MANSION OF HIS.

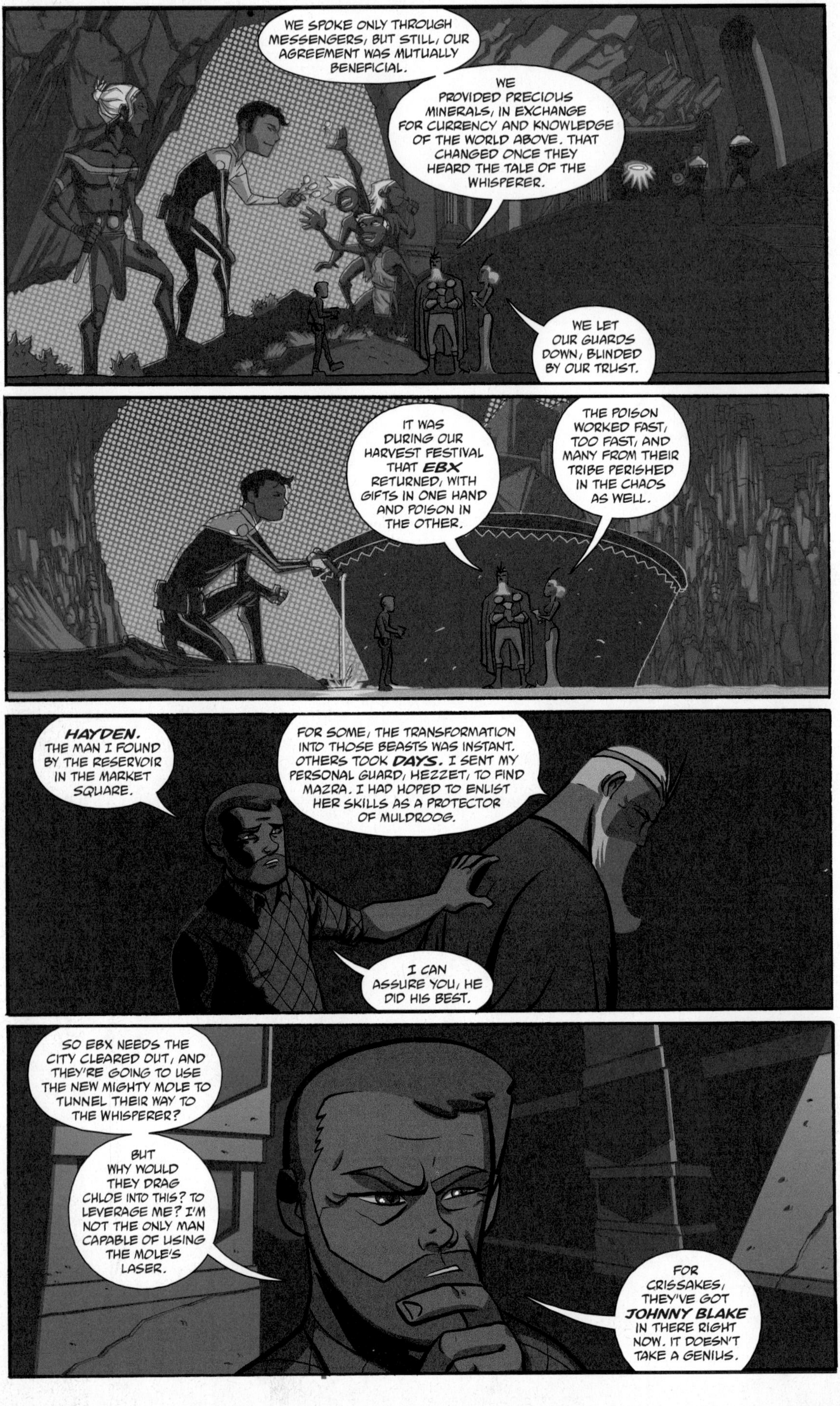
WE SPOKE ONLY THROUGH MESSENGERS, BUT STILL, OUR AGREEMENT WAS MUTUALLY BENEFICIAL.
WE PROVIDED PRECIOUS MINERALS, IN EXCHANGE FOR CURRENCY AND KNOWLEDGE OF THE WORLD ABOVE. THAT CHANGED ONCE THEY HEARD THE TALE OF THE WHISPERER.
WE LET OUR GUARDS DOWN, BLINDED BY OUR TRUST.
IT WAS DURING OUR HARVEST FESTIVAL THAT EBX RETURNED, WITH GIFTS IN ONE HAND AND POISON IN THE OTHER.
THE POISON WORKED FAST, TOO FAST, AND MANY FROM THEIR TRIBE PERISHED IN THE CHAOS AS WELL.
HAYDEN. THE MAN I FOUND BY THE RESERVOIR IN THE MARKET SQUARE.
FOR SOME, THE TRANSFORMATION INTO THOSE BEASTS WAS INSTANT. OTHERS TOOK DAYS. I SENT MY PERSONAL GUARD, HEZZET, TO FIND MAZRA. I HAD HOPED TO ENLIST HER SKILLS AS A PROTECTOR OF MULDROOG.
I CAN ASSURE YOU, HE DID HIS BEST.
SO EBX NEEDS THE CITY CLEARED OUT, AND THEY'RE GOING TO USE THE NEW MIGHTY MOLE TO TUNNEL THEIR WAY TO THE WHISPERER?
BUT WHY WOULD THEY DRAG CHLOE INTO THIS? TO LEVERAGE ME? I'M NOT THE ONLY MAN CAPABLE OF USING THE MOLE'S LASER.
FOR CRISSAKES, THEY'VE GOT JOHNNY BLAKE IN THERE RIGHT NOW. IT DOESN'T TAKE A GENIUS.

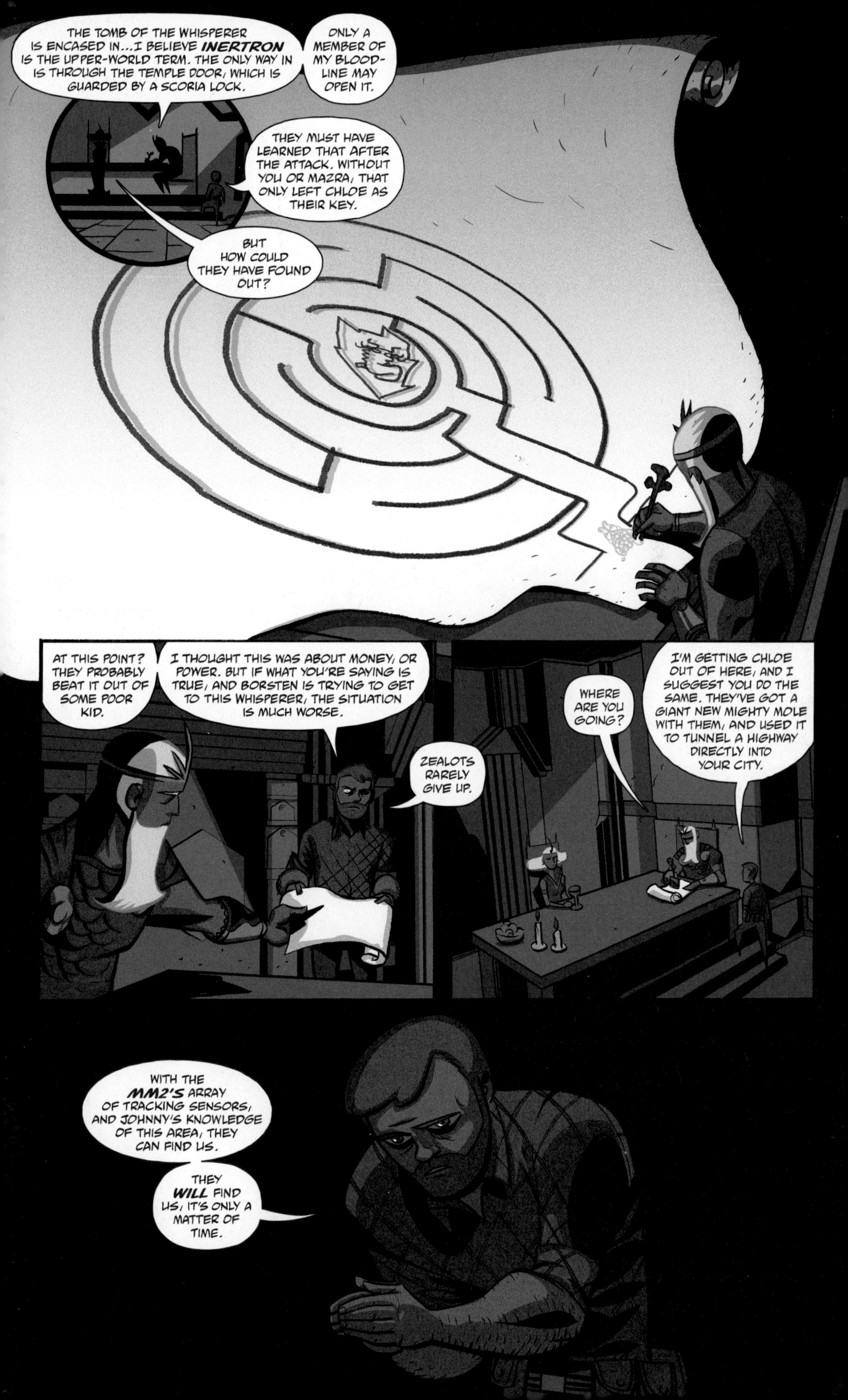
THE TOMB OF THE WHISPERER IS ENCASED IN...I BELIEVE INERTRON IS THE UPPER-WORLD TERM. THE ONLY WAY IN IS THROUGH THE TEMPLE DOOR, WHICH IS GUARDED BY A SCORIA LOCK.
ONLY A MEMBER OF MY BLOOD-LINE MAY OPEN IT.
THEY MUST HAVE LEARNED THAT AFTER THE ATTACK. WITHOUT YOU OR MAZRA, THAT ONLY LEFT CHLOE AS THEIR KEY.
BUT HOW COULD THEY HAVE FOUND OUT?
AT THIS POINT? THEY PROBABLY BEAT IT OUT OF SOME POOR KID.
I THOUGHT THIS WAS ABOUT MONEY, OR POWER. BUT IF WHAT YOU'RE SAYING IS TRUE, AND BORSTEN IS TRYING TO GET TO THIS WHISPERER, THE SITUATION IS MUCH WORSE.
ZEALOTS RARELY GIVE UP.
WHERE ARE YOU GOING?
I'M GETTING CHLOE OUT OF HERE, AND I SUGGEST YOU DO THE SAME. THEY'VE GOT A GIANT NEW MIGHTY MOLE WITH THEM, AND USED IT TO TUNNEL A HIGHWAY DIRECTLY INTO YOUR CITY.
WITH THE MM2'S ARRAY OF TRACKING SENSORS, AND JOHNNY'S KNOWLEDGE OF THIS AREA, THEY CAN FIND US.
THEY WILL FIND US, IT'S ONLY A MATTER OF TIME.

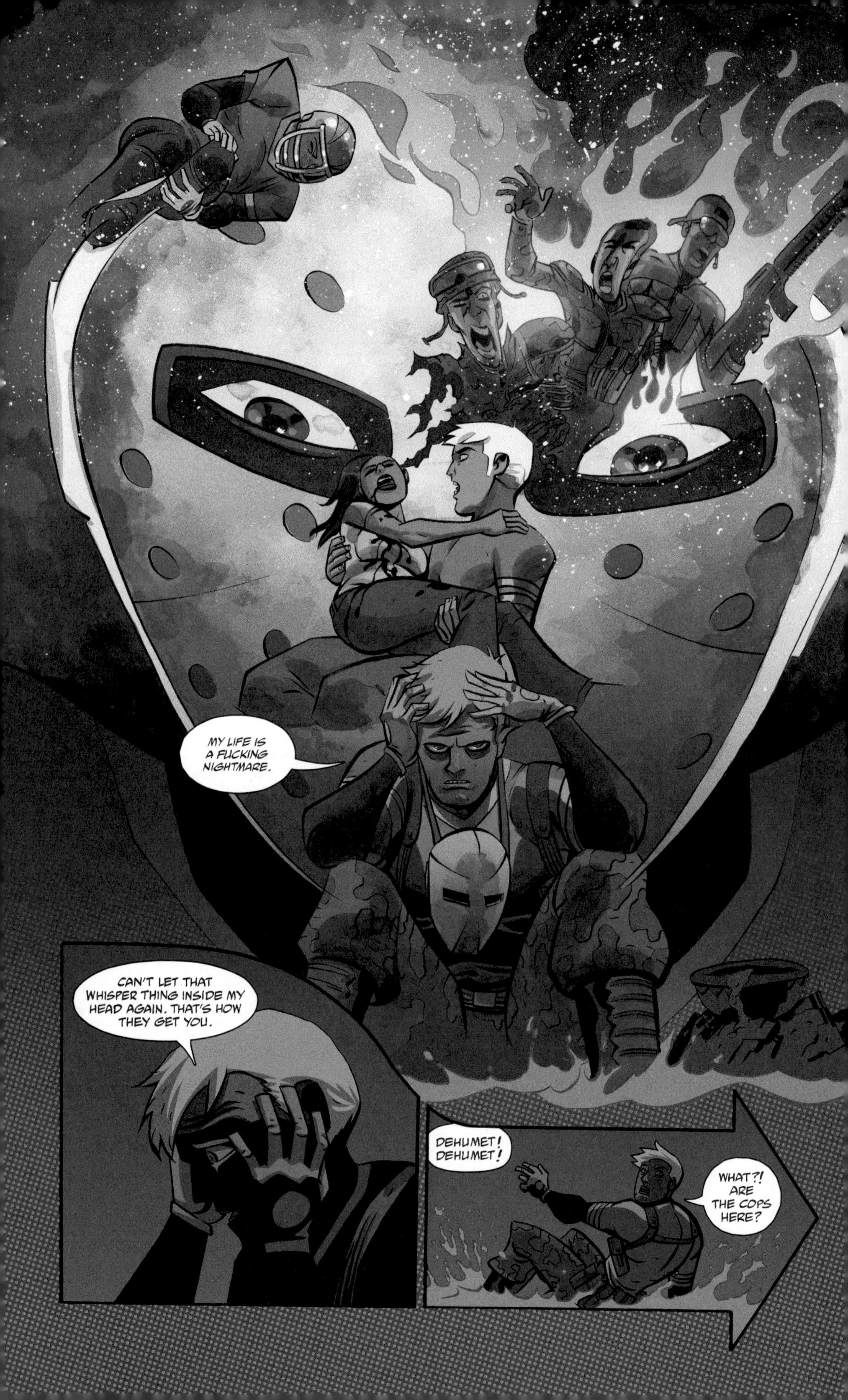
MY LIFE IS A FUCKING NIGHTMARE.
CAN'T LET THAT WHISPER THING INSIDE MY HEAD AGAIN. THAT'S HOW THEY GET YOU.
DEHUMET! DEHUMET!
WHAT?! ARE THE COPS HERE?

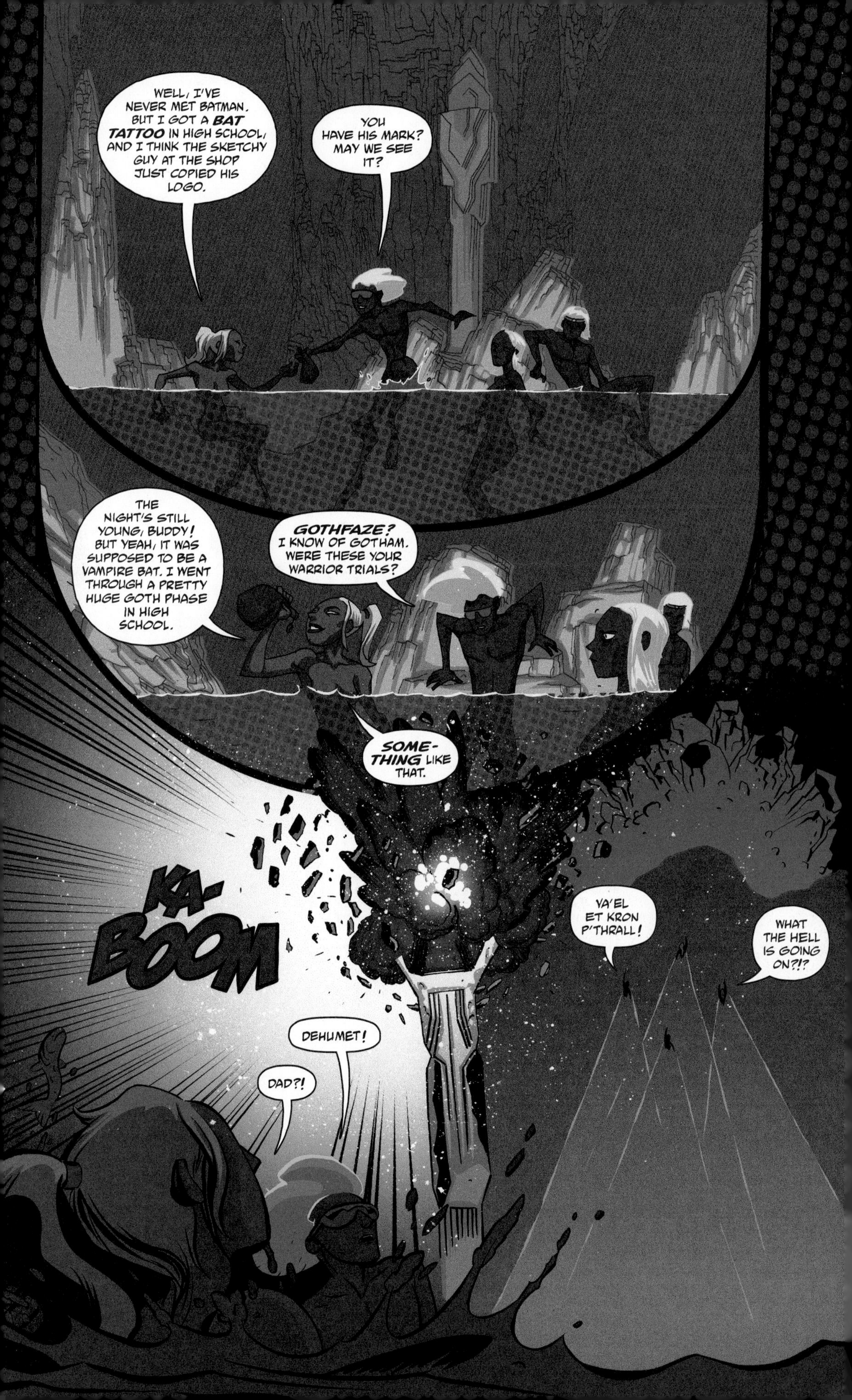
WELL, I'VE NEVER MET BATMAN. BUT I GOT A **BAT TATTOO** IN HIGH SCHOOL, AND I THINK THE SKETCHY GUY AT THE SHOP JUST COPIED HIS LOGO.
YOU HAVE HIS MARK? MAY WE SEE IT?
THE NIGHT'S STILL YOUNG, BUDDY! BUT YEAH, IT WAS SUPPOSED TO BE A VAMPIRE BAT. I WENT THROUGH A PRETTY HUGE GOTH PHASE IN HIGH SCHOOL.
GOTHFAZE? I KNOW OF GOTHAM. WERE THESE YOUR WARRIOR TRIALS?
SOME-THING LIKE THAT.
KA-BOOM
YA'EL ET KRON P'THRALL!
WHAT THE HELL IS GOING ON?!?
DEHUMET!
DAD?!

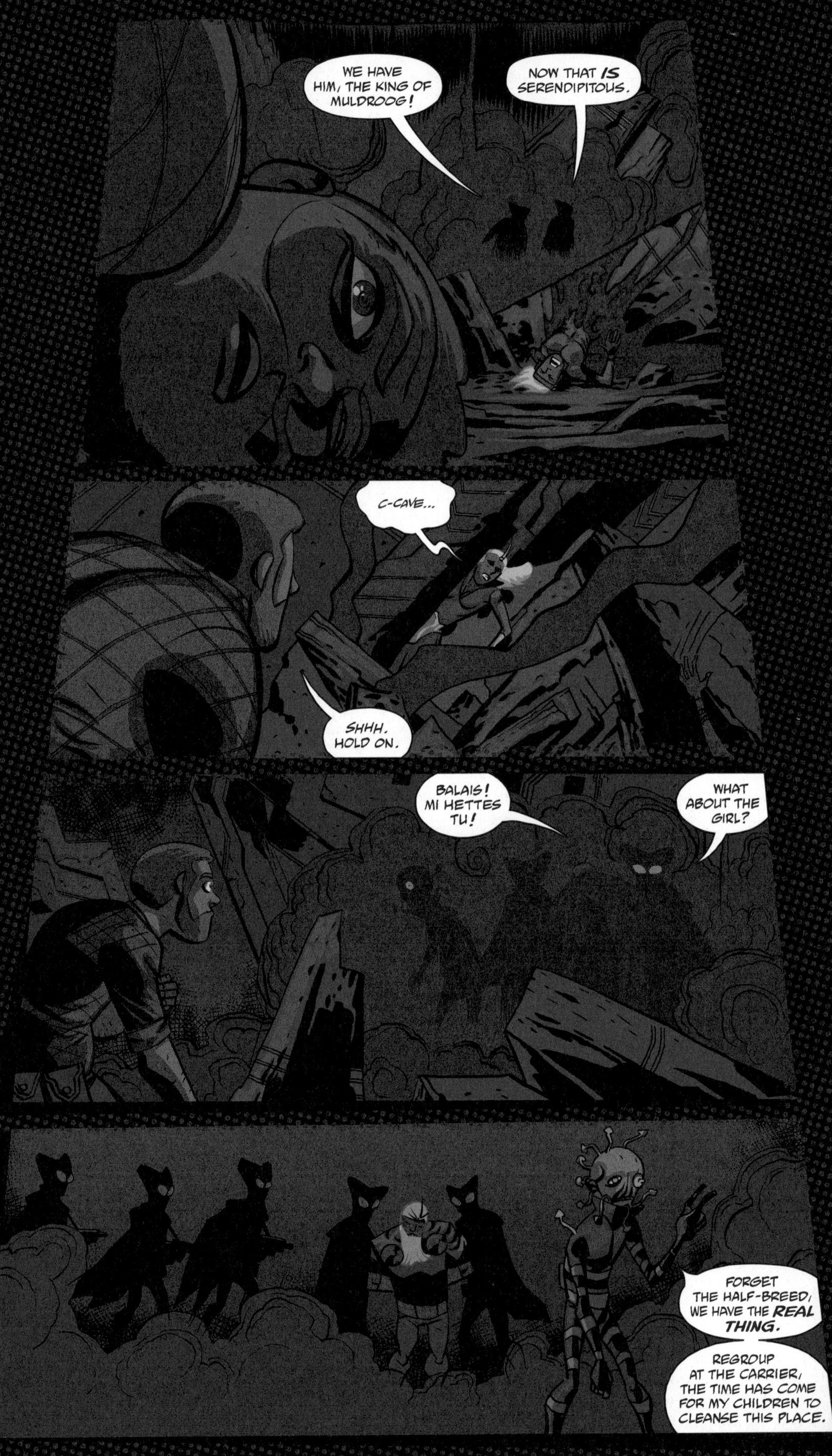
WE HAVE HIM, THE KING OF MULDROOG!
NOW THAT **IS** SERENDIPITOUS.
C-CAVE...
SHHH. HOLD ON.
BALAIS! MI HETTES TU!
WHAT ABOUT THE GIRL?
FORGET THE HALF-BREED, WE HAVE THE ***REAL THING.***
REGROUP AT THE CARRIER, THE TIME HAS COME FOR MY CHILDREN TO CLEANSE THIS PLACE.

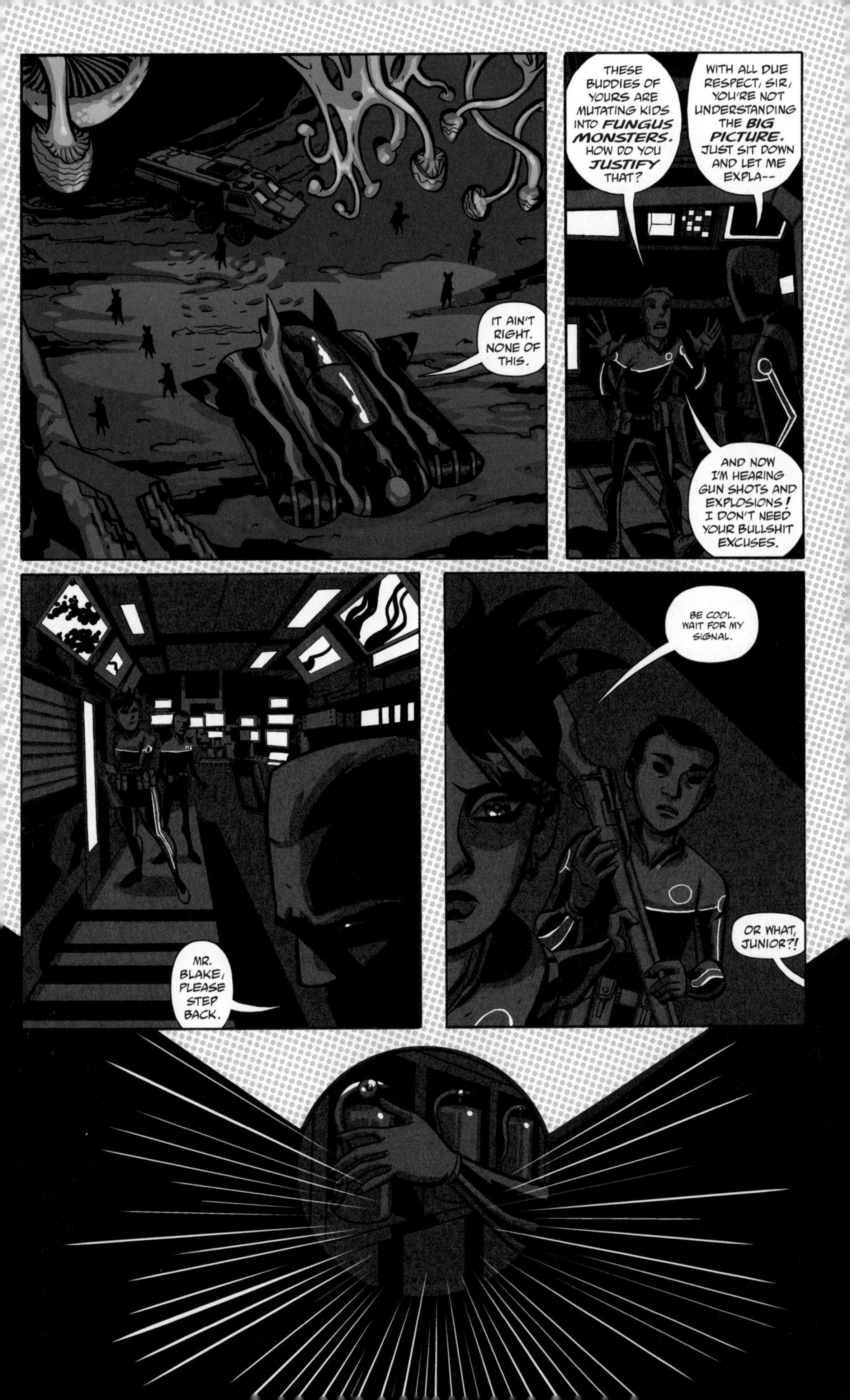
IT AIN'T RIGHT. NONE OF THIS.
THESE BUDDIES OF YOURS ARE MUTATING KIDS INTO FUNGUS MONSTERS. HOW DO YOU JUSTIFY THAT?
WITH ALL DUE RESPECT, SIR, YOU'RE NOT UNDERSTANDING THE BIG PICTURE. JUST SIT DOWN AND LET ME EXPLA--
AND NOW I'M HEARING GUN SHOTS AND EXPLOSIONS! I DON'T NEED YOUR BULLSHIT EXCUSES.
MR. BLAKE, PLEASE STEP BACK.
BE COOL. WAIT FOR MY SIGNAL.
OR WHAT, JUNIOR?!

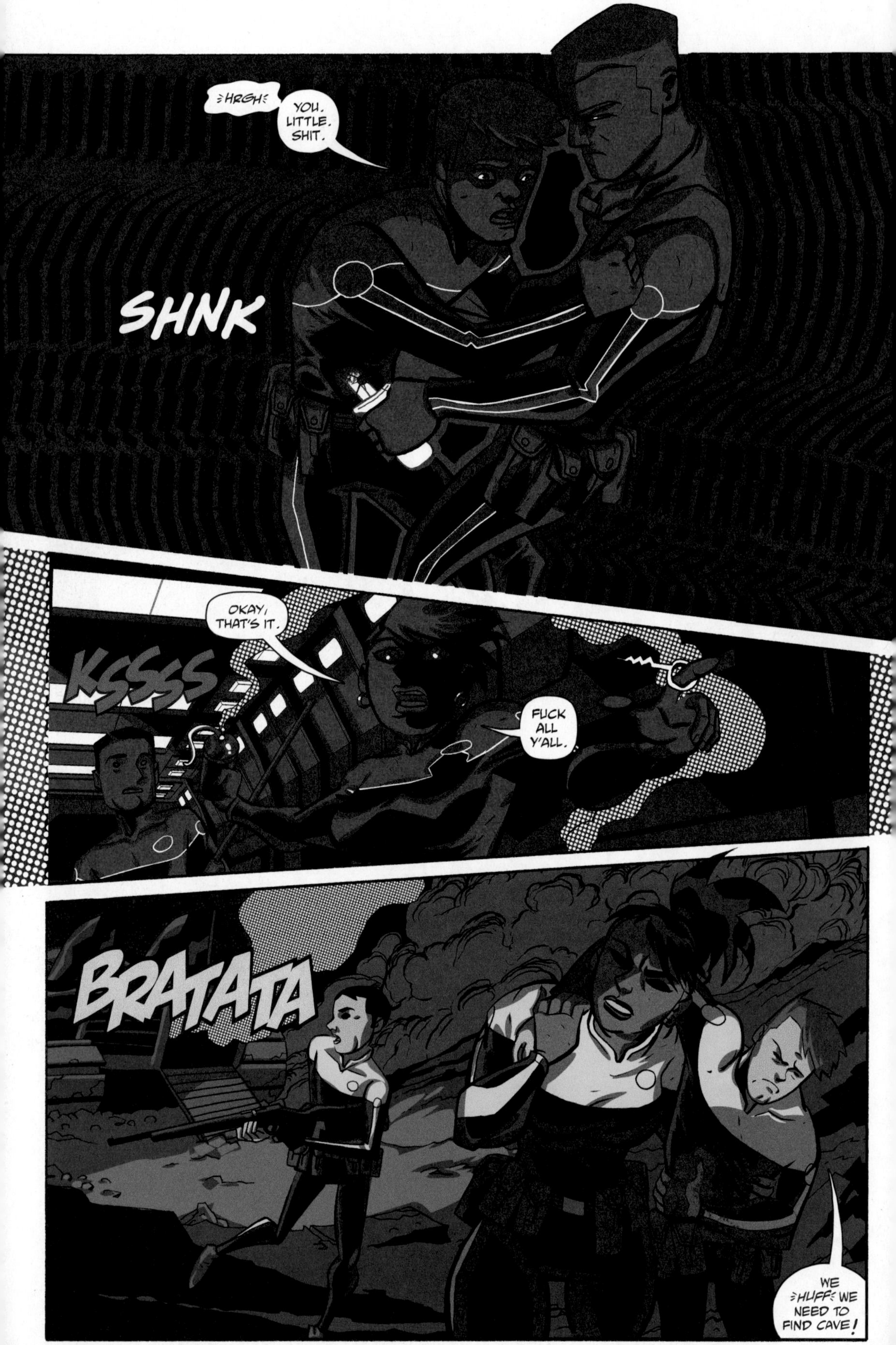
HRGH
YOU. LITTLE. SHIT.
SHNK
OKAY, THAT'S IT.
KSSSS
FUCK ALL Y'ALL.
BRATATA
WE HUFF WE NEED TO FIND CAVE!

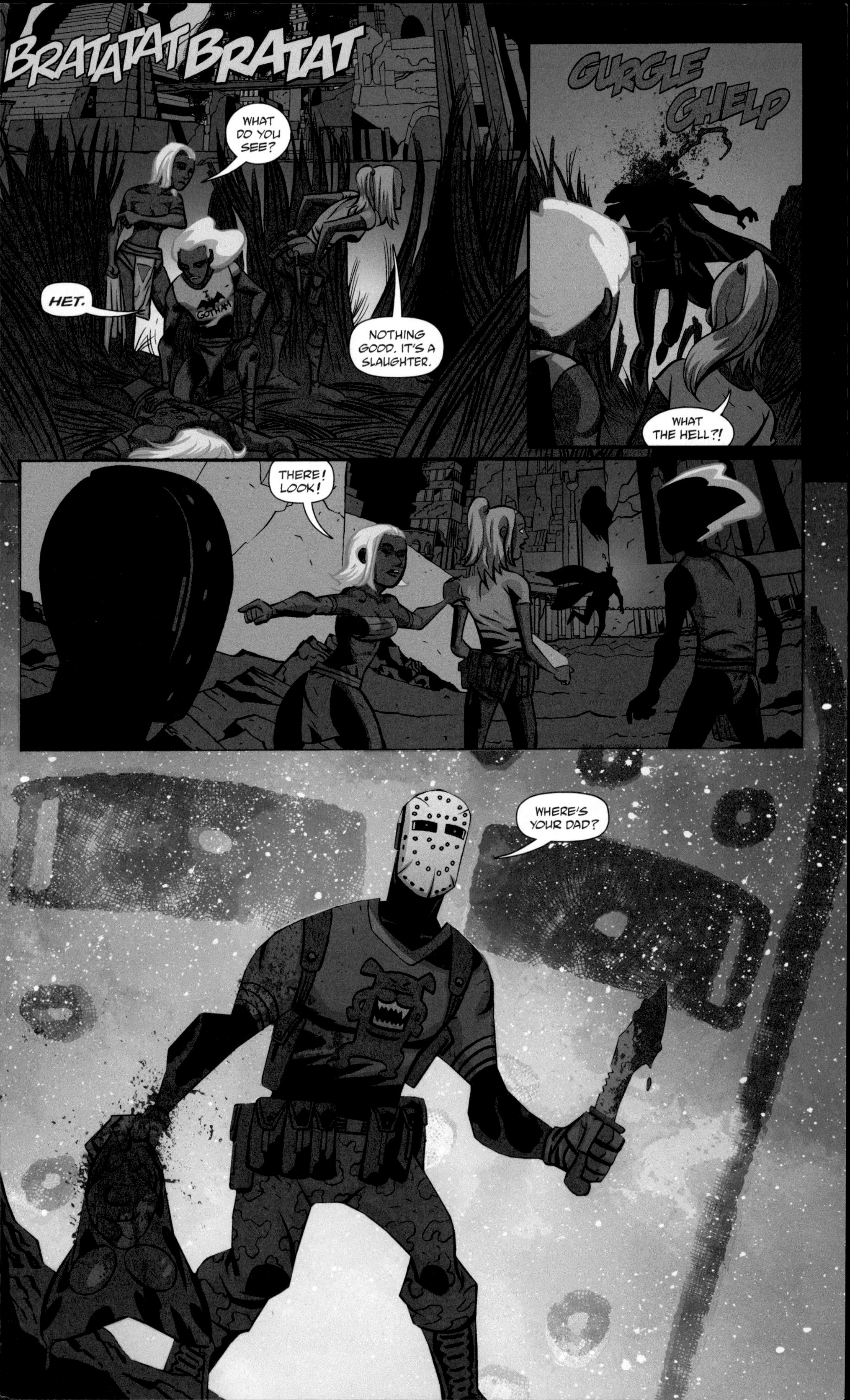
BRATATAT BRATAT
WHAT DO YOU SEE?
HET.
NOTHING GOOD. IT'S A SLAUGHTER.
GURGLE GHELP
WHAT THE HELL?!
THERE! LOOK!
WHERE'S YOUR DAD?

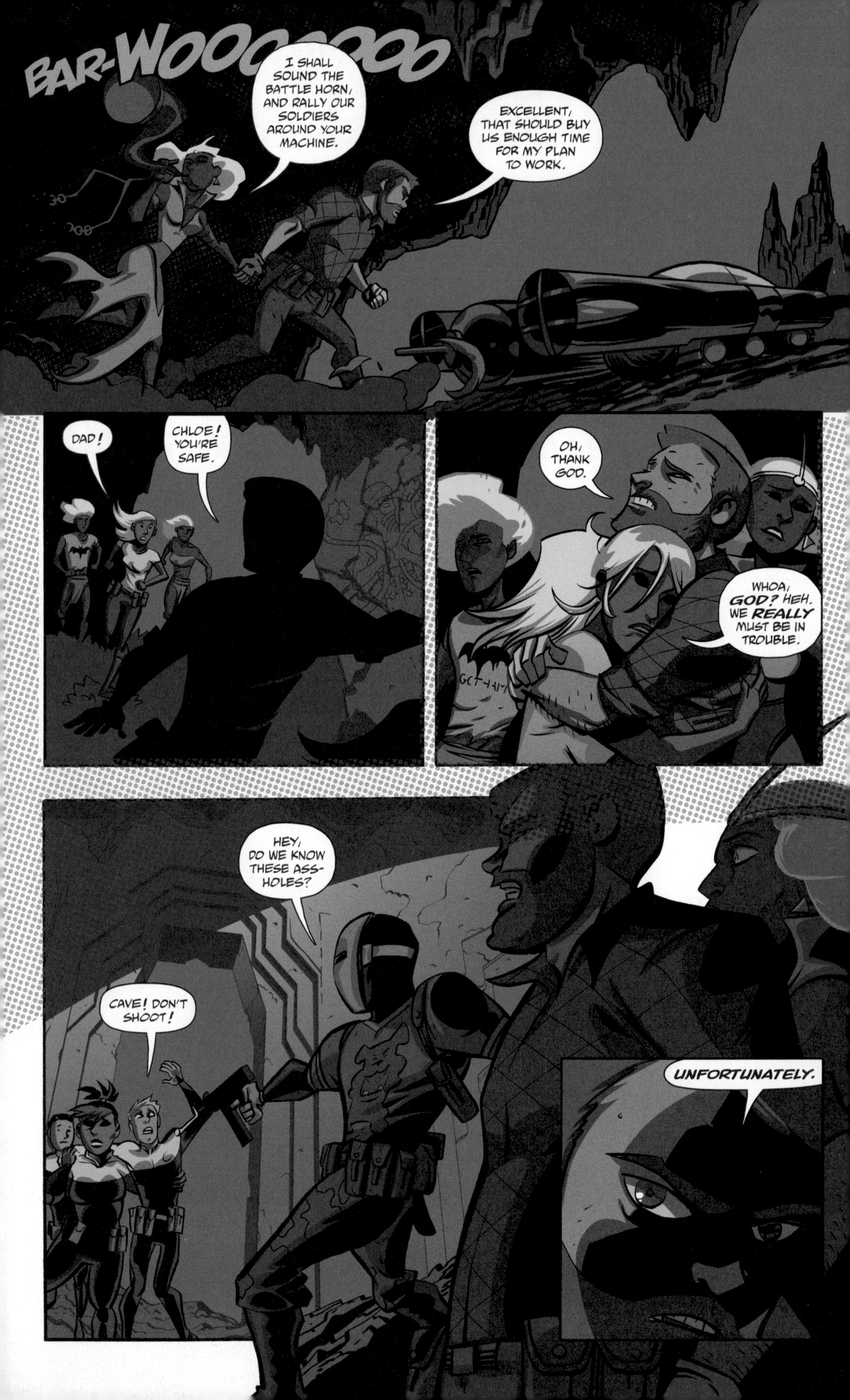
BAR-WOOOOOOO
I SHALL SOUND THE BATTLE HORN, AND RALLY OUR SOLDIERS AROUND YOUR MACHINE.
EXCELLENT, THAT SHOULD BUY US ENOUGH TIME FOR MY PLAN TO WORK.
DAD!
CHLOE! YOU'RE SAFE.
OH, THANK GOD.
WHOA, GOD? HEH. WE REALLY MUST BE IN TROUBLE.
HEY, DO WE KNOW THESE ASS-HOLES?
CAVE! DON'T SHOOT!
UNFORTUNATELY.

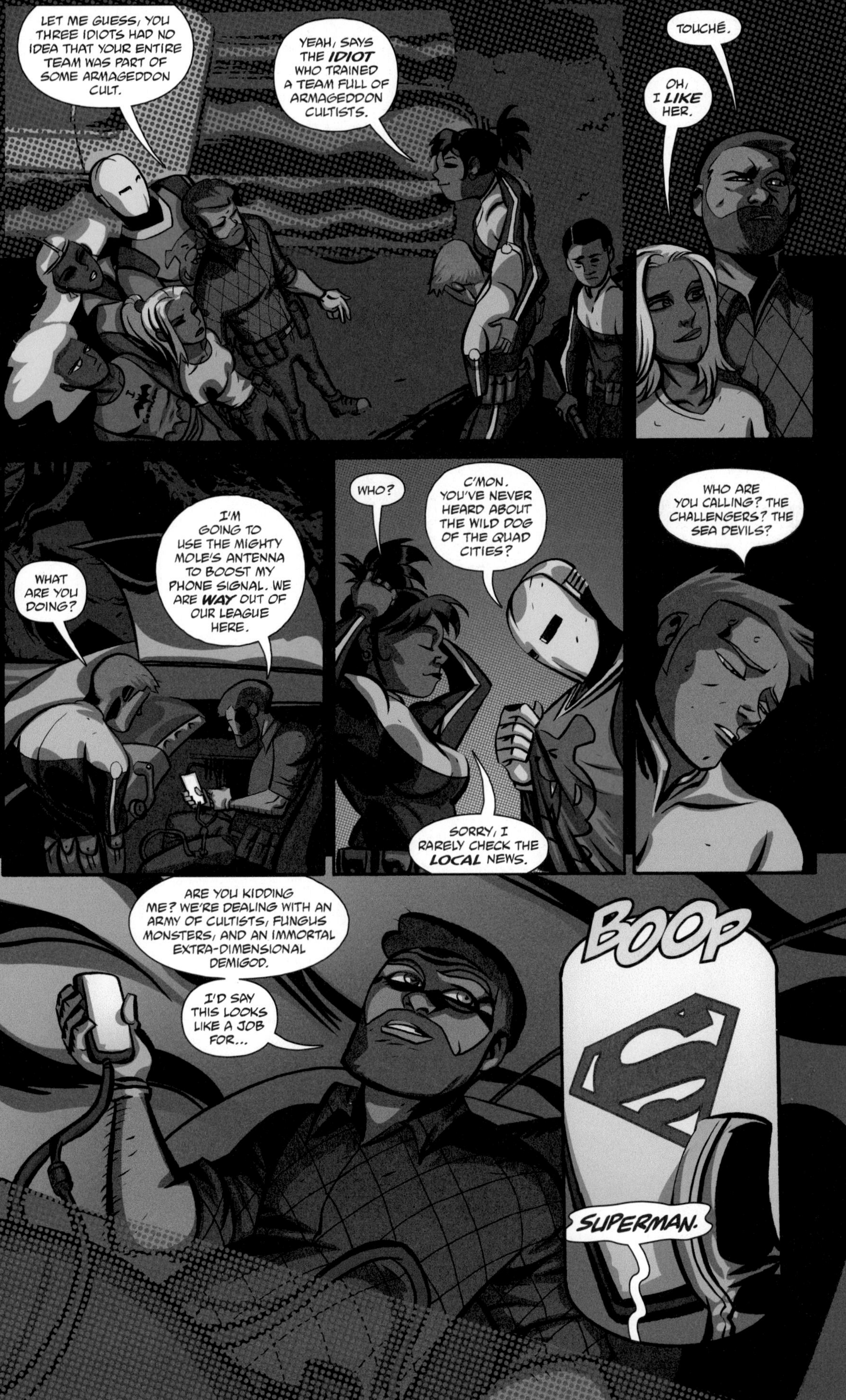
LET ME GUESS, YOU THREE IDIOTS HAD NO IDEA THAT YOUR ENTIRE TEAM WAS PART OF SOME ARMAGEDDON CULT.
YEAH, SAYS THE IDIOT WHO TRAINED A TEAM FULL OF ARMAGEDDON CULTISTS.
TOUCHÉ.
OH, I LIKE HER.
WHAT ARE YOU DOING?
I'M GOING TO USE THE MIGHTY MOLE'S ANTENNA TO BOOST MY PHONE SIGNAL. WE ARE WAY OUT OF OUR LEAGUE HERE.
WHO?
C'MON. YOU'VE NEVER HEARD ABOUT THE WILD DOG OF THE QUAD CITIES?
SORRY, I RARELY CHECK THE LOCAL NEWS.
WHO ARE YOU CALLING? THE CHALLENGERS? THE SEA DEVILS?
ARE YOU KIDDING ME? WE'RE DEALING WITH AN ARMY OF CULTISTS, FUNGUS MONSTERS, AND AN IMMORTAL EXTRA-DIMENSIONAL DEMIGOD.
I'D SAY THIS LOOKS LIKE A JOB FOR...
BOOP
SUPERMAN.

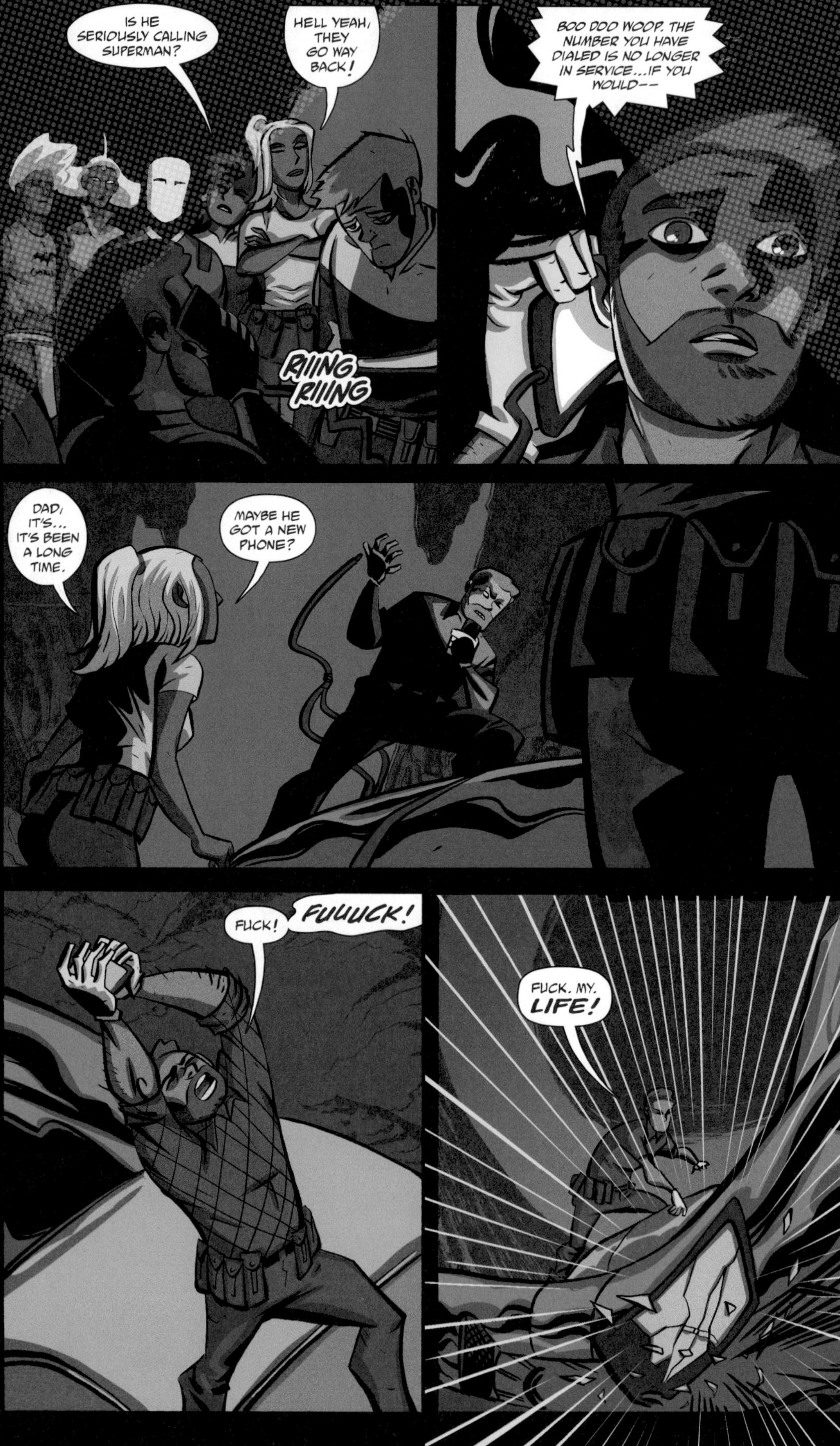

IS HE SERIOUSLY CALLING SUPERMAN?
HELL YEAH, THEY GO WAY BACK!
RIIING RIIING
BOO DOO WOOP. THE NUMBER YOU HAVE DIALED IS NO LONGER IN SERVICE...IF YOU WOULD--
DAD, IT'S... IT'S BEEN A LONG TIME.
MAYBE HE GOT A NEW PHONE?
FUCK!
FUUUCK!
FUCK. MY. LIFE!

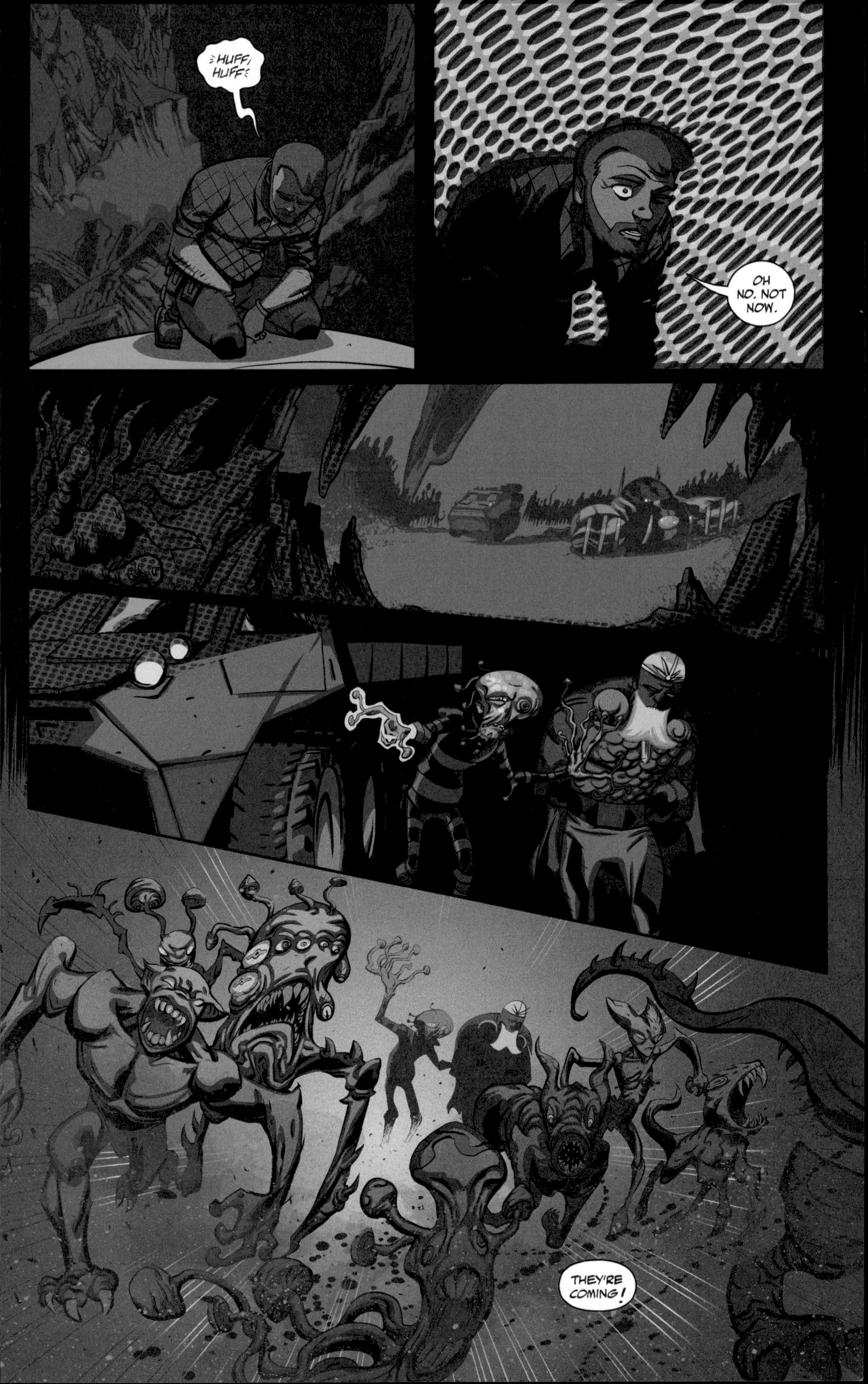
HUFF, HUFF
OH NO. NOT NOW.
THEY'RE COMING!

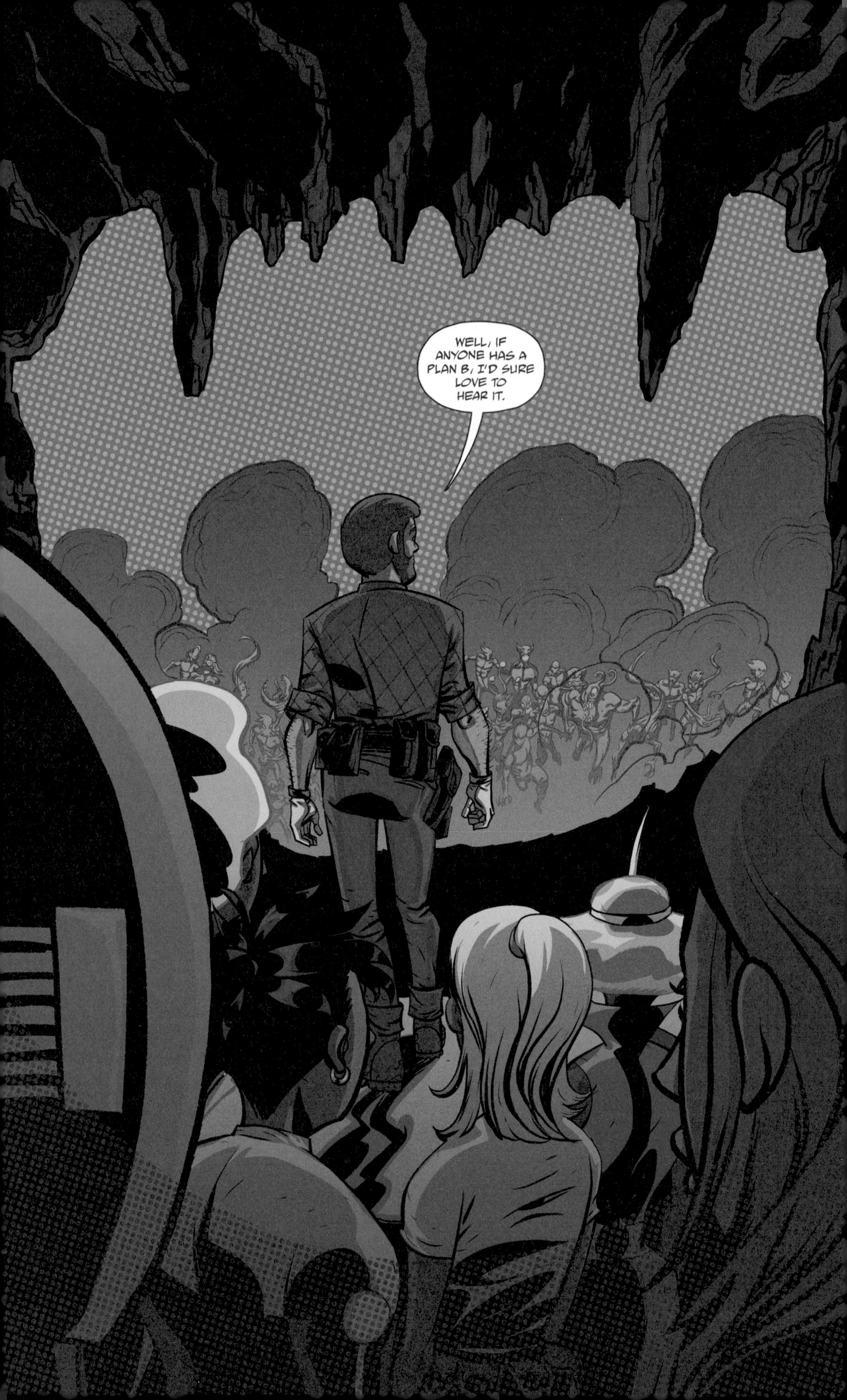
WELL, IF ANYONE HAS A PLAN B, I'D SURE LOVE TO HEAR IT.

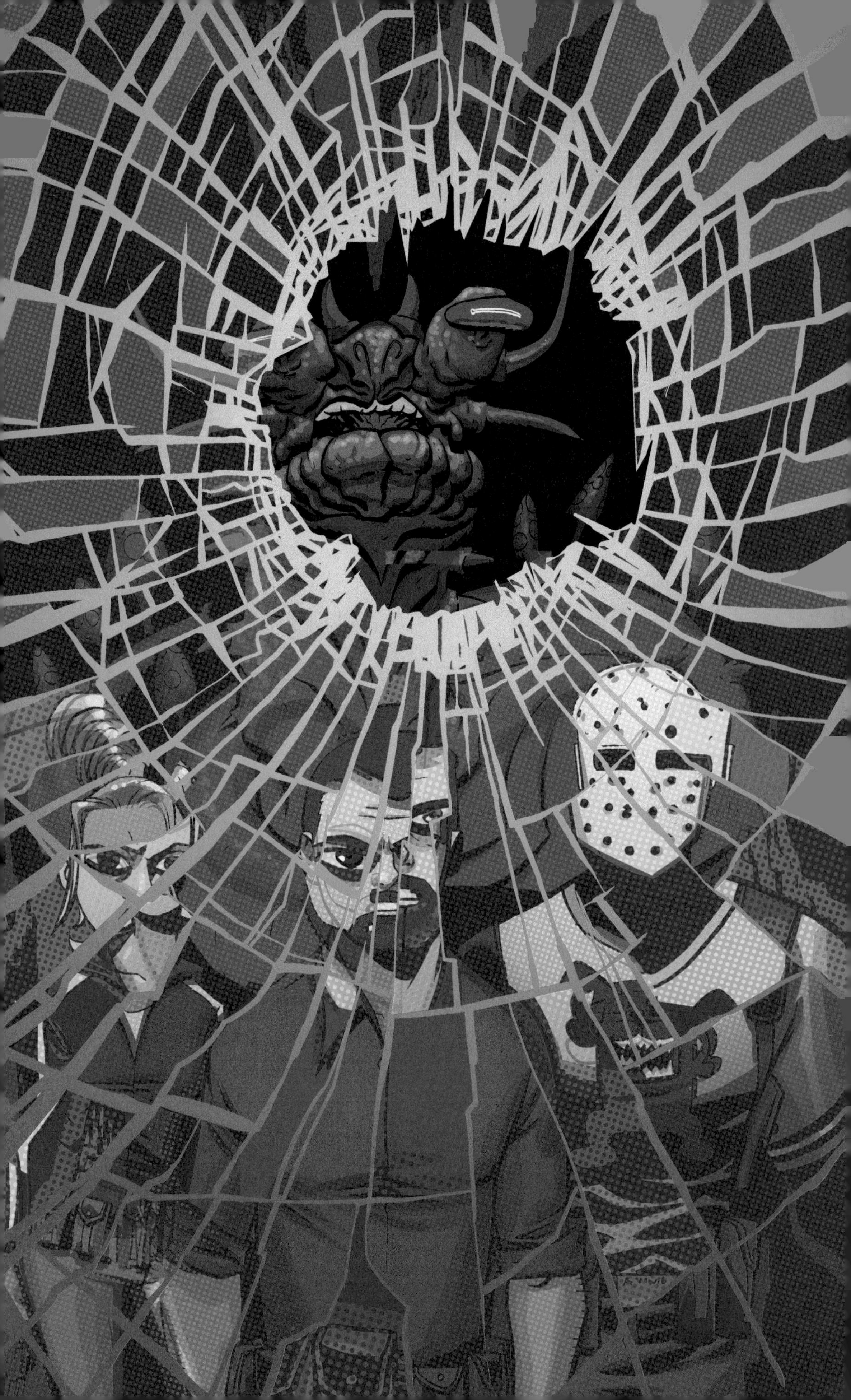

Variant cover art by Brendan McCarthy

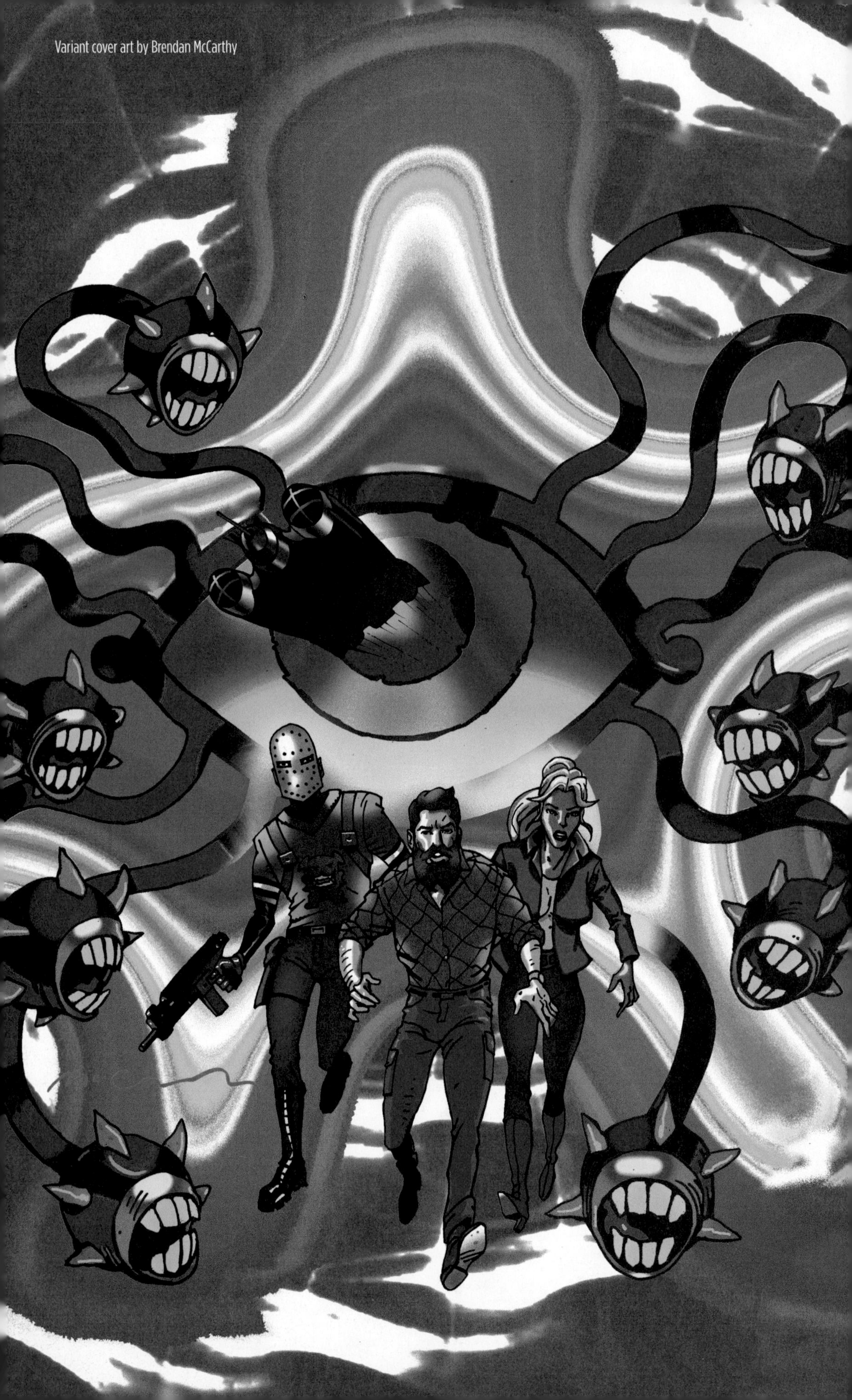

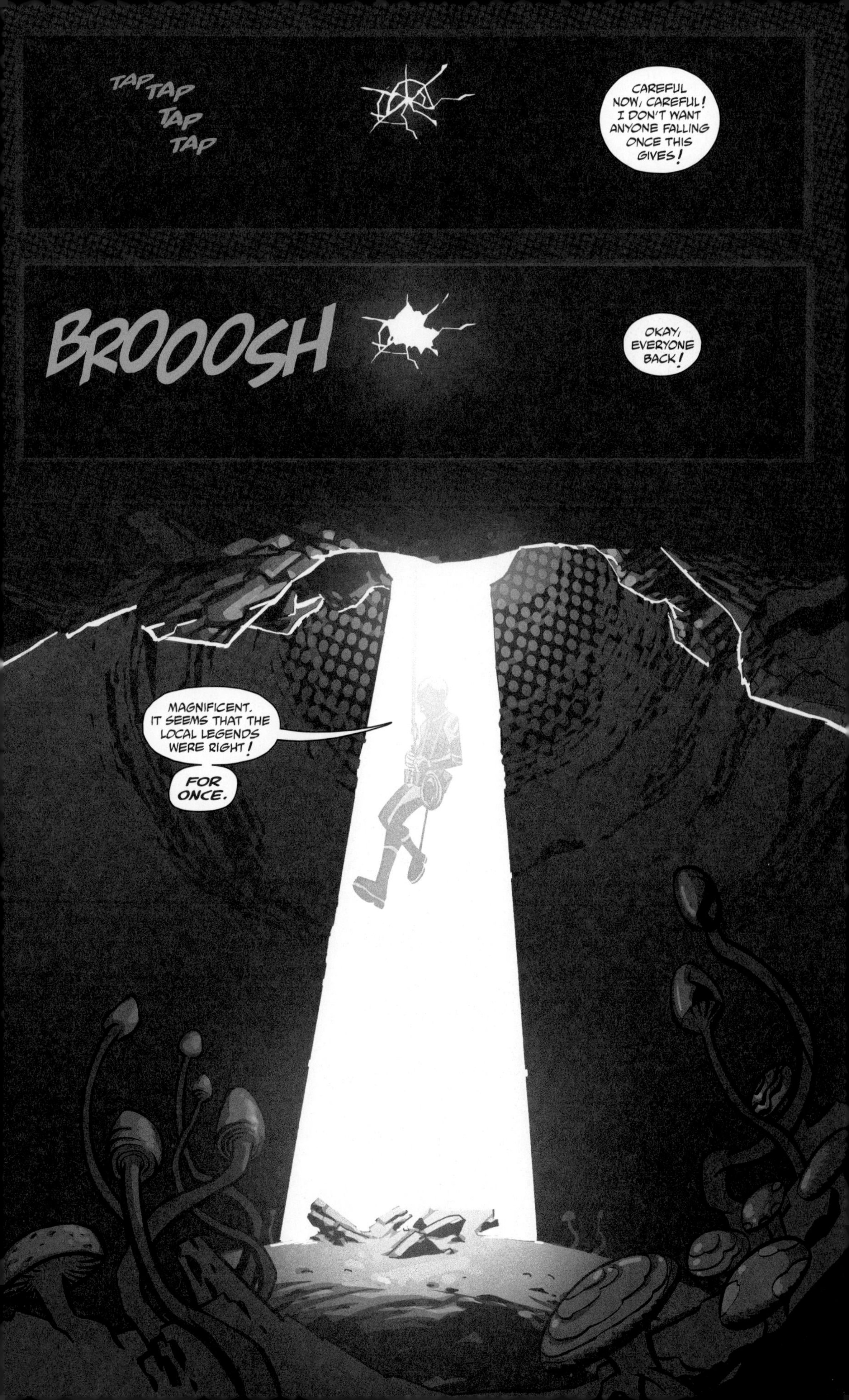
TAP TAP TAP TAP
CAREFUL NOW, CAREFUL! I DON'T WANT ANYONE FALLING ONCE THIS GIVES!
BROOOSH
OKAY, EVERYONE BACK!
MAGNIFICENT. IT SEEMS THAT THE LOCAL LEGENDS WERE RIGHT!
FOR ONCE.

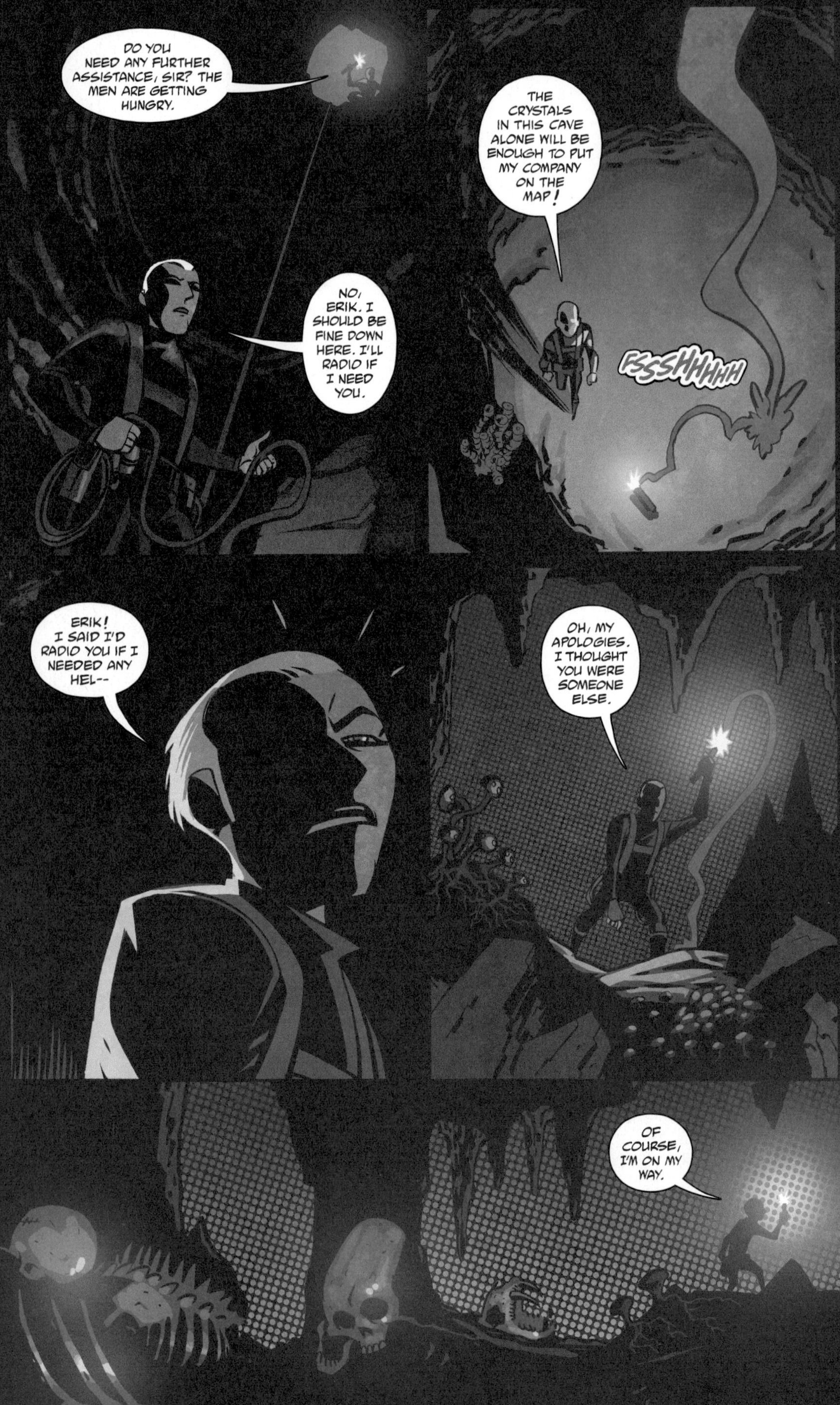
DO YOU NEED ANY FURTHER ASSISTANCE, SIR? THE MEN ARE GETTING HUNGRY.
NO, ERIK. I SHOULD BE FINE DOWN HERE. I'LL RADIO IF I NEED YOU.
THE CRYSTALS IN THIS CAVE ALONE WILL BE ENOUGH TO PUT MY COMPANY ON THE MAP!
FSSSHHHHH
ERIK! I SAID I'D RADIO YOU IF I NEEDED ANY HEL--
OH, MY APOLOGIES. I THOUGHT YOU WERE SOMEONE ELSE.
OF COURSE, I'M ON MY WAY.

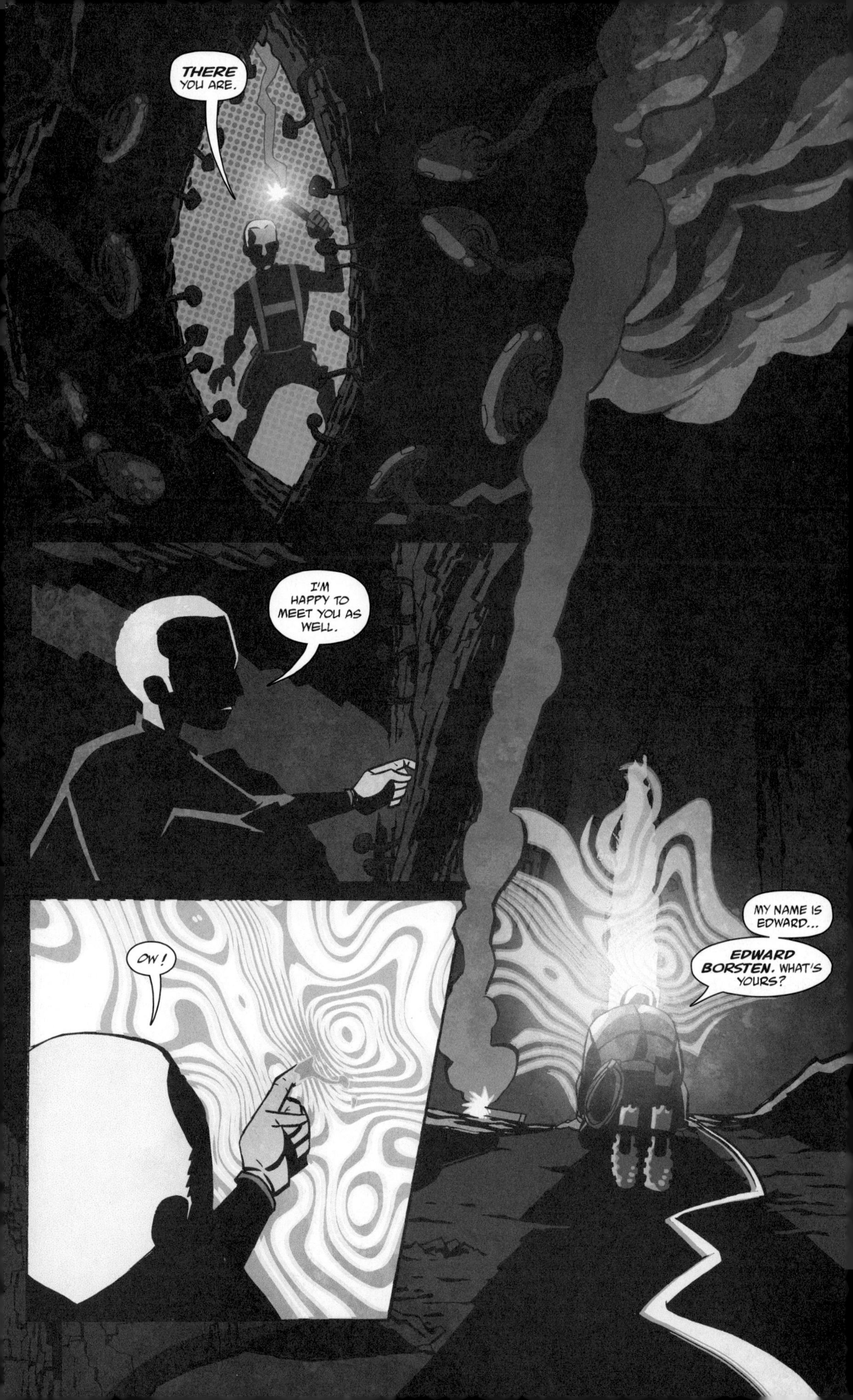
THERE YOU ARE.
I'M HAPPY TO MEET YOU AS WELL.
OW!
MY NAME IS EDWARD...
EDWARD BORSTEN. WHAT'S YOURS?

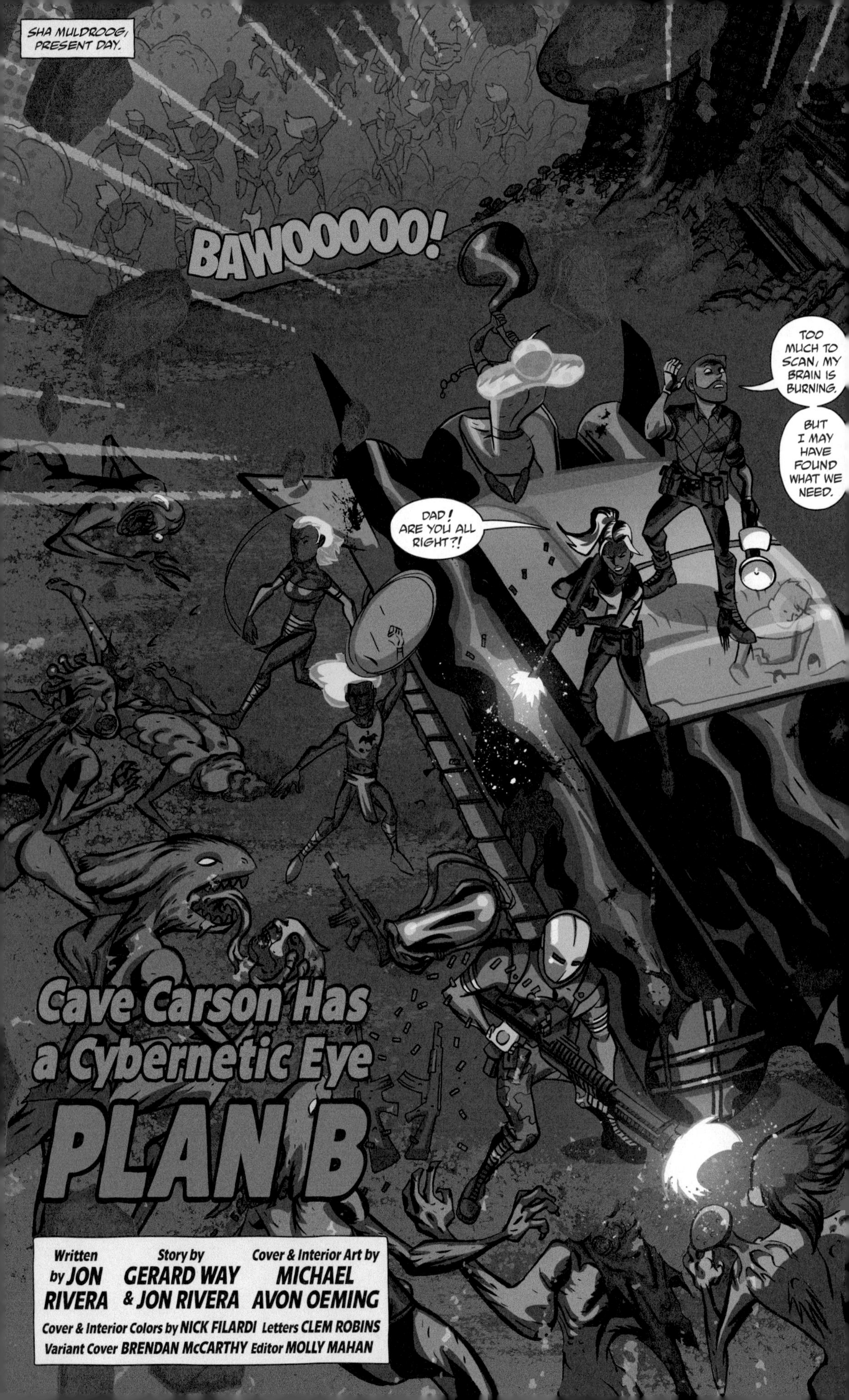
SHA MULDROOG, PRESENT DAY.
BAWOOOOO!
TOO MUCH TO SCAN, MY BRAIN IS BURNING.
BUT I MAY HAVE FOUND WHAT WE NEED.
DAD! ARE YOU ALL RIGHT?!
Cave Carson Has a Cybernetic Eye
PLAN B
Written by JON RIVERA
Story by GERARD WAY & JON RIVERA
Cover & Interior Art by MICHAEL AVON OEMING
Cover & Interior Colors by NICK FILARDI Letters CLEM ROBINS
Variant Cover BRENDAN McCARTHY Editor MOLLY MAHAN

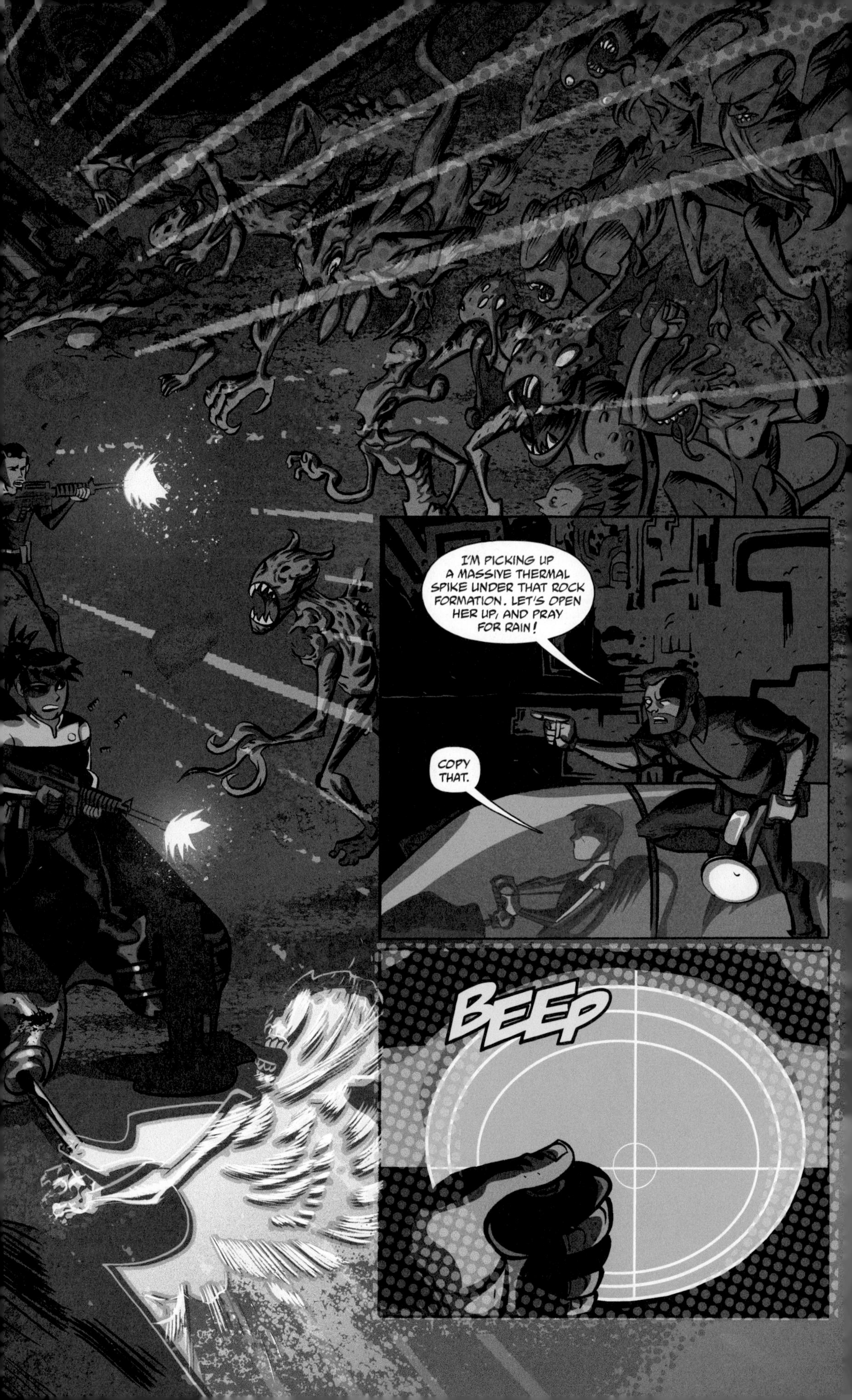
I'M PICKING UP A MASSIVE THERMAL SPIKE UNDER THAT ROCK FORMATION. LET'S OPEN HER UP, AND PRAY FOR RAIN!
COPY THAT.
BEEP

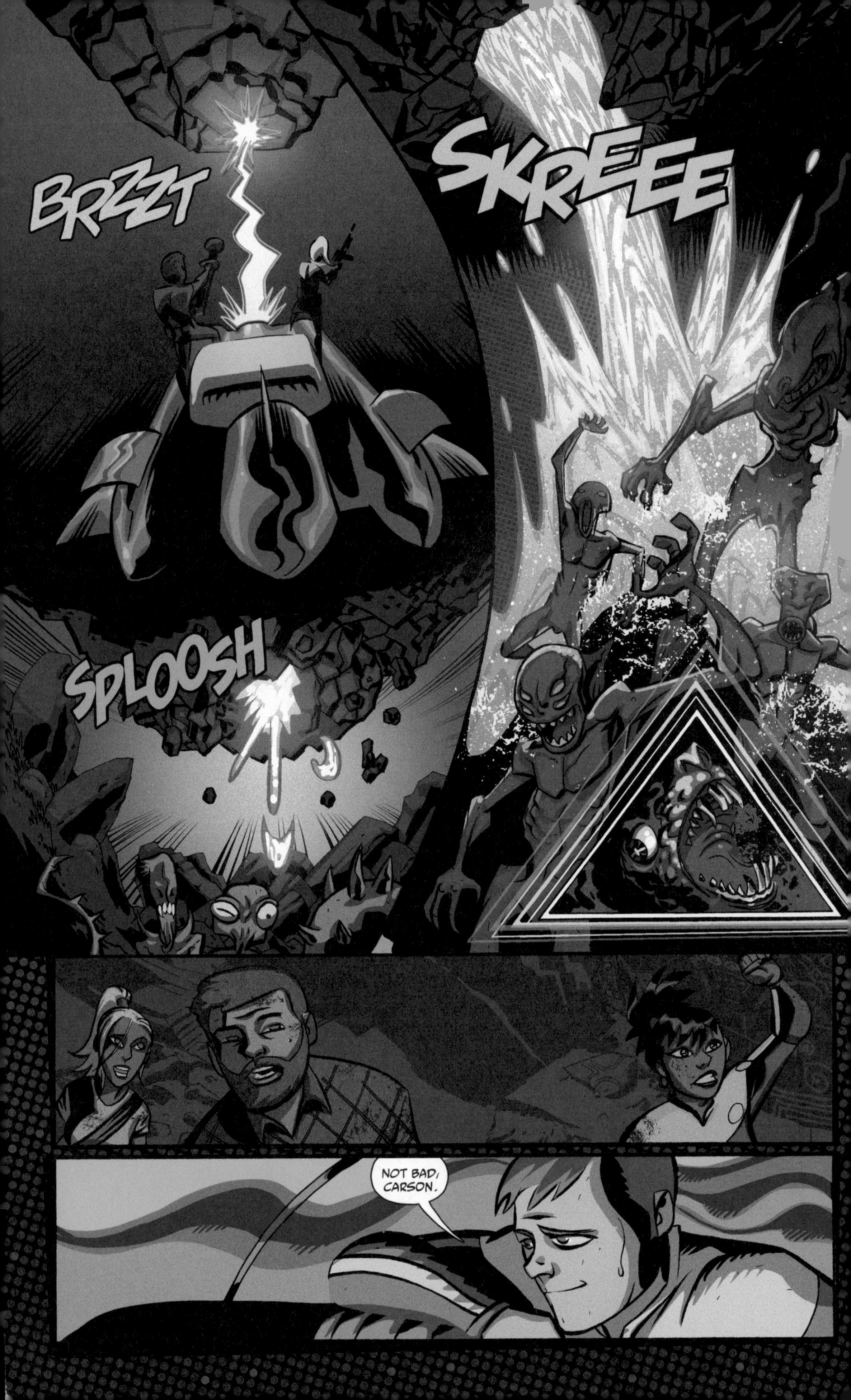
BRZZT
SKREEEE
SPLOOSH
NOT BAD, CARSON.

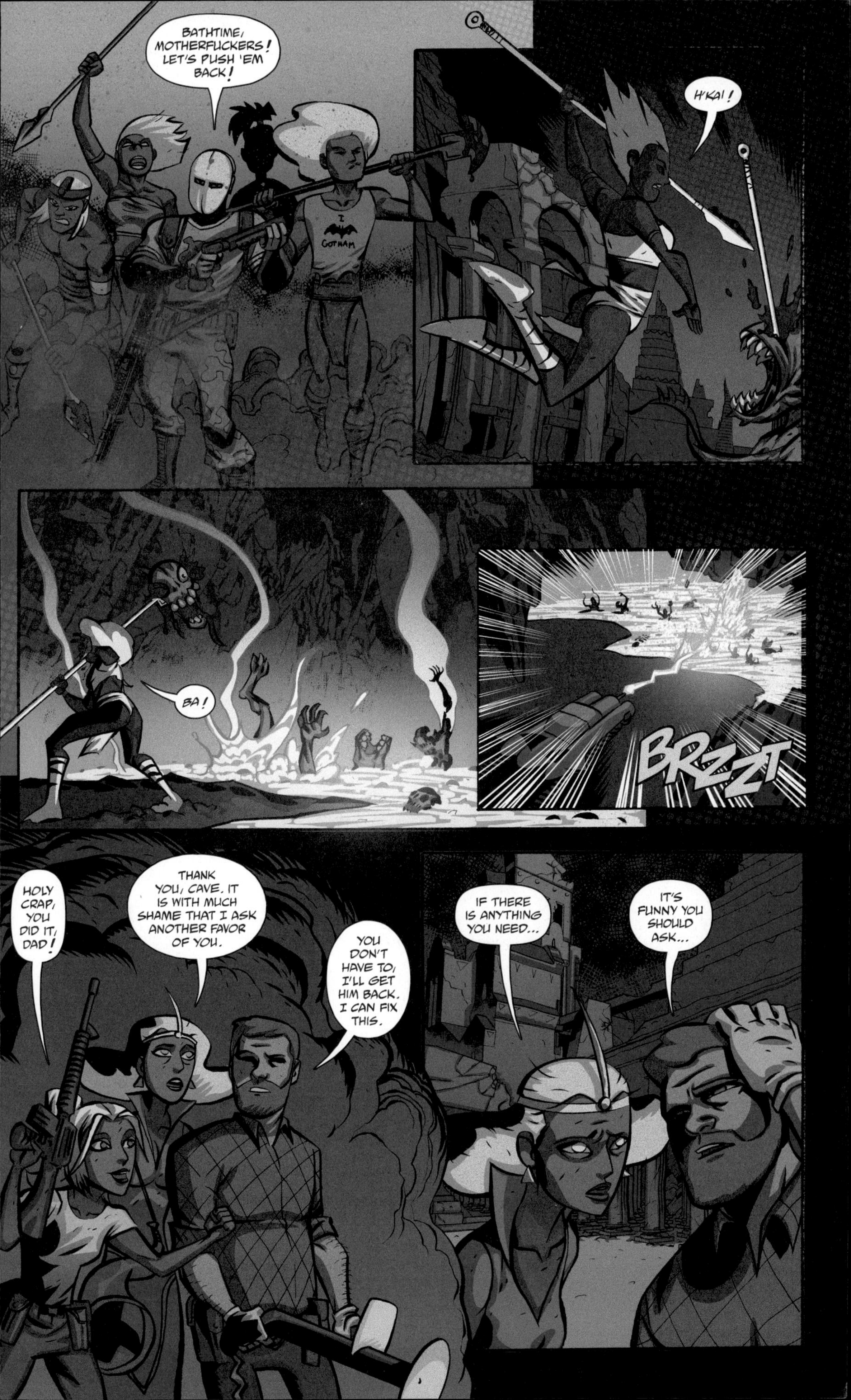
BATHTIME, MOTHERFUCKERS! LET'S PUSH 'EM BACK!
I [bat] GOTHAM
H'KAI!
BA!
BRZZT
HOLY CRAP, YOU DID IT, DAD!
THANK YOU, CAVE. IT IS WITH MUCH SHAME THAT I ASK ANOTHER FAVOR OF YOU.
YOU DON'T HAVE TO, I'LL GET HIM BACK. I CAN FIX THIS.
IF THERE IS ANYTHING YOU NEED...
IT'S FUNNY YOU SHOULD ASK...

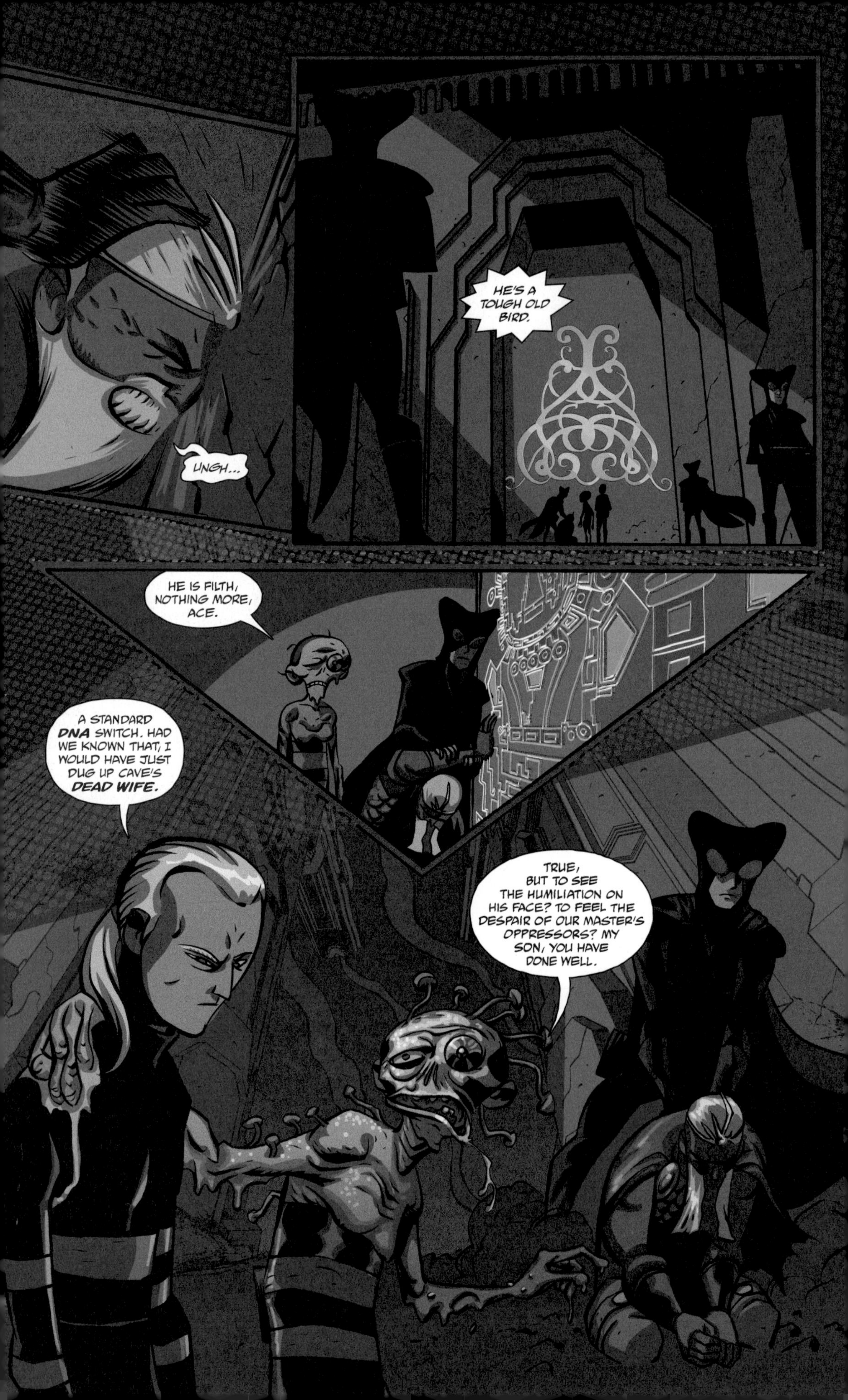
UNGH...
HE'S A TOUGH OLD BIRD.
HE IS FILTH, NOTHING MORE, ACE.
A STANDARD DNA SWITCH. HAD WE KNOWN THAT, I WOULD HAVE JUST DUG UP CAVE'S DEAD WIFE.
TRUE, BUT TO SEE THE HUMILIATION ON HIS FACE? TO FEEL THE DESPAIR OF OUR MASTER'S OPPRESSORS? MY SON, YOU HAVE DONE WELL.

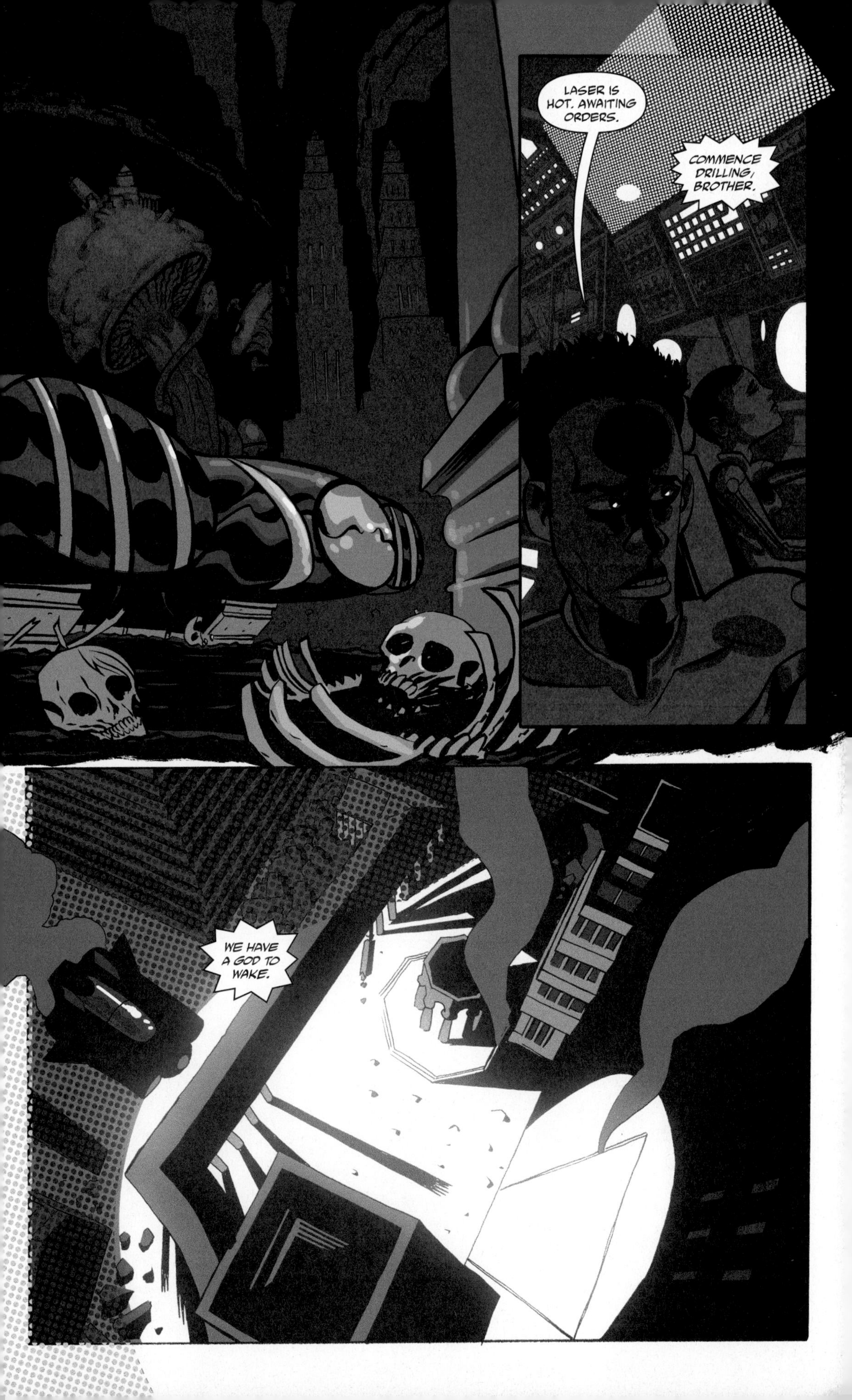
LASER IS HOT. AWAITING ORDERS.
COMMENCE DRILLING, BROTHER.
WE HAVE A GOD TO WAKE.

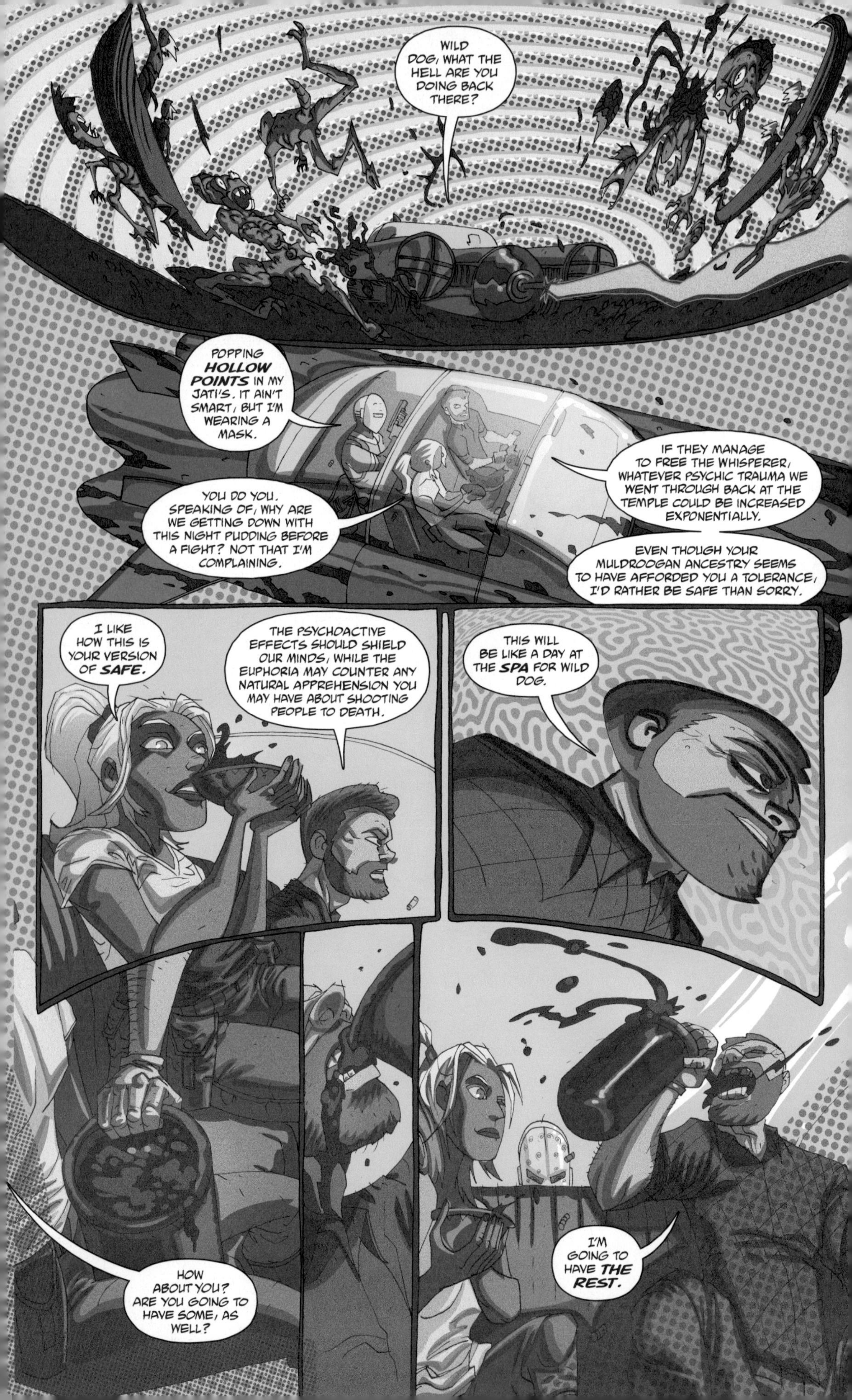

WILD DOG, WHAT THE HELL ARE YOU DOING BACK THERE?
POPPING HOLLOW POINTS IN MY JATI'S. IT AIN'T SMART, BUT I'M WEARING A MASK.
YOU DO YOU. SPEAKING OF, WHY ARE WE GETTING DOWN WITH THIS NIGHT PUDDING BEFORE A FIGHT? NOT THAT I'M COMPLAINING.
IF THEY MANAGE TO FREE THE WHISPERER, WHATEVER PSYCHIC TRAUMA WE WENT THROUGH BACK AT THE TEMPLE COULD BE INCREASED EXPONENTIALLY.
EVEN THOUGH YOUR MULDROOGAN ANCESTRY SEEMS TO HAVE AFFORDED YOU A TOLERANCE, I'D RATHER BE SAFE THAN SORRY.
I LIKE HOW THIS IS YOUR VERSION OF SAFE.
THE PSYCHOACTIVE EFFECTS SHOULD SHIELD OUR MINDS, WHILE THE EUPHORIA MAY COUNTER ANY NATURAL APPREHENSION YOU MAY HAVE ABOUT SHOOTING PEOPLE TO DEATH.
THIS WILL BE LIKE A DAY AT THE SPA FOR WILD DOG.
HOW ABOUT YOU? ARE YOU GOING TO HAVE SOME, AS WELL?
I'M GOING TO HAVE THE REST.

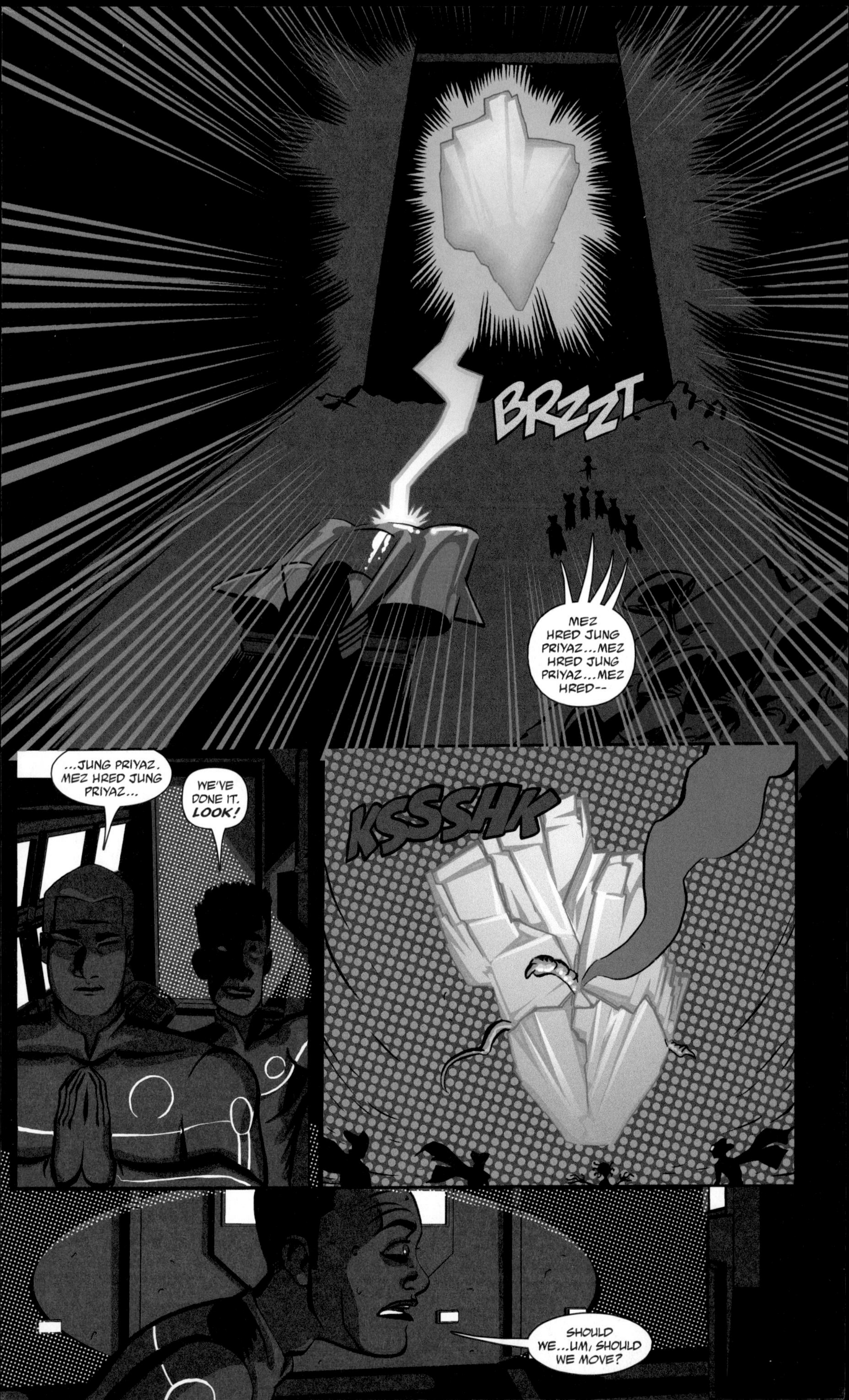
BRZZT
MEZ HRED JUNG PRIYAZ...MEZ HRED JUNG PRIYAZ...MEZ HRED--
...JUNG PRIYAZ. MEZ HRED JUNG PRIYAZ...
WE'VE DONE IT. LOOK!
KSSSHK
SHOULD WE...UM, SHOULD WE MOVE?

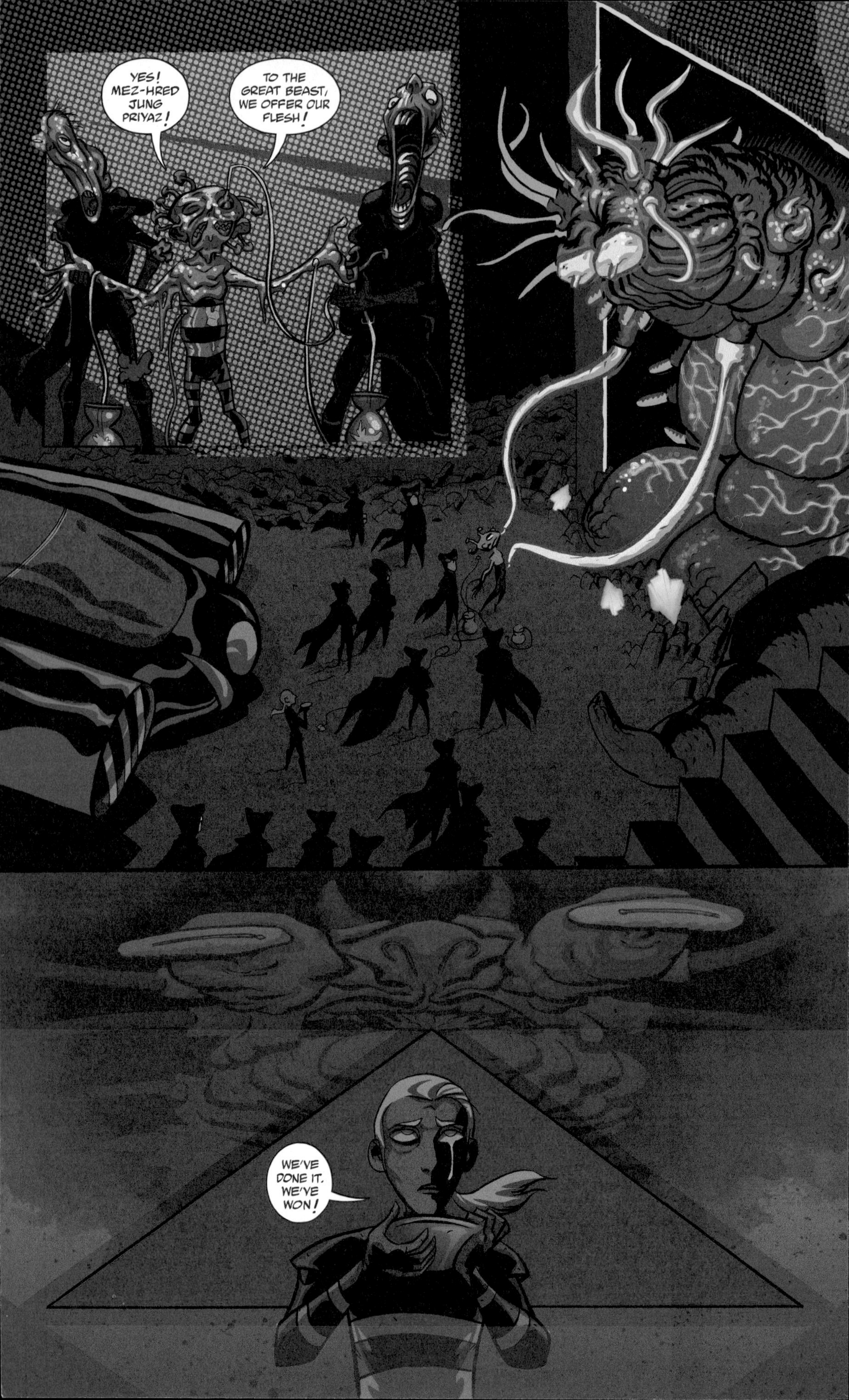
YES! MEZ-HRED JUNG PRIYAZ!
TO THE GREAT BEAST, WE OFFER OUR FLESH!
WE'VE DONE IT. WE'VE WON!

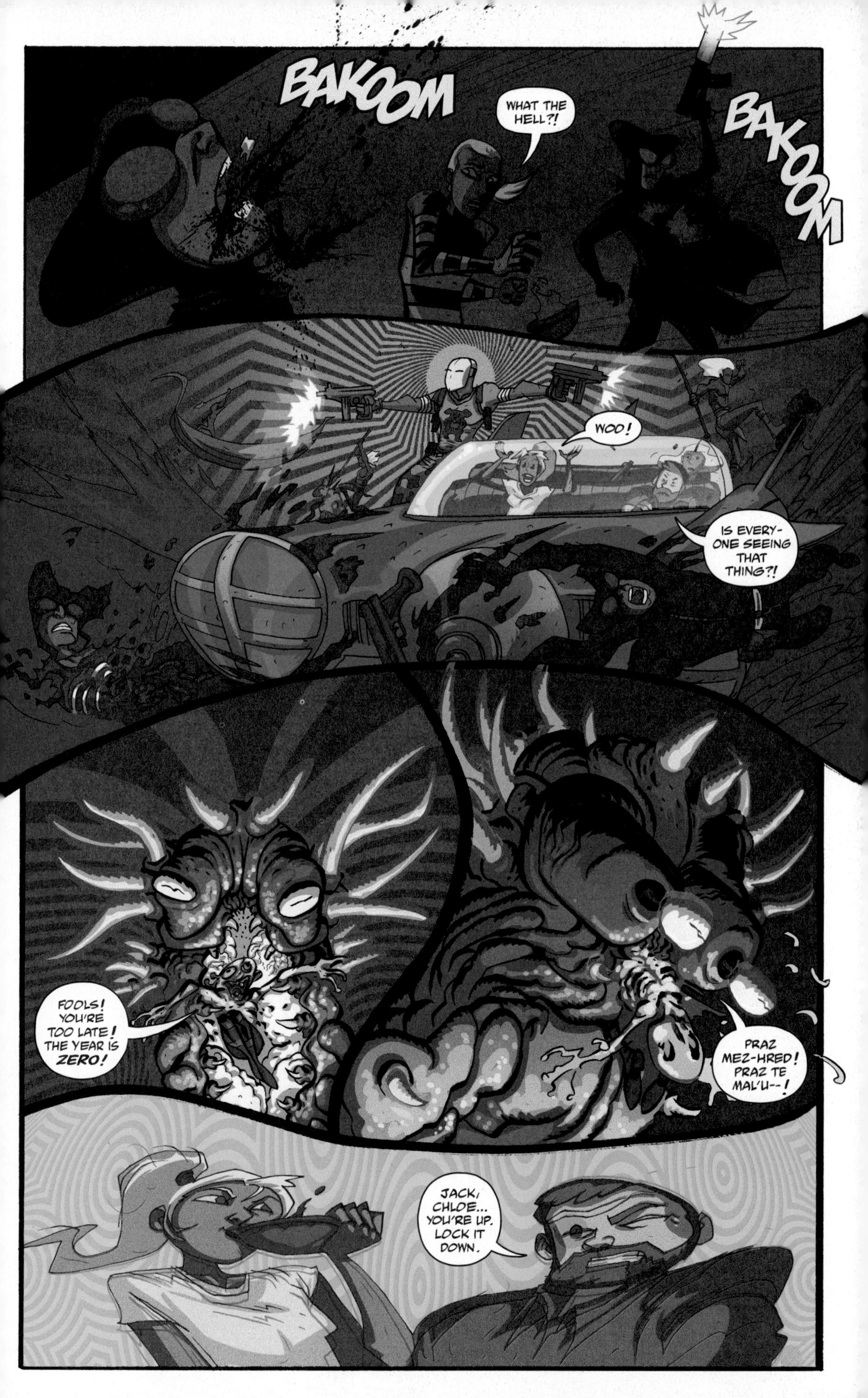
BAKOOM
WHAT THE HELL?!
BAKOOM
WOO!
IS EVERY-ONE SEEING THAT THING?!
FOOLS! YOU'RE TOO LATE! THE YEAR IS ZERO!
PRAZ MEZ-HRED! PRAZ TE MAL'U--!
JACK, CHLOE... YOU'RE UP. LOCK IT DOWN.

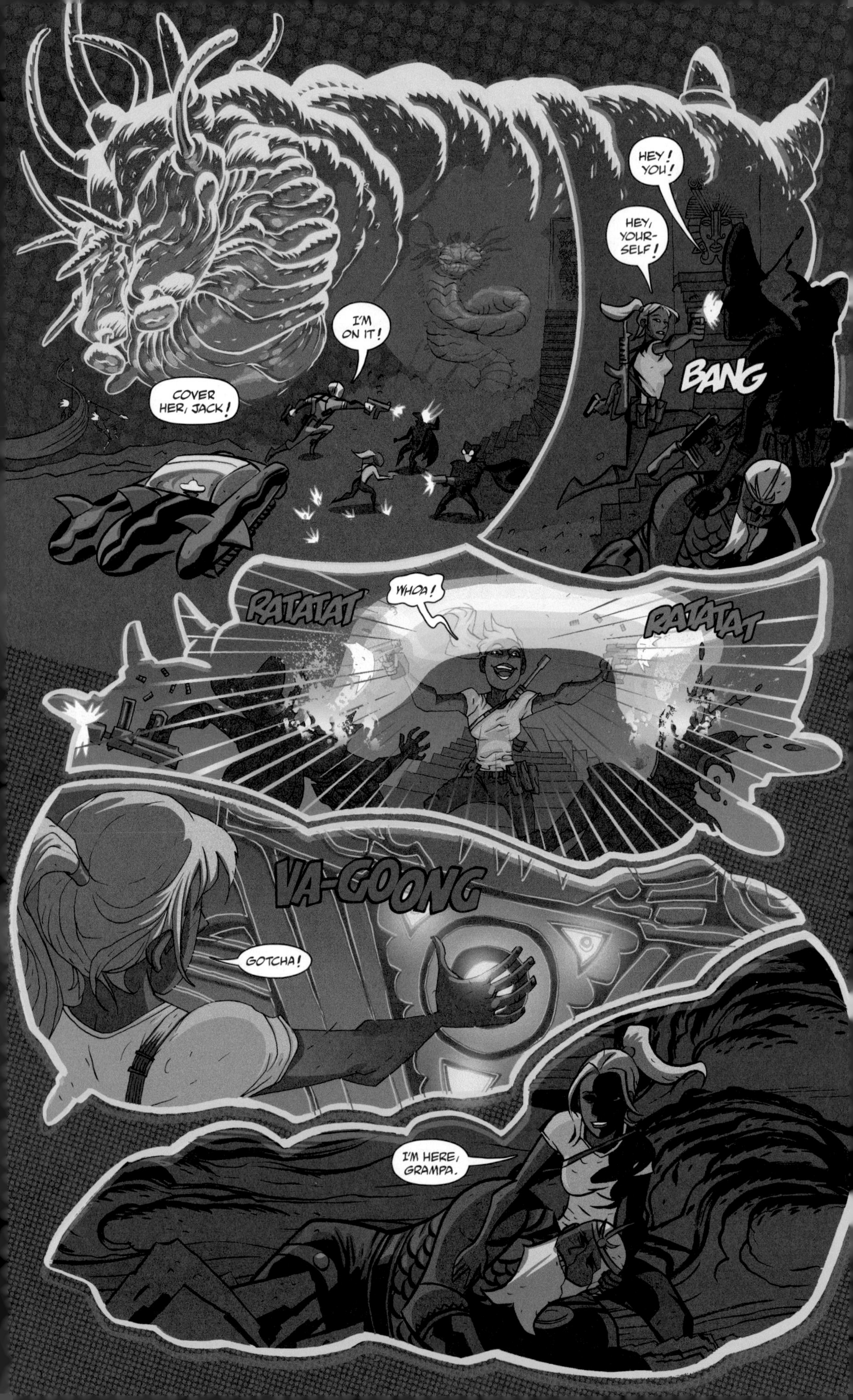
HEY! YOU!
HEY, YOURSELF!
I'M ON IT!
COVER HER, JACK!
BANG
RATATAT
WHOA!
RATATAT
VA-GOONG
GOTCHA!
I'M HERE, GRAMPA.

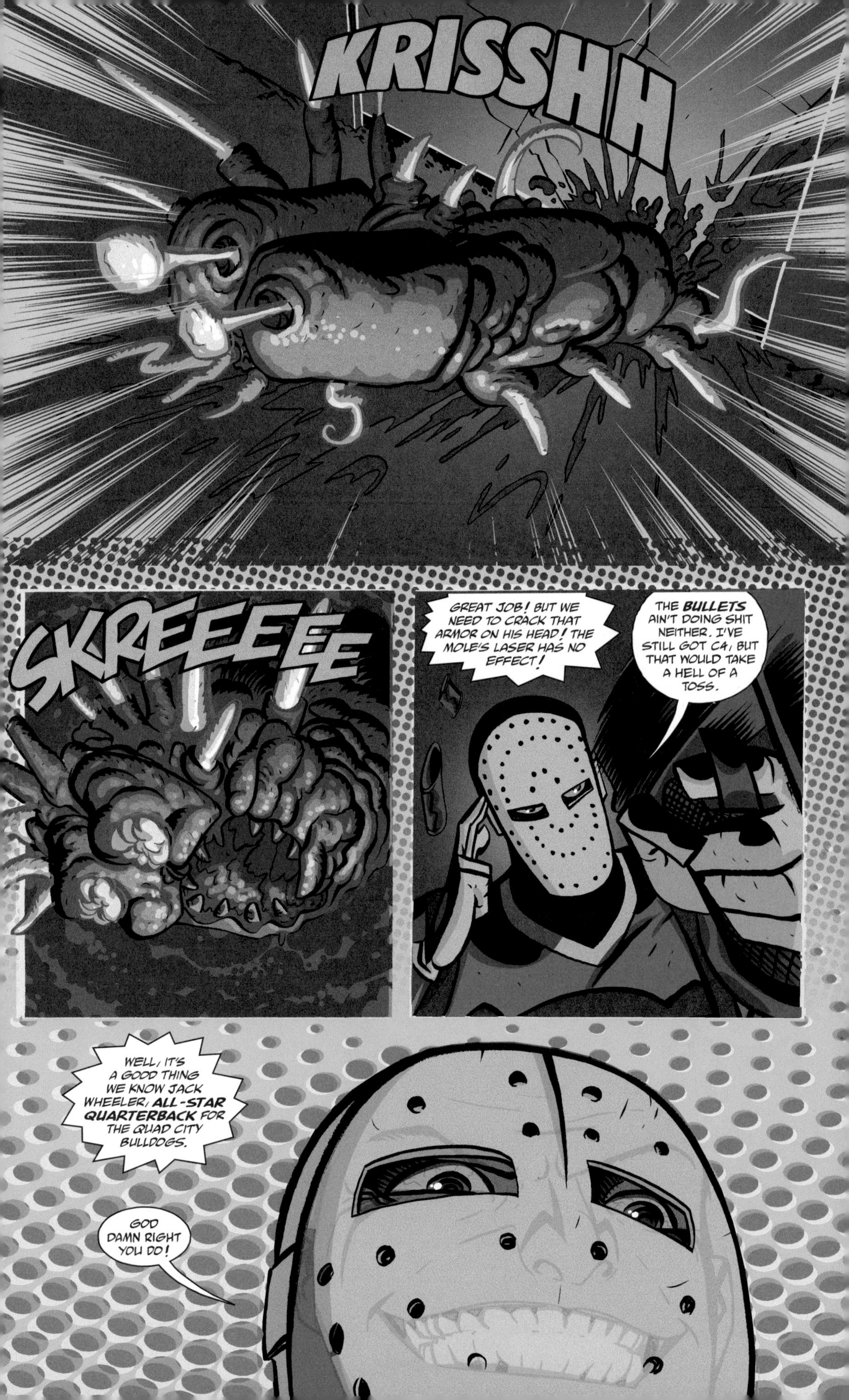
KRISSHH
SKREEEEEEE
GREAT JOB! BUT WE NEED TO CRACK THAT ARMOR ON HIS HEAD! THE MOLE'S LASER HAS NO EFFECT!
THE BULLETS AIN'T DOING SHIT NEITHER. I'VE STILL GOT C4, BUT THAT WOULD TAKE A HELL OF A TOSS.
WELL, IT'S A GOOD THING WE KNOW JACK WHEELER, ALL-STAR QUARTERBACK FOR THE QUAD CITY BULLDOGS.
GOD DAMN RIGHT YOU DO!

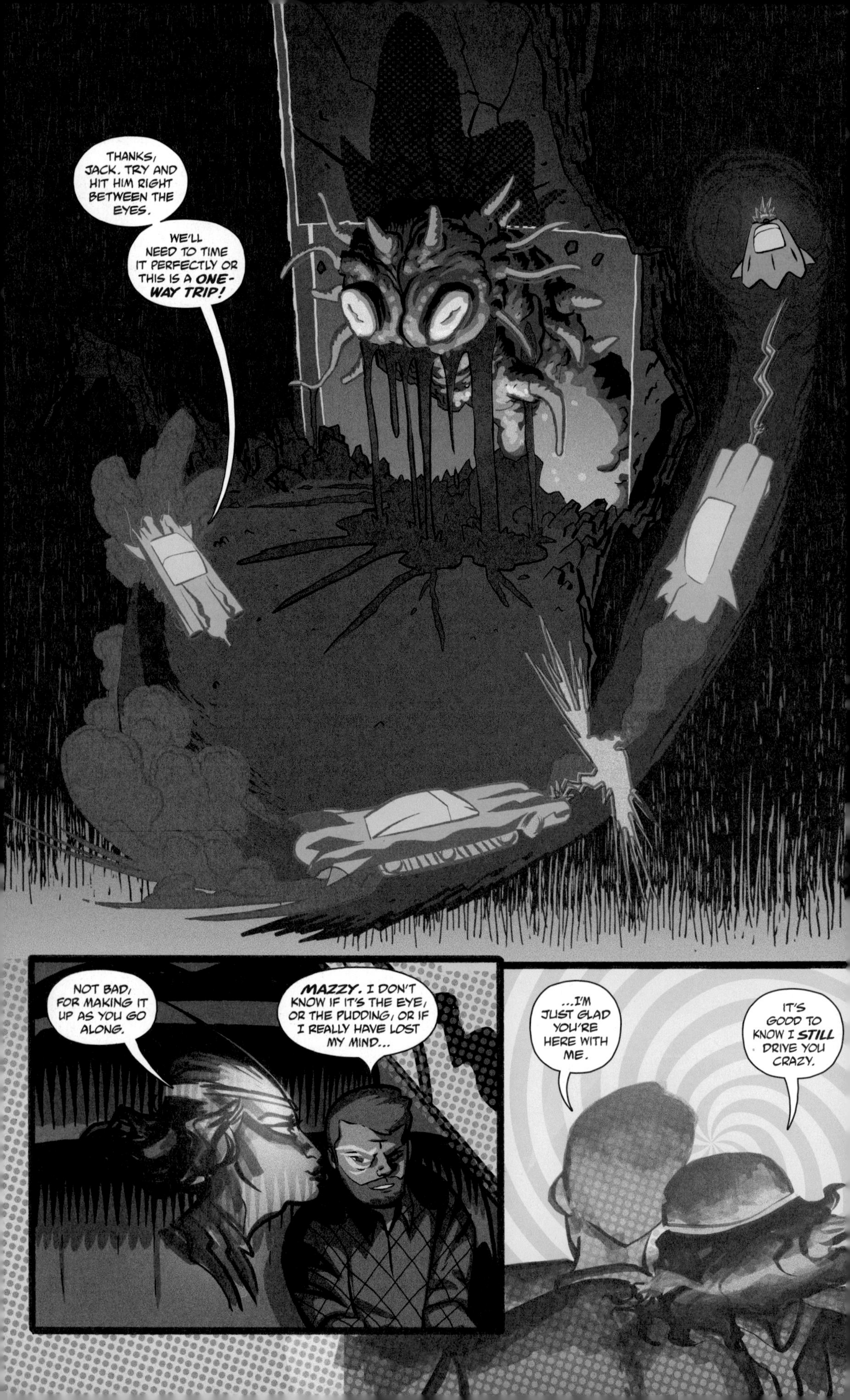
THANKS, JACK. TRY AND HIT HIM RIGHT BETWEEN THE EYES.
WE'LL NEED TO TIME IT PERFECTLY OR THIS IS A ONE-WAY TRIP!
NOT BAD, FOR MAKING IT UP AS YOU GO ALONG.
MAZZY. I DON'T KNOW IF IT'S THE EYE, OR THE PUDDING, OR IF I REALLY HAVE LOST MY MIND...
...I'M JUST GLAD YOU'RE HERE WITH ME.
IT'S GOOD TO KNOW I STILL DRIVE YOU CRAZY.

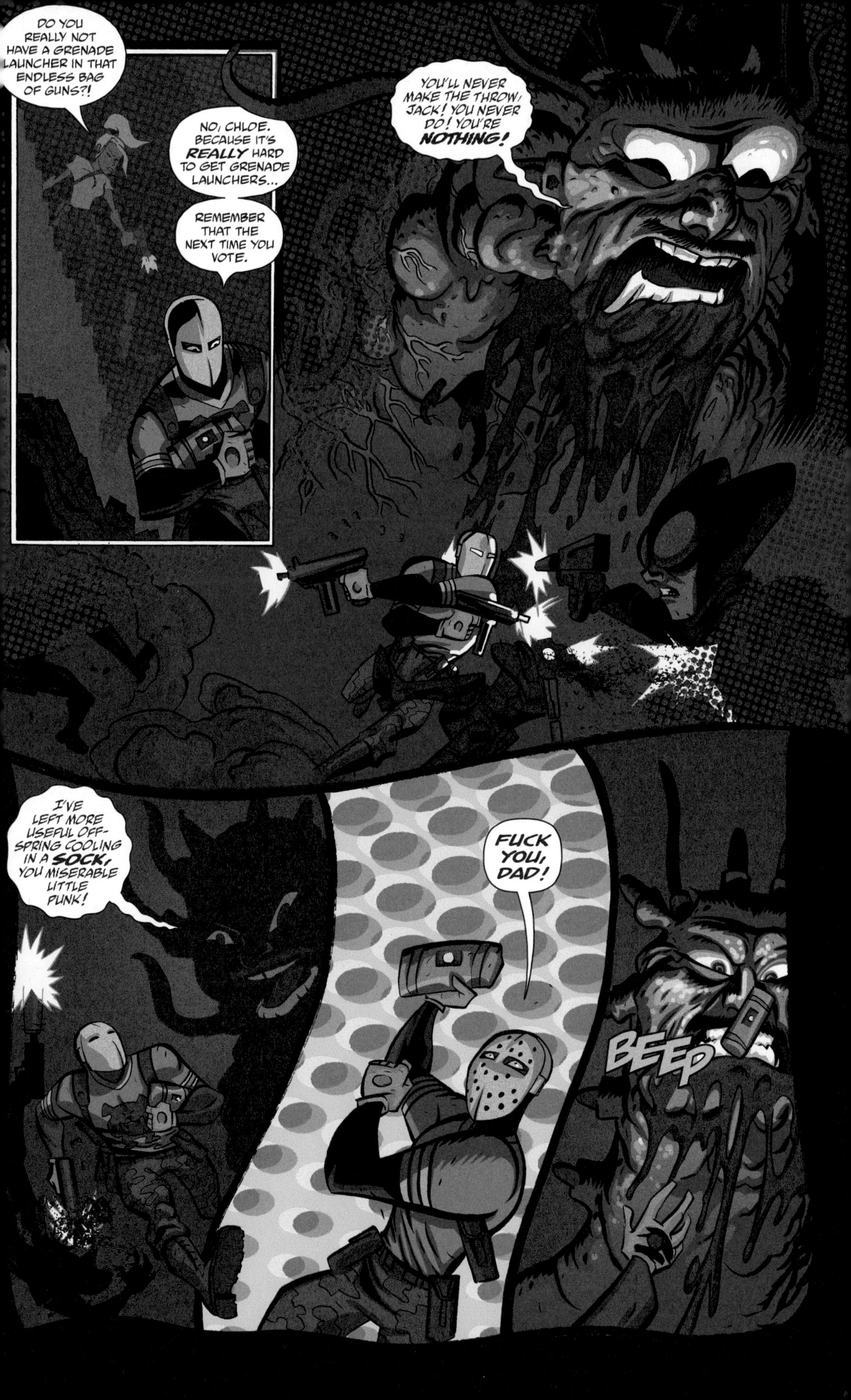
DO YOU REALLY NOT HAVE A GRENADE LAUNCHER IN THAT ENDLESS BAG OF GUNS?!
NO, CHLOE. BECAUSE IT'S REALLY HARD TO GET GRENADE LAUNCHERS...
REMEMBER THAT THE NEXT TIME YOU VOTE.
YOU'LL NEVER MAKE THE THROW, JACK! YOU NEVER DO! YOU'RE NOTHING!
I'VE LEFT MORE USEFUL OFF-SPRING COOLING IN A SOCK, YOU MISERABLE LITTLE PUNK!
FUCK YOU, DAD!
BEEP

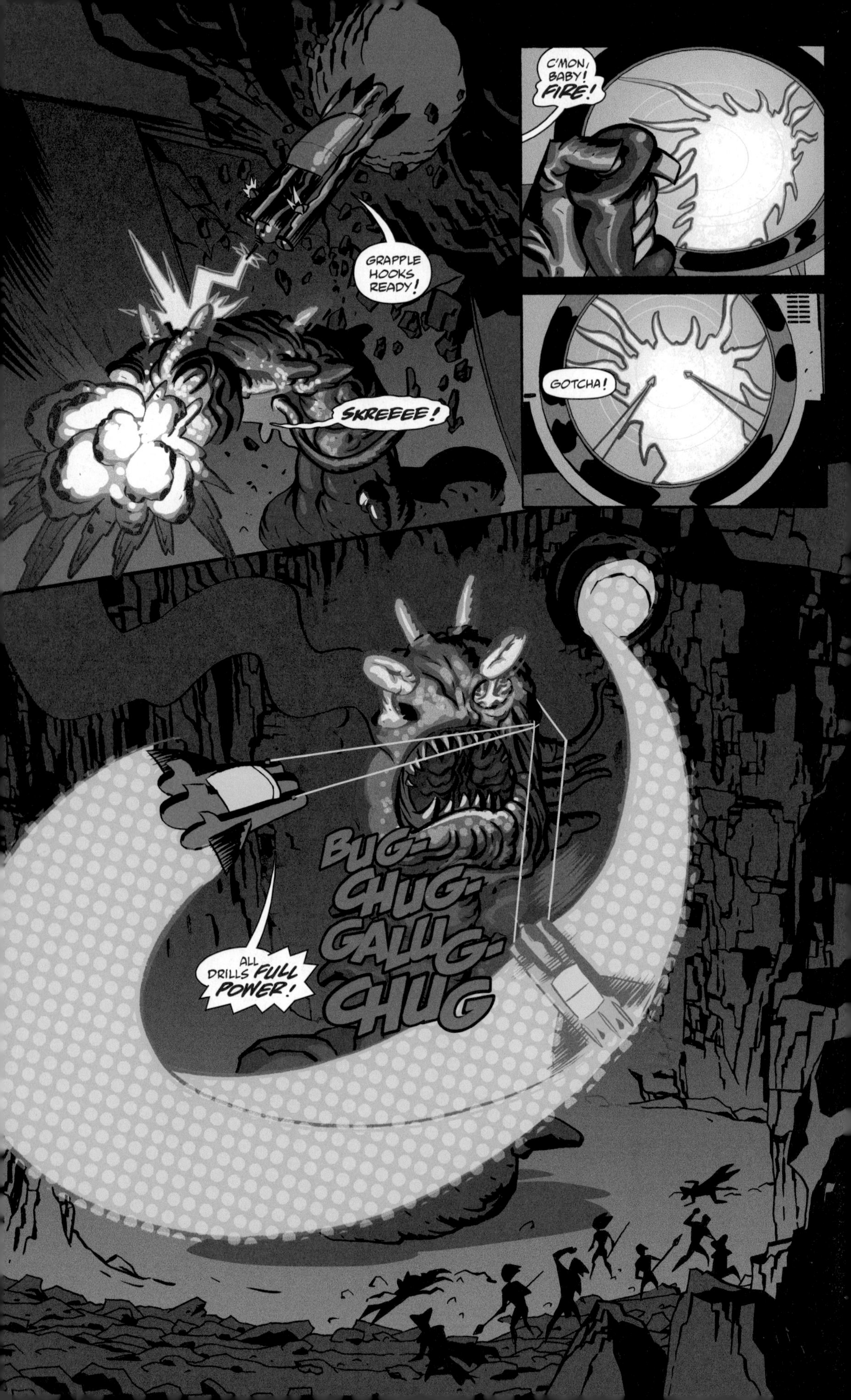

GRAPPLE HOOKS READY!
SKREEEE!
C'MON, BABY! FIRE!
GOTCHA!
BUG-CHUG-GALUG-CHUG
ALL DRILLS FULL POWER!

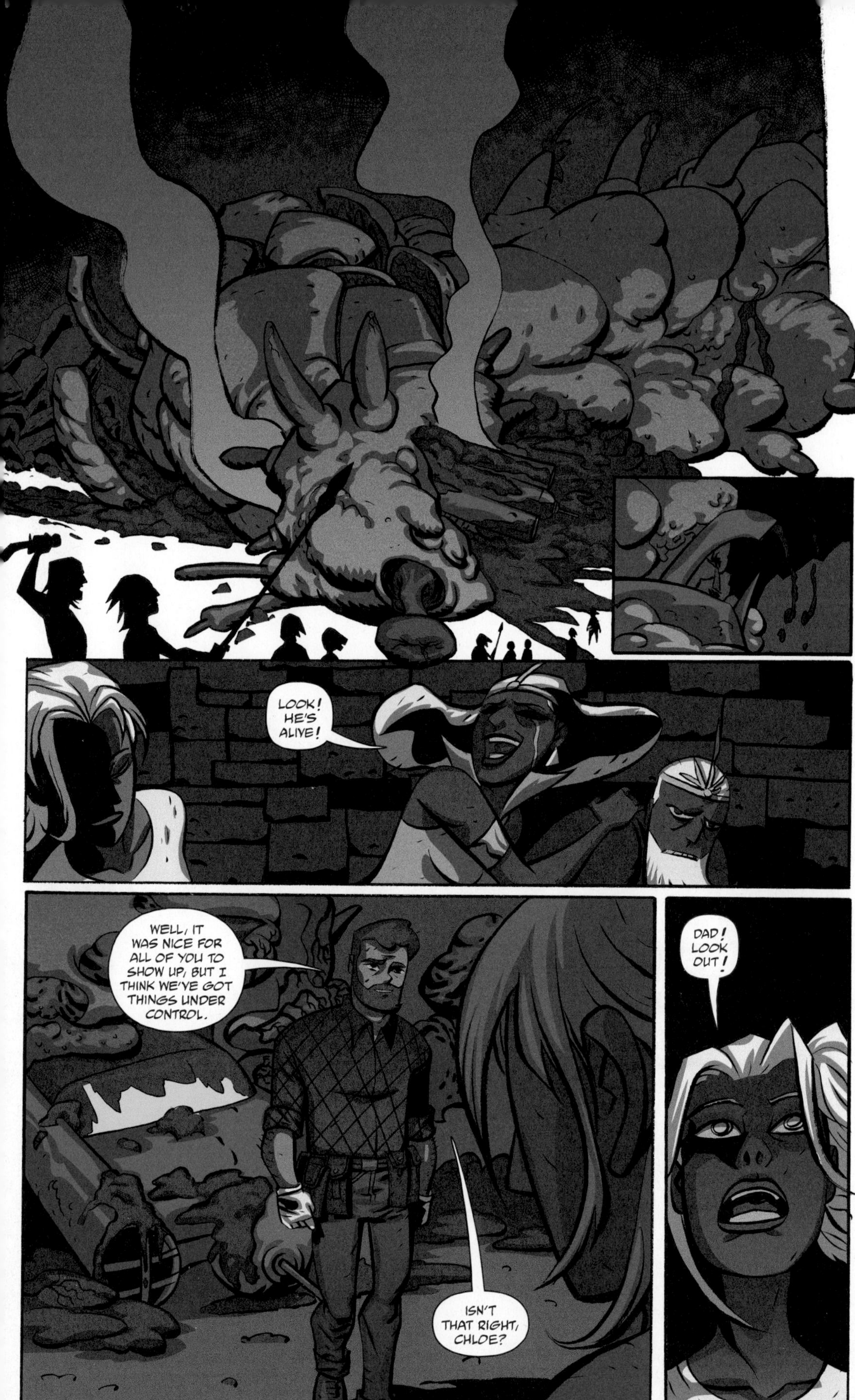
LOOK! HE'S ALIVE!
WELL, IT WAS NICE FOR ALL OF YOU TO SHOW UP, BUT I THINK WE'VE GOT THINGS UNDER CONTROL.
ISN'T THAT RIGHT, CHLOE?
DAD! LOOK OUT!

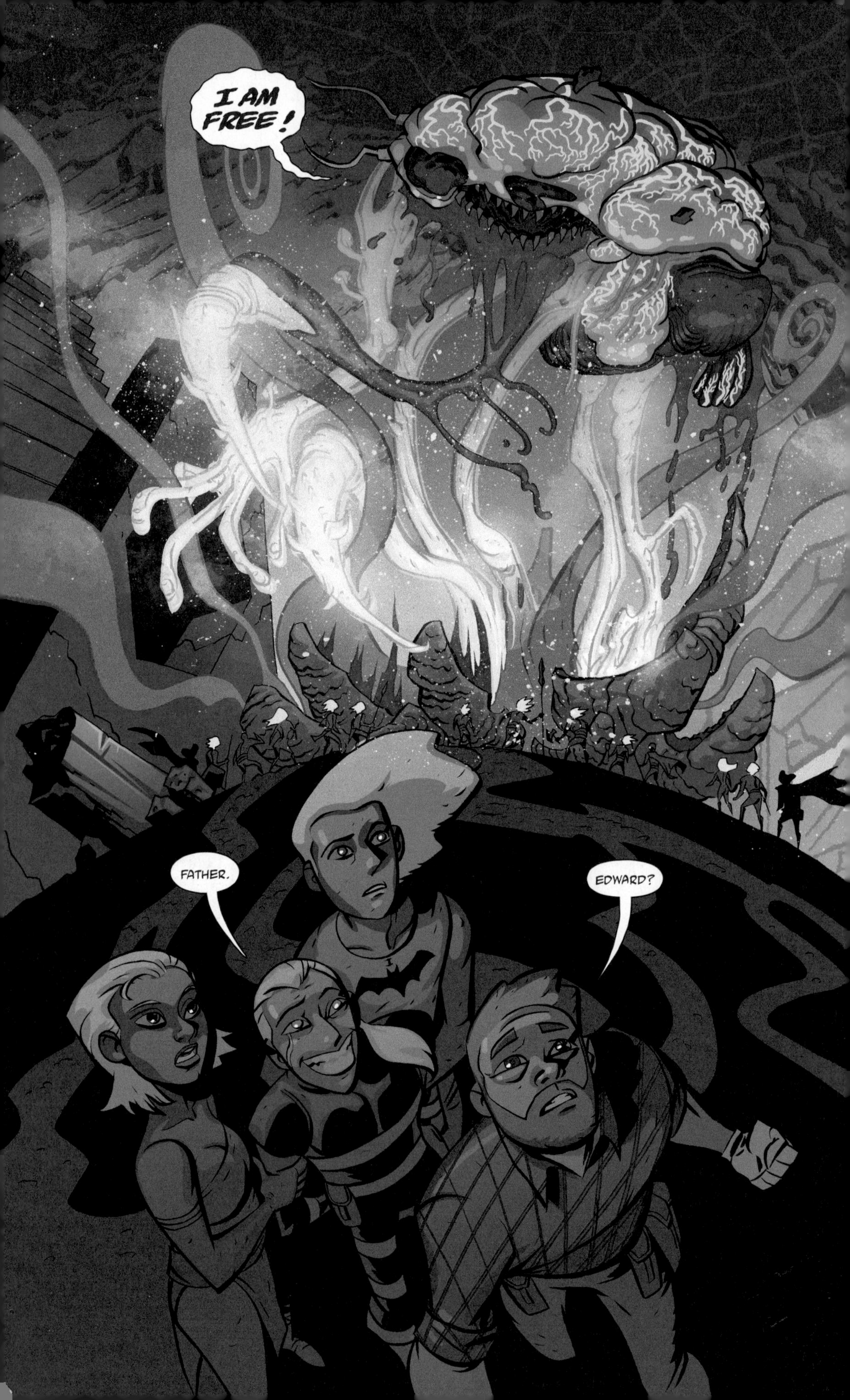
I AM FREE!
FATHER.
EDWARD?

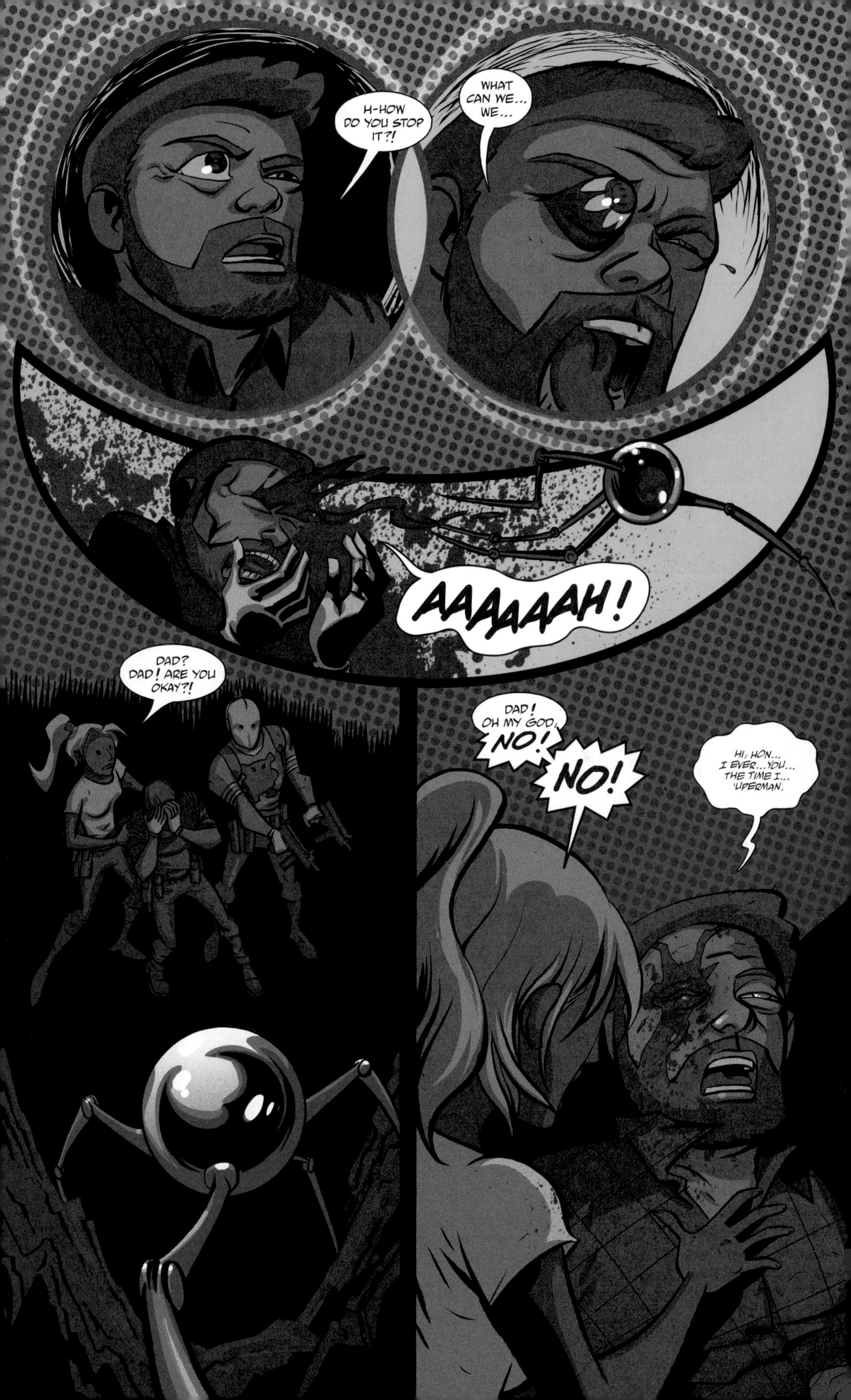
H-HOW DO YOU STOP IT?!
WHAT CAN WE... WE...
AAAAAAH!
DAD? DAD! ARE YOU OKAY?!
DAD! OH MY GOD, NO!
NO!
HI, HON... I EVER... YOU... THE TIME I... 'UPERMAN.

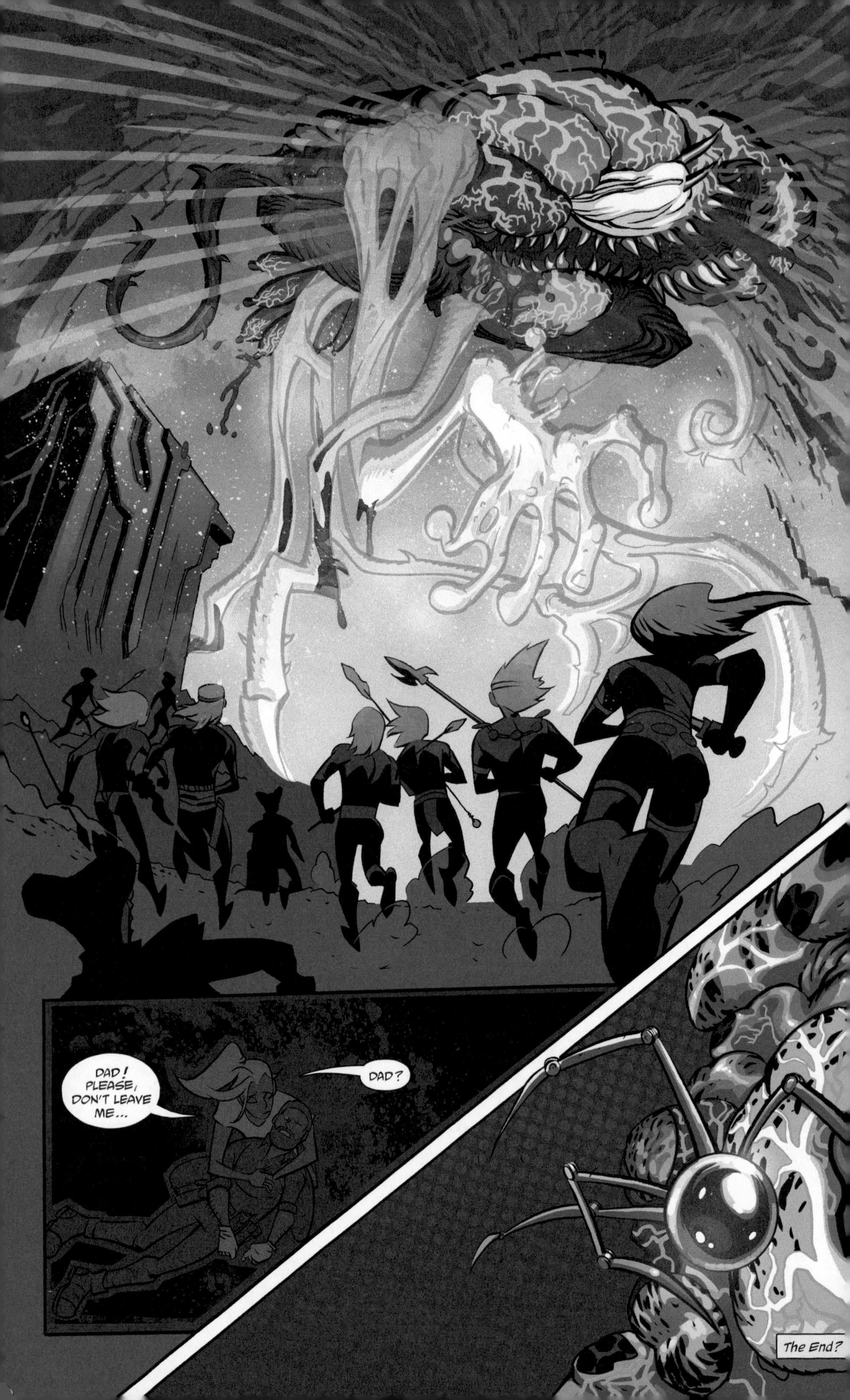
DAD! PLEASE, DON'T LEAVE ME...
DAD?
The End?

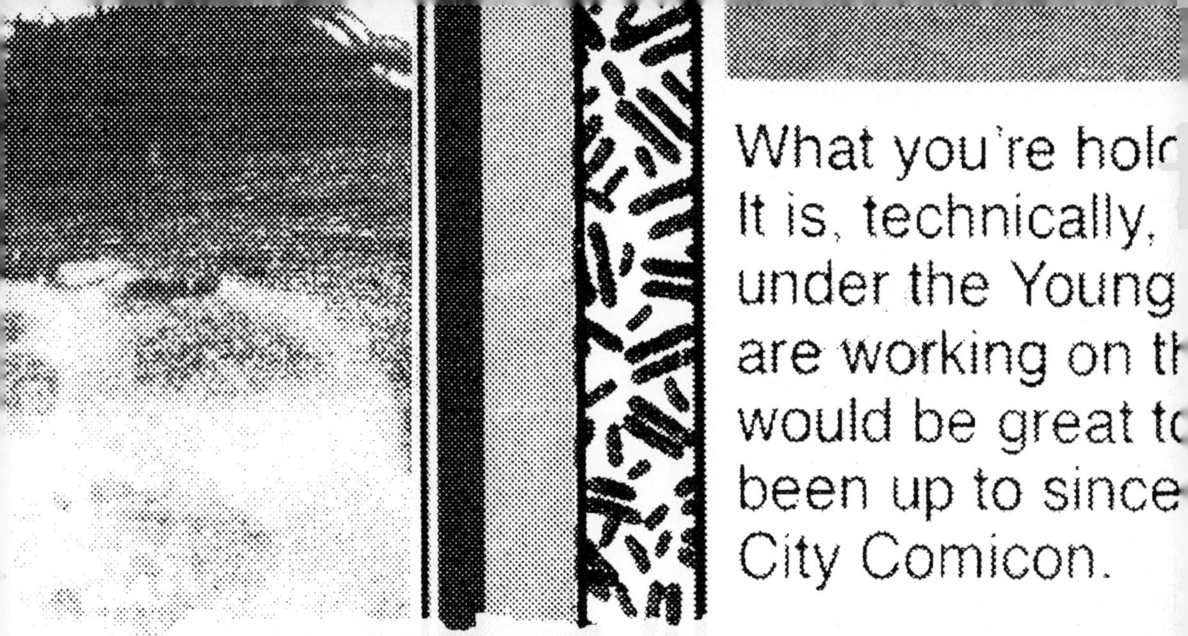
What you're hol
It is, technically,
under the Young
are working on t
would be great t
been up to since
City Comicon.

AFTERWORD By **Gerard Way**

So the story goes…

I find myself in Burbank, California, one day after coming home from a convention in South America. I'm sitting in Dan DiDio's office with Jim Lee, and we are talking about the possibilities of me working with DC Comics in some way. It's no secret that I've always loved DC—they put out some of the most important books to me growing up, books that shaped who I became. It's a really amazing meeting, and the energy in the room is fully charged. We talk about DOOM PATROL first—I explain that the version of DOOM PATROL I was working on was something entirely different from what was going on in more mainstream books, and that I wasn't sure where DOOM PATROL sat in that universe. I felt that if DOOM PATROL came out on its own, it would feel pretty lonely. It felt like it needed a movement behind it—the next wave of weird. At this point, Jim says "imprint," and we start rolling, we start talking about other characters. Shade, the Changing Man, comes up, and that feels good, but at this point Dan suggests we look outside of what Vertigo had done in the past. For us to start developing, we need to dig deeper. If we're going to create an imprint, it needs a new energy (even with old characters), a different trajectory. As the meeting is ending, Dan goes over to his shelf and hands me *The Encyclopedia of the DC Universe*. He then says, "Here you go, have fun with that." I can't wait to get home and see what's in there.

As a reader and creator, I've always had an affinity for obscure characters because I see them as being more malleable than the most well-known super-beings. I feel that creators who use them are able to take more risks and try new things. As a budding comics writer, I find them to be ripe for exploration because people may not have been paying much attention to them, or they might have gaps in their history, or readers don't really care what happens to them—and that feels like freedom. Obviously inspired by the semi-obscure nature of the characters in books like DOOM PATROL in the late '80s, I collected the fact-file comics that DC put out called WHO'S WHO IN THE DC UNIVERSE. My absolute favorite thing to do with those issues was to crack them open and look for hidden gems. I checked out characters I had never heard of before and then came up with my own take on them. I did this constantly, both because I was inspired by the books and because I thought it was a sneaky way to break into comics. I'd say to myself, "No one's using XYZ right now, so of course they'll let me use them, being 13 years old with no experience whatsoever." I'd put these crudely drawn and typed pitches together, mostly for myself, though I am fairly certain that I did send my revamp of the Inferior Five to the DC offices—of course it was a dark and gritty revamp, if you can imagine a character like Merryman being either of those things: a lot of open screaming mouths, blood, and action lines. I enjoyed the challenge of making something work (at least in my 13-year-old brain) and the flexibility that came along with it.

So, naturally, when I got home from my meeting at DC, I pulled out my favorite notebook and pen and started researching the dusty corners of the DCU. I wrote down names as they jumped out at me—even characters that I already knew but that maybe hadn't had a book in a while. Then I got to the "C" section.

I will never forget coming across the name Cave Carson. I may have seen him a long time ago in WHO'S WHO, but I didn't have every issue of that series when I was a kid, so there's a good chance that I had never heard of him. (I also like to think that if I *had* come across Cave as a kid, I just wasn't *ready* for him then.) Cave's entry in the *Encyclopedia* is roughly two inches long, and there's not a lot there. I checked out his stats at the top, and something grabbed my attention:

Special Powers/Abilities: *Highly intelligent, with a natural gift for his area of expertise; one eye is cybernetic.*

And that's it. There is some history involving his old crew, and a mention of their dip in popularity once the modern age of superheroes began (and a bit about him stealing a vehicle called the Mighty Mole from his employers), but statistically he was just a smart expert in geology with a cybernetic eye. I was in love. I knew what the title of the book was going to be, and I texted it to Dan: CAVE CARSON HAS A CYBERNETIC EYE. I am almost 100 percent positive that the title alone sold Dan on the whole imprint—he got it. Once we were able to look outside what had been done before, we found amazing things, and we stayed on that path.

We did some research but found out very little about the character. Most mysterious was how little information there was about his cybernetic eye. You would think that there would be some big story there, since it's the only thing really extraordinary about Cave, but there wasn't, so Dan became determined to find out where the eye had come from. Eventually he discovered that Cave had appeared in the final story arc of RESURRECTION MAN in the '90s, only with a new addition: a cybernetic eye. The brilliant creative team responsible—writers Dan Abnett and Andy Lanning, and artist Jackson Guice—never explained where the eye came from; its presence simply demonstrated that Cave had continued to have adventures during the time since his last comic book appearance, and that he had somehow acquired this high-tech peeper in the course of those adventures—a very clever narrative device, really, to show that life went on for Cave, even if he wasn't in any books. (He was also dressed in a kind of black leather bondage gear, but we really couldn't figure out that part.) This lack of information was a blessing,

and it made our job as storytellers even more fun—Cave and his eye were a relatively clean slate, aside from the awesome spelunking, experimental-vehicle-stealing, one-time-adventure-with-Superman-type thing he has going on.

CAVE CARSON HAS A CYBERNETIC EYE is truly a labor of love for the whole team. Everyone cares deeply about this character in the same way that you would if you had created him yourself. Cave does have a history, but there is so much room for filling in details and creating new adventures that it makes the title a joy to work on—and everyone completely pushes themselves to take the book to strange new places. Jon Rivera, my occasional writing partner, was absolutely the best choice for co-writing and eventually fully scripting this series, because I knew that we would have the same vision for it in our heads and that we would latch onto the same things about the character—but at the same time he would bring his own unique insights to the process. Jon also brings a warmth and humanity to the characters that I often overlook in my solo work, and I can't imagine anyone else writing Cave and Chloe.

Collaboration is key to the Young Animal imprint—and to comics in general. Everyone on a creative team is crafting their story together, and this series' crew constantly amazes me. Michael Avon Oeming is such a fantastic artist—I've always been a fan of his, but I feel like he is doing some of his greatest work on CAVE, and the chemistry between Michael and Nick Filardi on colors always makes us smile (and sometimes hallucinate). And thank god for Clem Robins, who makes a sometimes-wordy comic feel not so wordy and a pleasure to read. Of course, editor Molly Mahan brings all of us together, asks the right questions, gets great work out of us, and pushes us harder every time. I think you can feel the weight of everyone's dedication to this book from the first moment you hold it in your hands.

And did I mention that Wild Dog is in it?!?

See you around,
G

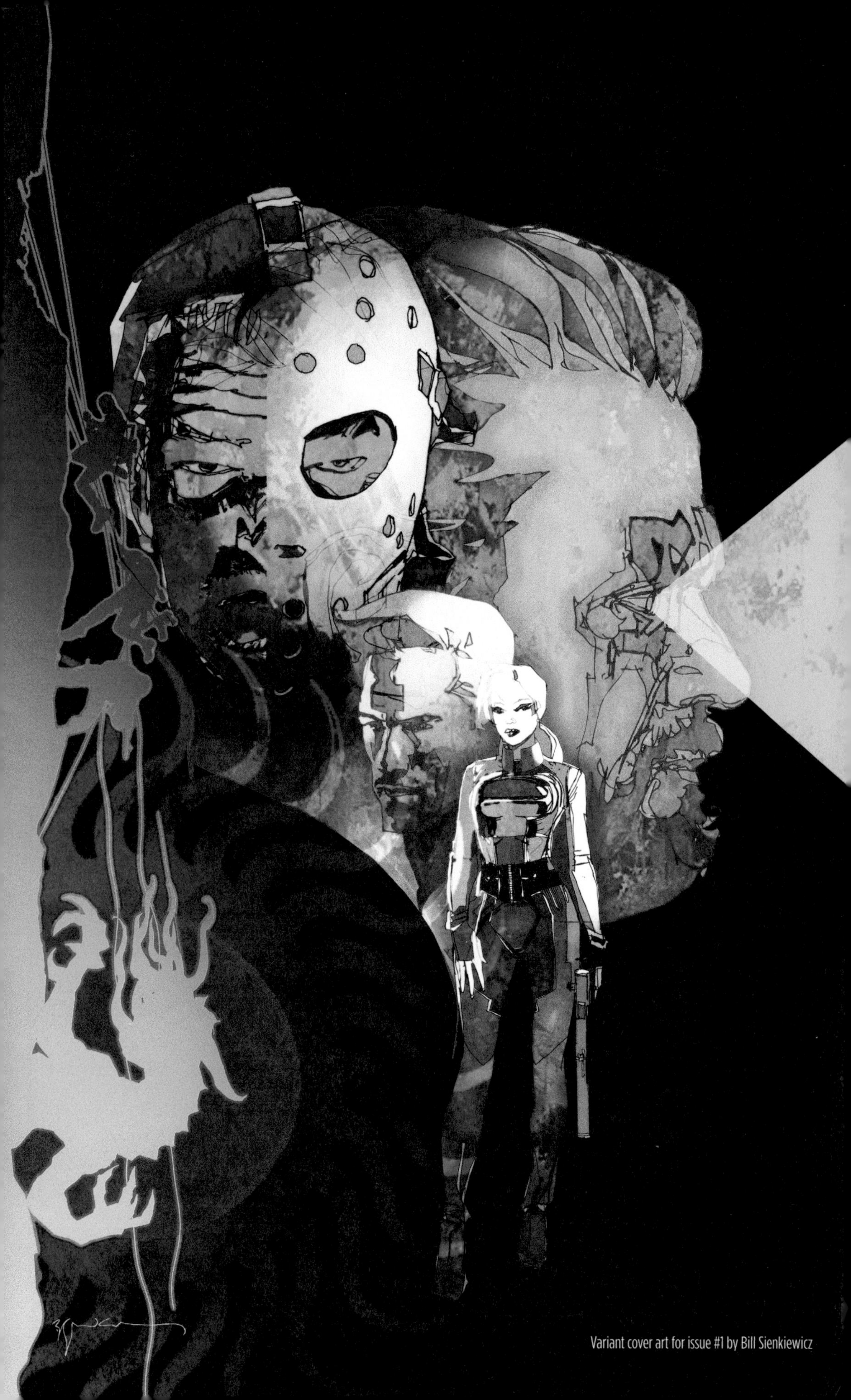

Variant cover art for issue #1 by Bill Sienkiewicz

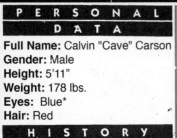

PERSONAL DATA

Full Name: Calvin "Cave" Carson
Gender: Male
Height: 5'11"
Weight: 178 lbs.
Eyes: Blue*
Hair: Red

HISTORY

Calvin "Cave" Carson has been many things in his life: teacher, scientist, thief, hero, and patron saint of the vibrant spelunking counterculture.

Once a promising young technician at E. Borsten & Sons, Cave helped develop the "Mighty Mole," an incredible machine capable of tunneling through the earth exponentially faster than any drill. However, once the project lost its funding from the military, Cave stole the Mighty Mole and assembled a crack team of adventurers and scientists to explore the hidden mysteries below the Earth's crust.

For ten years, Cave and his crew battled monsters, discovered ancient civilizations, helped Superman, and even filmed an award-winning documentary. During this period Cave met an accomplished fellow spelunker named Eileen Smith. They were married soon after and settled down, having a daughter named Chloe.

Adventuring was a family affair once Chloe became old enough to walk. By six years old, Chloe had already saved a small town in Iowa by discovering, and naming, a psychic worm controlling its citizens. (See: Boogeyworm.)

Time, and the world, moved on. The public's attention shifted toward outer space, and the exploits of superheroes with incredible powers. Cave and Eileen decided to hang up their gear and try for a "normal life" above ground.

Cave Carson

Cave Carson made amends with his former employer (now rebranded as EBX), returned the Mighty Mole, and began developing the next generation of tunneling technology.

Everything was working out, until Eileen got sick. Without their beloved wife and mother, Cave and Chloe now struggle to move forward. Cave spends his nights locked in his secret underground lab searching for purpose.

POWERS & WEAPONS

Possessing no true super-powers, Cave Carson is nonetheless a fair athlete and competent hand-to-hand combatant, with natural leadership ability.

*It is important to note that Cave has a cybernetic eye. Its origin, abilities, and circumstances surrounding its implantation are a complete mystery and should not be addressed in polite conversation.

PERSONAL DATA

Who's Who: Chloe Carson
Height: 5'7"
Weight: 125 lbs.
Eye Color: Blue
Hair Color: Strawberry blonde

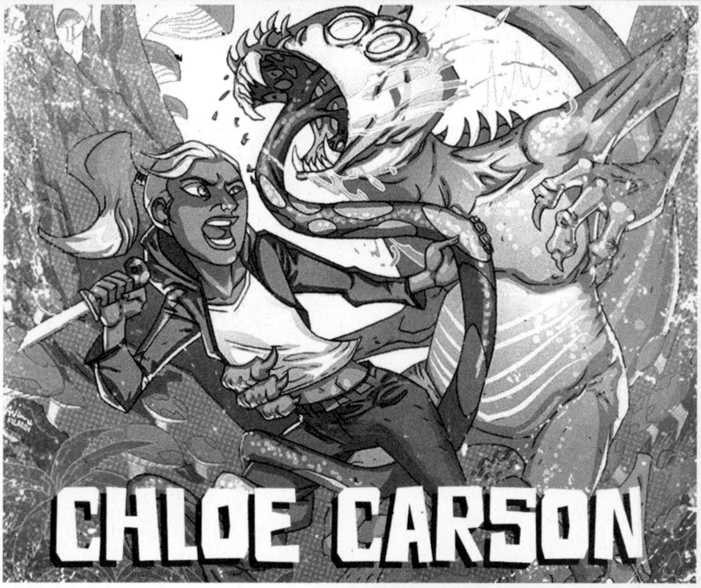
CHLOE CARSON

HISTORY

Chloe Carson is the teenage daughter of Cave and Eileen Carson, and she has lived a mostly normal life in the suburbs of the Quad Cities. She is currently a sophomore communications major with a minor in film at the University of Fawcett City.

Her birth marked the transition from the rather bohemian lifestyle enjoyed by Cave and Eileen (a.k.a. Mazra Tolten P'Thrall of the Clan Scoria, heir to the throne of Muldroog) in the years following the dissolution of Cave's original Mighty Mole Crew, and his status as an icon of the spelunking counterculture.*

Chloe's most notable contribution to the "family business" was her appearance in the now-infamous documentary *Into the Cave We Wander.* The partly staged film was mostly regarded as a desperate attempt to rebrand Cave as the leader and patriarch of an "adventuring family." Despite this, several more short films were created.

Due to her age, Chloe was only allowed on "softball missions" such as "The Secret of Rock Candy Mountain" and "Journey to the Penguin City." Her last adventure, "Night of the Boogieworm," was never released, due to a shocking scene of six-year-old Chloe being eaten by an abnormally large psychic worm.

Soon after, Chloe decided to leave "Team Carson," claiming that she wanted a normal life. Chloe's rejection encouraged Eileen to keep her own past a secret to her daughter, as well as ending Cave's dream of having his daughter someday carry on his work. Regrettably, it was also the moment that drove a wedge between father and daughter, one that would last until the death of Eileen.

* The spelunking counterculture was an artistic and ideological movement founded by Marc Bartow as a direct response to the general public's fascination with the space program at the time. Its most notable achievements are the seminal classic rock album *The Echo Anomaly* by Adam Starglider (co-produced by Cave Carson) and Carson's own controversial documentary, *Into the Cave We Wander*, which achieved cult status despite numerous legal troubles stemming from accusations of child endangerment.

POWERS & WEAPONS

Chloe still retains some of the combat and survival training she received as a young child. She has a rudimentary knowledge of "Kick Punching" (Eileen's made-up name for the real Muldroogan martial art Cret B'kar), as well as small-weapons training such as knives, axes, and pistols.

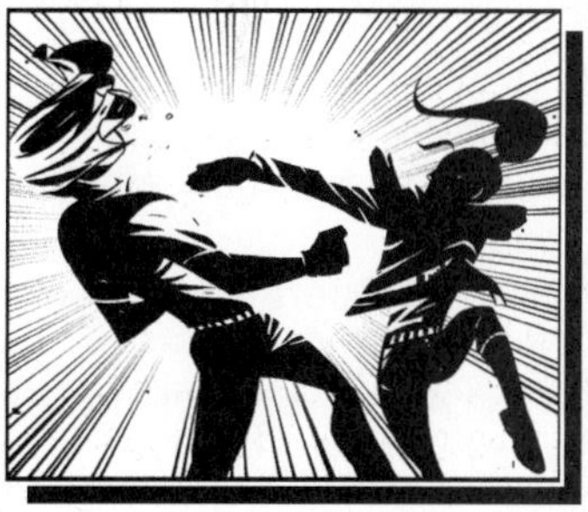

TEAM CARSON

DATA

Members: Cave Carson, Johnny Blake, Christine Madison, Bulldozer Smith, Lena the Lemur
Affiliation: Forgotten Heroes
Occupation: Professional spelunkers, miscellaneous
Mission: Uncovering the hidden secrets beneath the earth
Base of Operations: Inside the earth
First Appearance: BRAVE AND THE BOLD #31

HISTORY

The original Team Carson was put together after Cave Carson stole the Mighty Mole from his employer, E. Borsten & Sons, so that he could pursue his passion of uncovering underground discoveries, such as the remains of ancient cities and lost civilizations living underground. The team included ex-convict, strongman and tunneling expert Bulldozer Smith, renowned geologist Christine Madison, and devil-may-care adventurer and fellow spelunker Johnny Blake, as well as Bulldozer's pet lemur, Lena.

Dynamics in the group could be dfficult. Despite her engagement to Johnny, Cave vied for Christine's attention and affection, often at the expense of her fiancé. This tension, often hinging on Cave's ego and need for one-upmanship, could be seen as a reason for the team's minimized success and lack of renown, despite everyone's competence in skill and devotion to their mission. The group continued adventuring for many years, eventually being joined by Cave's wife, Mazra P'thrall, under her upper-world alias of Eileen Carson. The subject of the group's dissolution has remained a mystery, but some attribute it to the disappearance of Bulldozer Smith and Lena the Lemur, a subject, some would say, that was glossed over in Cave Carson's upcoming memoir, *The World on My Shoulders*.

DATA

Alias: Unknown at this time
Occupation: Malevolent deity
Purpose: Unknown
Current Location: Imprisoned in the God Stones of Muldroog

HISTORY

Little is known about the imprisoned deity known as The Whisperer. Locked away in a crystal prison, some believe it has been inside the earth since before the time of animal or man. Following a failed attempt at seducing followers to control an ancient subterranean civilization, the survivors swore an oath to trap the demon forever inside powerful crystals known as "God Stones." These guardians call themselves Muldroog, which translates to "Keepers of the Demon."

However, no prison is perfect. The Whisperer continues calling through the cracks and fissures in the earth hoping that someday someone will answer.

ABILITIES

The Whisperer is a powerful telepath, though the extent to which this power reaches is currently unknown. The Muldroog have found a way to deter its mind control, but there is no knowing what it could do to someone without proper training or immunity.

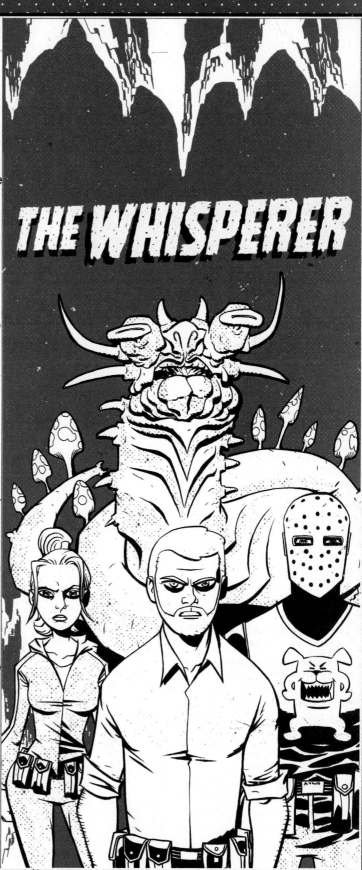

THE WHISPERER

CAVE PAINTINGS

CHARACTER DESIGNS BY MICHAEL AVON OEMING

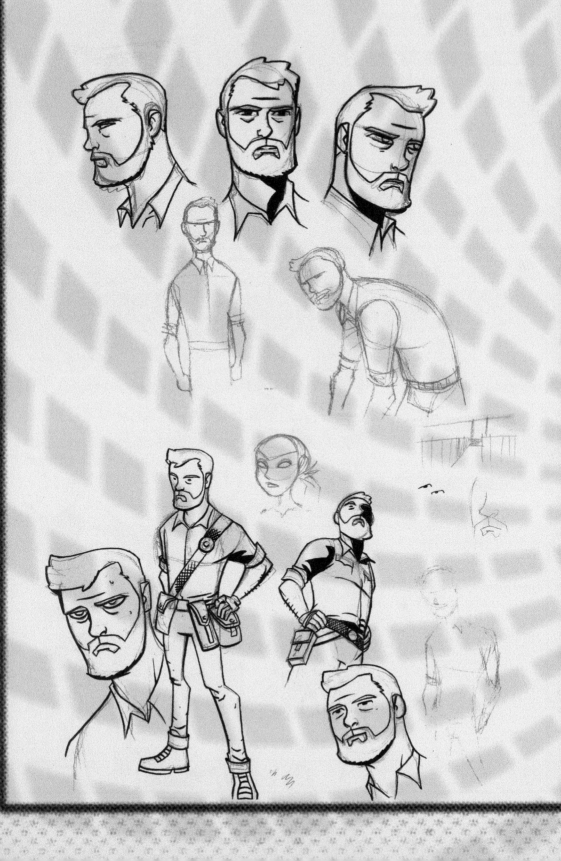

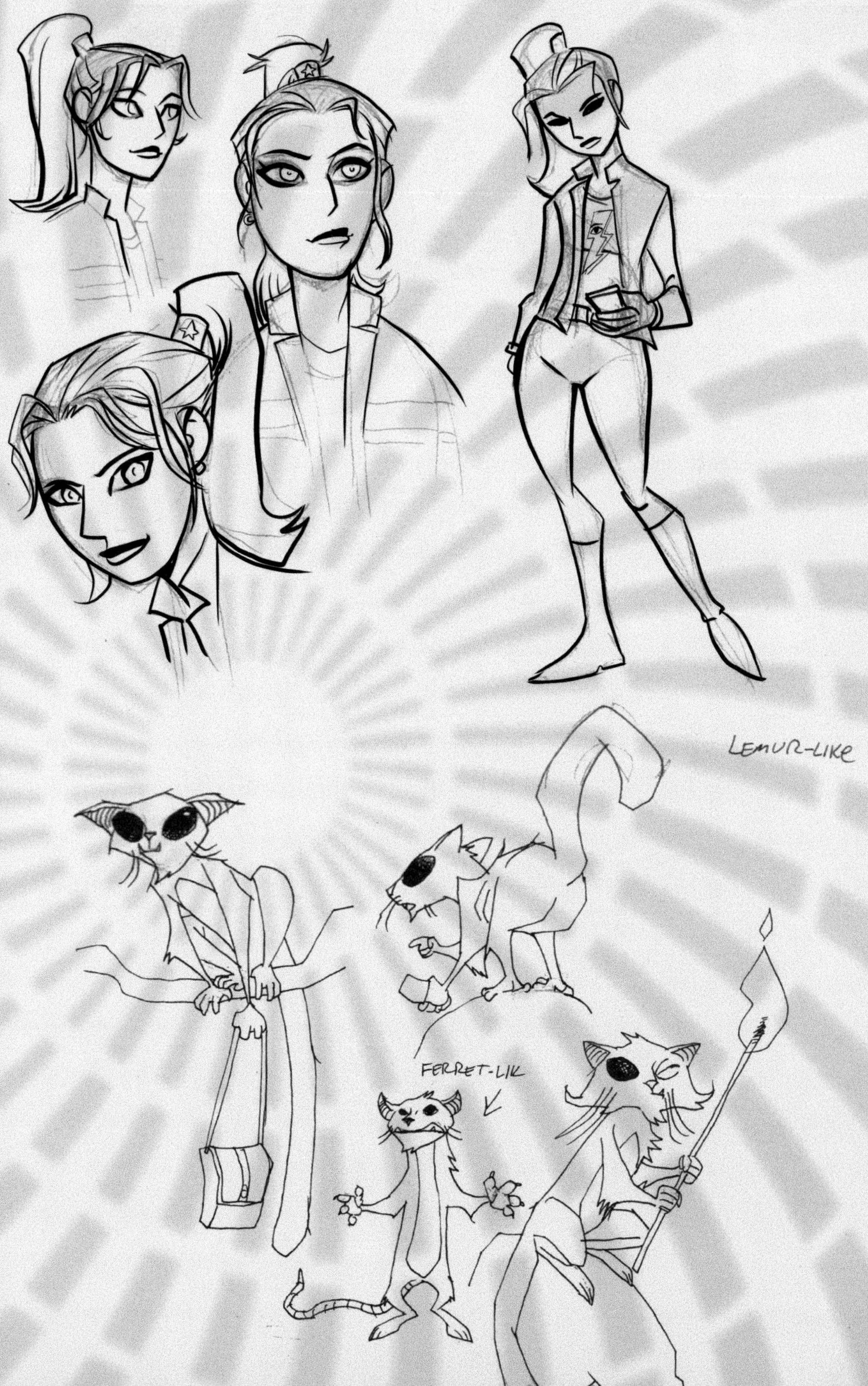
LEMUR-LIKE
FERRET-LIK

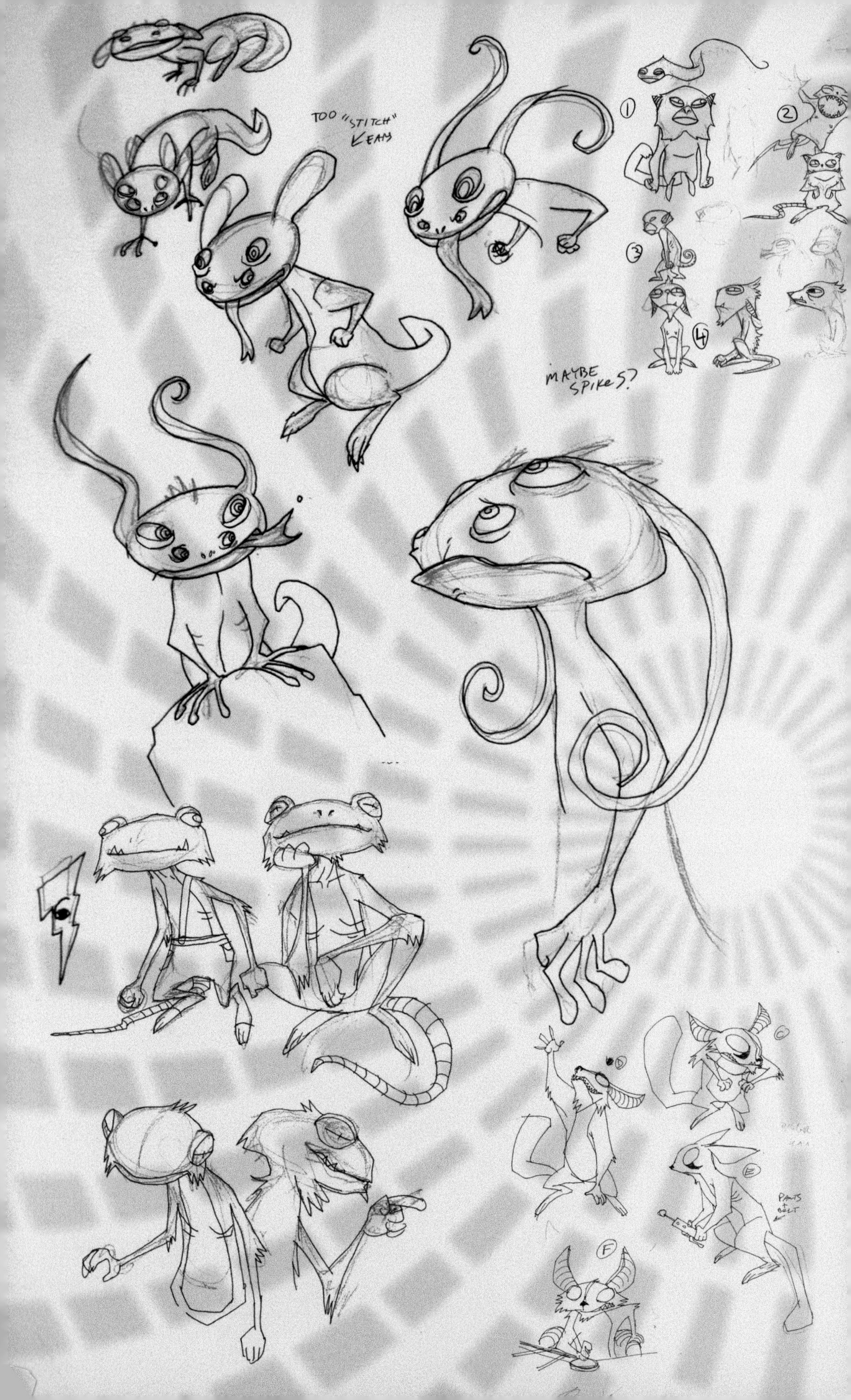

TOO "STITCH"
EARS
1
2
3
4
MAYBE SPIKES?
C
D
E
PANTS + BELT
F

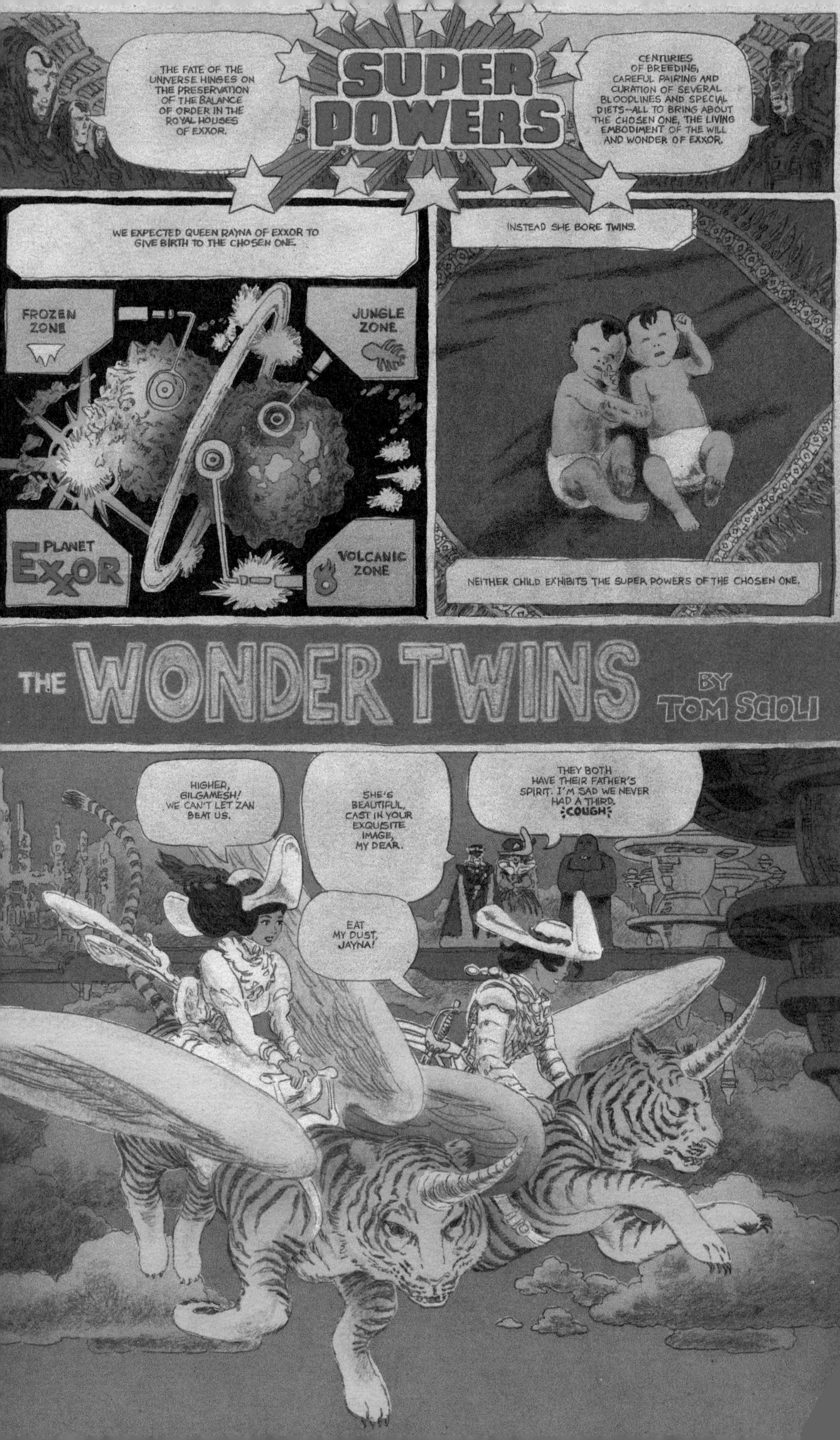

SUPER POWERS
THE FATE OF THE UNIVERSE HINGES ON THE PRESERVATION OF THE BALANCE OF ORDER IN THE ROYAL HOUSES OF EXXOR.
CENTURIES OF BREEDING, CAREFUL PAIRING AND CURATION OF SEVERAL BLOODLINES AND SPECIAL DIETS--ALL TO BRING ABOUT THE CHOSEN ONE, THE LIVING EMBODIMENT OF THE WILL AND WONDER OF EXXOR.
WE EXPECTED QUEEN RAYNA OF EXXOR TO GIVE BIRTH TO THE CHOSEN ONE.
FROZEN ZONE
JUNGLE ZONE
PLANET EXXOR
VOLCANIC ZONE
INSTEAD SHE BORE TWINS.
NEITHER CHILD EXHIBITS THE SUPER POWERS OF THE CHOSEN ONE.
THE WONDER TWINS
BY TOM SCIOLI
HIGHER, GILGAMESH! WE CAN'T LET ZAN BEAT US.
SHE'S BEAUTIFUL, CAST IN YOUR EXQUISITE IMAGE, MY DEAR.
THEY BOTH HAVE THEIR FATHER'S SPIRIT. I'M SAD WE NEVER HAD A THIRD. COUGH
EAT MY DUST, JAYNA!

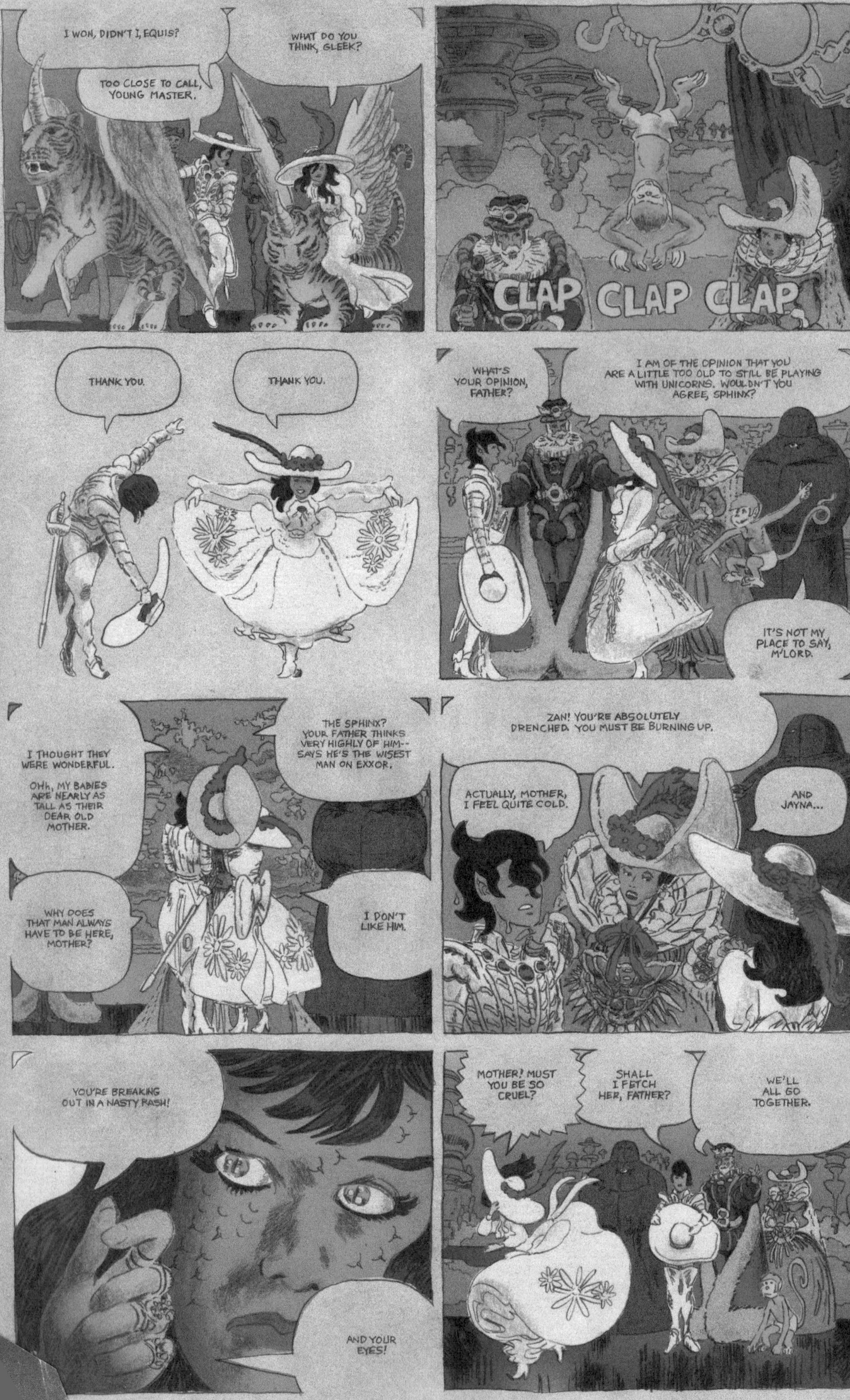
I WON, DIDN'T I, EQUIS?
TOO CLOSE TO CALL, YOUNG MASTER.
WHAT DO YOU THINK, GLEEK?
CLAP CLAP CLAP
THANK YOU.
THANK YOU.
WHAT'S YOUR OPINION, FATHER?
I AM OF THE OPINION THAT YOU ARE A LITTLE TOO OLD TO STILL BE PLAYING WITH UNICORNS. WOULDN'T YOU AGREE, SPHINX?
IT'S NOT MY PLACE TO SAY, M'LORD.
I THOUGHT THEY WERE WONDERFUL.
OHh, MY BABIES ARE NEARLY AS TALL AS THEIR DEAR OLD MOTHER.
THE SPHINX? YOUR FATHER THINKS VERY HIGHLY OF HIM-- SAYS HE'S THE WISEST MAN ON EXXOR.
WHY DOES THAT MAN ALWAYS HAVE TO BE HERE, MOTHER?
I DON'T LIKE HIM.
ZAN! YOU'RE ABSOLUTELY DRENCHED. YOU MUST BE BURNING UP.
ACTUALLY, MOTHER, I FEEL QUITE COLD.
AND JAYNA...
YOU'RE BREAKING OUT IN A NASTY RASH!
AND YOUR EYES!
MOTHER? MUST YOU BE SO CRUEL?
SHALL I FETCH HER, FATHER?
WE'LL ALL GO TOGETHER.

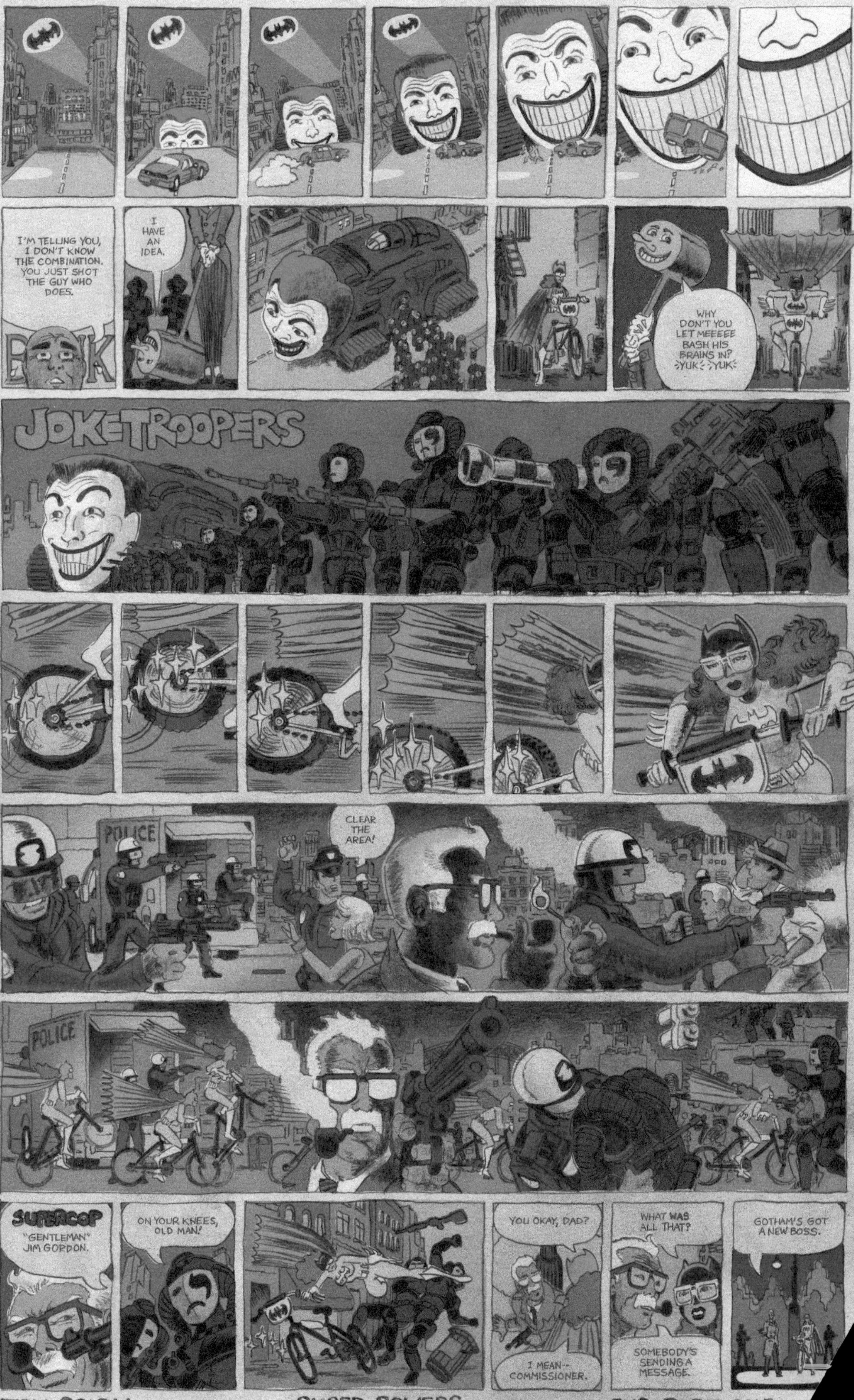
I'M TELLING YOU, I DON'T KNOW THE COMBINATION. YOU JUST SHOT THE GUY WHO DOES.
I HAVE AN IDEA.
WHY DON'T YOU LET MEEEEE BASH HIS BRAINS IN? YUK YUK
JOKETROOPERS
POLICE
CLEAR THE AREA!
POLICE
SUPERCOP "GENTLEMAN" JIM GORDON.
ON YOUR KNEES, OLD MAN!
YOU OKAY, DAD?
I MEAN-- COMMISSIONER.
WHAT WAS ALL THAT?
SOMEBODY'S SENDING A MESSAGE.
GOTHAM'S GOT A NEW BOSS.

TOM SCIOLI SUPER POWERS - END PART ONE -

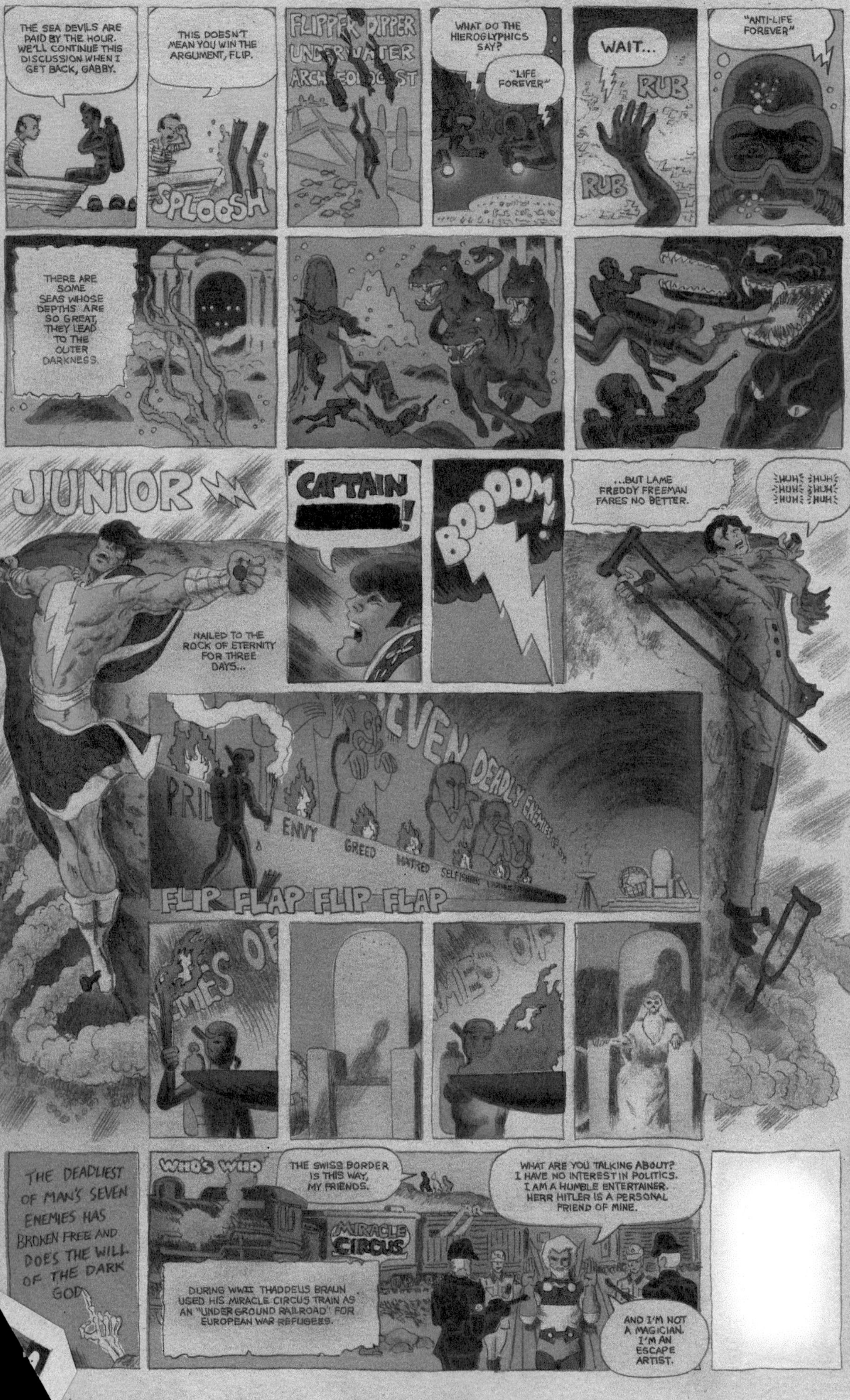

THE SEA DEVILS ARE PAID BY THE HOUR. WE'LL CONTINUE THIS DISCUSSION WHEN I GET BACK, GABBY.
THIS DOESN'T MEAN YOU WIN THE ARGUMENT, FLIP.
SPLOOSH
WHAT DO THE HIEROGLYPHICS SAY?
"LIFE FOREVER"
WAIT...
RUB
RUB
"ANTI-LIFE FOREVER"
THERE ARE SOME SEAS WHOSE DEPTHS ARE SO GREAT, THEY LEAD TO THE OUTER DARKNESS.
JUNIOR
CAPTAIN [redacted]!
BOOOOM!
...BUT LAME FREDDY FREEMAN FARES NO BETTER.
HUH HUH HUH HUH HUH HUH
NAILED TO THE ROCK OF ETERNITY FOR THREE DAYS...
ENVY
GREED
HATRED
FLIP FLAP FLIP FLAP
THE DEADLIEST OF MAN'S SEVEN ENEMIES HAS BROKEN FREE AND DOES THE WILL OF THE DARK GOD
WHO'S WHO
THE SWISS BORDER IS THIS WAY, MY FRIENDS.
WHAT ARE YOU TALKING ABOUT? I HAVE NO INTEREST IN POLITICS. I AM A HUMBLE ENTERTAINER. HERR HITLER IS A PERSONAL FRIEND OF MINE.
MIRACLE CIRCUS
DURING WWII THADDEUS BRAUN USED HIS MIRACLE CIRCUS TRAIN AS AN "UNDERGROUND RAILROAD" FOR EUROPEAN WAR REFUGEES.
AND I'M NOT A MAGICIAN. I'M AN ESCAPE ARTIST.

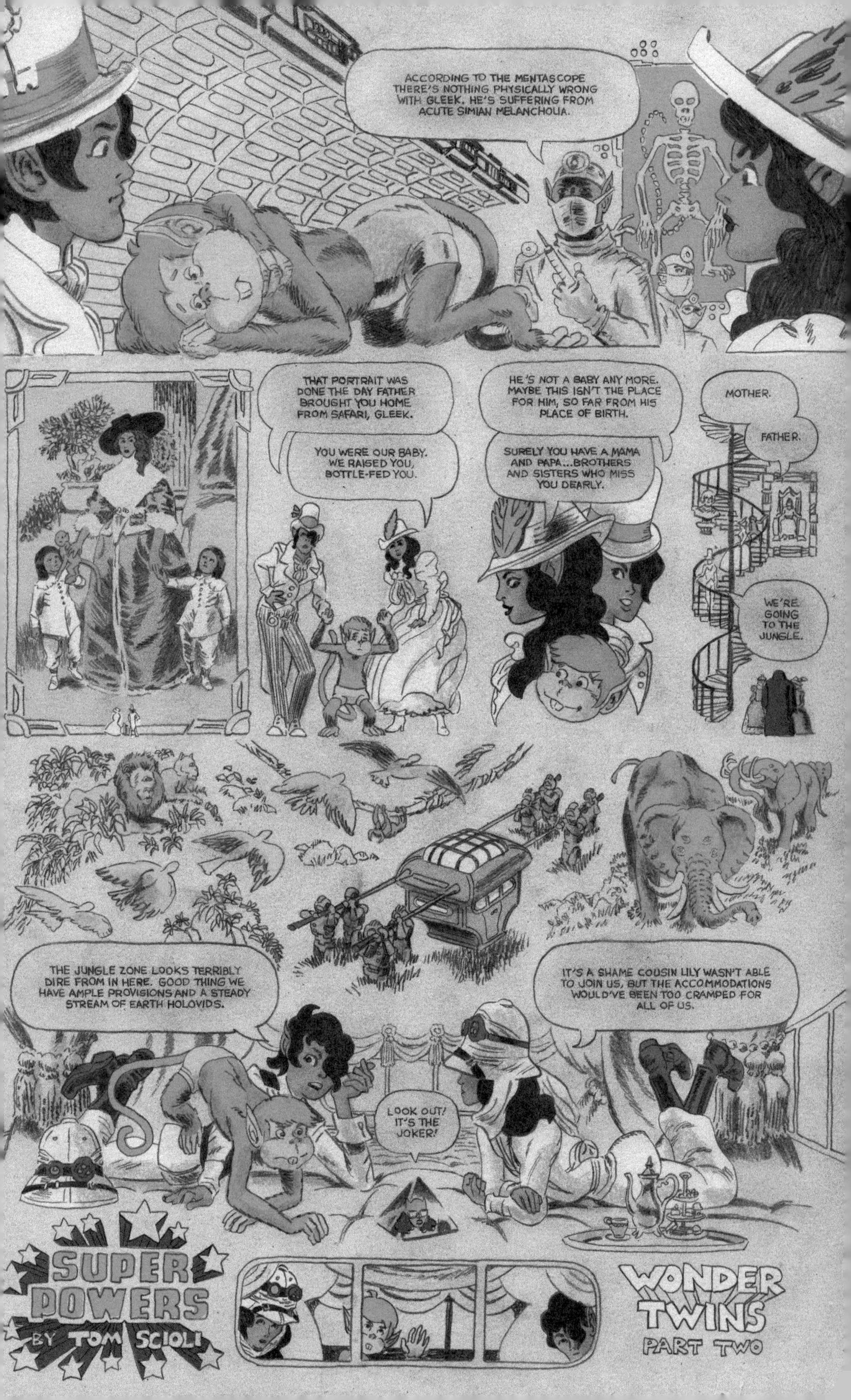
ACCORDING TO THE MENTASCOPE THERE'S NOTHING PHYSICALLY WRONG WITH GLEEK. HE'S SUFFERING FROM ACUTE SIMIAN MELANCHOLIA.
THAT PORTRAIT WAS DONE THE DAY FATHER BROUGHT YOU HOME FROM SAFARI, GLEEK.
YOU WERE OUR BABY. WE RAISED YOU, BOTTLE-FED YOU.
HE'S NOT A BABY ANY MORE. MAYBE THIS ISN'T THE PLACE FOR HIM, SO FAR FROM HIS PLACE OF BIRTH.
SURELY YOU HAVE A MAMA AND PAPA... BROTHERS AND SISTERS WHO MISS YOU DEARLY.
MOTHER.
FATHER.
WE'RE GOING TO THE JUNGLE.
THE JUNGLE ZONE LOOKS TERRIBLY DIRE FROM IN HERE. GOOD THING WE HAVE AMPLE PROVISIONS AND A STEADY STREAM OF EARTH HOLOVIDS.
LOOK OUT! IT'S THE JOKER!
IT'S A SHAME COUSIN LILY WASN'T ABLE TO JOIN US, BUT THE ACCOMMODATIONS WOULD'VE BEEN TOO CRAMPED FOR ALL OF US.
SUPER POWERS
BY TOM SCIOLI
WONDER TWINS
PART TWO

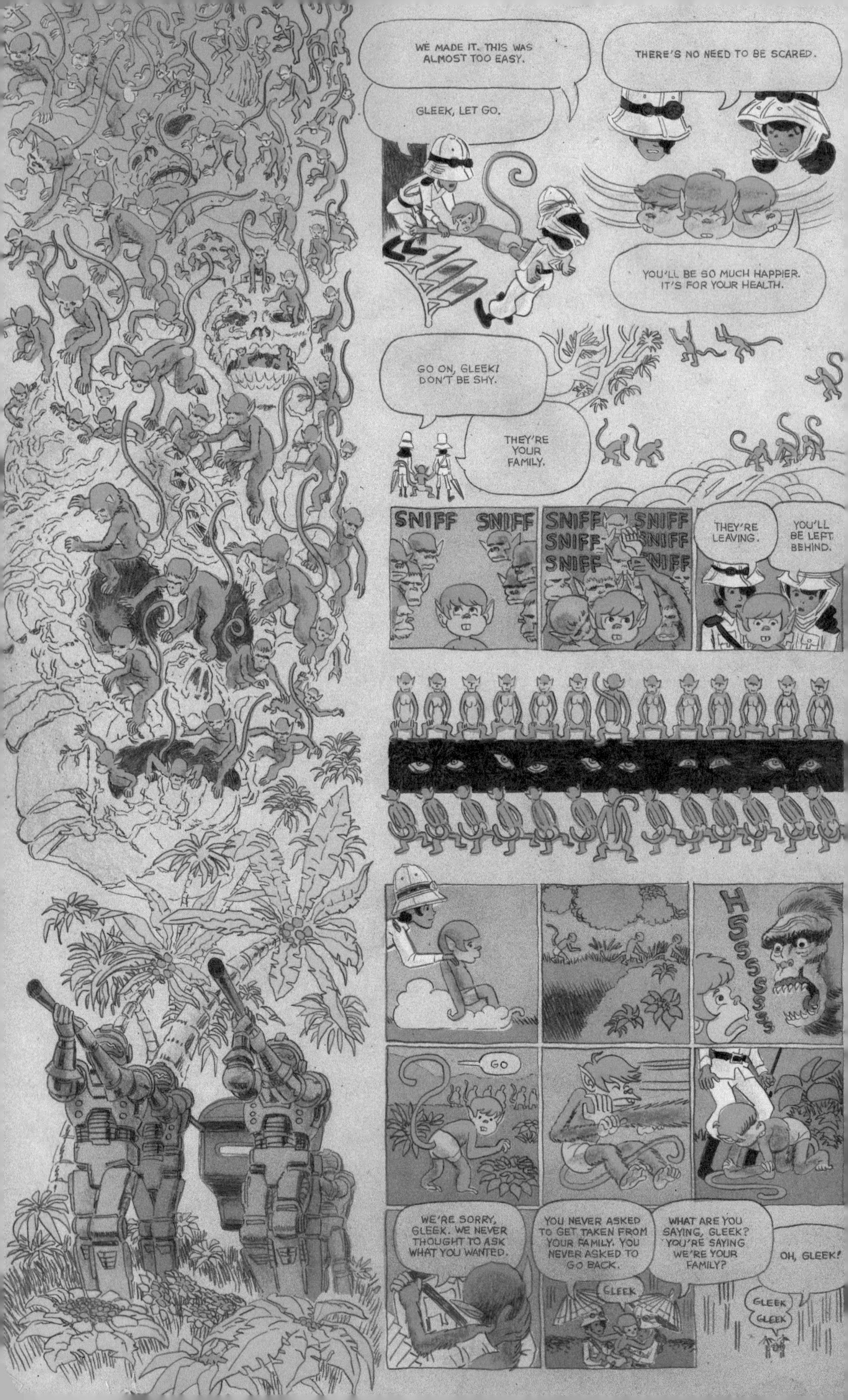
WE MADE IT. THIS WAS ALMOST TOO EASY.
GLEEK, LET GO.
THERE'S NO NEED TO BE SCARED.
YOU'LL BE SO MUCH HAPPIER. IT'S FOR YOUR HEALTH.
GO ON, GLEEK! DON'T BE SHY.
THEY'RE YOUR FAMILY.
SNIFF SNIFF
SNIFF SNIFF SNIFF SNIFF SNIFF SNIFF
THEY'RE LEAVING.
YOU'LL BE LEFT BEHIND.
HSSSSSSS
GO
WE'RE SORRY, GLEEK. WE NEVER THOUGHT TO ASK WHAT YOU WANTED.
YOU NEVER ASKED TO GET TAKEN FROM YOUR FAMILY. YOU NEVER ASKED TO GO BACK.
GLEEK
WHAT ARE YOU SAYING, GLEEK? YOU'RE SAYING WE'RE YOUR FAMILY?
OH, GLEEK!
GLEEK GLEEK

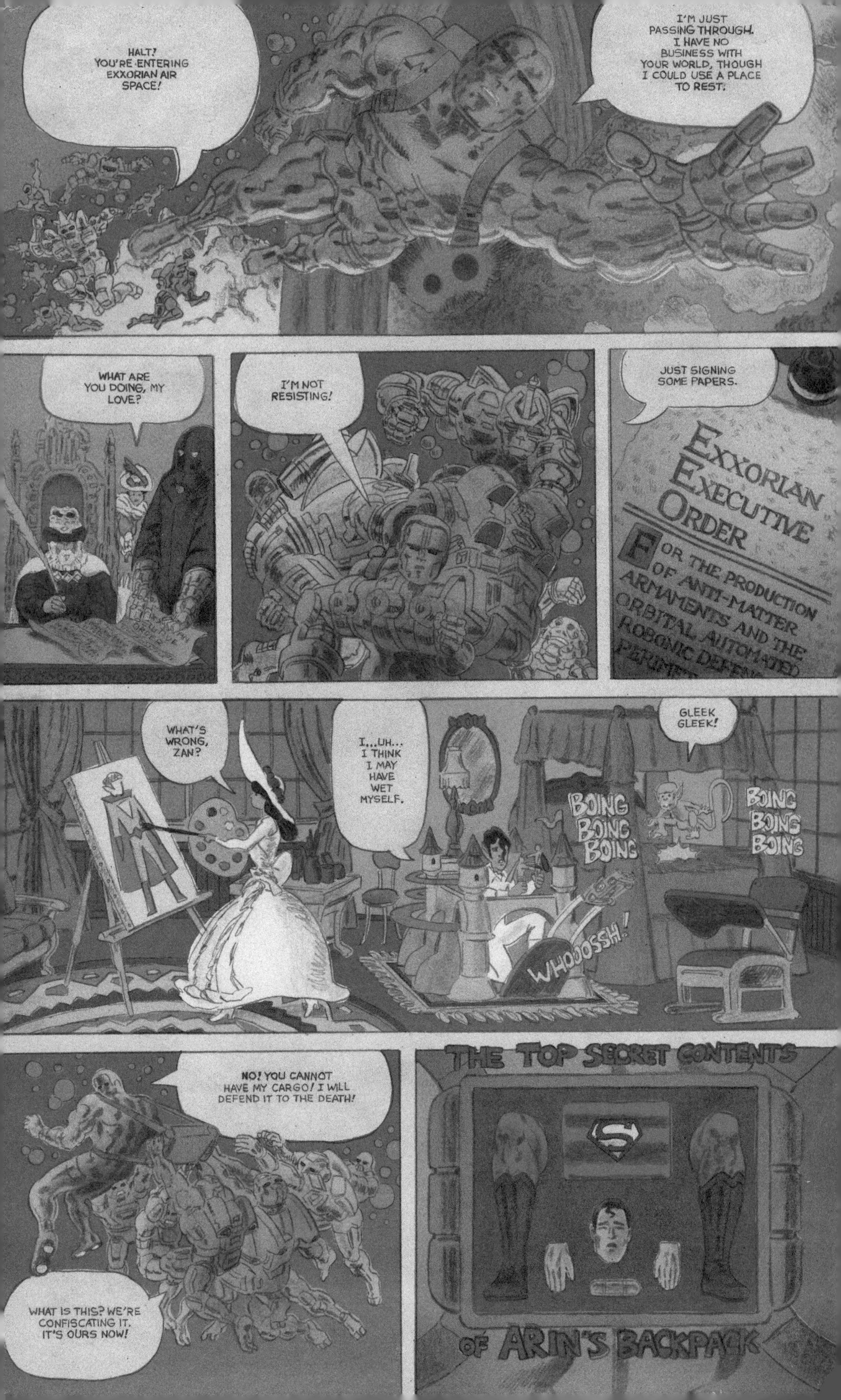
HALT? YOU'RE ENTERING EXXORIAN AIR SPACE!
I'M JUST PASSING THROUGH. I HAVE NO BUSINESS WITH YOUR WORLD, THOUGH I COULD USE A PLACE TO REST.
WHAT ARE YOU DOING, MY LOVE?
I'M NOT RESISTING!
JUST SIGNING SOME PAPERS.
EXXORIAN EXECUTIVE ORDER
FOR THE PRODUCTION OF ANTI-MATTER ARMAMENTS AND THE ORBITAL AUTOMATED ROBONIC DEFENS
WHAT'S WRONG, ZAN?
I...UH... I THINK I MAY HAVE WET MYSELF.
GLEEK GLEEK!
BOING BOING BOING
BOING BOING BOING
WHOOOSSH!
NO! YOU CANNOT HAVE MY CARGO! I WILL DEFEND IT TO THE DEATH!
WHAT IS THIS? WE'RE CONFISCATING IT. IT'S OURS NOW!
THE TOP SECRET CONTENTS
OF ARIN'S BACKPACK

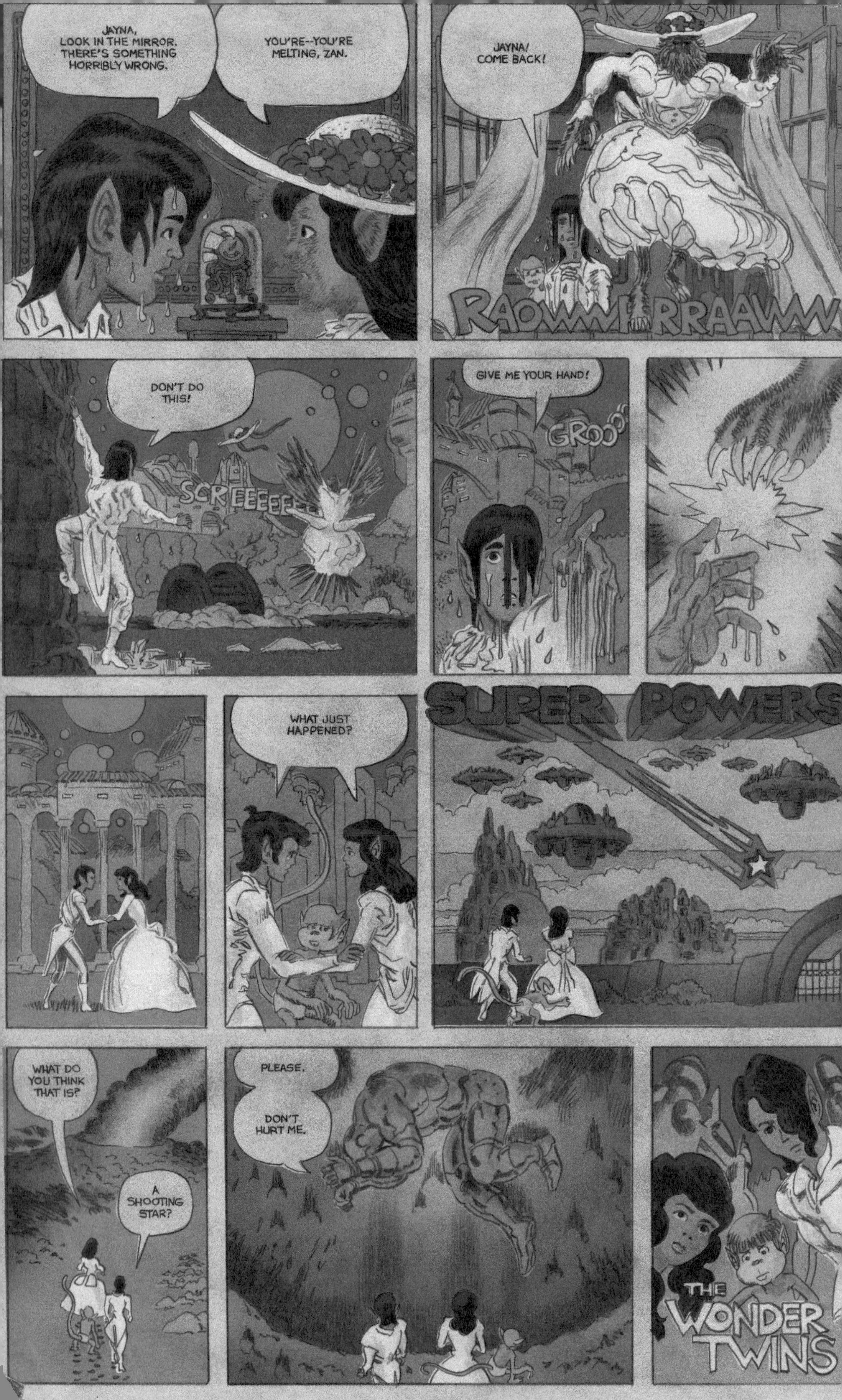

JAYNA, LOOK IN THE MIRROR. THERE'S SOMETHING HORRIBLY WRONG.
YOU'RE--YOU'RE MELTING, ZAN.
JAYNA! COME BACK!
RAOWWW RRAAWW
DON'T DO THIS!
SCREEEEEE
GIVE ME YOUR HAND!
GROOO
WHAT JUST HAPPENED?
SUPER POWERS
WHAT DO YOU THINK THAT IS?
A SHOOTING STAR?
PLEASE.
DON'T HURT ME.
THE WONDER TWINS

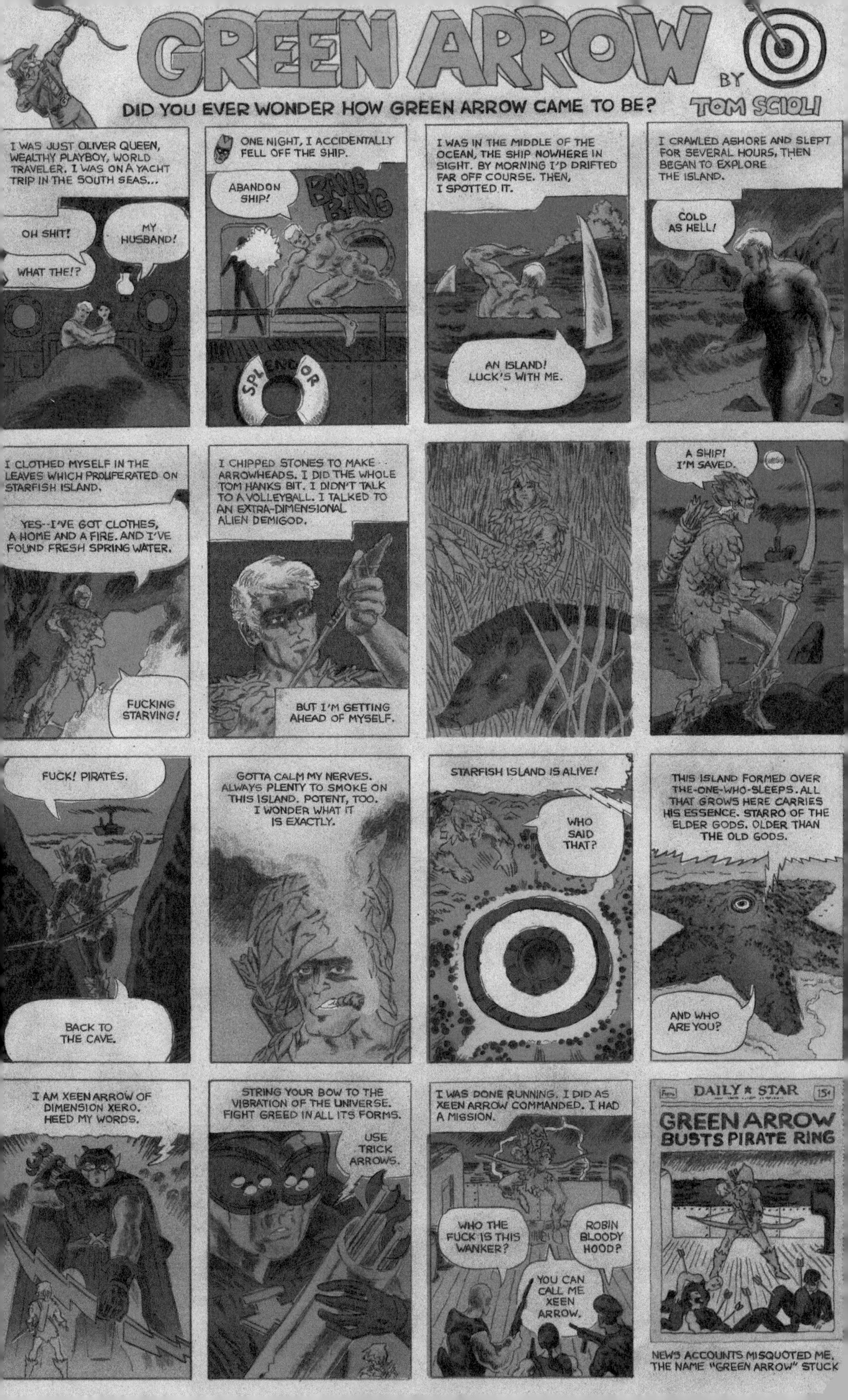
GREEN ARROW
BY
TOM SCIOLI
DID YOU EVER WONDER HOW GREEN ARROW CAME TO BE?
I WAS JUST OLIVER QUEEN, WEALTHY PLAYBOY, WORLD TRAVELER. I WAS ON A YACHT TRIP IN THE SOUTH SEAS...
OH SHIT!
MY HUSBAND!
WHAT THE!?
ONE NIGHT, I ACCIDENTALLY FELL OFF THE SHIP.
ABANDON SHIP!
BANG BANG
SPLENDOR
I WAS IN THE MIDDLE OF THE OCEAN, THE SHIP NOWHERE IN SIGHT. BY MORNING I'D DRIFTED FAR OFF COURSE. THEN, I SPOTTED IT.
AN ISLAND! LUCK'S WITH ME.
I CRAWLED ASHORE AND SLEPT FOR SEVERAL HOURS, THEN BEGAN TO EXPLORE THE ISLAND.
COLD AS HELL!
I CLOTHED MYSELF IN THE LEAVES WHICH PROLIFERATED ON STARFISH ISLAND.
YES--I'VE GOT CLOTHES, A HOME AND A FIRE. AND I'VE FOUND FRESH SPRING WATER.
FUCKING STARVING!
I CHIPPED STONES TO MAKE ARROWHEADS. I DID THE WHOLE TOM HANKS BIT. I DIDN'T TALK TO A VOLLEYBALL. I TALKED TO AN EXTRA-DIMENSIONAL ALIEN DEMIGOD.
BUT I'M GETTING AHEAD OF MYSELF.
A SHIP! I'M SAVED.
FUCK! PIRATES.
BACK TO THE CAVE.
GOTTA CALM MY NERVES. ALWAYS PLENTY TO SMOKE ON THIS ISLAND. POTENT, TOO. I WONDER WHAT IT IS EXACTLY.
STARFISH ISLAND IS ALIVE!
WHO SAID THAT?
THIS ISLAND FORMED OVER THE-ONE-WHO-SLEEPS. ALL THAT GROWS HERE CARRIES HIS ESSENCE. STARRO OF THE ELDER GODS. OLDER THAN THE OLD GODS.
AND WHO ARE YOU?
I AM XEEN ARROW OF DIMENSION XERO. HEED MY WORDS.
STRING YOUR BOW TO THE VIBRATION OF THE UNIVERSE. FIGHT GREED IN ALL ITS FORMS.
USE TRICK ARROWS.
I WAS DONE RUNNING. I DID AS XEEN ARROW COMMANDED. I HAD A MISSION.
WHO THE FUCK IS THIS WANKER?
ROBIN BLOODY HOOD?
YOU CAN CALL ME XEEN ARROW.
DAILY ★ STAR
15¢
GREEN ARROW BUSTS PIRATE RING
NEWS ACCOUNTS MISQUOTED ME. THE NAME "GREEN ARROW" STUCK

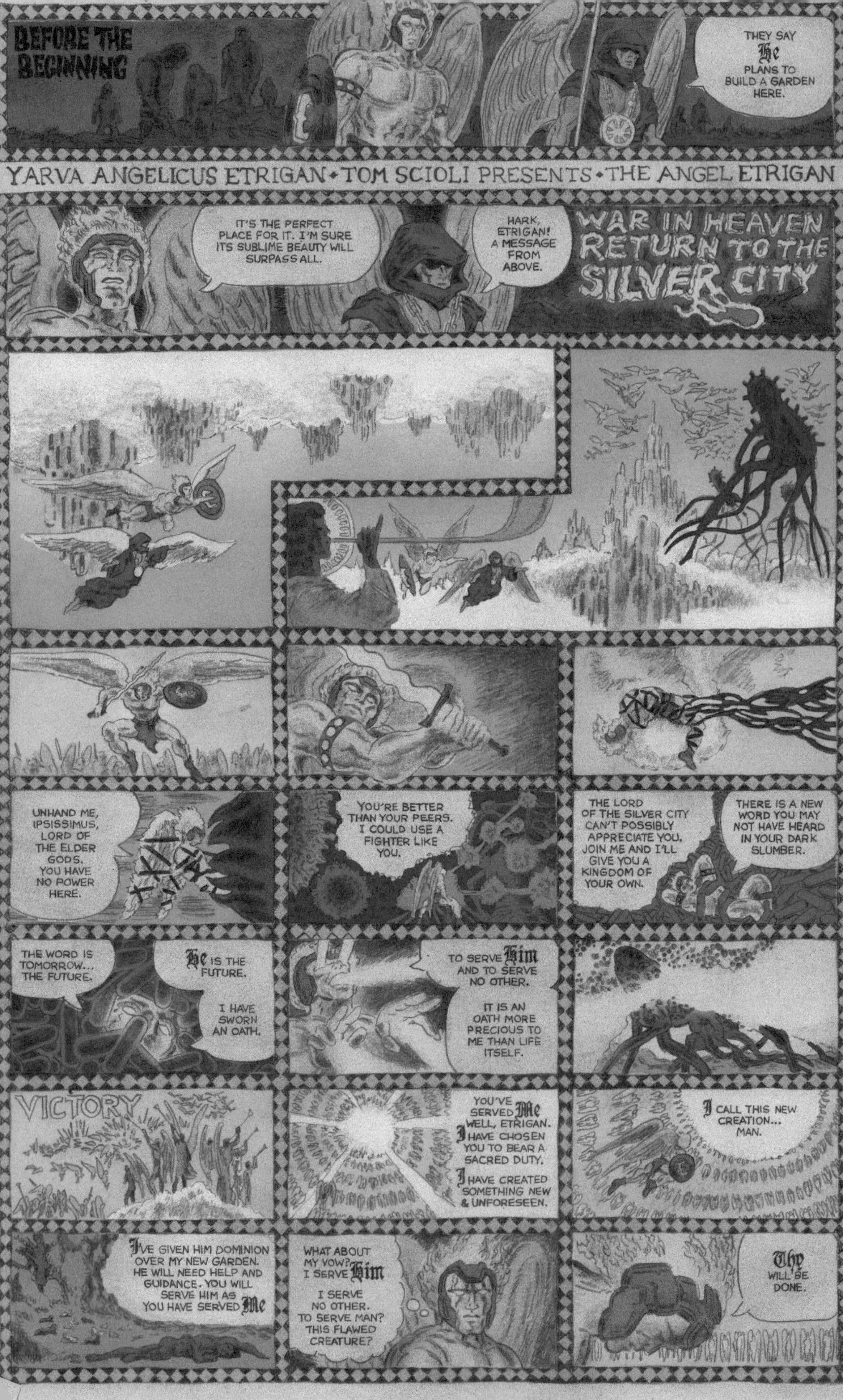

BEFORE THE BEGINNING
THEY SAY He PLANS TO BUILD A GARDEN HERE.
YARVA ANGELICUS ETRIGAN • TOM SCIOLI PRESENTS • THE ANGEL ETRIGAN
IT'S THE PERFECT PLACE FOR IT. I'M SURE ITS SUBLIME BEAUTY WILL SURPASS ALL.
HARK, ETRIGAN! A MESSAGE FROM ABOVE.
WAR IN HEAVEN RETURN TO THE SILVER CITY
UNHAND ME, IPSISSIMUS, LORD OF THE ELDER GODS. YOU HAVE NO POWER HERE.
YOU'RE BETTER THAN YOUR PEERS. I COULD USE A FIGHTER LIKE YOU.
THE LORD OF THE SILVER CITY CAN'T POSSIBLY APPRECIATE YOU. JOIN ME AND I'LL GIVE YOU A KINGDOM OF YOUR OWN.
THERE IS A NEW WORD YOU MAY NOT HAVE HEARD IN YOUR DARK SLUMBER.
THE WORD IS TOMORROW... THE FUTURE.
He IS THE FUTURE.
I HAVE SWORN AN OATH.
TO SERVE Him AND TO SERVE NO OTHER.
IT IS AN OATH MORE PRECIOUS TO ME THAN LIFE ITSELF.
VICTORY
YOU'VE SERVED Me WELL, ETRIGAN. I HAVE CHOSEN YOU TO BEAR A SACRED DUTY.
I HAVE CREATED SOMETHING NEW & UNFORESEEN.
I CALL THIS NEW CREATION... MAN.
I'VE GIVEN HIM DOMINION OVER MY NEW GARDEN. HE WILL NEED HELP AND GUIDANCE. YOU WILL SERVE HIM AS YOU HAVE SERVED Me
WHAT ABOUT MY VOW? I SERVE Him
I SERVE NO OTHER. TO SERVE MAN? THIS FLAWED CREATURE?
Thy WILL BE DONE.

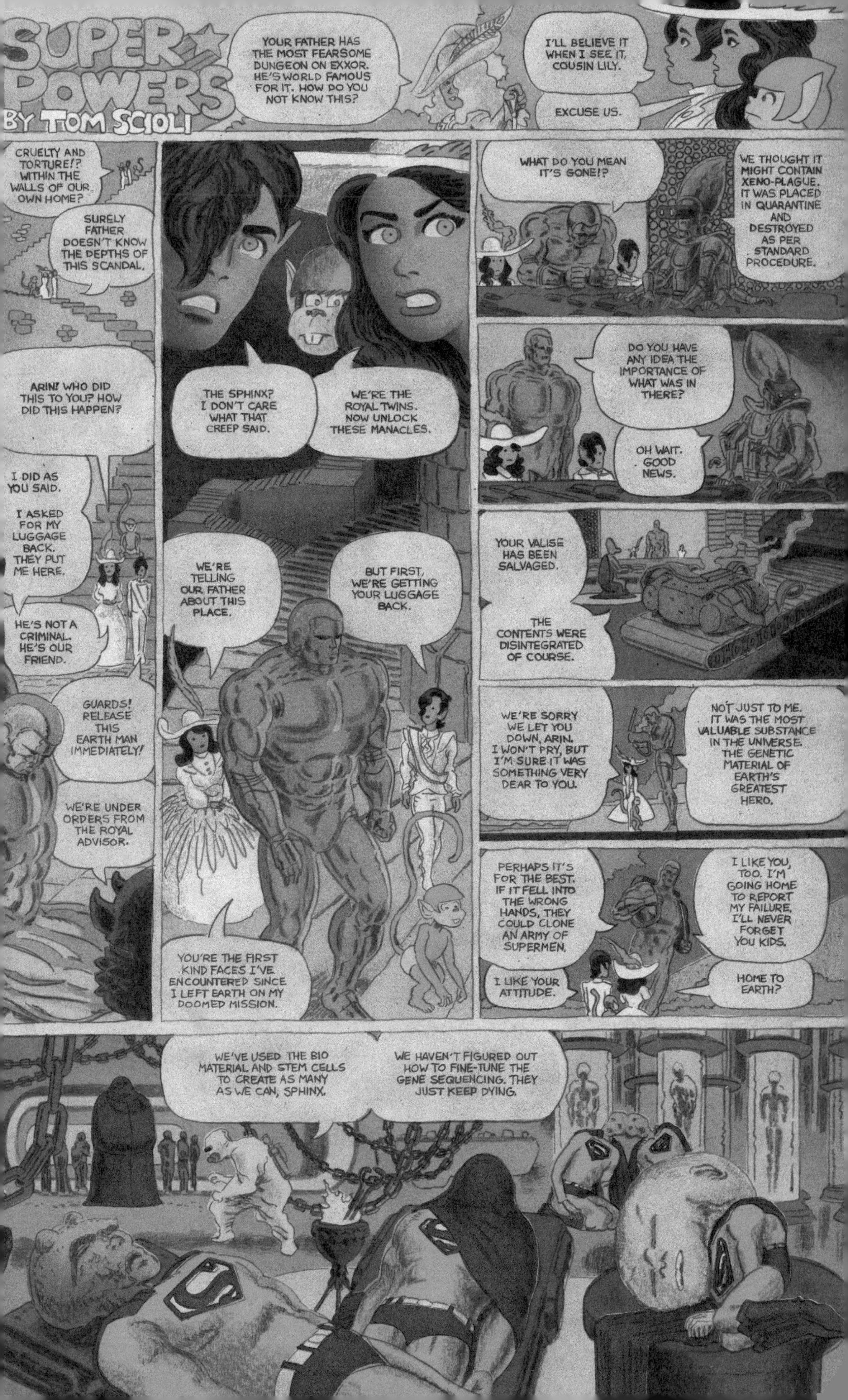
SUPER★POWERS
BY TOM SCIOLI
YOUR FATHER HAS THE MOST FEARSOME DUNGEON ON EXXOR. HE'S WORLD FAMOUS FOR IT. HOW DO YOU NOT KNOW THIS?
I'LL BELIEVE IT WHEN I SEE IT, COUSIN LILY.
EXCUSE US.
CRUELTY AND TORTURE!? WITHIN THE WALLS OF OUR OWN HOME?
SURELY FATHER DOESN'T KNOW THE DEPTHS OF THIS SCANDAL.
ARIN! WHO DID THIS TO YOU? HOW DID THIS HAPPEN?
I DID AS YOU SAID.
I ASKED FOR MY LUGGAGE BACK. THEY PUT ME HERE.
HE'S NOT A CRIMINAL. HE'S OUR FRIEND.
GUARDS! RELEASE THIS EARTH MAN IMMEDIATELY!
WE'RE UNDER ORDERS FROM THE ROYAL ADVISOR.
THE SPHINX? I DON'T CARE WHAT THAT CREEP SAID.
WE'RE THE ROYAL TWINS. NOW UNLOCK THESE MANACLES.
WE'RE TELLING OUR FATHER ABOUT THIS PLACE.
BUT FIRST, WE'RE GETTING YOUR LUGGAGE BACK.
YOU'RE THE FIRST KIND FACES I'VE ENCOUNTERED SINCE I LEFT EARTH ON MY DOOMED MISSION.
WHAT DO YOU MEAN IT'S GONE!?
WE THOUGHT IT MIGHT CONTAIN XENO-PLAGUE. IT WAS PLACED IN QUARANTINE AND DESTROYED AS PER STANDARD PROCEDURE.
DO YOU HAVE ANY IDEA THE IMPORTANCE OF WHAT WAS IN THERE?
OH WAIT. GOOD NEWS.
YOUR VALISE HAS BEEN SALVAGED.
THE CONTENTS WERE DISINTEGRATED OF COURSE.
WE'RE SORRY WE LET YOU DOWN, ARIN. I WON'T PRY, BUT I'M SURE IT WAS SOMETHING VERY DEAR TO YOU.
NOT JUST TO ME. IT WAS THE MOST VALUABLE SUBSTANCE IN THE UNIVERSE. THE GENETIC MATERIAL OF EARTH'S GREATEST HERO.
PERHAPS IT'S FOR THE BEST. IF IT FELL INTO THE WRONG HANDS, THEY COULD CLONE AN ARMY OF SUPERMEN.
I LIKE YOUR ATTITUDE.
I LIKE YOU, TOO. I'M GOING HOME TO REPORT MY FAILURE. I'LL NEVER FORGET YOU KIDS.
HOME TO EARTH?
WE'VE USED THE BIO MATERIAL AND STEM CELLS TO CREATE AS MANY AS WE CAN, SPHINX.
WE HAVEN'T FIGURED OUT HOW TO FINE-TUNE THE GENE SEQUENCING. THEY JUST KEEP DYING.

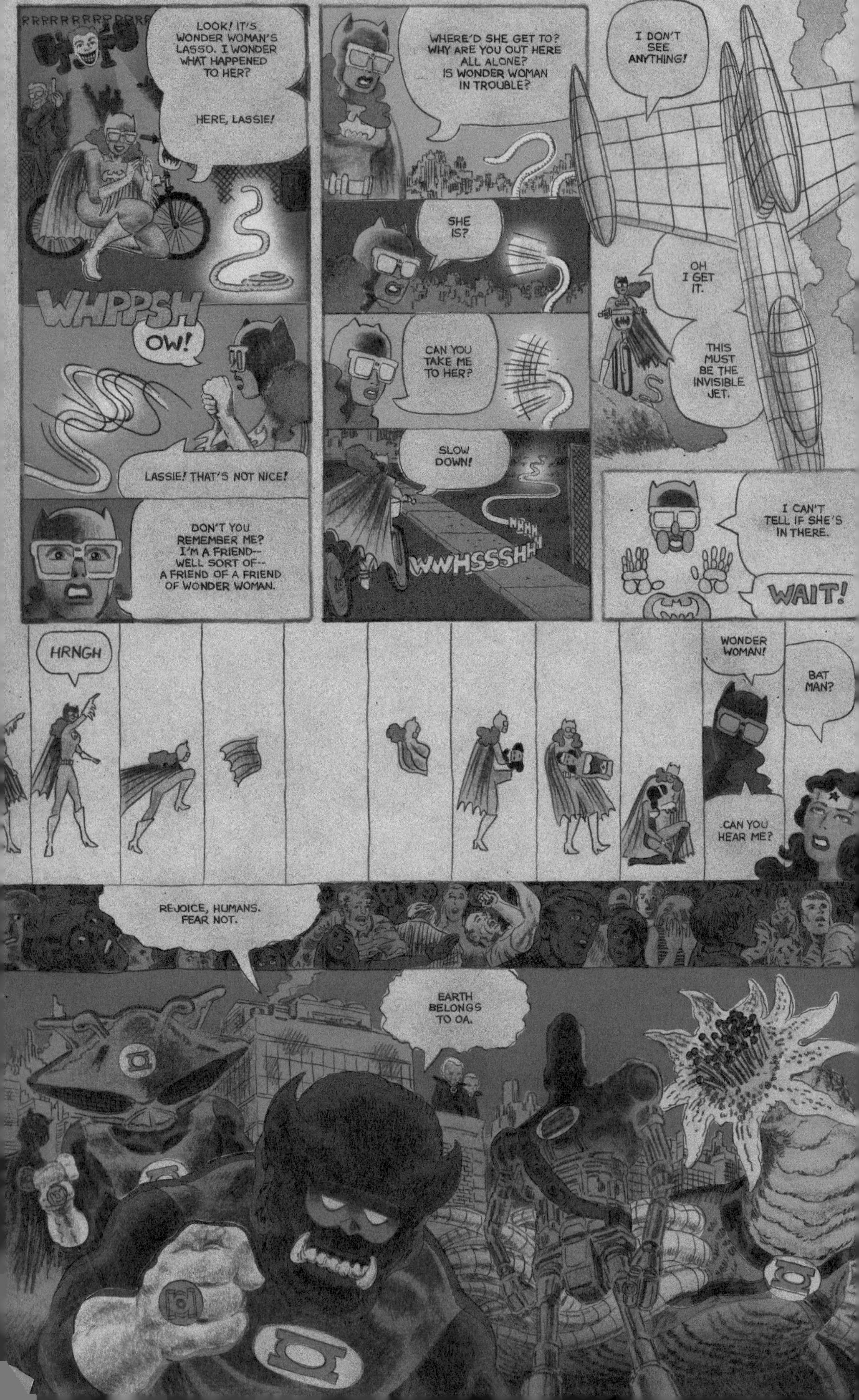
RRRRRRRRRRRRR
LOOK! IT'S WONDER WOMAN'S LASSO. I WONDER WHAT HAPPENED TO HER?
HERE, LASSIE!
WHPPSH
OW!
LASSIE! THAT'S NOT NICE!
DON'T YOU REMEMBER ME? I'M A FRIEND-- WELL SORT OF-- A FRIEND OF A FRIEND OF WONDER WOMAN.
WHERE'D SHE GET TO? WHY ARE YOU OUT HERE ALL ALONE? IS WONDER WOMAN IN TROUBLE?
SHE IS?
CAN YOU TAKE ME TO HER?
SLOW DOWN!
WWHSSSHHH
I DON'T SEE ANYTHING!
OH I GET IT.
THIS MUST BE THE INVISIBLE JET.
I CAN'T TELL IF SHE'S IN THERE.
WAIT!
HRNGH
WONDER WOMAN!
BAT MAN?
CAN YOU HEAR ME?
REJOICE, HUMANS. FEAR NOT.
EARTH BELONGS TO OA.

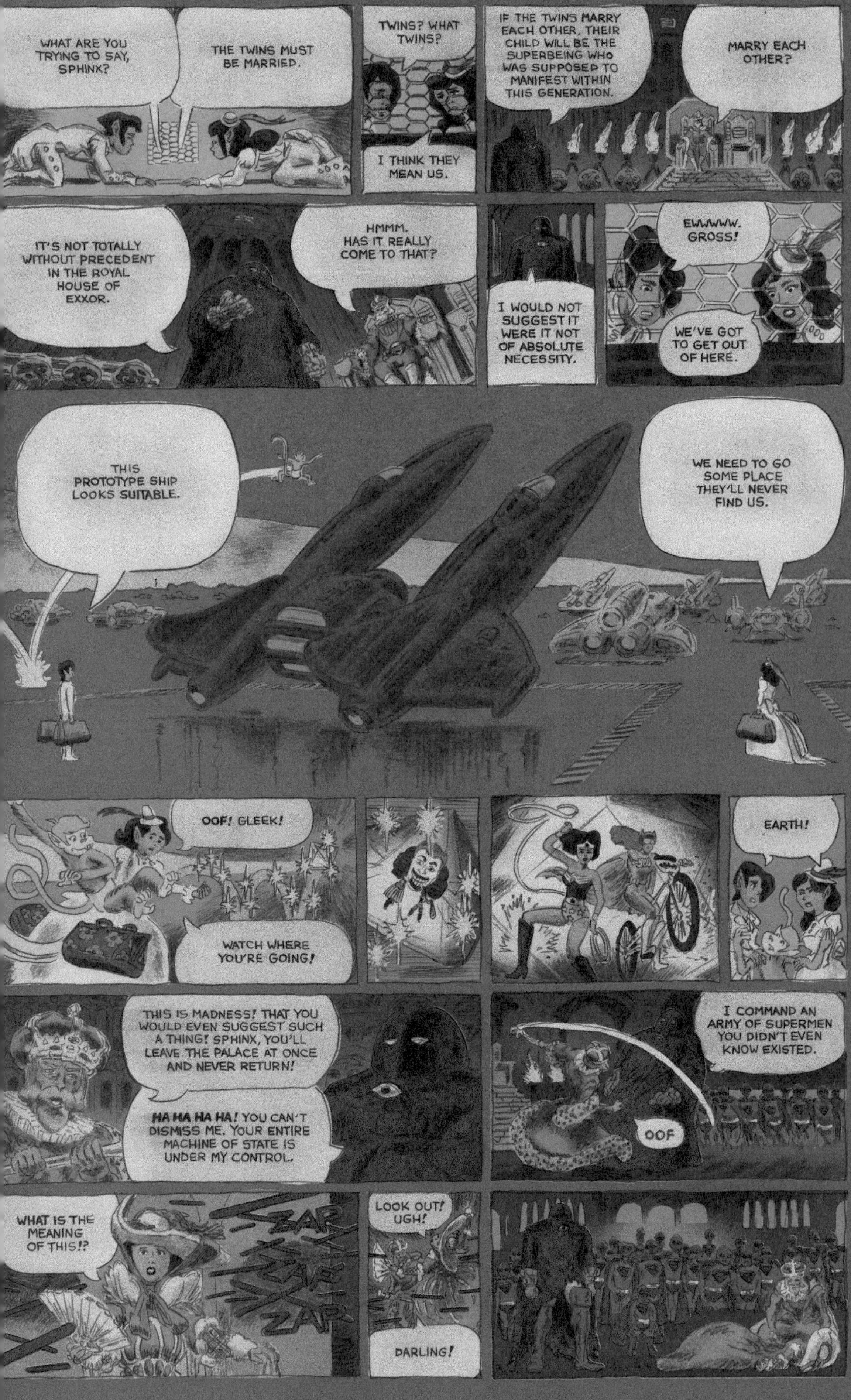

WHAT ARE YOU TRYING TO SAY, SPHINX?
THE TWINS MUST BE MARRIED.
TWINS? WHAT TWINS?
I THINK THEY MEAN US.
IF THE TWINS MARRY EACH OTHER, THEIR CHILD WILL BE THE SUPERBEING WHO WAS SUPPOSED TO MANIFEST WITHIN THIS GENERATION.
MARRY EACH OTHER?
IT'S NOT TOTALLY WITHOUT PRECEDENT IN THE ROYAL HOUSE OF EXXOR.
HMMM. HAS IT REALLY COME TO THAT?
I WOULD NOT SUGGEST IT WERE IT NOT OF ABSOLUTE NECESSITY.
EWWWWW. GROSS!
WE'VE GOT TO GET OUT OF HERE.
THIS PROTOTYPE SHIP LOOKS SUITABLE.
WE NEED TO GO SOME PLACE THEY'LL NEVER FIND US.
OOF! GLEEK!
WATCH WHERE YOU'RE GOING!
EARTH!
THIS IS MADNESS! THAT YOU WOULD EVEN SUGGEST SUCH A THING! SPHINX, YOU'LL LEAVE THE PALACE AT ONCE AND NEVER RETURN!
HA HA HA HA! YOU CAN'T DISMISS ME. YOUR ENTIRE MACHINE OF STATE IS UNDER MY CONTROL.
I COMMAND AN ARMY OF SUPERMEN YOU DIDN'T EVEN KNOW EXISTED.
OOF
WHAT IS THE MEANING OF THIS!?
ZAP
ZAP
ZAP
LOOK OUT! UGH!
DARLING!

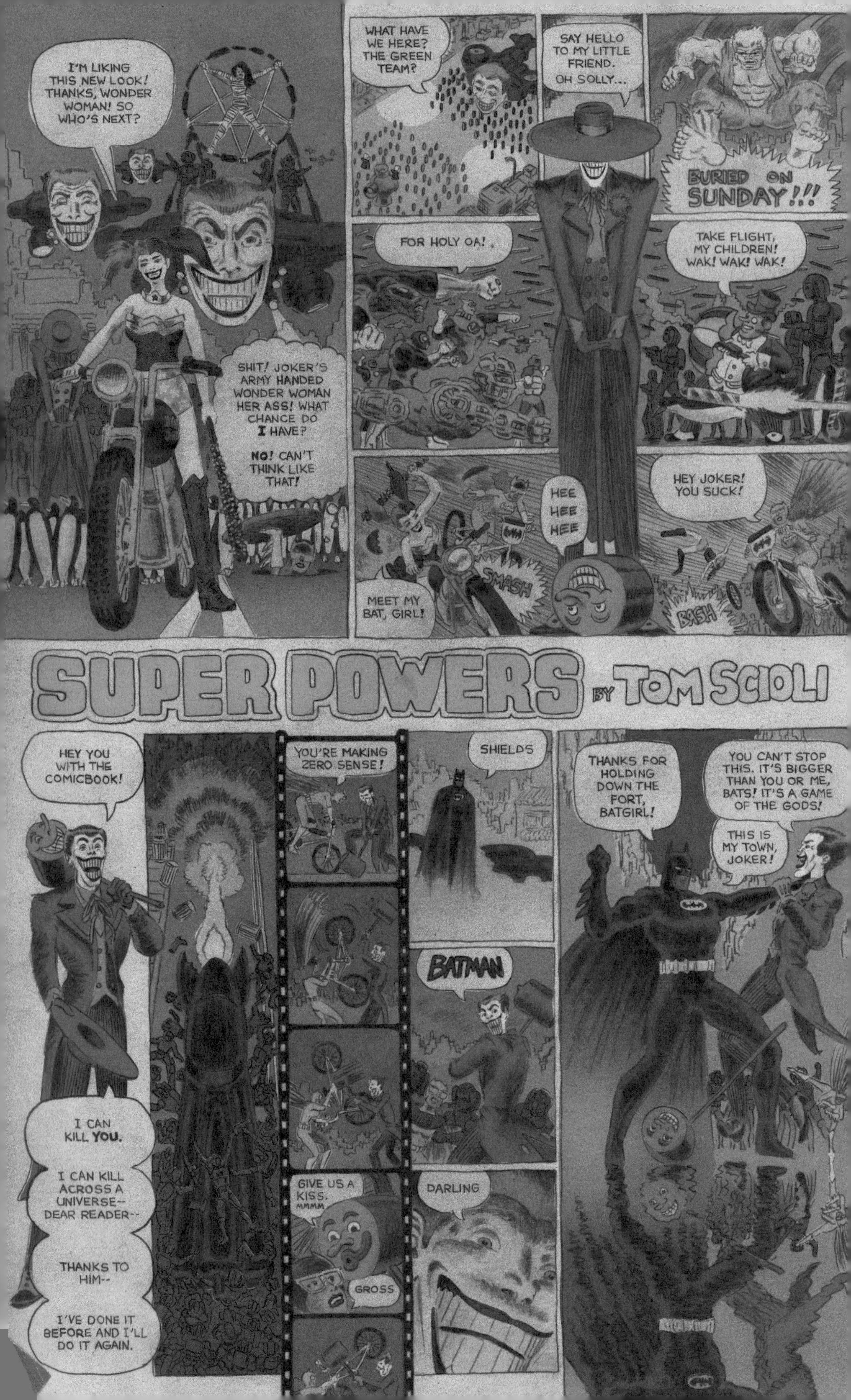
I'M LIKING THIS NEW LOOK! THANKS, WONDER WOMAN! SO WHO'S NEXT?
SHIT! JOKER'S ARMY HANDED WONDER WOMAN HER ASS! WHAT CHANCE DO I HAVE?
NO! CAN'T THINK LIKE THAT!
WHAT HAVE WE HERE? THE GREEN TEAM?
SAY HELLO TO MY LITTLE FRIEND. OH SOLLY...
BURIED ON SUNDAY!!!
FOR HOLY OA!
TAKE FLIGHT, MY CHILDREN! WAK! WAK! WAK!
HEE HEE HEE
MEET MY BAT, GIRL!
SMASH
HEY JOKER! YOU SUCK!
BASH
SUPER POWERS BY TOM SCIOLI
HEY YOU WITH THE COMICBOOK!
I CAN KILL YOU.
I CAN KILL ACROSS A UNIVERSE-- DEAR READER--
THANKS TO HIM--
I'VE DONE IT BEFORE AND I'LL DO IT AGAIN.
YOU'RE MAKING ZERO SENSE!
GIVE US A KISS. MMMM
GROSS
SHIELDS
BATMAN
DARLING
THANKS FOR HOLDING DOWN THE FORT, BATGIRL!
YOU CAN'T STOP THIS. IT'S BIGGER THAN YOU OR ME, BATS! IT'S A GAME OF THE GODS!
THIS IS MY TOWN, JOKER!

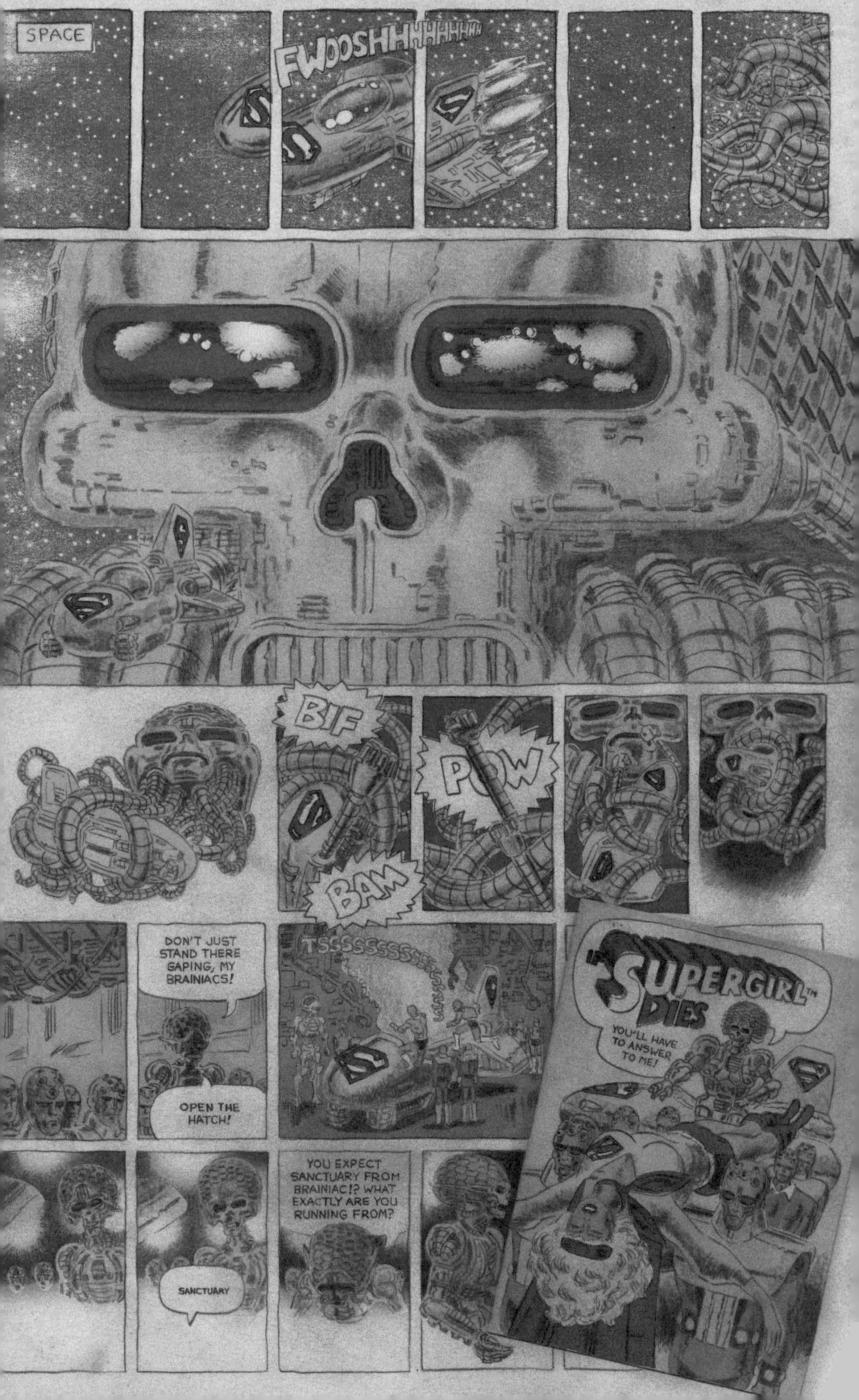
SPACE
FWOOSHHHHHHHH
BIF
POW
BAM
DON'T JUST STAND THERE GAPING, MY BRAINIACS!
OPEN THE HATCH!
TSSSSSSSSSSSSSS
"SUPERGIRL™ DIES"
YOU'LL HAVE TO ANSWER TO ME!
SANCTUARY
YOU EXPECT SANCTUARY FROM BRAINIAC!? WHAT EXACTLY ARE YOU RUNNING FROM?

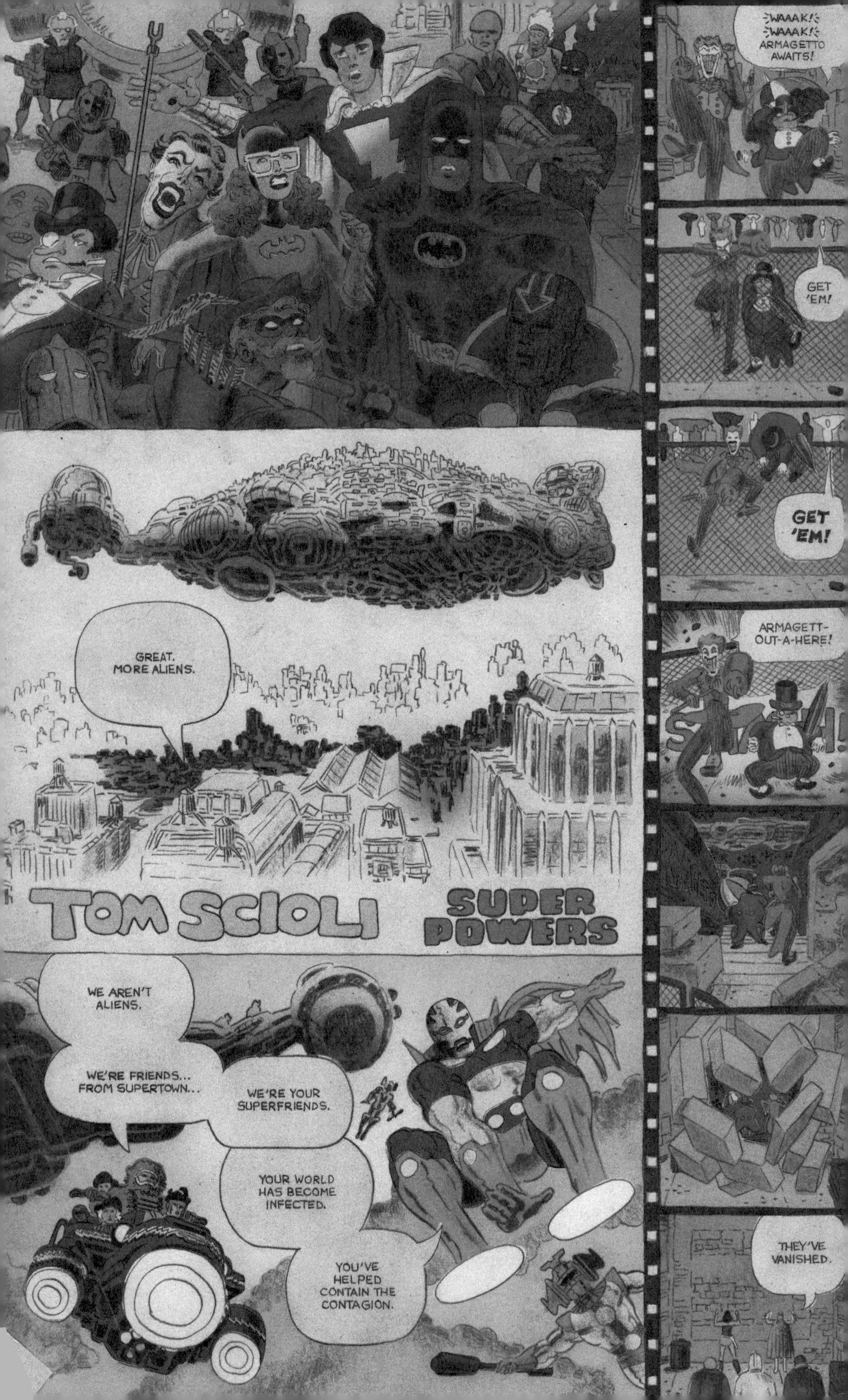
GREAT. MORE ALIENS.
TOM SCIOLI
SUPER POWERS
WE AREN'T ALIENS.
WE'RE FRIENDS... FROM SUPERTOWN...
WE'RE YOUR SUPERFRIENDS.
YOUR WORLD HAS BECOME INFECTED.
YOU'VE HELPED CONTAIN THE CONTAGION.
WAAAK! WAAAK! ARMAGETTO AWAITS!
GET 'EM!
GET 'EM!
ARMAGETT-OUT-A-HERE!
THEY'VE VANISHED.

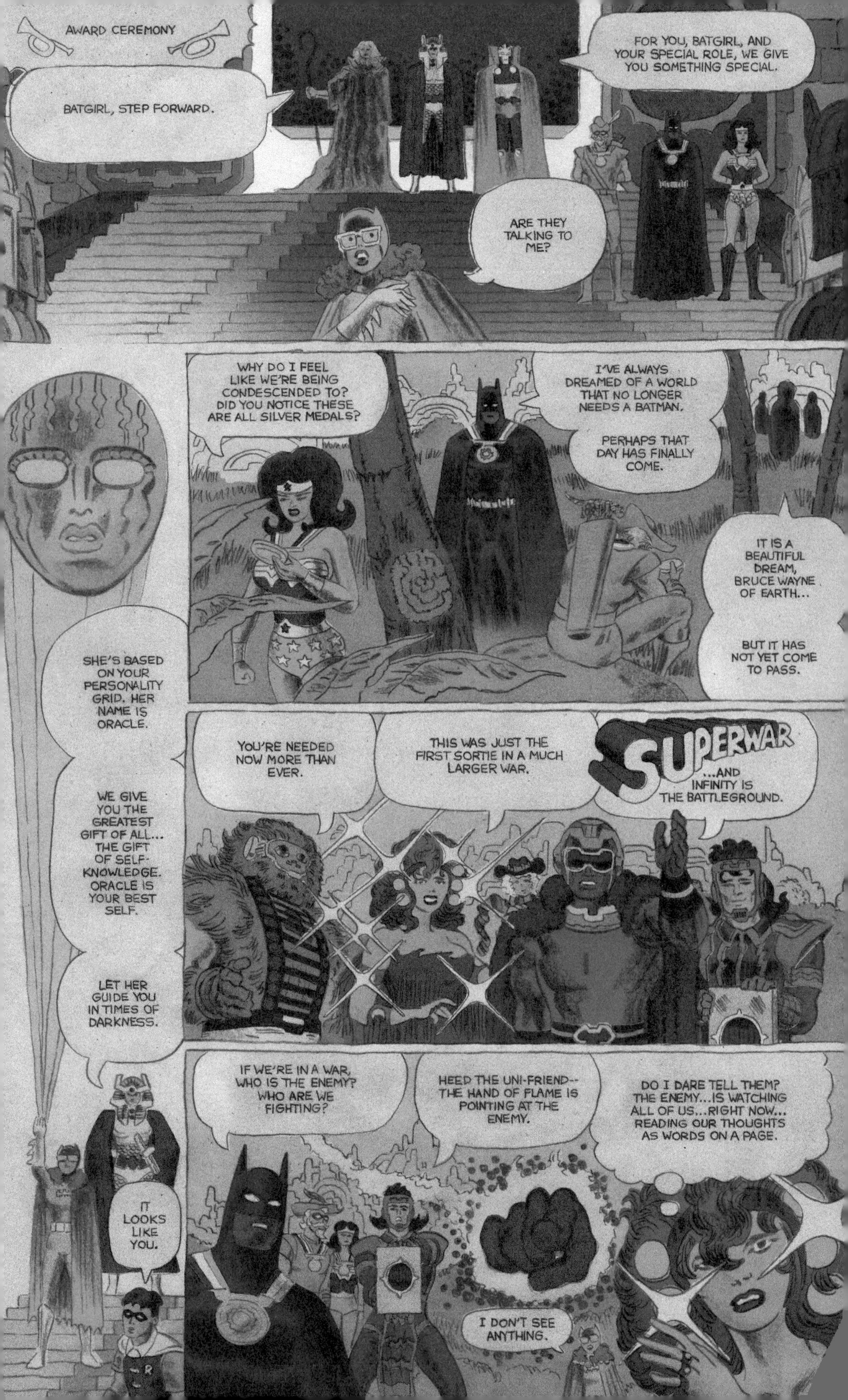
AWARD CEREMONY
BATGIRL, STEP FORWARD.
FOR YOU, BATGIRL, AND YOUR SPECIAL ROLE, WE GIVE YOU SOMETHING SPECIAL.
ARE THEY TALKING TO ME?
WHY DO I FEEL LIKE WE'RE BEING CONDESCENDED TO? DID YOU NOTICE THESE ARE ALL SILVER MEDALS?
I'VE ALWAYS DREAMED OF A WORLD THAT NO LONGER NEEDS A BATMAN.
PERHAPS THAT DAY HAS FINALLY COME.
IT IS A BEAUTIFUL DREAM, BRUCE WAYNE OF EARTH...
BUT IT HAS NOT YET COME TO PASS.
SHE'S BASED ON YOUR PERSONALITY GRID. HER NAME IS ORACLE.
WE GIVE YOU THE GREATEST GIFT OF ALL... THE GIFT OF SELF-KNOWLEDGE. ORACLE IS YOUR BEST SELF.
LET HER GUIDE YOU IN TIMES OF DARKNESS.
YOU'RE NEEDED NOW MORE THAN EVER.
THIS WAS JUST THE FIRST SORTIE IN A MUCH LARGER WAR.
SUPERWAR
...AND INFINITY IS THE BATTLEGROUND.
IF WE'RE IN A WAR, WHO IS THE ENEMY? WHO ARE WE FIGHTING?
HEED THE UNI-FRIEND-- THE HAND OF FLAME IS POINTING AT THE ENEMY.
DO I DARE TELL THEM? THE ENEMY...IS WATCHING ALL OF US...RIGHT NOW... READING OUR THOUGHTS AS WORDS ON A PAGE.
IT LOOKS LIKE YOU.
I DON'T SEE ANYTHING.

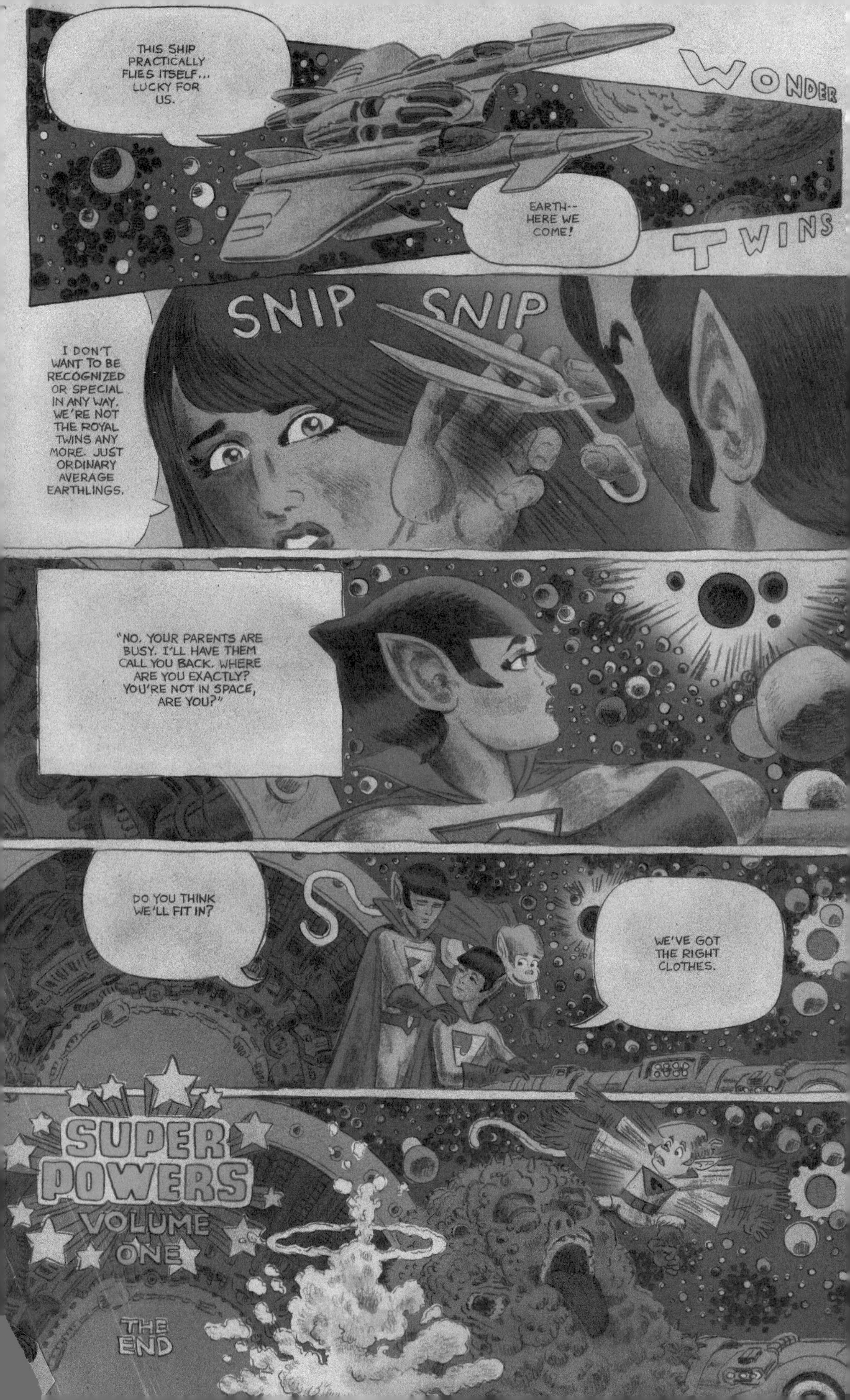
THIS SHIP PRACTICALLY FLIES ITSELF... LUCKY FOR US.
WONDER TWINS
EARTH-- HERE WE COME!
SNIP SNIP
I DON'T WANT TO BE RECOGNIZED OR SPECIAL IN ANY WAY. WE'RE NOT THE ROYAL TWINS ANY MORE. JUST ORDINARY AVERAGE EARTHLINGS.
"NO. YOUR PARENTS ARE BUSY. I'LL HAVE THEM CALL YOU BACK. WHERE ARE YOU EXACTLY? YOU'RE NOT IN SPACE, ARE YOU?"
DO YOU THINK WE'LL FIT IN?
WE'VE GOT THE RIGHT CLOTHES.
SUPER POWERS VOLUME ONE
THE END